Non-Violation Complaints in WTO Law

Studies in Global Economic Law
Studien zum globalen Wirtschaftsrecht
Études en droit économique mondial

edited by Thomas Cottier

Volume 9

PETER LANG
Bern · Berlin · Bruxelles · Frankfurt am Main · New York · Oxford · Wien

Dae-Won Kim

Non-Violation Complaints in WTO Law

Theory and Practice

PETER LANG
Bern · Berlin · Bruxelles · Frankfurt am Main · New York · Oxford · Wien

Bibliographic information published by Die Deutsche Bibliothek
Die Deutsche Bibliothek lists this publication in the Deutsche Nationalbibliografie; detailed bibliographic data is available on the Internet at ‹http://dnb.ddb.de›.

British Library and Library of Congress Cataloguing-in-Publication Data: A catalogue record for this book is available from *The British Library*, Great Britain, and from *The Library of Congress*, USA.

Published with a grant from the Faculty of Law, University of Bern, Switzerland.

ISSN 1423-9531
ISBN 3-03910-854-9
US-ISBN 0-8204-8043-6

Acknowledgements

The preparatory work for the thesis started at the University of Edinburgh in 1998. Having written my Master's thesis, I was strongly attracted to the non-violation. nullification or impairment (NVNI) concept in terms of legal reasoning. Furthermore, during 1998–2002 in Germany, the concept was reviewed from the standpoint of public international law. My analytical efforts applied to NVNI complaints were intensified and finalised at the World Trade Institute (WTI), University of Berne. Having had the privilege of the support of my supervisor, Professor Thomas Cottier, the managing director of the WTI, I was able to complete my thesis.

I would like to express my gratitude to those who offered wholehearted and patient help while I wrote this thesis. They particularly include Professor Thomas Cottier of the WTI for his careful supervision and several invaluable suggestions rendering the structures of the thesis more sophisticated. I am also indebted to the staff of the WTI. With regard to coherence, I appreciate useful comments from Professor Neil MacCormick at Edinburgh University. On the understanding of equity or the legitimate expectations requirement, a critical constituent in NVNI complaints, Professor Thomas Cottier deserves my utmost gratitude.

Professor Joost Pauwelyn at Duke University, USA, gave instructive advice on the nature of the remedies of NVNI complaints. Linguistic help was kindly given by Mr Jonathan Gage and Ms Susan Kaplan, WTI. Wholehearted gratitude is due to my wife: her uncompromising devotion and support during our odyssey in Europe will last forever.

Dae-Won KIM
Berne, June 2005

Contents

PREFACE XIII

SUMMARY XV

SELECT BIBLIOGRAPHY XVII

DOCUMENTS REFERENCES XXXIII

TABLE OF CASES CITED IN THIS DISSERTATION XXXV

STANDARD ABBREVIATIONS XLIII

Part One
The Concept of Non-Violation Nullification or Impairment in WTO Law

I. OUTLINE OF DISSERTATION 3
A. Non-Violation Complaints and GATT/WTO Jurisprudence 3
1. Negotiated Balance of Rights and Obligations in WTO 3
2. Non-Violation Complaints and Balance of Rights and Obligations 6
B. Aims and Structure of Dissertation 9
1. Aims of Dissertation 9
2. Structure of Dissertation 9

II. SIGNIFICANCE OF NON-VIOLATION COMPLAINTS 11
A. In General 11
1. Non-Violation as a Balancing Mechanism of Benefit 11

2. Theoretical Significance of Non-Violation Complaints 14
3. Practical Significance of Non-Violation Complaints. 16
B. The Origins of Non-Violation Complaints. 20
1. Historical Origin of Non-Violation Complaints till GATT 47 20
2. Institutional Origin of Non-Violation Complaints 29
3. Non-Violation Concept Elsewhere 42

III. THE DEVELOPMENT OF NON-VIOLATION COMPLAINTS 45
A. Non-Violation Complaints in GATT 47 45
B. Non-Violation Complaints in WTO Agreements 49
1. In General 49
2. General Agreement on Trade in Services (GATS) . . 52
3. Agreement on Trade-Related Aspects of Intellectual Property (TRIPS) 58
4. Anti-Competition Practices (Competition Policies). 66
5. WTO Jurisprudence 71
6. Survey of Non-Violation Complaints Cases: 1948 ~ 2005 78
7. The Jurisprudential Implications of Non-Violation: Sources Argument. 80

Part Two
The Established Interpretation of Non-Violation Complaints

IV. ESTABLISHED TREATY INTERPRETATION 87
A. Overview of the Vienna Convention Articles 31 and 32 87
1. In General 87
2. Uniformity and Flexibility in Interpretation 88

3. Textualism and Intentionalism ... 90
4. Coherent Interpretation between Two Sides ... 95
B. Typology of Interpretation of Non-Violation Complaints ... 97
1. Four Types of Interpretation ... 97
2. Textual Interpretation of Article XXIII:1(b) ... 98
3. Contextual Interpretation of Article XXIII:1(b) ... 101
4. Historical Interpretation of Article XXIII:1(b) of GATT ... 105
5. Teleological Interpretation of Article XXIII:1(b) ... 108
6. Summary: Coordination of Various Interpretations ... 112

V. Three Requirements of Non-Violation Complaints ... 115
A. In General ... 115
B. Application of a Measure ... 117
1. Notion of Measure ... 117
2. Application ... 121
C. An Accruing Benefit ... 122
1. Nature of "Benefit" ... 122
2. Legitimately Expected Benefits ... 125
D. "Nullified or Impaired ... as the Result of" (Causation) ... 126
1. Nullification or Impairment ... 126
2. Causation ("As the Result") of Non-Violation Complaints ... 131
3. Remedy ... 139
E. Different Scope of Interpretation ... 144
1. Narrow Interpretation (Restrictive Approach) ... 144
2. Broader Interpretation (Expansive Approach) ... 148
3. Two Variables Differentiating the Approaches ... 150

Part Three
Refining the Interpretation of Non-Violation Complaints

VI. Non-Violation Complaints in International Jurisprudence ... 155
A. General Jurisprudential Relevance of Non-Violation to Sources Argument ... 155
1. In Public International Law ... 155
2. In WTO Law ... 159
B. Procedural Relevance of Non-Violation to Causes of Action ... 162
1. Text in terms of Positive and Normative Dimensions ... 162
2. Text in terms of Consistent Rule-Making ... 165

VII. Theoretical Presumptions of the Refined Interpretation ... 167
A. Non-Violation Complaints in Legal Theory ... 167
B. Theories Underlying the Refined Interpretation ... 173
1. Different Theories of International Law ... 173
2. New International Law Process as a Counterpositivistic Approach ... 178
C. Dimensional Interpretation ... 184
1. Dimension of Gathering Legal Data of Non-Violation Complaints ... 184
2. Dimension of Analytic Studies of Non-Violation Complaints ... 186
3. Dimension of Normative Studies of Non-Violation Complaints ... 188

VIII. Institutional Presumptions of the Refined Interpretation ... 191
A. Non-Violation under Rule-Oriented Dispute Settlement Mechanism ... 191
1. Dispute, Negotiation and Adjudication ... 191
2. Characteristics of the Two Models ... 193

3. Desirable Model 194
4. Characteristics of Present WTO System: Mixed Character 196
B. Rule-Oriented WTO Dispute Settlement Mechanism . . 200
1. Dispute Settlement Mechanism of GATT 47 200
2. Dispute Settlement Mechanism of WTO 203
C. Dual Approach in Resolving Non-Violation Complaints 207
1. Two Aspects of WTO Rules 207
2. Two Modes for Resolving Non-Violation Complaints 212

IX. COHERENCE AS INTERPRETATIVE GUIDELINE OF ARTICLE XXIII : 1 217
A. Institutional Necessity for Coherent Interpretation: "Constitutionalisation" 217
1. Necessity from Institutional Presumption 217
2. Constitutionalisation of WTO DSM (1) 219
B. Theoretical Necessity for Coherent Interpretation . . . 222
1. Necessity from Theoretical Presumption 222
2. Constitutionalisation of WTO DSM (2) 223
C. The Notion of Coherence 224
1. Internal Coherence of Text of Article XXIII : 1(b) . . . 226
2. External Coherence of Text of Article XXIII : 1(b) . . 227

Part Four
Transforming the Non-Violation into Liability

X. INTERNAL COHERENCE AS AN ANALYTIC APPROACH 231
A. Structure of "Benefit" in GATT XXIII : 1 231
1. In General: Definitional Exactness and Reciprocity 231
2. Definitional Exactness and Benefit 232
3. Reciprocity and Benefit 234

B. Two-tried Track in "Benefits" of Article XXIII:1 237
1. From "Benefits" to "Rights" 237
2. Relationship between two Kinds of Benefits 243
C. Corresponding Structure of Obligations 246
1. Specific Obligations in Article XXIII:1(a) 246
2. General Obligations in Article XXIII:1(b) 247
3. Relationship of General Obligation to Legitimate Expectation 249
D. Non-Violation as State Liability 251

XI. External Coherence as a Normative Approach 257
A. General Principles of International Law 257
B. Roles of "Objective" of GATT Article XXIII:1 268
1. In General 268
2. GATT/WTO Jurisprudence on Objective 270
3. Bridging Role between Specific and General Obligations 274

XII. Standards Defining the Scope of Non-Violation Complaints 277
A. Introduction 277
B. Compensatory Adjustment Standard 280
1. Relevant Cases: Citrus and Uruguayan Recourse ... 280
2. Some Weaknesses of Compensatory Adjustment Standard 282
C. Expectation Standard 283
1. In General 283
2. Competitive Relationship Test 288
3. Market Access Test 291

Conclusion 295

Index 299

Preface

The law of the World Trade Organisation and of the multilateral trading system is characterised by a peculiar feature: liability is not only – and unlike in general international law – incurred by violating a legal obligation. Liability may also be incurred by acts which do not contradict obligations under the Agreements, but may otherwise nullify and impair the benefits under the Agreements or impede the attainment of one of their objectives. This peculiarity finds expression in Article XXIII of GATT and Article XXIII:3 of GATS. It reflects the concern that trade agreements are limited in scope, that measures outside this scope, while perfectly legal, could nevertheless nullify, impair or neutralise the benefits obtained. Such measures, in other words, could, despite being legal in nature, undermine the reciprocal balance of concessions entered into by Members of the WTO. These so called non-violation complaints, or non-violation nullification and impairment (NVNI) complaints have puzzled many scholars and raise a number of interesting questions. What is the nature of such a complaint? What is the theory behind it? How to explain it in legal theory? What is their relationship to ordinary legal complaints based upon an alleged violation of an obligation? How do they relate to general principles of law, in particular to the protection of good faith and equity, and particularly to the doctrine of protecting legitimate expectations – a core value and goal of all legal protection? What are the practical implications of these complaints? How often are they referred to in state practice and in WTO dispute settlement?

As the body of rights and obligations in the WTO system expands, non-violation complaints correspondingly tend to lose importance. At the same time, new areas emerge, in particular trade regulation in the field of services, and the boundaries in traditional areas are further pushed to reach frontiers, such as regulation of competition, properly speaking, non-violation complaints remain an important feature and cornerstone of the trading system. They are well worth being explored and examined in great detail. This is what Dr Dae Won Kim has done with great care and expertise in his doctoral dissertation, researched and written at the World Trade Institute in 2002/2003 and submitted to the Faculty of Law of Berne, Switzerland. The book offers a logical and convincing structure. It develops its theory step by step. Based upon an assessment of history, state practice and current interpretations, foundations for a theory are built. Dr Kim expands upon the the existing framework, taking into account theory and jurisprudence not commonly in touch with the discipline of international trade regulation. His wide interests in legal theory are put to work, enriching the discourse on non-violation complaints and WTO law, as much as his presence enriched the discourse and debates at the WTI during his stay at the Institute. For this, all the fellows were grateful and retain shared moments of interesting and lively debates.

Berne, October 2005 Professor Thomas Cottier

Summary

The main objective of this thesis is to set up an effective legal reasoning on Non-Violation Nullification or Impairment (NVNI) complaints of GATT Article XXIII : 1(b). It premises two basic characteristics of any norm structure, i. e. *positive* and *normative*. This dichotomy specifically relevant to the NVNI complaints can be judicially sorted out with the aid of the *Coherence* conception.

Every legal system is associated with elements of *uniformity* on the one hand, but *flexibility* on the other; while the former are connected with systematic mode of legal reasoning, the latter are seen as allowing or prompting a more purposive mode of reasoning. This is equally true at the level of WTO law. When reviewing GATT Article XXIII : 1(a), we see an application of a systematic approach, focusing on uniformly codified factors in WTO law; at the same time, the normative background of GATT Article XXIII : 1(b) is firmly related to a purposive approach, paying special attention to flexible factors hinging on underlying objectives of the WTO law. Therefore, the existence of the Article XXIII : 1(b) has its own sound reason from an analysis of general normative structure. Hence, the main stress must be laid upon its theorisation in the context of an optimal legal interpretation against *indeterminacy* in WTO law.

Because an inherent indeterminacy of the obligations of WTO Agreements has resulted from various relational combinations between *rules* and *values* in the WTO Agreements, suitable normative conceptions on certain ways of combining the rules and values clearly take priority in the interpretation. One of the concepts is *coherence,* in the sense that a rule should be related in a principled fashion to other rules of the same system. The coherence concept can be divided into *internal* and *external coherence*, according to how the principled fashion relates to the making of a rule.

As there is acceptance for a well-founded constitution of rules, the rules must show themselves to have *internal coherence*, in the sense that the very many rules of a legal system ought to be organised and not self-contradury. Since the rules are mainly composed of rights and obligations, regardless of their conceptual breadth, the best way for preventing possible contradictions among rules ought to make the rules in line with the *rights* (correspondingly obligations) concept.

Analysis of the *rights* (correspondingly obligations) concept is an important methodological point for a balanced comprehension of GATT Article XXIII : 1(b). By connecting GATT Article XXIII : 1(a) with complaints against specific, codified or *primary obligations*, the significance of the Article XXIII : 1(b) is in covering different complaints against uncertain, future or *secondary obligations*, i.e. *liability*. This is a reason why the NVNI complaints are to be understood as a kind of obligation complaint.

At the same time, since there are underlying *values* to set up rules, an exploration of the rules is likely to arrive at *an externally coherent structure*, in the sense that the multitudinous rules of legal systems should be pointless in case of their isolation from the values. From this external coherence, an existence of *value-nets* in legal systems, which makes sets of rules be regarded as their concrete manifestations, is confirmed. The values should present themselves in the form of a specific objective of the concerned law (e.g. *market access* in WTO law), or general principles of whole legal systems (e.g. *good faith, equity*). By reviewing the externally coherent interrelation between objective of WTO law and employment of indeterminate elements of Article XXIII : 1(b), *legitimate expectation* originated from *equity* figures prominently in catching roles of NVNI complaints. This is another reason why the NVNI complaints are to be grasped as a kind of obligation complaint.

With the above legal reasoning, we can avoid unnecessary arguments and interpret Article XXIII : 1 more consistently. GATT Article XXIII : 1 therefore *jurisprudentially* comprises three complaints: *Obligation* complaints [subsection (a)], *Liability* complaints [subsection (b)] and *Situation* complaints [subsection (c)]. The present wording of Article XXIII : 1 adopts unclear terminology inevitably causing systematic disturbance to the WTO system. For reducing the difficulty, we have to consider its amendment seriously.

Select Bibliography

Books

A NEGOTIATING HISTORY (1993)
The GATT Uruguay Round: A Negotiating History (1986–1992), Terence P. Stewart (ed.) (2 Volumes' Commentary) (Deventer: Kluwer Law and Taxation Publishers, 1993)

ANDERSON & HOEKMAN (EDS) (2002)
Kym Anderson and Bernard Hoekman (eds), The Global Trading System (4 Volumes) (London: I. B. Tauris, 2002)

AREND (1999)
Anthony Clark Arend, Legal Rules and International Society (Oxford: Oxford University Press, 1999)

ARROWSMITH (2002)
Sue Arrowsmith, Government Procurement In The WTO (Hague: Kluwer Law International, 2002)

AUST (2000)
Anthony Aust, Modern Treaty Law and Practice (Cambridge: Cambridge University Press, 2000)

BHAGWATI & PATRICK (EDS) (1990)
Jagdish Bhagwati and Hugh T. Patrick (eds), Aggressive Unilateralism: America's 301 Trade Policy and the World Trading System (Ann Arbor: The University of Michigan Press, 1990)

BHAGWATI & HUDEC (EDS) (1996)
Jagdish Bhagwati and Robert E. Hudec (eds), Fair Trade and Harmonization: Prerequisites for Free Trade? (2 Volumes) (Cambridge: MIT Press, 1996)

BLACK'S LAW DICTIONARY (ST. PAUL: WEST PUBLISHING, 1999)

BRIERLY (1945)
James Leslie Brierly, The Outlook for International Law (Oxford: Clarendon Press, 1945)

BRONCKERS & QUICK (EDS) (2000)
Marco Bronckers and Reinhard Quick (eds), New Directions In International Economic Law: Essays In Honour Of John H. Jackson (Hague: Kluwer Law International, 2000)

BROWNLIE (ED.) (1995)
Ian Brownlie (ed.), Basic Documents in International Law (Oxford: Clarendon Press, 1995)

BROWNLIE (1998)
Ian Brownlie, Principles of Public International Law (Oxford: Clarendon Press, 1998)
CAMERON & CAMPBELL (EDS) (1998)
James Cameron and Karen Campbell (eds), Dispute Resolution in the World Trade Organisation (London: Cameron May, 1998)
CHAYES ET AL. (1968)
Abram Chayes, Thomas Ehrlich and Andreas F. Lowenfeld, International Legal Process: Materials for an Introductory Course (2 volumes) (Boston: Little, Brown & co., 1968)
COTTIER & MAVROIDIS (EDS) (2000)
Thomas Cottier and Petros C. Mavroidis (eds), Regulatory Barriers and the Principle of Non-Discrimination in World Trade Law (Ann Arbor: The University of Michigan Press, 2000)
CRAWFORD (2002)
James Crawford, The International Law Commission's Articles on State Responsibility: Introduction, Text and Commentaries (Cambridge: Cambridge University Press, 2002)
DAM (1970)
Kenneth W. Dam, The GATT: Law And International Economic Organization (Chicago: University of Chicago Press, 1970)
D'AMATO (1995)
Anthony D'Amato, International Law: Process and Prospect (Irvington: Transnational Publishers, 1995)
D'AMATO (ED.) (1996)
Anthony D'Amato (ed.), ANALYTIC JURISPRUDENCE Anthology (Cincinnati: Anderson Pub.Co., 1996)
DURLING (2000)
James P. Durling, Anatomy of a Trade Dispute: A Documentary History of the Kodak Fuji Film Dispute (London: Cameron May, 2000)
DWORKIN (1997)
Ronald Dworkin, Law's Empire (Cambridge: Harvard University Press, 1997)
DWORKIN (2001)
Ronald Dworkin, Taking Rights Seriously (London: Duckworth, 2001)
ENCYCLOPEDIA
Encyclopedia of Public International Law, Rudolf Bernhardt (ed.) (4 volumes) (Amsterdam: North-Holland Publ., 1992, 1995, 1997, 2000)
FRANCK (1990)
Thomas M. Franck, The Power Of Legitimacy Among Nations (New York: Oxford University Press, 1990)
FRANCK (1995)
Thomas M. Franck, Fairness in International Law and Institutions (Oxford: Clarendon Press, 1995)

GATT ANALYTICAL INDEX (1995)
WTO, Analytical Index: Guide to GATT Law and Practice (2 volumes) (Geneva: World Trade Organization, 1995)
HANDBOOK OF WTO/GATT DISPUTE SETTLEMENT (1998)
Pierre Pescatore, William J. Davey and Andreas F. Lowenfeld, Handbook of WTO/GATT Dispute Settlement (2 volumes) (Irvington-on-Hudson: Transnational Juris Publications, 1998)
HART (1997)
H. L. A. Hart, The Concept of Law (Oxford: Clarendon Press, 1997)
HENKIN (1979)
Louis Henkin, How Nations Behave (New York: Columbia University Press, 1979)
HENKIN (1995)
Louis Henkin, International Law: Politics and Values (Dordrecht: Martinus Nijhoff Publishers, 1995)
HENKIN ET AL. (1993)
Louse Henkin, Richard Crawford Pugh, Oscar Schachter and Hans Smit, International Law in Theory and Practice (Dordrecht: Martinus Nijhoff Publishers, 1993)
HUDEC (1990)
Robert E. Hudec, The GATT Legal System And World Trade Diplomacy (Salem: Butterworth Legal Publisher, 1990)
HUDEC (1993)
Robert E. Hudec, Enforcing International Trade Law: The Evolution Of The Modern GATT Legal System (Salem: Butterworth Legal Publisher, 1993)
HUDEC (2000)
Robert E. Hudec, Essays on the Nature of International Trade Law (London: Cameron May, 2000)
JACKSON (1969)
John H. Jackson, World Trade And The Law Of GATT (Indianapolis: Bobbs-Merrill, 1969)
JACKSON (1990)
John H. Jackson, Restructuring The GATT System (London: The Royal Institute of International Affairs, 1990)
JACKSON (1997)
John H. Jackson, The World Trading System: Law And Policy Of International Economic Relations (Cambridge: MIT Press, 1997)
JACKSON (1998)
John H. Jackson, The World Trade Organization: Constitution and Jurisprudence (London: The Royal Institute of International Affairs, 1998)
JACKSON (2000)
John H. Jackson, The Jurisprudence Of The GATT And The WTO: Insights On Treaty Law And Economic Relations (Cambridge: Cambridge University Press, 2000)

JACKSON, DAVEY & SYKES (1995)
John H. Jackson, William J. Davey and Alan O. Sykes, Legal Problems of International Economic Relations: Cases, Materials and Text (St. Paul: West Publishing, 1995)

JENNINGS & WATTS (EDS) (1996)
Sir Robert Jennings, Sir Arthur Watts and Oppenheim Lassa Francis Lawrence, Oppenheim's International Law (2 volumes) (Harlow: Longman, 1996)

KAZAZI (1996)
Mojtaba Kazazi, Burden of Proof and Related Issues: A Study on Evidence Before International Tribunals (Hague: Kluwer Law International, 1996)

KELSEN (1961)
Hans Kelsen, General Theory of Law and State (Anders Wedberg trans.) (New York: Russell & Russell, 1961)

KELSEN (1966)
Hans Kelsen, Principles of International Law (New York: Holt Rinehart and Winston, 1966)

KRAMER ET AL. (2000)
Mattew H. Kramer, N. E. Simmonds and Hillel Steiner, A Debate Over Rights (Oxford: Clarendon Press, 2000)

KOSKENNIEMI (1989)
Martti Koskenniemi, From Apology to Utopia: The Structure of International Legal Argument (Helsinki: Kustannus, 1989)

KU & DIEHL (EDS) (1998)
Charlotte Ku and Paul F. Diehl (eds), International Law: Classic and Contemporary Readings (Boulder: Lynne Rienner, 1998)

THE LEGAL TEXTS (1995)
Final Act Embodying The Results Of The Uruguay Round Of Multilateral Trade Negotiations: The Legal Texts (WTO, 1995)

MACCORMICK (1995)
Neil MacCormick, Legal Reasoning and Legal Theory (Oxford: Clarendon Press, 1995)

MATSUSHITA ET AL. (2003)
Mitsuo Matsushita, Thomas J. Schoenbaum and Petros C. Mavroidis, The World Trade Organization: Law, Practice, and Policy (Oxford: Oxford University Press, 2003)

MCDOUGAL ET AL. (1994)
Myres S. Mcdougal, Harold D. Lasswell and Miller, James C., The Interpretation of international Agreements and World Public Order (New Haven: Martinus Nijhoff Publishers, 1994)

MCGOVERN (1995)
Edmond Mcgovern, International Trade Regulation (Exeter: Globefield Press, 1995)

OXFORD ENGLISH DICTIONARY (1993)
The New Shorter Oxford English Dictionary on Historical Principles, Lesley Brown (ed.) (2 volumes) (Oxford: Clarendon Press, 1993)
PETERSMANN (ED.) (1997A)
Ernst-Ulrich Petersmann (ed.), International Trade Law And The GATT/WTO Dispute Settlement System (London: Kluwer Law International, 1997)
PETERSMANN (1997B)
Ernst-Ulrich Petersmann, The GATT/WTO Dispute Settlement System: International Law, International Organizations and Dispute Settlement (London: Kluwer Law International, 1997)
PETERSMANN & HILF (EDS) (1991)
Ernst-Ulrich Petersmann and Meinhard Hilf (eds), The New GATT Round of Multilateral Trade Negotiation: Legal and Economic Problems (Deventer: Kluwer Law and Taxation Publishers, 1991)
PETERSMANN & JAENICKE (EDS) (1992)
Ernst-Ulrich Petersmann and Gunther Jaenicke (eds), Adjudication of International Trade Disputes in International and National Economic Law (Fribourg: University Press, 1992)
VAN DIJCK & FARBER (EDS) (1996)
Pitou van Dijck and Gerrit Farber (eds) Challenges to The New World Trade Organization (Hague: Kluwer Law International, 1996)
POSNER (1981)
Richard A. Posner, The Economics of Justice (Cambridge: Harvard University Press, 1981)
POSNER (1990)
Richard A. Posner, The Problems of Jurisprudence (Cambridge: Harvard University Press, 1990)
PROVOST (ED.) (2002)
Rene Provost (ed.), State Responsibility in International Law (Aldershot: Ashgate Dartmouth, 2002)
QURESHI (1996)
Asif H. Qureshi, The World Trade Organization: Implementing International Trade Norms (Manchester: Manchester University Press, 1996)
RUGGIE (1998)
John G. Ruggie, Constructing the World Polity: Essays on International Institutionalization (London: Routledge, 1998)
SCHACHTER (1997)
Oscar Schachter, International Law in Theory and Practice (Dordrecht: Martinus Nijhoff Publishers, 1997)
SCHAUER (1991), Frederick Schauer, Playing by the Rules (Oxford: Clarendon Press, 1991)
SEIDL-HOHENVELDERN (1999)
Ignaz Seidl-Hohenveldern, International Economic Law (Hague: Kluwer Law International, 1999)

SINCLAIR (1984)
Ian Sinclair, The Vienna Convention and the Law of Treaties (Manchester: University Press, 1984)
TREBILCOCK & HOWSE (2001)
Michael J. Trebilcock and Robert Howse, The Regulation of International Trade (London: Routledge, 2001)
VILLIGIER (1985)
Mark E. Villigier, Customary International Law and Treaties (Hague: Kluwer Law International, 1985)
VAN DIJCK & FABER (1996)
Pitou van Dijck and Gerrit Faber, Challenges to The New World Trade Organization (Hague: Kluwer Law International, 1996)
WAINCYMER (2002)
Jeff Waincymer, WTO Litigation: Procedural Aspects Of Formal Dispute Settlement (London: Cameron May, 2002)
WEILER (ED.) (2000)
J.H.H. Weiler (ed.), The EU, the WTO, and the NAFTA: Towards a Common Law of International Trade? (Oxford: Oxford University Press, 2000)
WEISS (ED.) (2000)
Friedl Weiss, Improving WTO Dispute Settlement Procedures: Issues and Lessons from the Practice of Other International Courts and Tribunals (London: Cameron May, 2000)
WINHAM (1992)
Gilbert R. Winham, The Evolution Of International Trade Agreement (Toronto: University of Toronto Press, 1992)
WITTGENSTEIN, LUDWIG
Remarks on the Foundations of Mathematics (Oxford: Basil Blackwell, 1978)
ZOLLER (1984)
Elisabeth Zoller, Peacetime Unilateral Remedies: An Analysis of Countermeasures (Dobbs Ferry: Transnational Publishers, 1984)

Articles and Book Chapters

Abbott (2000)
Frederick M. Abbott, *Report: TRIPS in Seattle: The Not-So-Surprising Failure and the Future of the TRIPS Agenda*, 18 Berkeley Journal of International Law 165 (2000)

Abels (1996)
Tracy M. Abels, *The World Trade Organization's First Test: The United States-Japan Auto Dispute,* 44 UCLA Law Review 467 (1996)

Akehurst (1985)
M. B. Akehurst, *International Liability for Injurious Consequences Arising out of Acts Not Prohibited by International Law,* XVI Netherlands Year Book of International Law ("NYIL") 4 (1985)

Alexander (1997)
Larry Alexander, *Incomplete Theorizing: A Review Essay of Cass R. Sunstein's Legal Reasoning and Political Conflict,* 72 Notre Dame Law Review 531 (1997)

Alexander & Kress (1997)
Larry Alexander and Ken Kress, *Against Legal Principles,* 82 Iowa Law Review 739 (1997)

Bagwell, Mavroidis & Staiger (2002)
Kyle Bagwell, Petros C. Mavroidis and Robert W. Staiger, *The Boundaries of the WTO: It's a Question of Market Access,* 96 American Journal of International Law ("AJIL") 56 (2002)

Barfield (2001)
Claude E. Barfield, *Free Trade, Sovereignty, Democracy: The Future of the World Trade Organization,* 2 Chicago Journal of International Law 403 (2001)

Barringer, William H., *Competition Policy and Cross Border Dispute Resolution: Lessons Learned from the US-Japan Film Dispute,* 6 George Mason Law Review 459 (1998)

Bederman (1994)
David J. Bederman, *Revivalist Canons and Treaty Interpretation,* 41 UCLA Law Review 953 (1994)

Bernhardt (1995)
Rudolf Bernhardt, 'Interpretation in International Law,' in 2 ENCYCLOPEDIA (1995) p. 1416

Bessko (1996)
Zsolt K. Bessko, *Going Bananas Over EEC Preferences?: A Look at the Banana Trade War and the WTO's Understanding On Rules and Procedures Governing the Settlement of Disputes,* 28 Case Western Reserve Journal of International Law 265 (1996)

Bhagwati (1996)
Jagdish Bhagwati, 'The Agenda of the WTO,' in VAN DIJCK & FARBER (EDS) (1996) p. 27

Bhala (1999)
Raj Bhala, *The Myth about Stare Decisis and International Trade,* 14 American University International Law Review 845 (1999)

Boyle (2002)
Alan E. Boyle, 'State Responsibility and International Liability for Injurious Consequences of Acts not Prohibited by International Law: A Necessary Distinction?' in PROVOST (ED.) (2002) p. 141

Burton (1985)
Steven J. Burton, *Review Essay: Law, Obligation, and a Good Faith Claim of Justice,* 73 California Law Review 1956 (1985)

Cass (2001)
Deborah Z. Cass, *The 'Constitutionalisation' Of International Trade Law: Judicial Norm-Generation As The Engine Of Constitutional Development In International Trade,* 12 European Journal of International Law ("EJIL") 39 (2001)

Charnovitz (1991)
Steve Charnovitz, *Exploring the Environmental Exceptions in GATT Article XX,* 25 JWT 37 (1991)

Charnovitz (2002)
Steve Charnovitz, *Triangulating the World Trade Organization,* 96 AJIL 28 (2002)

Cho (1998)
Sung-joon Cho, *GATT Non-Violation Issues in the WTO Framework: Are They the Achilles Heel of the Dispute Settlement Process?,* Harvard International Law Journal 311 (1998)

Chua (1998a)
Adrian T. L. Chua, *Reasonable Expectations and Non-Violation Complaints in GATT/WTO Jurisprudence,* 32 JWT 27 (1998)

Chua (1998b)
Adrian T. L. Chua, *Precedent and Principles of WTO Panel Jurisprudence,* 16 Berkeley Journal of International Law 171 (1998)

Cottier (1998a)
Thomas Cottier, *The Protection of Genetic Resources and Traditional Knowledge: Towards More Specific Rights and Obligations in World Trade Law,* 1 Journal of International Economic Law ("JIEL") 555 (1998)

Cottier (1998b)
Thomas Cottier, 'The Impact of the TRIPS Agreement on Private Practice and Litigation,' in CAMERON & CAMPBELL (EDS) (1998) p. 111

Cottier (1998c)
Thomas Cottier, *The WTO Dispute Settlement System: New Horizons,* 92 American Society of International Law Proceedings 86 (1998)

Cottier (2000)
Thomas Cottier, *Limits to International Trade: The Constitutional Challenge,* 94 American Society of International Law Proceedings 220 (2000)
Cottier & Mavroidis (2000)
Thomas Cottier and Petros C. Mavroidis, 'Regulatory Barriers and the Principle of Non-Discrimination in WTO Law: An Overview,' in COTTIER & MAVROIDIS (EDS) (2000) p. 3
Cottier & Mueller (1995)
Thomas Cottier and Joerg Paul Mueller, 'Estoppel,' in 2 ENCYCLOPEDIA (1995) p. 116
Cottier & Schefer (1997)
Thomas Cottier and Krista Nadakavukaran Schefer, 'Non-Violation Complaints in WTO/GATT Dispute Settlement: Past, Present, and Future,' in PETERSMANN (ED.) (1997A) p. 145
Cottier & Schefer (1998)
Thomas Cottier and Krista Nadakavukaren Schefer, *The Relationship Between World Trade Organisation Law, National And Regional Law,* 1 JIEL 83 (1998)
Cottier & Schefer (2000)
Thomas Cottier and Krista Nadakavukaran Schefer, 'Good Faith and the Protection of Legitimate Expectations in the WTO,' in BRONCKERS & QUICK (EDS) (2000) p. 47
Daul (1995)
David A. Daul, *A Picture Worth For More than a Thousand Words: A Unique Cause of Action at the World Trade Organization to Enforce American Trade Rights against Japan,* 17 Hamline Journal of Public Law and Policy (1995)
Dillon (1999)
Sara Dillon, *Fuji-Kodak, the WTO, and the Death of Domestic Political Constituencies,* 8 Minnesota Journal of Global Trade 197 (1999)
Dunoff (1997)
Jeffrey L. Dunoff, *Recent Developments in Trade Policy and Scholarship – and Their Surprising Political Implications,* 17 Northwestern Journal of International Law and Business 759 (1996–97)
Durling & Lester (1998)
James P. Durling and Simon N. Lester, *Original Meaning and the Film Dispute: The Drafting History, Textual Evolution, and Application of the Non-Violation Nullification or Impairment Remedy,* 32 George Washington Journal of International Law and Economics 211 (1999)
Ehlermann & Ehring (2003)
Claus-Dieter Ehlermann and Lothar Ehring, *WTO Dispute Settlement and Competition Law: Views from the Perspective of the Appellate Body's Experience,* 26 Fordham International Law Journal 1505 (2003)

Eskridge & Frickey (1994)
William N. Eskridge, Jr., and Philip P. Frickey, 'An Historical and Critical Introduction to the Legal Process,' in HENRY M. HART, JR., & ALBERT M. SACKS, THE LEGAL PROCESS: BASIC PROBLEMS IN THE MAKING AND APPLICATION OF LAW (WILLIAM N. ESKRIDGE, JR., & PHILIP P. FRICKEY EDS, 1994)
Fallon (1987)
Richard H. Fallon, Jr. *A Constructive Coherence Theory of Constitutional Interpretation,* 100 Harvard Law Review 1189 (1987).
Fiss (1982)
Owen M. Fiss, *Objectivity and Interpretation,* 34 Stanford Law Review 739 (1982)
Franck (1988)
Thomas M. Franck, *Legitimacy in The International System,* 82 AJIL 705 (1988)
Geller (1995)
Paul Edward Geller, *Intellectual Property in the Global Marketplace: Impact of TRIPs Dispute Settlements?,* 29 The International Lawyer 99 (1995)
Goldie (1985)
L. F. E. Goldie, *Concepts of Strict and Absolute Liability and the Ranking of Liability in terms of Relative Exposure to Risk,* XVI NYIL 175 (1985)
Hall (2001)
Stephen Hall, *The Persistent Spectre: Natural Law, International Order And The Limits Of Legal Positivism,* 12 EJIL 269 (2001)
Hart (1958)
H. L. A. Hart, *Positivism and the Separation of Law and Morals,* 71 Harvard Law Review 593 (1958)
Henkin (1998)
Louis Henkin, 'The Politics of Law-Making', in KU & DIEHL (EDS) (1998)
Hilf (2001)
Meinhard Hilf, *Power, Rules and Principles – Which Orientation for WTO/ GATT Law?,* 1 JIEL 111 (2001)
Hindley (1996)
Brian Hindley, 'Competition Law and the WTO: Alternative Structures for Agreement,' in 2 BHAGWATI & HUDEC (EDS) (1996) p. 333
Hoekmann & Mavroidis (1994)
Bernard M. Hoekman and Petros C. Mavroidis, *Competition, Competition Policy and the GATT,* 17 World Economy 121 (1994)
Howse (2000)
Robert Howse, 'Adjudicative Legitimacy and Treaty Interpretation in International Trade Law: The Early Years of WTO Jurisprudence,' in WEILER (ED.) (2000) p. 35
Howse (2002)
Robert Howse, *From Politics to Technocracy – and Back Again: The Fate of the Multilateral Trading Regime,* 96 AJIL 94 (2002)

Howse & Trebilcock (1996)
Robert Howse and Michael J. Trebilcock, *The Fair Trade Debate: Trade, Labor, and the Environment*, 16 International Review of Law and Economics 61 (1996)
Hudec (1970)
Robert E. Hudec, *The GATT Legal System: A Diplomat's Jurisprudence*, 4 JWT 615 (1970)
Hudec (1975)
Robert E. Hudec, *Retaliation Against "Unreasonable" Foreign Trade Practices: The New Section 301 and GATT Nullification and Impairment*, 59 Minnesota Law Review 461 (1975)
Hudec (1980)
Robert E. Hudec, *GATT Dispute Settlement after the Tokyo Round: An Unfinished Business,* 13 Cornell International Law Journal 145 (1980)
Hudec, Robert E. 'Thinking About the New Section 301: Beyond Good and Evil,' in BHAGWATI & PATRICK (EDS) (1990) p. 113
Huhn (2003)
Wilson Huhn, *The Stages of Legal Reasoning: Formalism, Analogy, and Realism,* 48 Villanova Law Review 305 (2003)
Jackson (2002)
John H. Jackson, 'Designing and Implementing Effective Dispute Settlement Procedures: WTO Dispute Settlement, Appraisal and Prospects,' in 2 ANDERSON & HOEKMAN (ED.) (2002) p. 103
Janis (1995)
M. W. Janis, 'Equity in International Law,' in 2 ENCYCLOPEDIA (1995) p. 109
Kennedy (1998)
Kevin C. Kennedy, *The GATT-WTO System At Fifty*, 16 Wisconsin International Law Journal 421 (1998)
Kennedy (2001)
Kevin C. Kennedy, *Foreign Direct Investment and Competition Policy at the World Trade Organization, 33* George Washington International Law Review *585 (2001)*
Koh (1991)
Harold Hongju Koh, *Transnational Public Law Litigation*, 100 Yale Law Journal 2347 (1991)
Koh (1997)
Harold Hongju Koh, *Why Do Nations Obey International Law?*, 106 Yale Law Journal 2599 (1997)
Kuyper (1994)
Pieter Jan Kuyper, *The Law of GATT as a Special Field of International Law,* XXV NYIL 227 (1994)
Lennard (2002)
Michael Lennard, *Navigating by the Stars: Interpreting the WTO Agreements,* 5 JIEL 17 (2002)

Lichtenbaum (1998)
Lichtenbaum Peter, *Procedural Issues in WTO Dispute Resolution,* 19 Michigan Journal of International Law 1195 (1998)
Linarelli (2000)
John Linarelli, *The Role of Dispute Settlement in World Trade Law: Some Lessons from the Kodak-Fuji Dispute,* 31 Law and Policy in International business 263 (2000)
MacCormick (1984)
Neil MacCormick, *Coherence in Legal Justification,* in THEORY OF LEGAL SCIENCE: PROCEEDINGS OF THE CONFERENCE ON LEGAL THEORY AND PHILOSOPHY OF SCIENCE (ALEKSANDER PECZENIK ET AL., EDS, 1984) p. 37
Maki (2000)
Peter C. Maki, *Interpreting GATT Using the Vienna Convention on the Law of Treaties: A Method to Increase the Legitimacy of the Dispute Settlement System,* Minnesota Journal of Global Trade 343 (2000)
Marceau (1999)
Gabrielle Marceau, *A Call for Coherence in International Law: Praises for the Prohibition Against "Clinical Isolation" in WTO Dispute Settlement,* 33 JWT87 (1999)
Marceau & Trachtman (2002)
Gabrielle Marceau and Joel P. Trachtman, *The Technical Barriers to Trade Agreement, the Sanitary and Phytosanitary Meaures Agreement, and the General Agreement on Tariffs and Trade: A Map of the World Trade Organization Law of Domestic Regulation of Goods,* 36 JWT 881 (2002)
Moore (1985)
Michael S. Moore, *A Natural Law Theory of Interpretation,* 58 Southern California Law Review 279 (1985)
Morawetz (1992)
Thomas Morawetz, *Understanding Disagreement, the Root of Jurisprudence: Applying Wittgenstein to Positivism, Critical Theory, and Judging,* 141 University of Pennsylvania Law Review 371 (1992)
Nichols (1996a)
Philip M. Nichols, *GATT Doctrine,* 36 Virginia Journal of International Law 379 (1996)
Nichols (1996b)
Phillip M. Nichols, *Trade Without Values,* 90 Northwestern University Law Review 658 (1996)
O'Connel (1999)
Mary Ellen O'Connel, *New International Legal Process,* 93 AJIL 334 (1999)
Palmeter (2000)
David Palmeter, *The WTO as a Legal System,* 24 Fordham International Law Journal 444 (2000).

Palmeter & Mavroidis (1998)
D. Palmeter and P. C. Mavroidis, *The WTO Legal System: Sources of Law*, 92 AJIL 398 (1998)
Pauwelyn (1998)
Joost Pauwelyn, *Evidence, Proof and Persuasion in WTO Dispute Settlement: Who Bears the Burden?*, 1 JIEL 227 (1998)
Pauwelyn (2000)
Joost Pauwelyn, *Enforcement and Countermeasures in the WTO: Rules are Rules – Towards a more Collective Approach*, 94 AJIL 335 (2000)
Pauwelyn (2001)
Joost Pauwelyn, *Public International Law in the WTO System: How Far Can We Go?* 95 AJIL 535 (2001)
Petersmann (1991)
Ernst-Ulrich Petersmann, *Violation-complaints and Non-violation Complaints in Public International Trade Law*, 34 German Yearbook of International Law 175 (1991)
Petersmann (1994)
Ernst-Ulrich Petersmann, *The Dispute Settlement System of the World Trade Organization and the Evolution of the GATT Dispute Settlement System since 1948*, 31 Common Market Law Review 1157 (1994)
Petersmann (1998)
Ernst-Ulrich Petersmann, 'How to Promote the International Rule of Law? Contributions by the WTO Appellate Review System,' in CAMERON & CAMPBELL (EDS) (1998) p. 75
Petersmann (2003)
Ernst-Ulrich Petersmann, 'From Negative Integration in the WTO: The TRIPS Agreement and the WTO Constitution,' in COTTIER & MAVROIDIS (EDS) (2003) p. 21
Pescatore (1993)
Pierre Pescatore, *The GATT Dispute Settlement Mechanism – Its Present Situation and its Prospects*, 27 JWT 5 (1993)
Posner (1979)
Richard Posner, *Some Uses and Abuses of Economics in Law*, 46 University of Chicago Law Review 281 (1979)
Reichman (1998)
Jerome H. Reichman, *Securing Compliance with the TRIPS Agreement after US v India*, 1 JIEL 585 (1998)
Roessler (1997)
Frieder Roessler, 'The Concept of Nullification and Impairment in the Legal System of the World Trade Organization,' in PETERSMANN (ED.) (1997A) p. 125
Roessler (1999)
Frieder Roessler, *Should Principles of Competition Policy Be Incorporated into WTO Law Through Non-Violation Complaints?*, 2 JIEL 413 (1999).

Samahon (2000)
Tuna N. Samahon, *TRIPS Copyright Dispute Settlement after the Transition and Moratorium: Nonviolation and Situation Complaints against Developing Countries,* 31 Law and Policy in International Business 1051 (2000)
Schachter (1971)
Oscar Schachter, '*Towards a Theory of International Obligation,*' in THE EFFECTIVENESS OF INTERNATIONAL DECISIONS 9–10 (STEPHEN M. SCHWEBEL, ED., 1971)
Schoenbaum (1998)
Thomas J., Schoenbaum, *WTO Dispute Settlement: Praise and Suggestions for Reform*, 47 International and Comparative Law Quarterly 647 (1998)
Simma & Paulus (1999)
Bruno Simma and Andreas L. Paulus, *Responsibility of Individuals for Human Rights Abuses in Internal Conflicts: A Positivist View*, 93 AJIL 302 (1999)
Sullivan (1992)
Kathleen M. Sullivan, *The Justices of Rules and Standards*, 106 Harvard Law Review 22 (1992)
Sykes (1998)
Alan O. Sykes, *Comparative Advantage and The Normative Economics Of International Trade Policy,* 1 JIEL 49 (1998)
Sykes (1999)
Alan O. Sykes, *Regulatory Protectionism and the Law of International Trade,* 66 University of Chicago Law Review 1 (1999)
Swan (1999)
Alan C. Swan, *"Fairness" and "Reciprocity" in International Trade Section 301 and the Rule of Law*, 16 Arizona Journal of International and Comparative Law 37 (1999)
Tarullo (2000)
Daniel K. Tarullo, *Norms and Institutions in Global Competition Policy*, 94 AJIL 478 (2000)
Terrell (1984)
Timothy P. Terrell, *Flatlaw: An Essay on the Dimension of Legal Reasoning and the Development of Fundamental Normative Principles*, 72 California Law Review 288 (1984)
Tkacik (1997)
Michael Patrick Tkacik, *Post-Uruguay Round GATT/WTO Dispute Settlement: Substance, Weakness, and Causes for Concern*, 9 International Legal Perspectives 169 (1997)
Tietje (1997)
Christian Tietje, *The Concept of Coherence in the Treaty on European Union and the Common Foreign and Security Policy,* 2 European Foreign Affairs Review 211 (1997)

Trachtman (1999)
Joel P. Trachtman, *The Domain of WTO Dispute Resolution*, 40 Harvard International Law Journal 333 (1999)
Van Alstine (1998)
Michael P. Van Alstine, *Dynamic Treaty Interpretation,* 146 University of Pennsylvania Law Review 687 (1998)
Villalpando (2002)
Santiago M. Villalpando, *Attribution Of Conduct To The State: How The Rules Of State Responsibility May Be Applied Within The WTO Dispute Settlement System,* 5 JIEL 393 (2002)
Virally (1983)
Michael Virally, *Good Faith in Public International Law (review essay),* 77 AJIL 130 (1983)
Von Bogdandy (1992)
Armin Von Bogdandy, *The Non-Violation Procedure of Article XXIII: 2, GATT – Its Operations Rationale,* 26 JWT 95 (1992)
Wright (1985)
Richard W. Wright, *Causation in Tort Law,* 73 California Law Review 1735 (1985)
Zdouc (1999)
Werner Zdouc, *WTO Dispute Settlement Practice Relating to the GATS,* 2 JIEL 295 (1999)

Documents References*

A. Drafting of the General Agreement and the Havana Charter

1. First Session of the Preparatory Committee of the United Nations Conference on Trade and Employment (London, October–November 1946)

E/PT/T/33	Final Report of the First Session ("London Draft")
E/PC/T/PV/1–6	Plenary Session Verbatim Reports
E/PC/T/C.II/PRO/PV/5–15	Committee II, Sub-Committee on Procedures, Verbatim Reports

2. Second Session of the Preparatory Committee of the United Nations Conference on Trade and Employment (Geneva, April–October 1947)

E/PC/T/186	Report of the Second Session of the Preparatory Committee of the United Nations Conference on Trade and Employment (Geneva, April–October 1947) ("Geneva Draft")
E/PC/T/W/23–344	Plenary Working Papers
E/PC/T/A/PV/1–43	Commission A, Verbatim Reports

3. United Nations Conferences on Trade and Employment (Havana, November 1947 to March 1948)

E/CONF.2/1–78	Plenary Documents
E/CONF.2/78	Havana Charter
E/CONF.2/C.8/1–28	Committee VIII (Central Drafting Committee)

B. Interim Commission for the International Trade Organization

ICITO/I/1–39	Documents and Summary Records
ICITO/1/W.1–4	Working Papers

* These headings are as outlined in: WTO, 1 ANALYTICAL INDEX: GUIDE TO GATT LAW AND PRACTICE 9–19 (updated 6th ed., 1995).

C. GATT Documents

1. CONTRACTING PARTIES

   Basic Instruments and Selected Documents ("BISD")

2. Uruguay Round Document Series

MTN.GNG/NG13	Negotiating Group on Dispute Settlement
MTN.GNG/NG13/W/31	Group of Negotiations on Goods-Negotiating Group on Dispute Settlement – Non-Violation Complaints under GATT Article XXIII.2 (Note by the Secretariat on 14 July 1989)

D. WTO Documents**

1. GATT 94
2. GATS: (S/* or GATS/* or TN/S/*)
3. TRIPS: (IP/* or TN/IP/*)

IP/C/* Council for Trade-Related Aspects of Intellectual Property Rights ("TRIPS Council")

IP/C/M/* TRIPS Council – Minutes of Meeting

** All WTO Documents cited in this dissertation are taken from WTO website (www.wto.org).

Table of Cases Cited in this Dissertation*

Argentina – Bovine Hides
WTO Panel Report, *Argentina – Measures Affecting the Export of Bovine Hides and the Import of Finished Leather,* WT/DS155/R, adopted 16 February 2001

Argentina – Footwear and Apparel (AB)
Appellate Body Report, *Argentina – Measures Affecting Imports of Footwear, Textiles, Apparel and Other Items,* WT/DS56/AB/R, adopted 27 March 1998

Argentina – Footwear Safeguards (AB)
Appellate Body Report, *Argentina – Safeguard Measures on Imports of Footwear,* WT/DS121/AB/R, adopted 12 January 2000

Australia – Salmon (AB)
Appellate Body Report, *Australia – Measures Affecting Importation of Salmon,* WT/DS18/AB/R, adopted on 6 November 1998

Australian Subsidy (NVNI) **
GATT Working Party Report, *Australian Subsidy on Ammonium Sulphate,* GATT/CP.4/39, GATT BISD II/188, adopted on 3 April 1950

Canada – Alcoholic Drinks
GATT Panel Report, *Canada – Import, Distribution and Sale of Certain Alcoholic Drinks by Provincial Marketing Agencies,* DS17/R, BISD 39S/27, adopted on 18 February 1992

Canada – Beef
GATT Panel Report, *European Economic Community – Imports of Beef from Canada,* L/5099, BISD 28S/92, adopted on 10 March 1981

Canada – Ice Cream
GATT Panel Report, *Canada – Import Restrictions on Ice Cream and Yoghurt,* L/6568, BISD 36S/68, adopted 4 December 1989

Canada – Dairy (AB)
Appellate Body Report, *Canada – Measures Affecting the Importation of Milk and the Exportation of Dairy Products,* WT/DS103/AB/R, WT/DS113/AB/R and Corr.1, adopted 27 October 1999

* All cases cited in this dissertation are taken from Worldtradelaw.net (www.worldtradelaw.net); The Short Title of each case will be used in this dissertation. For example, *EC – Asbestos (AB)* means Appellate Body Report *on European Communities-Measures Affecting Asbestos and Asbestos-Containing Products (Complaint by Canada).*

** NVNI: Non-Violation Nullification or Impairment

Canada – FIRA
GATT Panel Report, *Canada – Administration of the Foreign Investment Review Act,* L/5504, BISD 30S/140, adopted 7 February 1984

Canada – Herring and Salmon
GATT Panel Report, *Canada – Measures Affecting Exports of Unprocessed Herring and Salmon,* L/6268, 35S/985, adopted 22 March 1988

Canada – Periodicals (AB)
Appellate Body Report *Canada – Certain Measures Concerning Periodicals,* WT/DS31/AB/R, adopted 30 July 1997

DISC
GATT Panel Report, *United States Tax Legislation (DISC),* L/4422, 23S/98, adopted 7–8 December 1981

EC – Asbestos (AB) (NVNI)
Appellate Body Report, *European Communities-Measures Affecting Asbestos and Asbestos-Containing Products – Complaint by Canada,* WT/DS135/AB/R, adopted 5 April 2001

EC – Asbestos (NVNI)
WTO Panel Report, *European Communities-Measures Affecting Asbestos and Asbestos-Containing Products (Complaint by Canada),* WT/DS135/R, adopted (as modified) by the Appellate Body on 5 April 2001

EC – Bananas I
GATT Panel Report, *EEC – Member States' Import Regime for Bananas,* DS32/R, adopted 3 June 1993

EC – Bananas II
GATT Panel Report, *EEC – Import Regime for Bananas,* DS38/R, adopted 11 February 1994

EC – Bananas III (Ecuador)
WTO Panel Report, *European Communities – Regime for the Importation, Sale and Distribution of Bananas,* WT/DS27/R/ECU (circulated 22 May 1997), adopted (as modified) 25 September 1997

EC – Bananas (AB)
Appellate Body Report, *European Communities – Regime for the Importation, Sale and Distribution of Bananas,* WT/DS27/AB/R, adopted 25 September 1997

EC – Canned Fruit (NVNI)
GATT Panel Report, *European Economic Community – Production Aids Granted on Canned Peaches, Canned Pears, Canned Fruit Cocktail and Dried Grapes,* L/5778, circulated 20 February 1985 (unadopted)

EC – Citrus (NVNI)
GATT Panel Report, *European Community – Tariff Treatment on Imports of Citrus Products from Certain Countries in the Mediterranean Region,* L/5776, circulated 7 February 1985 (unadopted)

EC – Computer Equipment (AB)
Appellate Body Report, *European Communities – Customs Classifications of Certain Computer Equipment,* WT/DS62/AB/R, adopted 22 June 1998

EC – Dessert Apples
European Economic Community – Restrictions on Imports of Dessert Apples – Complaint by Chile, L/6491, 36S/93, adopted 22 June 1989

EC – Hormones (Panel) (US)
WTO Panel Report, *EC Measures Concerning Meat and Meat Products (Hormones),* WT/DS26/R/USA (circulated 18 August 1997), adopted (as modified) 13 February 1998

EC – Hormones (Panel) (Canada)
WTO Panel Report, *EC Measures Concerning Meat and Meat Products (Hormones),* WT/DS48/R/CAN (circulated 18 August 1997), adopted (as modified) 13 February 1998

EC – Hormones (AB)
Appellate Body Report, *European Communities – Measures Concerning Meat and Meat Products (Hormones),* WT/DS26,48/AB/R, adopted 13 February 1998

EC-Oilseeds I (or Oilseeds) (NVNI)
GATT Panel Report, *European Economic Community-Payments and Subsidies Paid to Processors and Products of Oilseeds and Related Animal-Feed Proteins,* L/6627, BISD 37S/86, adopted 25 January 1990

EC – Oilseeds II (NVNI)
GATT Panel Report, *European Economic Community – Follow-up on the Panel Report, Payments and Subsidies Paid to Processors and Producers of Oilseeds and Related Animal-Feed Proteins,* DS28/R, BISD 39S/91, circulated 31 March 1992 (unadopted)

EC – Poultry (AB)
Appellate Body Report, *European Communities – Measures Affecting the Importation of Certain Poultry Products,* WT/DS69/AB/R, adopted 13 July 1998

EC – Sugar
GATT Panel Report, *European Communities – Refunds on Exports of Sugar,* L/4833, BISD 26S/290, adopted 6 November 1979

Germany – Starch
GATT Panel Report, *German Import Duties on Starch and Potato Flour,* W.9/178, BISD 3S/77, adopted 16 February 1955

Germany – Sardines (NVNI)
GATT Panel Report, *Treatment by Germany of Imports of Sardines,* G/26, BISD 1S/53, adopted 31 October 1952

Guatemala – Cement
WTO Panel Report, *Guatemala – Anti-Dumping Investigation Regarding Portland Cement from Mexico,* WT/DS60/R, adopted (as reversed) 25 November 1998

India – Patent I
WTO Panel Report, *India – Patent Protection for Pharmaceutical and Agricultural Chemical Products,* WT/DS50/R, adopted (as modified) 16 January 1998

India – Patent I (AB)
Appellate Body Report, *India – Patent Protection for Pharmaceutical and Agricultural Chemical Products*, WT/DS50/AB/R, adopted 16 January 1998.

Italian Agriculture Machinery
GATT Panel Report, *Italian Discrimination Against Imported Agricultural Machinery*, L/833, 7S/607, adopted 23 October 1958

Japan – Agricultural Products
GATT Panel Report, *Japan – Restrictions on Imports of Certain Agricultural Products*, L/6253, 35S/163 adopted 18 November 1987

Japan – Alcoholic Beverages (AB)
Appellate Body Report, *Japan – Taxes on Alcoholic Beverages*, WT/DS 8,10,11/AB/R, adopted 1 November 1996

Japan – Customs Duties
GATT Panel Report, *Japan – Customs Duties, Taxes and Labelling Practices on Imported Wines and Alcoholic Beverages*, L/6216, 34S/83, adopted 10/11 November 1987

Japan – GATT Objectives
GATT Panel Report, *Japan – Nullification and Impairment of Benefits and Impediment to the Attainment of GATT Objectives*, L/5479, adopted 8 April 1983

Japan – Imports Leather
GATT Panel Report, *Japanese Measures on Imports Leather*, L/5623, BISD 31S/94, adopted 15/16 May 1984

Japan – Film (or Film) (NVNI)
WTO Panel Report, *Japan – Measures Affecting Consumer Photographic Film and Paper*, WT/DS44/R, adopted on 31 March 1998

Japan – Semi-Conductors (NVNI)
GATT Panel Report, *Japan – Trade in Semi-Conductors*, L/6309, 35S/116, adopted 4 May 1988

Korea – Alcoholic Beverages (AB)
Appellate Body Report, *Korea – Taxes on Alcoholic Beverages*, WT/DS 75,84/AB/R, adopted 17 February 1999

Korea – Beef
WTO Panel Report, *Korea – Measures Affecting Imports of Fresh, Chilled and Frozen Beef*, WT/DS161/R and WT/DS169/R, adopted (as modified) 10 January 2001

Korea – Dairy (AB)
Appellate Body Report, *Korea – Definitive Safeguard Measure on Imports of Certain Dairy Products*, WT/DS98/AB/R, adopted 12 January 2000

Korea – Polyacetal Resins
GATT Panel Report, *Korea – Antidumping Duties on Imports of Polyacetal Resins*, ADP/92, 40S/205, adopted by the Anti-Dumping ("ADP") Committee on 27 April 1993

Korea – Procurement
WTO Panel Report, *Korea – Measures Affecting Government Procurement,* WT/DS163/R, adopted 19 June 2000

New Zealand – Imports of Electrical Transformers
GATT Panel Report, *New Zealand – Imports of Electrical Transformers from Finland,* L/5814, 32S/55, adopted 18 July 1985

Spain – Soyabean Oil (NVNI)
GATT Panel Report, *Spain – Measures Concerning Domestic Sale of Soyabean Oil,* L/5142, circulated 17 June 1981 (unadopted)

Uruguayan Recourse to Article XXIII (NVNI)
GATT Panel Report, *Uruguayan Recourse to Article XXIII,* adopted 16 November 1962, L/1923, BISD 11S/95

US – Anti-Dumping Act of 1916
WTO Panel Report, *United States – Anti-Dumping Act of 1916,* WT/DS136/R, adopted 26 September 2000

US – Copyright Act
WTO Panel Report, *United States – Section 110(5) of the US Copyright Act,* WT/DS160/R, adopted 27 July 2000

US – Cotton and Underwear (AB)
Appellate Body Report, *United States-Restrictions on Import of Cotton and Man-Made Fibre Underwear,* WT/DS24/AB/R, adopted 25 February 1997

US – Cotton Yarn (AB)
Appellate Body Report, *United States – Transitional Safeguard Measure on Combed Cotton Yarn from Pakistan,* WT/DS192/AB/R, adopted 5 November 2001

United States Customs User Free
GATT Panel Report, *United States Customs User Free,* L/6264, BISD 35S/245, adopted 2 February 1988

US – FSC (AB)
Appellate Body Report, *United States – Tax Treatment for "Foreign Sales Corporations,"* WT/DS108/AB/R, adopted 20 March 2000.

US – Gasoline
WTO Panel Report, *United States – Standards for Reformulated and Conventional Gasoline,* WT/DS2/R (circulated 29 January 1996), adopted (as modified) 20 May 1996

US – Gasoline (AB)
Appellate Report, *United States – Standards for Reformulated and Conventional Gasoline,* adopted 20 May 1996

US – Hot-Rolled Steel (AB)
Appellate Body Report, *United States – Anti-Dumping Measures on Certain Hot-Rolled Steel Products from Japan,* WT/DS184/AB/R, adopted 23 August 2001

US – Lamb
WTO Panel Report, *United States – Safeguard Measures on Imports of Fresh, Chilled or Frozen Lamb Meat from New Zealand and Australia,* WT/DS177/R and WT/DS178/R, adopted (as modified) 16 May 2001

US – Malt Beverages
GATT Panel Report, *United States – Measures Affecting Alcoholic and Malt Beverages,* DS 23/R, 39S/206, adopted 19 June 1992

US – Nicaragua (NVNI)
GATT Panel Report, *United States – Trade Measures Affecting Nicaragua,* L/6053, circulated 13 October 1986 (unadopted)

US – Offset Act
WTO Panel Report, *United States – Continued Dumping and Subsidy Offset Act of 2000,* WT/DS 217, 234/R, adopted 16 January 2003

US – Offset Act (AB)
Appellate Body Report, *United States – Continued Dumping and Subsidy Offset Act of 2000,* WT/DS217, 234/AB/R, adopted 16 January 2003

US – Restrictions on Imports of Sugar
GATT Panel Report, *United States – Restrictions on Imports of Sugar,* L/6514, BISD 36S/331, adopted 22 June 1989

US – Section 337
GATT Panel Report, *United States – Section 337 of the Tariff Act of 1930,* L/6439, BISD 36S/345, adopted 7 November 1989

US – Shirts and Blouses (AB)
Appellate Body Report, *United States – Measure Affecting Imports of Woven Wool Shirts and Blouses from India,* WT/DS33/AB/R, adopted 23 May 1997

US – Shrimp
WTO Panel Report, *United States – Import Prohibition of Certain Shrimp and Shrimp Products,* WT/DS58/R (circulated 5 May 1998), adopted (as modified) 6 November 1998

US – Shrimp (AB)
Appellate Body Report, *United States – Import Prohibition of Certain Shrimp and Shrimp Products,* WT/DS58/AB/R, adopted 6 November 1998

US – Shrimp (21.5)
WTO Panel Report, *United States – Import Prohibition of Certain Shrimp and Shrimp Products, Recourse to Article 21.5 by Malaysia,* WT/DS58/RW, adopted 15 June 2001

US – Sugar Waiver (NVNI)
GATT Panel Report, *United States – Restrictions on the Importation of Sugar and Sugar-Containing Products Applied under the 1955 Waiver and under the Headnote to the Schedule of Tariff Concessions,* L/6631, BISD 37S/228, adopted 7 November 1990

US – Superfund
GATT Panel Report, *United States – Taxes on Petroleum and Certain Imported Substances,* L/6175, 34S/136, adopted 17 June 1987

US – Tobacco
GATT Panel Report, *United States – Measures Affecting the Importation, Internal Sale and Use of Tobacco.* DS44/R, adopted 4 October 1994

US – Section 301
WTO Panel Report, *United States – Sections 301–310 of the Trade Act of 1974*, WT/DS152/R, adopted 27 January 2000

US – Tuna I
GATT Panel Report, *United States – Restrictions on Imports of Tuna*, DS21/R, 39S/155, adopted 3 September 1991

US – Tuna II
GATT Panel Report, *United States – Restrictions on Imports of Tuna*, DS 29/R, adopted 16 June 1994

US – Wool Shirts
WTO Panel Report, *United States-Measure Affecting Imports of Woven Wool Shirts and Blouses from India*, WT/DS33/R (circulated 6 January 1997), adopted as upheld by the Appellate Body on 23 May 1997

US – Wool Shirts (AB) Appellate Body Report, *United States – Measure Affecting Imports of Woven Wool Shirts and Blouses from India*, WT/DS33/AB/R and Corr.1, adopted 23 May 1997

Value-Added Tax and Threshold
GATT Panel Report, *Value-Added Tax and Threshold*, GPR/21, BISD 31S/247, Adopted by the Committee on Government Procurement on 16 May 1984

Standard Abbreviations

AB	WTO Appellate Body
AJIL	American Journal of International Law
BISD	GATT, Basic Instruments and Selected Documents. The citation "BISD 36S/86 (1990)" means "page 86 of the 36th Supplement to BISD, published in 1990"
DSB	Dispute Settlement Body
DSU	WTO Dispute Settlement Understanding
DSM	Dispute Settlement Mechanism
GATS	General Agreement on Trade in Service
GATT	General Agreement on Tariff and Trade
EC	European Economic Community
EJIL	European Journal of International Law
E/PC/T	United Nations Documents of 1946–1947
EU	European Union
HAVANA (ITO) CHARTER	Havana Charter for an International Trade Organisation, U.N. ESCOR, U.N. Doc. E/CONF. 2/78 (24 March 1948)
ICJ	International Court of Justice
ICJ Reports	Reports of Judgments, Advisory Opinions and Orders of International Court of Justice
ILC	International Law Commission
ILC Yearbook	Yearbook of the International Law Commission
IMF	International Monetary Fund
ITO	International Trade Organisation
JIEL	Journal of International Economic Law
JWT	Journal of World Trade
MFN	Most-Favoured-Nation
PCIJ Series A	Permanent Court of International Justice, Judgments and Orders 1922–30
TMB	Textiles Monitoring Body
TRIPS	Trade-Related Aspects of Intellectual Property Rights
U.N. ESCOR	United Nations Economic and Social Council Official Records
U.N. G.A.	United Nations General Assembly Official Records
US	United States
USC	United States Code
WIPO	World Intellectual Property Organisation
WTO	World Trade Organisation

Special Abbreviations

- AB — Appellate Body
- NVNI — Non-Violation Nullification or Impairment
- THE LEGAL TEXTS (1995) — WTO, FINAL ACT EMBODYING THE RESULTS OF THE URUGUAY ROUND OF MULTILATERAL TRADE NEGOTIATIONS: THE LEGAL TEXTS (1995)
- Most articles cited in this dissertation are taken from "Lexis-Nexis Legal Database" and "Westlaw Legal Database"
- For articles appearing in *1* [Journal] *1, 10 (2003)* means Volume 1 of [Journal], the article Starting at 1 with a Specific reference to page 10, Year of publication was 2003
- 'at' refers to the page or pages in any reference; 'p.' or 'pp.' refers to the page or pages in a subsection of the edited book; '§' refers to 'section' of the book
- *Words in italics within main body are the emphasis of the writer of this dissertation unless otherwise indicated*; underlying is employed to highlight a comparison
- Words enclosed with " " means quoted from the reference

Part One

The Concept of Non-Violation Nullification or Impairment in WTO Law

It appears to me that what [GATT causes of action] say[s] is this: in this wide world of sin there are certain sins which we have not yet discovered and which after long examination we cannot define; but there being such sins, we will provide for some sort of punishment for them if we find out what they are and if we find anybody committing them.

Dr Holloway, Geneva Report (1947)

I. Outline of Dissertation

A. Non-Violation Complaints and GATT/WTO Jurisprudence

1. Negotiated Balance of Rights and Obligations in WTO

International trade relations came to be regulated within the framework of World Trade Organisation (WTO) established by one of the five agreements composing the Uruguay Round Agreements.[1] The

1 The five agreements consist of the Marrakesh Agreement Establishing the World Trade Organisation (WTO Agreement), the Multilateral Trade Agreements, the Understanding on Rules and Procedures Governing the Settlement of Disputes (Dispute Settlement Understanding or DSU), the Trade Policy Review Mechanism, and the Plurilateral Trade Agreements. The Multilateral Trade Agreements are located in Annex 1 of the WTO Agreement. The Dispute Settlement Understanding is located in Annex 2. The Trade Policy Review Mechanism is located in Annex 3. The Plurilateral Trade Agreements are located in Annex 4. *See* THE LEGAL TEXTS (1995), at 7; For a history of the Uruguay Round from its inception in 1986 to 1992, *see* A NEGOTIATING HISTORY (1993); The most prominent innovation of the WTO Agreement is its "single undertaking approach" which aims, as noted in the Preamble of the Agreement, "to develop an integrated, more viable and durable multilateral trading system." *See* THE LEGAL TEXTS, at 6. This Agreement consists of a series of annexed additional agreements and legal instruments dealing with trade in goods and services as well as intellectual property rights. These are referred to as the "WTO Agreements" or "covered agreements." The most important of these are the annex entitled "Multilateral Agreements on Trade in Goods," which includes the text of General Agreement on Tariffs and Trade 1994 (GATT 94), with six Understandings concerning the interpretation of its Articles, and 12 substantive agreements, running from the Agreement on Agriculture to the Agreement on Safeguards; the General Agreement on Trade in Services (GATS); and the Agreement on Trade-Related Aspects of Intellectual Property Rights (TRIPS).

establishment of the WTO provides for a multilateral institutional structure[2] for regulating trade relations among its Members.[3] The creation of WTO as an actual trade organisation was a marked improvement over the WTO's predecessor, the General Agreement on Tariffs and Trade 1947 ("GATT 47"),[4] which never formed an organisation *per se*. Among the many improvements to the GATT 47, the WTO Agreement substantially changed the mechanism for dispute settlement. This change, codified as the Understanding on Rules and Procedures Governing the Settlement of Disputes (Dispute Settlement Understanding or DSU),[5] was initially hailed as a great improvement over the GATT dispute settlement provisions whenever conflicts on *negotiated balance between rights and obligations* arose.

2 The structure of the WTO is made up of a Ministerial Conference and a General Council, each composed of representatives of all the Members, which meet at least once every two years and as appropriate, respectively. The General Council basically takes over the functions of the Ministerial Conference in between its meetings by carrying out the functions of the WTO, making decisions on all matters under any of the multilateral trade agreements, and taking any necessary actions to such effect. The General Council is also in charge of discharging the responsibilities of the Dispute Settlement Body provided for in the Understanding. Finally, councils and committees are created for various elements under the WTO, such as trade in goods, services, and intellectual property, and development, finance, and the budget. *See* WTO Agreement, Article IV, in THE LEGAL TEXTS 8 (1995).

3 The "Members" of the WTO are governments or separate customs territories exercising full autonomy in matters provided for in the WTO Agreement and the annexed Multilateral Trade Agreements, *see* WTO Agreement, Article XII : 1; The primary purpose of the WTO are two-fold: to ensure the reduction of tariffs and other barriers to trade, and the elimination of discriminating treatment in international trade relations, *see* the Preamble of the WTO Agreement; The original GATT 47 mentioned "any contracting party" rather than "a Member," *see* Article 2(a) of GATT 94.

4 General Agreement on Tariffs and Trade (GATT 1947), THE LEGAL TEXTS, at 485–558; For the historical background of the postwar global economic situations and the birth of GATT, *see generally* WINHAM (1992), at 43–52; HUDEC (1990), at 3–61; DAM (1970), at 10–16; For a general review on the progressive transformation of GATT 47 from temporary contract on the reciprocal liberalization of tariffs into a complex system of multilateral trade agreement, *see* GATT, GATT STATUS OF LEGAL INSTRUMENT (GENEVA: GATT, 1993).

5 *See* THE LEGAL TEXTS (1995), at 404–33.

This institutional development allows the global trade relations to be more dynamic and interdependent than it has been in past decades.[6] With the increased interdependence of the global economy,[7] the negotiated balance of rights and obligations in WTO have a greater importance since any deviation from the balance is more likely than ever to affect WTO Members.[8] The growing international interdependence in the trade relations, on the other hand, is expected to complicate possible trade disputes[9] because each Member will try to protect *domestic* commercial, social and political stability, using measures to the extent of not shattering *international*

6 *See, e.g.* Bhagwati (1996) p. 28; JACKSON (1997), at 6–8.

7 The economic interdependency, rather than the concept of State sovereignty, lays the foundation of international economic law, *see* Miquel Montatna i Mora, *A GATT with Teeth: Law wins over Politics in the Resolution of International Trade Disputes,* 31 Columbia Journal of Transnational Law 103, 105 (1993); For the importance and implications of interdependency in international economic activities, *see, e.g.*, JACKSON, DAVEY & SYKES (1995), at 87; Cottier (1998c), at 86 (stating that foreign and domestic economic regulation can be no longer separated); Marsha A. Echols, *Food Safety Regulation in the European Union and the United States: Different Cultures, Different Laws,* 4 Columbia Journal of European Law 525 (1998) (stating that the globalization and interdependence affect regulation of food safety); John H. Jackson, *Global Economics and International Economic Law,* 1 Journal of International Economic Law (JIEL) 1, 1–23 (1998); Julie Mertus, *From Legal Transplants to Transformative Justice: Human Rights and the Promise of Transnational Civil Society,* 14 American University of International Law Review 1335 (1999); Alex Y. Seita, *Globalisation and the Convergence of Values,* 30 Cornell International Law Journal 429 (1997); Renato Ruggiero, Ex-Director-General of WTO, *The Global Challenge: Opportunities and Choices in the Multilateral Trading System,* Address to Harvard University (16 October 1995) (last visited 15 January 2003) at <http://www. wto.org/english/news_e/sprr_e/harvar_e.htm>

8 *See, e.g.*, WTO Appellate Body Report, *EC – Bananas (AB),* para. 136. The Appellate Body agreed with the following Panel's statement: "[…] with the increased interdependence of the global economy, […] Members have a greater stake in enforcing WTO rules than in the past since any deviation from the negotiated balance of rights and obligations is more likely than ever to affect them, directly or indirectly."

9 *See, e.g.* JAGDISH. BHAGWATI, 'Fair Trade, Reciprocity and Harmonization: The New Challenge to the Theory and Policy of Free Trade,' in 3 ANDERSON & HOEKMAN (EDS) (2002), pp. 27–31; JACKSON (2000), at 414–48.

stability negotiated in the WTO.[10] This "liberal"[11] international trading system initiated from the temporary legal structure of the GATT 47 has been retained in the WTO legal system[12] in the shape of negotiated rights and obligations.

2. *Non-Violation Complaints and Balance of Rights and Obligations*

One of the most intriguing jurisprudential issues for WTO judicial bodies[13] concerning the balance between rights and obligations in WTO law is the somewhat "dazzling" claims under Article XXIII : 1(b)

10 This kind of a delicate balancing setting from the historical backgrounds of GATT, and its successor WTO as well, has functioned as an apparatus of avoiding extreme protectionist measures that is disastrous for the global economy. This setting is said to have "widely perceived by the founders of the Bretton Woods system to have led eventually to perilous instability in the interstate system and economic catastrophe in the interwar years-which phenomena were seen as having contributed to the climate that made fascism, and the Second World War itself, possible," *see* Howse (2002), at 95; For a general overview, *see* JACKSON (2000), at 458–61.

11 *See* RUGGIE (1998), at 62–84. He explained the essence of the *embedded liberalism* compromise as "Unlike the economic nationalism of the thirties, [embedded liberalism] would be multilateral in character; unlike the liberalism of the gold standard and free trade, its multilateralism would be predicted upon domestic interventionism," *see id.*, at 72–73; *See also* JACKSON (1990), at 11–14.

12 From a legal perspective, a "system" would indicate a specific legal order which links the various principles and objectives to form a coherent unit. *See* Hilf (2001), at 112.

13 "WTO judicial bodies" indicate the WTO Panels and the Appellate Body. Curtis Reitz discussed the similarities of the WTO Appellate Body and a judicial court, *see* CURTIS REITZ, *Enforcement of the General Agreement on Tariffs and Trade,* 17 University of Pennsylvania Journal of International Economic Law 555, 583 (1996); *But cf.* Richard L. Matheny, III, *"Like Products" and Cultural Products after the World Trade Organisation's Decision in Canada Certain Measures Concerning Periodicals,* 147 University of Pennsylvania Law Review 245, 249 n. 21 (1998). He argued that "There are, however, important differences, [...]. For instance, the precedential weight of panel appellate body reports is an open question, as is the authority of the appellate body to resolve issues not litigated before the panel". *Idem.*

and (c) of the General Agreement on Tariffs and Trade 1994 ("GATT 94").[14] It secures a WTO member's claim against measures by another member, even if the measures do not violate specific WTO obligations, if these measures nullify or impair "any benefit" or impede "any objective" of the Agreement.[15] This is known as a "GATT's equity concept"[16] of Non-Violation Nullification or Impairment ("NVNI") because the measures alleged to violate WTO obligations under this provision do not have to be an explicit breach of any provision in a WTO agreement or of any concessions made by the other WTO member.[17] Article XXIII : 1 of the GATT provides for three legally-distinct *causes of action*[18] on which a member may base a complaint. It distinguishes between so-called *violation*, *non-violation* and *situation* complaints under subparagraph (a), (b) and (c) respectively. Because neither complaints raised under subparagraph 1(b) nor 1(c) concern violations, they are sometimes referred to collectively as "non-violation complaints."[19] They read:

14 THE LEGAL TEXTS (1995), Annex 1A (incorporating the provisions of the GATT 47). The only textual difference between the two instruments is that GATT 94 also consists of a number of additional legal instruments, including the texts of protocols of accession to GATT 47, decisions under GATT 47 and several understandings arrived at by the parties to GATT 1947, *see* THE LEGAL TEXTS, Annex 1A, para. 1. In this dissertation, "GATT" refers to the texts of both GATT 47 and GATT 94.

15 Article XXIII : 1 of GATT. This dissertation focuses on the NVNI complaints under the GATT 94. The NVNI concept thus contains the case in which a measure does not directly violate a covered agreement, yet impedes the attainment of objectives of a covered agreement. This case was coined as "non-violation impediment to objectives," *see* DAUL (1995), at 137 n. 113.

16 Robert E. Hudec, *A Statistical Profile of GATT Dispute Settlement Cases: 1948–1989,* 2 Minnesota Journal of Global Trade 1, 6 (1993); *See also* COTTIER & SCHEFER (2000), p. 48.

17 *See, e.g.* PETERSMANN (1997B), at 147–50; TREBILCOCK & HOWSE (2001), at 80; WAINCYMER (2002), at 92–117; *See also* COTTIER & SCHEFER (1997), p. 146; DURLING & LESTER (1998), at 212; ROESSLER (1997), p. 125; CHO (1998), at 313.

18 *Cause of action* is defined as "A group of operative facts giving rise to one or more bases for suing." *See* BLACK'S LAW DICTIONARY (1999), at 214.

19 However, the term "non-violation complaints" has never been precisely defined by the CONTRACTING PARTIES. Nor have the differences between claims under Article XXIII : 1(b) and (c), or the relationship between "situations" in

> 1. If any contracting party should consider that any benefit accruing to it directly or indirectly under this Agreement is being nullified or impaired or that the attainment of any objective of the Agreement is being impeded as the result of…
>
> (b) the application by another contracting party of any measure, whether or not it conflicts with the provisions of this Agreement, or
>
> (c) the existence of any other situation,
>
> the contracting party may, with a view to the satisfactory adjustment of the matter make written representations or proposals to the other contracting party or parties which it considers to be concerned.[20]

With regards to the Article XXIII : 1(c), commonly known as "situation" complaints, there have been very little traces in the GATT/ WTO jurisprudence.[21] This dissertation deals mainly with Article XXIII : 1(b) of GATT [Article XXIII : 1(b) or GATT Article XXIII : 1(b)] non-violation nullification or impairment complaints under the abbreviation of NVNI complaints.

---

terms of Article XXIII : 1(c) and "situations" mentioned in other safeguard clauses such as Article XII, XVIII and XIX, been specifically regulated in the text of Article XXIII. *See* Uruguay Round Document, MTN.GNG/NG13/W/31, para. 4; WTO Appellate Body Report, *EC-Asbestos (AB),* para. 185.

20 Article XXIII : 1 of GATT, in THE LEGAL TEXTS (1995), at 521.

21 A "situation" complaint can be teased out of the complaints in two GATT cases. *See Uruguayan Recourse to Article XXIII* and *Japan – GATT Objectives.* The details of the two cases are given in HUDEC (1993), at 445–46 & 512. The latter case is a 1983 complaint by the EC against Japan that the benefits of successive negotiations with Japan had not been realised due to factors peculiar to the Japanese economy that had allegedly resulted in a lower level of imports. The EC ultimately did not pursue its complaint, *see* GATT ANALYTICAL INDEX (1995), at 670–71; There have been no GATT panel decisions recognizing non-violation claims based on Article XXIII : 1(c), *see* JACKSON, DAVEY & SYKES (1995). at 364; Matsushita, Schoenbaum & Mavroidis expect that "In the future, situation complaints seem unlikely," *see* MATSUSHITA et al. (2003), at 84; For a more concrete review, *see* WAINCYMER (2002), at 110–11; ROESSLER (1997), p. 139; In competition law context, Kevin Kennedy dealt with "situation" complaints, *see* Kennedy (2001), at 644–46; In addition, Article XXIII : 1(c) "has never been the foundation for a recommendation or ruling of the GATT CONTRACTING PARTIES or the Dispute Settlement Body," *see* WTO Appellate Body Report, *India – Patent I(AB),* para. 39.

B. Aims and Structure of Dissertation

1. *Aims of Dissertation*

There are two broad aims of this dissertation.

First, this dissertation seeks to develop a theory of adjudicating NVNI complaints. It assesses how adjudicators have decided NVNI cases and suggests how they ought to decide such cases. It concerns thus a *theory of legal reasoning or interpretation.*

Second, the dissertation theorises a NVNI complaint as a *sort of violation complaint* or *liability*. This theorisation will use a *coherent interpretation* so that WTO adjudicators can assess the applicable scope of the NVNI complaint, and interpret trade issues not expressly covered by WTO provisions.

2. *Structure of Dissertation*

This dissertation proceeds in four specific steps.

Part One examines the significances of NVNI complaints and summarises conceptual development of the NVNI complaints. *First*, the conceptual origins of NVNI complaints are investigated, referring to historical and institutional backgrounds of the concept. *Second*, the conceptual development of the NVNI complaints will be illustrated using GATT/WTO cases and the current WTO Agreements. We employ the Vienna Convention on the Law of Treaties (Vienna Convention) to find out the jurisprudential roots of NVNI complaints.

Part Two will review NVNI complaints within the conventional interpretation of the Vienna Convention. This review is intended to find out the *conceptual identity* of NVNI complaint in terms of international jurisprudence. *First*, the various interpretations of NVNI complaints will be categorised from the standpoint of the Vienna Convention. *Second*, in the course of this categorisation three requirements for a successful NVNI complaint will be explained. These analyses render the *conceptual identity* of NVNI complaints as *liability* in international jurisprudence which *procedurally* triggers a *cause of action* of GATT Article XXIII: 1. Moreover, these invoke also a more refined interpretation to *clarify the conceptual constituents* and *applicable scopes of the liability* in NVNI complaints.

Part Three concerns explorations of conceptual constituents and applicable scopes of the NVNI complaints under a refined interpretation. First, it will address the NVNI complaints under a *rule-oriented* WTO dispute settlement mechanism, highlighting the dichotomy of *positive* and *normative* aspects of NVNI complaints. This necessitates an interpretation (or legal reasoning) process to contain both the positive and normative aspects of NVNI complaints. Second, such a legal reasoning process will be depicted, centering on International Law Process (ILP) discourse. The elaboration on the ILP will converge on an interpretive guideline (i.e. *coherence*) to efficiently include the positive and normative aspects of NVNI complaints.

Part Four will elaborate a *coherent interpretation* which contains a couple of subcomponents within it. First, in terms of *internal coherence* of Article XXIII: 1, the most appropriate meanings of some critical terms (e.g., "benefits," or "objective") are sought. Second, *external coherence* in the interpretive process will connect the theoretical rationale of *legitimate expectation* with the Article XXIII: 1. Through these reviews, the *existence of a liability* or a *constituent of legal obligation* and *its applicable scope* in the Article XXIII: 1(b) will be confirmed.

Conclusion presents the implications of the perspective of liability for the current negotiating round.

II. Significance of Non-Violation Complaints

A. In General

1. Non-Violation as a Balancing Mechanism of Benefit

In effect, Article XXIII of GATT 47 was developed in the 1920s and 1930s in bilateral trade agreements[1] and made necessary for preventing reciprocally balanced tariff concessions from being frustrated by non-tariff trade barriers[2] or by other governmental measures.[3] Furthermore, in order to prevent frustrating a treaty's goal by lawful measures, unorthodox remedies such as NVNI or situation complaints were adopted. The drafters of the GATT must have realised that the intended effect of tariff reductions could be easily undermined by measures that the GATT did not address and regulate such as competition policy, subsidies and product regulations serving proper domestic policy goals.[4] However, due to inadequate standards with the lawful measures and their incomplete procedure-bases, procedures were needed for adjusting tariff concessions following the introduction of such measures. The Article XXIII: 1(b) and (c) must have been envisaged to carry out that role. From a

1 COTTIER & SCHEFER (1996), p. 166; Hudec (1970), at 616; For a detailed historical origin, *see* PART ONE-II-B of this dissertation.

2 Non-tariff barriers (NTBs) include manoeuvres such as internal taxation on foreign goods and changing a product's tariff classification to defeat the value of the negotiated tariff. For a general approach to the NTBs, *see* JACKSON (1997), at 154–55.

3 PETERSMANN (ED.) (1997A), at 143–44.

4 HUDEC (1990), at 46. He asserted that "The draftmen [of GATT/International Trade Organisation] perceived that matters outside the legal code could cause serious controversy and instability". He also explained the nullification or impairment clause in terms of a "regulatory system." *Id.*

lawyer's viewpoint, this combination of substantive basis and its procedural enforcement in the remedy was unusual and even incomplete. To put it another way, NVNI complaints clearly present "a diplomat's concept of legal order"[5] and were used as a remedy to expand the reach of the written provisions of the GATT.[6]

Therefore, the GATT Article XXIII : 1 differs from the dispute settlement provisions of most other international agreements in several respects. Traditionally, the dispute settlement provisions of international treaties focus on legal concepts such as the rights and obligations of the Member countries, infringement of treaty obligations, or "legal disputes concerning: (a) the interpretation of a treaty; (b) any question of international law; (c) the existence of any fact which, if established, would constitute a breach of an international obligation; (d) the nature or extent of the reparation to be made for the breach of an international obligation".[7]

By contrast, Article XXIII makes use of certain concepts that are rather unique in the international law. It proceeds from the concept of "nullification or impairment of any benefit [...] accruing under this Agreement" that can give the GATT "regulatory powers to subsequent events".[8] Therefore, international responsibility in WTO law is not assessed only in terms of compliance with specific provisions of the relevant WTO Agreements. Rather, it is the idea of *nullification or impairment of benefits* that determines whether rights to complain arise under the GATT.[9] In other words, what is actionable under the WTO is not so much the breach of obligations, but "the upsetting of the negotiated balance of benefits consisting of rights, obligations and additional trade concessions."[10] Even

5 HUDEC (1993), at 7 ("At least, [the diplomat's concept of legal order] is the way [GATT] started out").
6 COTTIER & SCHEFER (1997), p. 166.
7 Article 36 of the Statute of the International Court of Justice (ICJ), *see* BROWNLIE (ED.) (1995), at 447–48.
8 HUDEC (1990), at 47 ("Legal arrangements of this kind [of nullification or impairment] are not common, for governments do not easily entrust the eventual shape of an institution's regulatory powers to subsequent events").
9 COTTIER & SCHEFER (1997), p. 146.
10 PAUWELYN (2000), at 341.

breaches of obligations are described in GATT practice as "*prima facie* nullification or impairment of benefits". In addition, many other seemingly "unusual" legal concepts (e.g. "impediment of any objective", "any situation") have neither been defined in the GATT itself nor in subsequent GATT practices. This legal uncertainty has been on the one hand criticised as reducing the legal predictability of the WTO dispute settlement mechanism[11] and yet on the other hand assessed as offering more flexibility of the legal obligation.[12]

This *nullification or impairment approach* in *causes of action* directly parallels two possible remedies: either the losing party removes the trade restricting measure or the prevailed party enacts its own trade restriction by removing an earlier trade concession. The resulting enforcement regime was, however, both lenient and strict.[13] While the customary consequences linked to a breach of an international law obligation, cessation and reparation[14] were avoided, the system was uniquely strict: parties were held responsible not only for breaches of GATT obligations, but also for nullification or impairment caused by conduct whether it conflicted with any specific GATT provision or not.[15]

One commentator suggested that if the drafters of the GATT had focused on specified legal obligations, which must have ossified the dispute settlement mechanism of the GATT and thereby made the mechanism unenforceable, the balancing of tariff concessions should have been more difficult or even impossible.[16] Con-

11 PETERSMANN (1997B), at 142–50.
12 HUDEC (1990), at 46–47.
13 PAUWELYN (2000), at 340.
14 For the definitions and commentaries on the "cessation" and "reparation", *see* CRAWFORD (2002), at 196–206.
15 PAUWELYN (2000), *id.*
16 HUDEC (1990), at 36 ("The beauty of this [diplomat's] technique was its safety. Just as it permitted administrators to turn away from legal conclusions that proved unenforceable, so would it permit retreat when more adventurous suggestions of legal authority proved unacceptable"); *See also* HUDEC, *id.*, at 46 ("The nullification and impairment provision is a classic example of how the various elements of law's authority can be assembled without necessarily following the model of conventional legal systems").

trary to the previous observation, another scholar pointed out that, since the notion of the nullification or impairment can no longer be accommodated as easily in the more rigorous legal environment of the new dispute settlement procedure of WTO, the requirement of a nullification finding becomes increasingly pointless.[17]

2. *Theoretical Significance of Non-Violation Complaints*

The significance of NVNI complaints can be divided into two parts. From a *theoretical* viewpoint of the WTO legal system, the complaints are said to confuse the whole GATT/WTO system.[18] The complaints often use broad legal principles like "legitimate expectation"[19] which is neither defined in WTO Agreements nor clear from the texts of DSU. The requirements for the NVNI complaints have been mainly supplemented through the judicial decisions of the WTO Dispute Settlement Body (DSB).[20] Hence a critic has argued that such a complaint is "a legal fantasy [...] and dangerous construction".[21]

Contrasted with this extreme negative opinion about the utility of NVNI complaints, most scholars seem to recognise the function of the complaints, ranging from supporting restrained use[22] to broadening the use of NVNI complaints over the entire

17 PETERSMANN (1997B), at 142–50; Moreover, he argued that the concept of NVNI makes no sense at all in the TRIPS agreement, *id.*, at 149–50.

18 *See, e.g.,* CHO (1998), at 313.

19 *See, e.g.,* COTTIER & SCHEFER (1997), pp. 162–63.

20 CHUA (1998), at 39; DSB consists of representatives of every WTO Members. Article IV:3 of the WTO Agreement provides that the General Council shall convene as appropriate to discharge the responsibilities of the DSB as provided for in the DSU. Article 2 of the DSU provides for the DSB to administer the rules and procedures; The original GATT 47 referred to "CONTRACTING PARTIES" rather than "Dispute Settlement Body," *see* Article 2(b) of GATT 94.

21 PESCATOR (1993), at 19 (claiming that the NVNI construction resulted from "a merely grammatical turn of the words in the General Agreement: 'whether or not'").

22 *See, e.g.,* JACKSON (1997), at 114–15; CHO (1998), at 321–33; COTTIER & SCHEFER (1997), at 181–82; HUDEC (1993), at 7; PETERSMANN (1994), at 1188; ROESSLER (1999), at 418.

WTO.[23] Previous opinion is that the provision of Article XXIII: 1(b) sets forth dangerously broad language that should be construed narrowly.[24] On the other hand, it is the same opinion that Article XXIII: 1(b) has the potential to be an important piece of the WTO Agreements architecture.[25] Provoked by the Panel Report on *Japan – Film*,[26] many have analysed the claims under Article XXIII: 1(b),[27] intensifying the arguments over the significance of NVNI complaints. These theoretical controversies mainly take into account the *causes of action* of Article XXIII: 1(b) of the GATT and the "sources of obligations" of WTO law.[28] Given the pro-

23 *See, e.g.* BENEDEK (1990), at 290–91; ABELS (1996), at 526; BAGWELL, Mavroidis & STAIGER (2002), at 67; DAUL (1995), at 148–50; ROBERT HOWSE & MICHAEL J. TREBILCOCK, *The Fair Trade Debate: Trade, Labor, and the Environment*, 16 International Review of Law and Economy 61 (1996); HINDLEY (1996), p. 333; LINARELLI (2000), at 266–67; VON BOGDANDY (1992), at 98–99.

24 *See, e.g.*, ROESSLER (1997), at 134 ("[G]iven the broad extension of the multilateral trade order into the area of domestic policies, the field of potential application of [Article XXIII: 1(b)] has diminished significantly").

25 *See, e.g.* LINARELLI (2000), at 266 ("It provides WTO members with the twin incentives of providing concessions to one another during successive rounds of multilateral negotiations and of avoiding circumvention of agreed-upon concessions after the conclusion of the negotiating rounds").

26 WTO Panel Report, *Japan – Measures Affecting Consumer Photographic Film and Paper*, WT/DS44/R, adopted on 31 March 1998.

27 *See* PETERSMANN (1997B), at 221–22; WILLIAM H. BARRINGER, *Competition Policy and Cross Border Dispute Resolution: Lessons Learned from the US-Japan Film Dispute*, 6 George Mason Law Review 459 (1998); Cho (1998), at 311–13; MITSUO MATSUSHITA, 'Restrictive Business Practices and the WTO/GATT Dispute Settlement Process,' in PETERSMANN (1997B), pp. 362–63; DILLON (1999); DUNOFF (1997); WILLIAM H. BARRINGER & JAMES P. DURLING, *Out of Focus: The Use of Section 301 to Address Anticompetitive Practices in Foreign Markets*, 1 UCLA Journal of International Law & Foreign Affairs 99, 99–101 (1996); CHARLES D. LAKE II & JENNIFER DANNER RICCARDI, *Market Access Barriers in the Japanese Consumer Photographic Film and Paper Sector: Can Section 301 Address the Problem?*, 1 UCLA Journal of International Law & Foreign Affairs 143 (1996).

28 *See generally* LORAND BARTELS, *Applicable Law in WTO Dispute Settlement Proceedings*, 35 JWT 3, 499 n. 3 (2001). This discussions are centering around whether all of the sources of law set out in Article 38(1) of the Statute of the International Court of Justice could be potential sources of WTO law or not. *See* PALMETER & MAVROIDIS (1998); SCHOENBAUM (1998); MARCEAU (1999), at 109–115; TRACHTMAN (1999), at 342 n. 41; For a different view, *see* PAUWELYN (2001).

gressive move to a "rule-oriented" dispute settlement mechanism (DSM)[29] and growing potential conflicts among trade-related areas, a theoretical legal clarification on NVNI complaints is becoming increasingly important.

3. Practical Significance of Non-Violation Complaints

The complaints are also *practically* important in developing WTO law. The requirements of the NVNI complaints could affect several domestic commercial policies, e.g. competition standard,[30] labor standards, the regulation on environmental policy,[31] and technical

29 The WTO dispute settlement mechanism is presided over by DSU which has created the DSB to administer the DSU. The DSB has compulsory jurisdiction to resolve disputes initiated by WTO Members and has its own rules and presidency. Its functions are, *inter alia*, to establish panels at the request of a complaining party, to adopt panel reports, to monitor the implementation of its decisions, and to authorize compensatory measures when appropriate. Both the adoption of the panel and the Appellate Body reports are decisions to be taken automatically, unless the DSB decides by consensus not to adopt the report *(negative consensus)*. *See* Article 2 of the DSU.

30 *See, e.g.*, Hoekman & Mavroidis (1994); Hindley (1996), pp. 333–48; Roessler (1999); The complaining party of *Japan-Film*, the United States tried to determine, by the claim of NVNI complaint, whether the existing WTO Agreements would sufficiently regulate anti-competitive behaviour in the absence of an explicit agreement within the WTO framework that deals with competition policy. The great deal of discussion as to whether the WTO framework should include an international agreement that deals with competition questions has failed to generate any consensus; As a result of the Singapore Ministerial Conference, a Working Group on Trade and Competition Policy has been established to look at this question, but with no concrete results as yet. *See infra* p. 67, note 90.

31 *See* Bagwell, Mavroidis & Staiger (2002), at 74 (proposing that in addressing non-pecuniary externalities associated with labour and environmental standards, the existing implicit enforcement links between the WTO and other organisations – as embodied in the non-violation nullification-or-impairment and renegotiation provisions of the WTO Agreements – should be encouraged); Howse & Trebilcock (1996), at 78 ("Where a Contracting Party views the 'beggar-thy-neighbor' but technically GATT-legal conduct of another Party

trade barriers.[32] In addition, NVNI claims can be used as a means of challenging free-trade area rules of origin that allegedly "raise barriers to the trade of other contracting parties with such territories."[33] Consequently the scope of NVNI complaints will be a practical gauge of whether a specific domestic regulation can cause international legal consequences including trade compensation or retaliation. The NVNI case of *EC – Asbestos* attracted considerable attention because it suggests that WTO can balance fostering multilateral trade against non-trade policies involving, for example, the environment, health and the treatment of workers.[34] This situation typically arises in the specific WTO Agreements relating to technical barriers and sanitary and phytosanitary measures.[35] The NVNI complaints have been said to prevent circumventing GATT provisions and negotiated tariff concessions through GATT-consistent trade measures.[36] However, if we apply the NVNI complaints over

---

as undermining the existing cooperative equilibrium of GATT rules and concessions, it may seek GATT approval of ultimate recourse to unilateral trade measures through making a case that non-violation nullification or impairment has occurred").

32 Technical trade barriers are defined as regulations and standards governing the sale of products into national markets that have as their *prima facie* objective the correction of market inefficiencies stemming from externalities associated with the production, distribution, and consumption of these products. For the connection of technical barriers with NVNI complaints, *see* Gabrielle Marceau & Joel P. Trachtman, *The Technical Barriers to Trade Agreement, the Sanitary and Phytosanitary Meaures Agreement, and the General Agreement on Tariffs and Trade: A Map of the World Trade Organization Law of Domestic Regulation of Goods,* 36 JWT 811, 873 (2002).

33 *See* GATT Article XXIV: 4; Richard H. Steinberg, *Antidotes to Regionalism: Responses to Trade Diversion Effects of the North American Free Trade Agreement,* 29 Stanford Journal of International Law 315, 342 (1993).

34 WTO Appellate Body Report, *EC – Asbestos (AB),* paras. 172, 175 & 192.

35 *See, e.g.* Atsuko Okubo, *Environmental Labeling Programs and the GATT/WTO Regime,* 11 Georgetown International Environmental Law Review 599, 627–30 (1999).

36 *See, e.g.* GATT Panel Report, *EC – Oilseeds I* (1990), para. 144; GATT, *US – Sugar Waiver* (1990), para. 41; *India – Patent I (AB)* para. 5.21.

whole WTO Agreements, it could abstain a Member from undermining *market access* by way of WTO-consistent measures.[37] Therefore the NVNI complaints require much more systematic scrutiny in the WTO era.

First, given the additional new rules in GATS and TRIPS, and given the ambiguity on whether certain measures violate GATT rules, the arguments on the applicability of NVNI complaints has been fierce.[38] Furthermore the increasing concerns over "trade disorders" between trade liberalisation and specific domestic policies,[39] for example, trade measures taken pursuant to multilateral environmental agreements or health-based measures, raise the issue of whether the measures justified under the exceptions in GATT Article XX are open to be challenged under the NVNI complaints.[40] This significance is clearly seen in the Appellate Body Report of *EC – Asbestos*:

> An important aspect of the European Communities' [Appellee] argument is that a Member cannot have reasonable expectations of continued market access for products which are shown to pose a serious risk to human life or health. However, the paragraphs of the Panel Report appealed by the European Communities involve *exclusively* the Panel's findings on the threshold issues of the scope of application of Article XXIII : 1(b). This particular argument of the European Communities, important as it is, simply does not relate to those threshold issues. Rather, the European Communities' argument relates to the substance of a claim that has been determined to fall within the scope of application of Article XXIII : 1(b) and, in particular, *concerns the issue whether a "benefit" has been "nullified or impaired" by a measure restricting market access for products posing a health risk*[41] [emphasis added]

37 *See* ROESSLER (1997), p. 133; PETERSMANN (1997B), at 172.
38 *See* PART ONE-III-B of this Dissertation.
39 JACKSON (2000), at 414.
40 JACKSON (2000), at 417–23. He mentioned the concept of "externalities" in the context of general policy of liberalizing trade and environmental protection, *see id,* AT 418; *See also* CHUA (1998a), at 38; For the implications of "externalities" on NVNI complaints, *see* LINARELLI (2000), at 354–56;
41 WTO Appellate Body Report, *EC – Asbestos (AB),* para. 190.

In line with this relevance of NVNI complaints to the exceptions in GATT XX, the remedies for "waivers" are also worth much attention.[42]

Second, given the evolution of WTO system "in the direction of rule orientation"[43] and subsequent increasing role of DSB to monitor various conflicts from "regulatory protectionism,"[44] the potentials of Article XXIII cases for the DSB is likely to be enormous.[45] Furthermore, supposing that any multilateral trade has a co-ordination effect among the Members, the NVNI complaints may also facilitate such co-ordination because of its flexible approach to a certain trade conflicts.[46]

42 Understanding in respect of Waivers of Obligations under the General Agreement on Tariffs and Trade 1994, *see* THE LEGAL TEXTS (1995), at 35 ("Any Member considering that a benefit accruing to it under GATT 1994 is being nullified or impaired as a result of: [...] (b) the application of *a measure consistent with the terms and conditions of the waiver* may invoke the provisions of Article XXIII of GATT 1994 as elaborated and applied by the Dispute Settlement Understanding") *(emphasis added).*

43 JACKSON (2000), at 455.

44 SYKES (1999), at 3–5. He defined "regulatory protectionism" as "any cost disadvantage imposed on foreign firms by a regulatory policy that discriminates against them or that otherwise disadvantages them in a manner that is unnecessary to the attainment of some genuine, non-protectionist regulatory objective." *See id,* at 3.

45 *See, e.g.* LINARELLI (2000), at 337; *But cf.* COTTIER & SCHEFFER (1997), at 182 ("With the expansion of trade law into areas other than tariffication and quotas, the WTO no longer needs the non-violation structures developed in the 1920s"); *See also* ROESSLER (1997), at 134 ("Given the broad extension of the multilateral trade order into the area of domestic policies, the field of potential application of [Article XXIII: 1(b)] has diminished significantly"); John Jackson discussed the potential for numerous NVNI Complaints if the WTO admitted China before China fully complied with various GATT trade rules, *see* JOHN JACKSON, 'The Institutional Ramifications of China's Accession to the WTO,' in CHINA IN THE WORLD TRADING SYSTEM: DEFINING THE PRINCIPLES OF ENGAGEMENT,' 75, 78–79 (FREDERICK M. ABBOTT ED., 1998).

46 CHUA (1998a), at 39.

B. The Origins of Non-Violation Complaints

1. *Historical Origin of Non-Violation Complaints till GATT 47*

The chronological origins of NVNI concept can be divided into six stages in the textual evolution of NVNI complaints: (1) July 1933 by League of Nations suggestion on Equitable Treatment Draft; (2) the various bilateral trade agreements from the 1930s and 1940s; (3) the September 1946 Suggested Charter for International Trade Organization ("ITO"); (4) the November 1946 London Draft; (5) the June 1947 Geneva Draft; and (6) finally the October 1947 GATT text.[47]

First, the NVNI concept was originated to control government tariff policies affecting international trade in the 1920s.[48] Along with consistently discouraging high tariffs, the League of Nations tried to deal with "indirect protectionism".[49] These were unregulated substitute measures to evade the promised tariff concessions. During the London Monetary and Economic Conference (London Conference) held in 1933 under the auspices of the League of Nations, the so-called "Equitable Treatment Draft" was presented by Fred Nielsen, the US delegate. It stated:

> The High Contracting Parties agree that, if one of the Contracting Parties introduces, after the conclusion of the present treaty, *any measure even of an internal nature, capable of materially altering the de facto situation created by the present treaty,* to the prejudice of the other Party, the first Party shall not refuse to consider in a friendly spirit any complaints or proposals that may be made by the other Party, or to enter into negotiations with that Party *with a view to seeking the best means of re-establishing the disturbed equilibrium.*[50] [emphasis added]

47 The framework of this drafting history is based largely on the review of DURLING & LESTER (1998) and the documents are quoted from their review.

48 DURLING & LESTER (1998), at 218.

49 *Id.*

50 *Draft Report Prepared by the Drafting Committee Appointed to Combine in a Single Text the Various Drafts Submitted for the Equitable Treatment Clause and other Questions of Indirect Protectionism,* League of Nations Doc. Conf. M.E./C.E.86 (1933) ["Equitable Treatment Draft"].

Subsequently, this language was modified in the final report on the suggestion of Mr Nielsen. The final text of the clause read:

> If, subsequent to the conclusion of the treaty, one of the Contracting Parties introduces any measure, which even though it does not result in an infringement of terms of the treaty, is considered by the other Party to be of such a nature as to *have the effect of nullifying or impairing any object of the treaty*, the former shall not refuse to enter into negotiations with the purpose either of an examination of proposals made by the latter or of the friendly adjustment of any complaint preferred by it.[51] [emphasis added]

In comparing the above two texts, the first formulation of the NVNI concept was changed from "materially altering the de facto situation" to "have the effect of nullifying or impairing any object of the treaty."[52] Thus, the phrase "nullification or impairment," which has persisted in all subsequent treaty drafting of the NVNI concept was born.[53] In the end, the London Conference adopted the text suggested by Mr Nielsen.[54]

Second, with the recommendations from the League of Nations that countries insert an equitable treatment clause into their bilateral trade agreements,[55] the United States' reciprocal trade agreements in the 1930s and 1940s played a crucial role in developing the NVNI concept. For example, Article XIV of the US – Honduras Trade Agreement stated:

> In the event that the United States of America or the Republic of Honduras adopts any measure which, even though it does not conflict with the terms of this Agreement, is considered by the Government of the other country to

51 Suggestion Submitted by the Delegate of USA. Concerning Doc. M.E./C.E./86, League of Nations Doc. M.E./C.E./86 (1933).

52 *Id.*

53 DURLING & LEISTER (1998), at 224.

54 *Monetary and Economic Conference Reports Approved by the Conference on July 27th, 1933 and Resolutions Adopted by the Bureau and the Executive Committee*, at 18, League of Nations Doc. C.435 M.220 1933. II (1933). The purpose of the text was to deal with government actions not currently addressed, rather than acts already regulated by commercial treaties. *See* DURLING & LEISTER (1998), at 224 n. 70.

55 DURLING & LEISTER (1998), at 224.

> *have the effect of nullifying or impairing any object of the Agreement*, the Government of the country which has adopted any such measure shall consider such representations and proposals as the Government of the other country may make with a view to effecting a mutually satisfactory adjustment of the matter.[56]

The only notable difference from the equitable clause of the London Conference is the omission of specific language that the government measure had to be subsequent to the negotiation of the treaty.[57] Most of the bilateral trade agreements signed by the United States (US) during this period contained virtually identical language.[58] These bilateral agreements preceded the ITO negotiations, where the US encouraged including and expanding the *equitable clause* into the dispute settlement provisions during the ITO negotiations.[59]

One of the characteristics of the bilateral agreements and consequently GATT 47 was the employment of provisions to protect Contracting Parties[60] from the nullification and impairment of benefits by measures not directly marked in the agreements itself.[61] Such provisions have entailed not only a cautious balancing between acceptable sets of trade barriers and the legal measures em-

56 Reciprocal Trade Agreement, Dec. 18, 1935, US-Hond., Article XIV, 49 Stat. 3851, 3863 (entered into force on 2 March 1936; terminated 28 February 1961).

57 Hudec (1990), at 25 ("The typical U.S, trade agreement provision… spoke only of a single cause of action called 'nullification and impairment,' a term which applied to 'any measure [...] even though it does not conflict with the terms of this agreement").

58 *See* Durling & Leister (1998), at 227 n. 88; Other major trading countries also were signing similar bilateral agreements with each other. And many of the agreements signed by these other countries contained an equitable treatment clause. *See id.*, at 228–30.

59 The specific language of the NVNI clauses of these bilateral treaties is "highly uniform and strikingly similar" to the present text of Article XXIII: 1(b). *See* Cottier & Schefer (1997), p. 150.

60 In GATT practice, individual parties were referred to with initial capitals as "Contracting Parties," while the term "CONTRACTING PARTIES" referred to actions of all of the parties acting collectively. *See* GATT Article XXV: 1.

61 Cottier & Schefer (1997), p. 149.

ployed to discipline them,[62] but also some thorny exception or emergency provisions,[63] which reflected the recognition that in some cases an individual state might actually have needed to increase trade protection to manage a crisis in an adequate manner.[64]

Third, in negotiating for the ITO, the NVNI remedy was proposed in the Suggested Charter submitted in September 1946 by the United States.[65] The initial version of the NVNI clause appeared as Article 30 of the Commercial Policy Chapter, entitled "Nullification or Impairment," and applied only to that chapter:

> If any Member should consider that *any measure* adopted by any other Member, *whether or not it conflicts with the terms of this Chapter*, has the effect of

62 There may be four core legal commitments through which the tarde barriers are controlled. "(1) the unconditional most-favored nation ("MFN") obligation that prohibits importing countries from discriminating against or giving preferences to any other country, regardless of whether the latter has made any trade concessions to the former; (2) the national treatment obligation, which requires that imports be treated the same as the like domestic product insofar as taxes and other domestic regulations are concerned; (3) binding commitments to reduce tariffs on imports; and (4) the elimination of quotas on imports." *See* KENNEDY (1998), at 425.

63 There may be three kinds of exception categories: "First, an importing country facing a balance-of-payments shortfall may temporarily impose 'quantitative restrictions' (i.e. quotas) on imported goods until its balance-of-payments position improves [Article XII of GATT]. Second, domestic industries seriously injured by imports of competing products may receive 'safeguard' relief from their home government [Article XIX of GATT] (known in the United States as Section 201 escape clause relief). Such relief can take the form of a temporary increase in tariffs, the imposition of quotas, or both, on competing imports. The third exception is a set of GATT exceptions. They are found in Articles XX and XXI, covering public health and safety measures, inter alia, and national security, respectively." *See* KENNEDY (1998), *id.*

64 This flexible balancing could be resulted from, what John Ruggie calls, the "embedded liberalism" bargain of GATT system, *see supra* p. 6, note 11.

65 *Suggested Charter for an International Trade Organisation, Article 30, Dep't St. Publ. No. 2598, Com. Pol'y Series No. 93, at 23* (September 1946) ["Suggested Charter"]. This Charter consisted of five substantive chapters: Commercial Policy; Employment Policy; Economic Development; Restrictive Business Practices; and Commodity Agreements. It included also a dispute settlement procedure applicable to all five chapters.

> *nullifying or impairing any object of this Chapter*, such other Member shall give sympathetic consideration to such written representations or proposals as may be made with a view to effecting a mutually satisfactory adjustment of the matter.[66] [emphasis added]

Fourth, at the first negotiating session for the ITO (London, November 1946), the NVNI provision of the Suggested Charter was altered, mainly at the suggestion of the US Delegate Connie Hawkins,[67] in two points:[68] (1) the word "Chapter" was changed to "Charter," which made the provision applicable to all five Chapters of the proposed ITO Charter;[69] (2) a separate clause now provided for consultations in the event that "any situation has arisen".[70]

Fifth, at the next substantive negotiating session (Geneva, 1947), the broad scope of NVNI provision was a big concern among the delegates.[71] The Geneva negotiations redrafted[72] the provision to

66 *Id.*

67 He supported the expansion of the NVNI provision and noted that the nullification or impairment provision involves "a complaint by one party that another is not carrying out the letter of the Charter… or is not carrying out its spirit." *See* Verbatim Report of the Preparatory Committee of the U.N. Conference on Trade and Employment, U.N. ESCOR, 2nd Sess., 9th mtg., at 21, U.N. Doc. E/PC/T/C.II/PRO/PV/9 (1946) ["U.N. Conf.–9th Mtg."].

68 *Report of the First Session of the Preparatory Committee of the United Nations Conference on Trade and Employment,* U.N. Doc. E/PT/T/33 (1946) ["London Draft"].

69 Hudec (1990), at 39.

70 *Id.*

71 In this process, the South African delegate criticised the NVNI concept very strongly. He argued that under the current language, sanctions were available as a remedy against countries that nullified or impaired benefits as a result of measures that did not conflict with the proposed ITO Charter. He regarded the NVNI remedy as a source of new obligations where none had previously existed. *See* Hudec (1990), at 39. The South African delegate's opinion was that, although sanctions were legitimate where a party could show an actual breach of obligations, consultations were enough in the case of the NVNI complaints. *See* Verbatim Report of the Preparatory Committee of the U.N. Conference on Trade and Employment, U.N. ESCOR, 2nd Sess., 5th mtg., at 10, U.N. Doc. E/PC/T/A/PV/5 (1947).

72 *Report of the Second Session of the Preparatory Committee of the United Nations Conference on Trade and Employment,* U.N. Doc. E/PC/T/186 (1947) ["Geneva Draft"].

avoid the unlimited scope of the earlier London Draft:[73] the London Draft had singled out any measure that "has the effect of nullifying or impairing any object of this Charter."[74] In Geneva, the NVNI complaint was reformulated with more clearly specified the measures subject to a complaint. The Australian delegate offered language allowing a complaint if: (1) "any benefit accorded to it directly or indirectly by this Charter is being nullified or impaired;" or (2) "the promotion by it of any of the Purposes of this Charter is being impeded."[75] In addition, he offered three distinct types of *causes of action*: (i) the application by another Member of any measure, whether or not it conflicts with the provisions of this Charter; or (ii) the failure of another Member to carry out its obligations under this Charter; or (iii) the existence of any other situation.[76] Thus, several notable alterations were revealing to examine the components of a NVNI complaint. These have been well-summarized in the Durling and Leister's article:

> First, the ITO now protected "benefits accruing" under the Charter and prevented the objectives of Article I from being impeded. This language replaced the previous reference to preventing nullification or impairment of "any object of the Charter." The "benefits accruing" language more precisely defined the possible scope of the remedy. Second, the three types of claims – violation, non-violation, and situation – were clearly defined as three separate categories. The violation claim appeared first because of the expectation that it would be the most frequent type of complaint. The structure also reflected the concern that the other complaints might well require different

73 In London Draft, US Delegate Connie Hawkins noted that NVNI provision involves "a complaint by one party that another is not carrying out the letter of the Charter… or is not carrying out its spirit." Thus, any measure in NVNI formulation by a party that undermines the "spirit" of the Charter is actionable. *See* U.N. Conf.–9th Mtg., at 21.

74 London Draft, at 33.

75 Amendment Proposed by the Australian Delegation, U.N. ESCOR, 2nd Sess., at 1, U.N. Doc. E/PC/T/W/170 (1947).

76 Verbatim Report of the Preparatory Committee of the U.N. Conference on Trade and Employment, U.N. ESCOR, 2nd Sess., 12th mtg. at 8, UN Doc. E/PC/T/A/PV/12 (1947) ["U.N. Conf.–12th Mtg.U.N."].

> standards of proof. Finally, the drafters moved the NVNI provision out of the Commercial Policy chapter to make clear that the provision applied to the entire proposed ITO Charter.[77] [footnotes omitted]

Sixth, prior to the final negotiations for the proposed ITO Charter (Havana, 1948),[78] some countries, led by the US, initiated a round of tariff negotiations even before the ITO's establishment. As a result, 23 countries signed the GATT on October 30, 1947.[79] Along with this temporary setting of GATT 47, discussions in London, New York, Geneva and Havana from 1946 through 1948, produced a proposed ITO Charter to address commercial policy.[80] The failure to ratify the ITO Charter left the organisation stillborn. Hence, the GATT "incidentally" came to serve as the final agreement on commercial policy of the ITO and to represent the first multilateral set

77 DURLING & LEISTER (1998), at 238.

78 Havana Charter for an International Trade Organization, U.N. Doc. E/Conf. 2178 (24 March 1948) ["Havana Charter"]; The Havana Charter provided for the creation of an International Trade Organisation which would take its place beside the other institutions of Bretton Woods, the IMF and World Bank. On a substantive level, the Havana Charter comprised, in addition to the Chapter IV which are reproduced in the GATT 47, Chapters relating to employment and economic activity, economic development and reconstruction, restrictive trade practices, as well as agreements on primary products. The Charter never entered into force, because of the US failure to ratify the Havana Charter. *See* PAUL DEMARET, *The Metamorphoses of the GATT: From the Havana Charter to the World Trade Organization,* 34 Columbia Journal of Transnational Law 123, 126–27 (1995).

79 GATT 1947, in THE LEGAL TEXTS (1995), at 486; A Drafting Committee, under the auspices of the Preparatory Committee charged with drafting the ITO charter, produced a full draft of the GATT at Lake Success, New York, in 1947. Based on this text and the schedules of tariff commitments made by the 25 governments, the "Geneva Final Act" was drawn. It also included a "Protocol of Provisional Application" ("PPA"), which intended to be a temporary skeleton, but ended up being fundamental to GATT for its 47-year operation. *See* Final Act Adopted at the Conclusion of the Second of the Preparatory Committee of the United Nations Conference on Trade and Employment, UN Sales No. 1947.II/10;55 UNTS 187 (1947); *See also* JACKSON (1969), at 60–63 ("§ 3.2 Provisional Application").

80 *See* JACKSON (1969), at 42–46.

of trade rules.[81] Simultaneously, it meant that the only dispute settlement procedure in the GATT was a *nullification or impairment provision almost identical to the Geneva draft of the ITO Charter.*[82] The final text of the nullification or impairment provision was included in Article XXIII of GATT 47[83] that has been retained in the WTO Agreements as GATT 94. It is also noteworthy to compare the provisions of GATT Article XXIII: 1 with its corresponding ITO Charter Article 94, which provides insights into the developments of the drafting history of Article XXIII: 1(b).

Table 1: Overview of the Development of Non-Violation Complaints

6 Chronological Stages	
Equitable Treatment Clause (1933) ⇒ Various Bilateral Trade Agreements (1930s and 1940s) ⇒ Suggested Charter (1946) ⇒ London Draft (1946) ⇒ Geneva Draft (1947) ⇒ GATT (1947) ⇒ Havana Charter (1947) *Cf.* NAFTA (1992)	
4 Important Stages (emphasis added)	
Equitable Treatment Draft (1933)	"The High Contracting Parties agree that, if one of the Contracting Parties introduces, after the conclusion of the present treaty, any measure even of an internal nature, capable of materially *altering the de facto situation* created by the present treaty, to the prejudice of the other Party, the first Party shall not refuse to consider in a friendly spirit any complaints or proposals that may be made by the other Party, or to enter into negotiations with that Party with a view to seeking the best means of re-establishing the disturbed equilibrium."
Bilateral Agreements (1930s and 40s)	"In the event that the United States of America or the Repub lic of Honduras adopts any measure which, even though it does not conflict with the terms of this Agreement, is considered by the Government of the other country to *have the effect of nullifying or impairing any object of the Agreement,* the Government of the country which has adopted any such measure shall consider such representations and proposals as the Government of the other country may make with a view to effecting a mutually satisfactory adjustment of the matter."

81 HUDEC (1990), at 49–52.

82 *Id.*, at 52.

83 This text made only minor changes to the Geneva draft, including removal of all references to the powers of the "Organization." The Contracting Parties themselves had to resolve disputes, because no ITO existed to administer the rules. *See* Durling & Leister (1998), at 239.

Table 1: Overview of the Development of Non-Violation Complaints (cont.)

GATT (1947)	**Nullification or Impairment** "1. If any contracting party should consider that *any benefit* accruing to it directly or indirectly under this Agreement is being nullified or impaired or that the attainment of *any objective* of the Agreement is being impeded as the result of (a) the failure of another contracting party to carry out its obligations under this Agreement, or (b) the application by another contracting party of any measure, *whether or not* it conflicts with the provisions of this Agreement, or (c) the existence of any other situation, the contracting party may, with a view to the satisfactory adjustment of the matter, make written representations or proposals to the other contracting party or parties which it considers to be concerned. Any contracting party thus approached shall give sympathetic consideration to the representations or proposals made to it."
Havana Charter (1947)	**Consultation and Arbitration** "1. If any Member considers that *any benefit accruing to it directly or indirectly, implicitly or explicitly*, under any of the provisions of this Charter other than Article 1, is being nullified or impaired as a result of, (a) a breach by a Member of an obligation under this Charter by action or failure to act, or (b) the application by a Member of a measure *not conflicting with* the provisions of this Charter, or (c) the existence of any other situation the Member may, with a view to the satisfactory adjustment of the matter, make written representations or proposals to such other Member or Members as it considers to be concerned, and the Members receiving them shall give sympathetic consideration thereto."
	Cf. NAFTA (1992)
	Annex 2004: Nullification and Impairment "1. If any Party considers that any benefit it could *reasonably have expected to accrue to it under any provision* of [...] is being nullified or impaired as a result of the application of any measure that is *not inconsistent with* this Agreement, the Party may have recourse to dispute settlement under this Chapter."

2. Institutional Origin of Non-Violation Complaints

a. "Embedded Liberalism" in Bretton Woods System

In the regime of WTO, as it succeeded the GATT in the post-Second World War era, there is a conceptual foundation that harmonizes the classic economic insights of absolute and comparative advantage from unilateral free trade with the interdependency of different states' trade and economic policies.[84] This sort of harmonization under a liberal structure[85] was widely perceived by the founders of the Bretton Woods system.[86] They wanted to keep the classical polio-economic theory of comparative advantage which dictated the removal of import restrictions on an international level, while they also recognised the realities of different

84 *See generally* TREBILCOCK & HOWSE (2001), CH. 1; SYKES (1998), at 49–57.

85 Liberalism is the invitation to act in a self-interested manner, without impediment from other entities, as long as what we do not harm them. *See generally* J. S. MILL, ON LIBERTY, 70–86 (NORTON ED., 1975); In this context, the TRIPS Agreement was composed a bit differently, since it obligates WTO Members to undertake measures to protect property interests in intangibles both within and at their own borders, *see* GELLER (1995), at 105.

86 Historically, the origin of Bretton Woods System dates back to the Atlantic Charter of August 14, 1941, between the United States and the United Kingdom contained commitments for post-war policies in the fields of: (1) civil, political and social human rights; (2) national self-determination; (3) global organization and security; (4) freedom from individual want; and (5) commitment to international economic cooperation. The Bretton Woods Conference of 1944 culminated in the establishment of the International Monetary Fund (IMF) and the International Bank for Reconstruction and Development (World Bank). It also provided a major catalyst for the US Proposals of December 1945, which led to the U.N.-sponsored Conference on Trade and Employment. The U.N. Conference consisted of a series of meetings from October 1946 to March 1948. The Conference prepared the draft Charter for the proposed ITO and, as an appendix, the GATT 47. *See* LAING (1996), at 263; Since the Bretton Woods conference in 1944 was mainly focused on monetary and banking issues, the attention to GATT legal structure might not so high, *see* JACKSON (1990), at 10–11; *See also* JACKSON (2000), at 408–10 ("The WTO as a Bretton Woods partner").

countries' sovereign policy preferences would resist the removal of trade restrictions.[87]

In formatting the postwar financial and trade institutions, such as the International Monetary Fund (IMF),[88] the World Bank,[89] and the GATT 47,[90] the founders were keen to design an institutional structure which would enable countries to manage their domestic economies, in a manner consistent with political and social stability, without the risk of setting off a "protectionist race to the bottom".[91] Although the GATT pushes economies in many ways towards greater efficiency,[92] GATT rules permit rampant inefficiency

87 *See* SYKES (1999), at 2–5. His critical question in the context of *EC – Hormones* case was "Why are protective tariffs, subsidies, and quotas (under specified circumstances) perfectly legal under WTO law, while protectionism in the form of a regulatory measure such as the hormones regulation is illegal?," *see id.*, at 3.

88 The IMF, a creation of the Bretton Woods Conference, was established to promote international monetary cooperation and exchange stability. *See generally* DEBORAH E. SIEGEL, *Legal Aspects of the IMF/WTO Relationship: The Fund's Articles of Agreement and the WTO Agreements*, 96 AJIL 561 (2002). To enable members to overcome shortages of foreign exchange, the IMF in 1969 established currency reserve units called Special Drawing Rights. *Id.;* For a comparison between GATT 47 and IMF, *see* JACKSON (1990), at 10–11; For a useful historical review, *see* Dukgeun Ahn, *Linkages Between International Financial and Trade Institutions: IMF, World Bank and WTO*, 34 JWT 1, 3–5 (2000).

89 The World Bank, a specialised agency of the United Nations, was established, along with the International Monetary Fund, by the Bretton Woods Agreement (1944) to assist Europe in its postwar recovery. On the organisational co-operation of World Bank with IMF and GATT, *see* AHN, *id.*, at 7–8.

90 Many follow the origins of the GATT to discussions between the US, the UK, and Canada in 1942 about provisions of the Lend-Lease programme and the postwar economy. *See* HUDEC (1990), at 49.

91 Howse (2002), at 95; During the late 1940s, many US and European political leaders believed that the trade wars of the 1920s and 1930s, and the resulting political conflicts, detonated World War II. Toward the end of the war, a series of initiatives was launched to develop global trade and monetary organizations that could help avoid future trade wars, *see* JACKSON (1990), at 7; This is also related to the argument of "inefficiency" of GATT/WTO rules, *see generally* CHARNOVITZ (2002), at 34–35.

92 For example, reducing tariffs and preventing more efficient import protection can improve efficiency of GATT/WTO, *see* Sykes (1999), at 7–10.

through trade policy,[93] and discrimination through preferential trading arrangements.[94] This liberal structure of trade regulations has often promoted governments[95] to depart from their GATT obligations of free trade and non-discriminatory competition.[96] This is the first institutional sense in which the postwar trading order addressed the very conception and structure of NVNI complaints.

b. "Functionalist" Mechanism of GATT

The leading institutional insights, as seen above, affected the "temporary"[97] and "functionalist"[98] construction of the GATT 47, designed to cover the period prior to the entry into force of the Havana

93 *See generally* SYKES (1999), at 13–15; Allowance to retain protectionism through tariffs and antidumping duties, and through textile/apparel quotas until 2005 can be examples. *Cf.* GATT Article II, Agreement on the Implementation of Article VI ("Anti-dumping Agreement"), and Agreement on Textiles and Clothing.

94 *See* JACKSON (1969), at 575–623; *Cf.* GATT Article XXIV; Understanding on the Interpretation of Article XXIV of the General Agreement on Tariffs and Trade 1994, *see* THE LEGAL TEXTS (1995), at 31–34.

95 The actual text of NVNI provision refers to "Contracting Party," not "government". Because the GATT Contracting Parties were all governments, here the words of "government" and "Contracting Parties" are used interchangeably.

96 *See* PETERSMANN (1994), at 1160.

97 The GATT was a provisional agreement designed to cover the period prior to the entry into force of the ITO. To avoid the possibility of tariff concessions being indirectly undermined, GATT reproduced the content of Chapter IV of the ITO Charter relating to trade policy. Technically, the basic treaty comprising the GATT has never come into force, being applied through a 1947 "Protocol of Provisional Application" (PPA), *see* JACKSON (1990), at 1; John Jackson suggested that the ambiguity of the original GATT dispute settlement procedures can be attributed to the temporary GATT structure, in that there was a need to obtain compliance, and that some mechanism was necessary for ensuring "continued reciprocity and balance of concessions in the face of possibly changing circumstances." *See* JACKSON (1969), at 169–70.

98 COTTIER (2000), at 221. He assessed that "functionalist" approach in GATT were much more successful than that of the International Trade Organisation (ITO). *Id.*

Charter for stillborn ITO.[99] It obligated states not to impose quotas or related import restrictions on the one hand, but allowed the states to control their import tariffs within the conceded boundaries on the other.[100] In other words, "the legal structure of the [GATT] was designed to facilitate [such] concessions and make them binding, but it did not require them".[101] This legal construction, maintaining the basic "embedded liberalism" of the Bretton Woods political system, was founded on a contradiction, in the sense that each contracting party wants freedom to engage in the pursuit of its own domestic policy, yet wants security from harm by other parties. Furthermore, from its inception, the GATT 47 contained institutional provisions designed to be temporary, pending the establishment of the ITO.[102] Thus, the main challenge of GATT legal design was fundamentally to ensure that, even if one or several parties had to renounce on their trade commitments, this would not trigger a general crisis of specific confidence in the GATT system and of the general integrity of the international legal order.[103]

This understanding of the trade commitments has appeared to result in the observation that the main concern of dispute settlement of GATT, and successively of WTO, revolves around the concept of *nullification or impairment of any benefits* accruing from trade commitments rather than on violations of the treaty language.[104] The

99 Since the diplomats who negotiated the GATT were eager to bring it into force as quickly as possible, even though the ITO negotiations had not been completed, the parties to the GATT entered into the PPA, through which the General Agreement would be applied until the entire ITO Charter came into force. *See generally* 1 GATT ANALYTICAL INDEX (1995), at 3–6; For more elaborate dispute settlement mechanisms of the ITO, *see* JACKSON (1997), at 113–14.

100 *See generally* KENNEDY (1998), at 433–35.

101 HOWSE (2002), at 95.

102 LAING (1996), at 264.

103 According to Robert Hudec, the legal obligations in GATT were originally just one option among various kinds of diplomatic instruments for securing the tariff concessions. *See* Hudec (1970), at 616–36.

104 *See, e.g.* COTTIER & SCHEFER (1997), p. 146; ROESSLER (1997), p. 125; *Cf.* Memorandum from Fred Nielsen to US Secretary of State 5 (June 17, 1933) *quoting* from DURLING & LESTER (1998), at 213 ("From the standpoint of logic, and

legal structure of the GATT therefore was composed of conflicting and multi-dimensional legal factors inevitably.[105] This originally "open-texture" legal structure,[106] which has supported the liberal political structure of Bretton Wood arrangements, despite its strong merits of "flexibility," has caused serious difficulties in proceeding with legal reasoning properly. The difficulties may bring about considerable damages to the normative power of GATT, especially in light of securing the trade commitments or legal obligations in the GATT.

c. Non-Violation Complaints as a Balancing Tool

Several solutions coping with such difficulties might be possible. One is simply to leave the *ad-hoc* untidy but flexible structure, taking each individual party's risks and premium seriously.[107] Since legal positivism in international law which holds that "everything that was not explicitly prohibited was considered to be lawful",[108] was prevailing in the time of formatting the GATT 47, a proposal of leaving the untidy structure might have been persuasive.[109]

---

more specifically speaking, from the standpoint of principles of legal interpretation, it may seem somewhat incongruous to speak of nullifying purposes of a treaty by acts [that] do not infringe terms of the treaty").

105 This background led Keynes to call lawyers the *poets* of Bretton Woods, *see* ANNE-MARIE SLAUGHTER, 'Regulating the World: Multilateralism, International Law, and the Projection of the New Deal Regulatory State,' in THE WORLD TRADING SYSTEM: CRITICAL PERSPECTIVES ON THE WORLD ECONOMY 50 (ROBERT HOWSE ED., 1988).

106 This famous description of the indeterminacy of law originated with H. L. A. Hart, *see* HART (1997), at 128–36 (discussing the indeterminacy and "open texture" inherent in both precedent and legislation).

107 HOWSE (2002), at 96 (saying that "when you sign an agreement that disciplines certain kinds of measures, you take the other public policies of the signatories as you find them and accept the risk that those policies might be changed, charging a premium as it were to bear such risks, the premium being, for example, higher levels of concessions from others").

108 COTTIER & SCHEFER (1997), p. 164.

109 Actually, one of the delegates from the secretariat sustained this proposal and noted that it would be better to trust "the loyalty of States assuring each other equitable treatment" than to refrain the States from taking certain administra-

Another logical and political solution is to convene persistent negotiations to all public policies that might undermine trade concessions, enacting specific disciplines on those policies.[110] In some sense, the GATT/WTO system, as the forum for many multilateral rounds of trade issues, has sustained by this way.[111] For example, through the Kennedy Round negotiations (1964–1967), the tariffs, a most common trade barrier, came to be reduced by an average of thirty-five percent, and left average tariffs afterwards at seven percent.[112] Subsequently, the Tokyo Round (1973–1979) had as its principal objective the reduction of non-tariff barriers to trade,[113] and the Contracting Parties have concluded a number of "Side Agreements" which are technically independent and thus only applied to those countries which join them.[114] More recently, the Uruguay Round resulted in five multilateral agreements, establishing prin-

---

tive actions that could be used to burden imports." *See* 21 League of Nations J. of the Monetary and Econ. Conference (League of Nations, London, U.K.), July 4, 1933, at 141–42 (1933), *quoting* from Durling & Lester (1998), at 223 n. 50.

110 HOWSE (2002), at 96.

111 *See generally* HUDEC (1993), at 3–10; 2 A NEGOTIATING HISTORY (1993), at 1895–1995 ('Functioning of the GATT System').

112 *See* JOHN B. REHM, *Developments in the Law and Institutions of International Economic Relations: The Kennedy Round of Trade Negotiations*, 62 AJIL. 403 (1968); *See also* 1 NEGOTIATING HISTORY (1993), at 393.

113 *See* Declaration of Ministers adopted at Tokyo on September 14, 1973, GATT, Basic Instruments and Selected Documents ("BISD"), 20S/20.

114 The Tokyo Round negotiations resulted in agreements on: 1) Technical Barriers to Trade; 2) Government Procurement; 3) Subsidies; 4) Bovine Meat; 5) Dairy Products; 6) Customs Valuation; 7) Import Licensing Procedures; 8) Trade in Civil Aircraft; and 9) Antidumping, *see* GATT BISD, 26S/3–191. The technique of using "side agreements" entailed the "balkanisation" of GATT system, because each agreement was subject to its own dispute settlement procedure, even though each was also based on the general procedure that had been developed within the framework of the GATT. On the other hand, these side agreements served to reduce the effective scope of the "grandfather clause," designed to allow the United States to enforce legislation incompatible with the GATT to its foreign trade where such legislation pre-dated the General Agreement.

ciples which are defined and expanded in several annexes.[115] It is in these annexes that the GATT 94, GATS,[116] TRIPS[117] as well as the DSU are to be found. Thus, the original GATT 47 became the foundation and point of departure for the present WTO system of more than one hundred protocols, agreements, understandings, and other instruments.[118]

The third answer to the difficulties is to generate a middle position. This can be done, for example, by employing a "catch-all" type provision or a utilitarian calculus of global economic community that would bridge the gap between the Bretton Woods institutional insights and the inherent requirements of GATT as a legal system. Thus some tools were invented to protect the concessions granted under the essentially loose GATT regulatory framework.[119] One such "procedural rule" tool, to be found in the GATT 47 and subsequently retained in the WTO Agreements, was NVNI complaints.[120] Such a tool would provide guidance in choosing between the seemingly irreconcilable opposites of the liberal institutional and strict legal system. This method of mediating fundamental

115 *See supra* p. 1, note 1.

116 THE LEGAL TEXTS (1995), at 325–64.

117 *Id.*, at 365–403.

118 Because WTO system has been evolved in this diverse fashion, it is lacking somewhat in coherence as a general framework, *see* QURESHI (1996), at 11.

119 "The concept of nullification and impairment originated in bilateral trade agreements negotiated in the 1920s and 1930s. In order to protect the agreed tariff reductions as well as the reciprocal 'balance of concessions' from being undermined by non-tariff trade barriers or by other governmental measures (e. g. outside the trade sphere), those agreements made use of three complementary legal techniques: (1) *substantive legal rules* prohibiting or limiting the use of trade restricting or distorting trade policy measures; (2) *procedural rules* providing for legal remedies not only in case of treaty violations but also in situations where the commercial opportunities protected by those trade agreements were being nullified by other (e. g. purely domestic) measures; and (3) *termination clauses* allowing a disappointed party to terminate the trade policy obligations altogether on short notice (mostly three to six months)" [emphasis added]. *See* Uruguay Round Doc. MTN.GNG/NG13/W/31, para. 5; *See also* PETERSMANN (1991), at 192.

120 *See* GATT, Article XXIII : 1(b); GATS, Article XXIII : 3.

contradictions seeks to provide a "super-standard" that can guide the adjudicators of dispute resolution, who have to choose between the contradictory settings of freedom of sovereign states' policy-making and security of arranged tariff concessions in particular instances. This third approach was introduced by the provision of NVNI complaints of GATT Article XXIII: 1(b), as a *super-standard* for GATT dispute resolution. This is the second and legal sense in which the dispute resolution of GATT addressed the conception and structure of NVNI complaints.

d. Non-Violation Complaints as an Equity Clause

Because the Bretton Woods system was constructed under US leadership, it would be natural that much of the systemic elements including the legal structure of the GATT 47 were imported from those of the US.[121] It is assessed that much of the "form and substance" of GATT 47 was originated from the US bilateral trade agreements in the decades immediately preceding World War II, which emphasised bilateral tariff reductions on reciprocal bases.[122] However, the reciprocal bases of tariff reductions had a deeper origin. It was first seen as the "equitable treatment clause"[123] in discussion at economic conferences held by the League of Nations in the 1920s, eventually in the bilateral trade agreements negotiated in the 1930s and 1940s.[124] The United States not only drafted the original "equitable treatment clause" but it also pushed for the inclusion and expansion of this idea into the dispute settlement provisions during the ITO negotiations.[125]

121 *See* Hudec (1990), at 50 ("The [GATT] had to be framed as a 'trade agreement' within the meaning of the U.S. trade agreements legislation").
122 *See* Hudec (1970), at 616–36; Petersmann (1994), at 1171.
123 This clause sought to promote the fulfillment of trade agreement obligations in good faith in the absence at that time of general principles of equity in international law, *see* Durling & Lester (1998), at 214.
124 *See* Cottier & Schefer (1997), pp. 149–52; Roessler (1997), p. 126; *See also* Petersmann (1997b), at 143.
125 Hudec (1990), at 17: Laing (1996), at 261.

The prevailing purpose of the trade agreements at that time was "the exchange of tariff reduction".[126] The purpose was to be achieved in two ways: by promoting the use of commercial treaties that discouraged high tariffs and by preventing *indirect protection* by erecting barriers other than tariffs. Since the tariff reduction could easily be impeded by various indirect protection measures of domestic commercial policy, it was urged that some legal tools against possible non-reciprocal measures, which caused an adverse effect on the balance of the tariff reductions or economic interests, be introduced. For example, at the London Economic and Monetary Conference of 1933, the need for more broad provisions designed "in terms of the effect (nullification and impairment) rather than the specific cause" was raised.[127]

However, as the futility of defining a comprehensive list of impermissible measures became apparent,[128] the focus then moved to a more general formulation that would address the concerns about indirect protection measures not specifically covered by existing agreements. This formulation became the basis for the "equitable treatment clause" and, ultimately, for the NVNI complaints under the GATT 47. This is the third and legal sense in which the GATT system addressed the conception and structure of NVNI complaints.

126 In the aftermath of World War I, multilateral discussions among countries about economic matters was made under the auspices of the League of Nations and in order to dealing with significant economic matters a Provisional Economic and Financial Committee in 1920 was established. The main focus of these committees was on government policies affecting international trade, mainly on placing restrictions on the use of tariffs, because tariffs had the most direct effect on the flow of the international trade. For more detailed situations, *see* DURLING & LESTER (1998), at 216–219.

127 HUDEC (2000), at 19.

128 One of the German delegates in the Monetary and Economic Conference of League of Nations in 1933 suggested that drafting a complete list of examples of indirect protection would become helpful and thus submitted a list of indirect protection measures. *See* Observations by the German Delegation, League of Nations Doc. Conf. M.E./C.E./54 (1933).

e. Non-Violation Complaints as a Safeguard Tool

The balancing process based on equitable treatment became more delicate when the huge number of non-trade or not explicitly trade-based policies which individual Contracting Parties could implement, and which could ultimately undermine the value of the negotiated tariff concessions and legal disciplines supporting the concessions, were introduced. Thus the protection of the binding tariff concession, on the reciprocal base of *equity*, became a paramount goal for the bilateral agreements, as well as for the GATT 47. One of tools for the tariff concession protection was NVNI complaints that served as a "general clause of compensation" for policy change, where the value of negotiated concessions was affected.[129] This point was cogently explained by the panel on *EC – Oilseeds I* (1990):[130]

129 Howse (2002), at 97.

130 Because *EC – Oilseeds I* case is an important for understanding NVNI concept, more detailed factual background is worth noting: In 1961, the EC and the US agreed to reciprocal tariff concessions for whole, crushed, or broken soybeans, rape seeds and sunflower seeds, and oilcakes (all collectively referred to as "oilseeds"). In order to stimulate domestic oilseeds production, the EC established a price subsidisation regime for the Community oilseeds market in 1966. Beginning in the early 1980s, EC production subsidies under this regime caused a sharp increase in EC oilseeds production, which in turn reduced U.S. oilseeds exports to the EC. In 1987, the U.S. government responded to industry petitions for relief filed pursuant to Section 301 of the Trade Act of 1974, and requested consultations with the EC to remedy the situation. After failing the consultations, the US in May of 1988 requested that a GATT panel convene to examine the matter. In December 1989, the panel submitted its report, finding that the EC practices were inconsistent with the GATT. The panel recommended that the GATT CONTRACTING PARTIES suggest "ways and means to eliminate the impairment". In deference to the EC, however, the panel recommended that "the CONTRACTING PARTIES take no further action [...] until the Community has had reasonable opportunity to adjust its Regulations [...]". Two years later, the EC purported to remedy the impairment by enacting a Council Regulation establishing a new support system for the producers of oilseeds. In fact, this regulation merely shifted subsidies from the processor to the producer and left the impairment intact. The United States again requested GATT assistance, and the original

> The idea underlying [the provisions of Article XXIII: 1(b)] is that the improved competitive opportunities that can legitimately be expected from a tariff concession can be frustrated not only by measures proscribed by the General Agreement but also by measures consistent with that Agreement. *In order to encourage contracting parties to make tariff concessions they must therefore be given a right of redress when a reciprocal concession is impaired by another contracting party as a result of the application of any measure, whether or not it conflicts with the General Agreement.*[131] [emphasis added]
> [...]
> The Panel considered that the main value of a tariff concession is that it provides an assurance of better market access through improved price competition. Contracting parties negotiate tariff concessions primarily to obtain that advantage. They must therefore be assumed to base their tariff negotiations on the expectation that the price effect of the tariff concessions will not be systematically offset. *If no right of redress were given to them in such a case*

---

panel was reconvened. After further meetings with the disputants and with interested third parties, the panel concluded that benefits reasonably expected by the United States under the tariff concessions continued to be impaired by the EC's new subsidy scheme. Consequently, the panel called for the EC to "act expeditiously to eliminate the impairment." Rather than correcting the problem, the EC sought to renegotiate its previously-agreed tariff concessions and to compensate injured U.S. and third-party industries, as provided under Article XXVIII: 4 of the GATT, and three months of negotiations then commenced. During the course of these meetings, the EC made it apparent that its real intention was to delay and to further limit U.S. export opportunities. The United States sought binding arbitration as a last-ditch effort to obtain redress, but the EC rejected this possibility in September 1992. Faced with mounting losses by U.S. producers and an increasingly uncooperative EC, the U.S. government requested authorisation from the GATT CONTRACTING PARTIES to employ self-help by suspending concessions, as provided by Article XXIII: 2 of the GATT. As with the panel mandates and the request for arbitration, the EC again frustrated the U.S. request by blocking consensus in the GATT Council. GATT remedies thus completely exhausted, the United States announced on November 5, 1992 that it would increase import duties to 200% on $ 300 million worth of white wines, wheat gluten, and rape seed oil beginning December 5. *See* James R. Arnold, *The Oilseeds Dispute and the Validity of Unilateralism in a Multilateral Context*, 30 Stanford Journal of International Law 187, 189–92 (1994).

131 GATT Panel Report, *EC – Oilseeds I*, para. 144. This passage was quoted with approval in the WTO panel report on *Japan – Film*, para. 10.35.

> *they would be reluctant to make tariff concessions and the General Agreement would no longer be useful as a legal framework for incorporating the results of trade negotiations.*[132] [emphasis added]

In relation to the second part of the above quotation, the following insight of *EC – Citrus* Panel (1985) is, notwithstanding being on a different track from the most GATT jurisprudence on the NVNI complaints, worthy to consider:

> The Panel noted that the basic purpose of Article XXIII : 1(b) was *to provide for offsetting or compensatory adjustment* in situations in which the balance of rights and obligations of the contracting parties had been disturbed (see page 5 of document E/PC/T/A/PV/6 of 2 June 1947). One of the fundamental benefits accruing to the contracting parties under the General Agreement, therefore, was the right to such adjustment in situations in which the balance of their rights and obligations had been upset to their disadvantage.[133] [emphasis added]

132 *EC-Oilseeds I,* para. 148; *Japan-Film,* para. 10.50 ("We reach this conclusion in considering the purpose of Article XXIII : 1(b), which is to protect the balance of concessions under GATT by providing a means to redress government actions not otherwise regulated by GATT rules that nonetheless nullify or impair a Member's legitimate expectations of benefits from tariff negotiations. To achieve this purpose, in our view, it is important that the kinds of government actions considered to be measures covered by Article XXIII : 1(b) should not be defined in an unduly restrictive manner"); *EC-Asbestos (P),* para. 8.258 ("The Community reasoning is also wrong because it does not concur with the preparatory work on the GATT 1947, which shows that the objective of Article XXIII : 1(b) is to prevent abuse of the provisions of the General Agreement"); *India-Patent I,* para. 41 ("'Non-violation' complaints are rooted in the GATT's origins as an agreement intended to protect the reciprocal tariff concessions negotiated among the contracting parties under Article II. In the absence of substantive legal rules in many areas relating to international trade, the 'non-violation' provision of Article XXIII : 1(b) was aimed at preventing contracting parties from using non-tariff barriers or other policy measures to negate the benefits of negotiated tariff concessions") (footnote deleted).

133 *EC-Citrus,* para. 4.37.

Although the *EC – Citrus* decision did mention the broad balancing function of NVNI complaints, not referring specifically to the tariff concessions, the decision can be equated to the opinion of *EC-Oilseeds I* on the purpose of NVNI complaints, in the sense that the tariff concession's value is intended to provide "an assurance of better market access," which is no less than an "adjustment in situations in which the balance of their rights and obligations had been upset to [contracting parties'] disadvantage." This more expanded description is also found in the Appellate Body Report of the *US – Wool Shirts* case as follows:

> The foundation of dispute settlement under Article XXIII of the GATT 1994 is the assurance to Members of *the benefits accruing directly or indirectly to them under the GATT 1994*. This was true as well of dispute settlement under the GATT 1947. If any Member should consider that its benefits are nullified or impaired as the result of circumstances set out in Article XXIII, then dispute settlement is available.[134] [emphasis added]

Thus, the *safeguard function* of NVNI complaint for assuring "better market access" to all WTO Members is the fourth and legally more expanded sense of the NVNI complaints.[135] Based on the safeguard function, the NVNI complaints furthermore enable the parties to obtain proper information about barriers to trade that exist in the economies of other Members, to reach agreement on tariff concessions, and to monitor compliance with concessions. On WTO multilateral negotiations process, these complaints can function as an incentive device to encourage negotiations.[136]

134 WTO Appellate Body Report, *US – Wool Shirts*, at 13.

135 *See Japan – Film*, para. 10.35 ("Clearly, the safeguarding of the process and the results of negotiating reciprocal tariff concessions under Article II is fundamental to the balance of rights and obligations to which all WTO Members subscribe").

136 *See* LINARELLI (2000), at 276.

3. Non-Violation Concept Elsewhere

NVNI complaints are not unique to the WTO. For example, the North American Free Trade Agreement ("NAFTA")[137] contains NVNI complaints.[138] The relevant provisions are as follows:

> Article 2004: Recourse to Dispute Settlement Procedures
>
> Except for the matters covered in Chapter Nineteen (Review and Dispute Settlement in Antidumping and Countervailing Duty Matters) and as otherwise provided in this Agreement, the dispute settlement provisions of this

137 North American Free Trade Agreement, Dec. 17. 1992, US-Can.-Mex., 32 I.L.M. 289 (containing chs. 1–9), 32 I.L.M. 605 (containing chs. 10–22) [hereinafter NAFTA]. Some of the dispute settlement mechanisms of NAFTA are found in several chapters of the agreement: Chapter 11 (settlement of disputes between a party and an investor of another party), Chapter 19 (review and dispute settlement in antidumping and countervailing duty matters), and Chapter 20 (institutional arrangements and dispute settlement procedures). The other two NAFTA dispute settlement mechanisms are contained within the two supplemental agreements negotiated after the NAFTA text on labor and environmental issues. *See* North American Agreement on Labor Cooperation, Sept. 14, 1993, Can.-Mex.-US, Article 29, 39 I.L.M 1499, 1509–10; North American Agreement on Environmental Cooperation, Sept. 14, 1993, Can.-Mex.-US, Article 24, 32 I.L.M. 1480, 1490–91. Article 1801:1 of the US-Canadian Free Trade Agreement. *See generally* FREDERICK M. ABBOT, LAW AND POLICY OF REGIONAL INTEGRATION: THE NAFTA AND WESTERN HEMISPHERIC INTEGRATION IN THE WORLD TRADE ORGANISATION SYSTEM 97–117 (1995); Cherie O'Neal Taylor, *Dispute Resolution as a Catalyst for Economic Integration and an Agent for Deepening Integration: NAFTA and MERCOSUR?,* 17 Northwestern Journal of International Law and Business 850, 899 n. 161 (1997).

138 NAFTA applies the NVNI complaint to Chapter Seventeen on intellectual property. Though there are exceptions, a party could access NAFTA's State dispute settlement mechanism in order to determine whether another party had initiated a novel measure which, while not inconsistent with NAFTA, nullified or impaired a benefit expected under Chapter Seventeen. Potential actions that could trigger a NVNI complaint include new laws on cigarette packaging, domestic content in broadcasting, and reference-based pricing for pharmaceutical drugs. *See* Owen Lippert, *One Trip to the Dentist is Enough: Reasons to Strengthen Intellectual Property Rights through the Free Trade Area of the Americas,* Fordham Intellectual Property, Media & Entertainment Law Journal 241, 296–99 (1998).

Chapter shall apply with respect to the avoidance or settlement of all disputes between the Parties regarding the interpretation or application of this Agreement or wherever a Party considers that an actual or proposed measure of another Party is or would be inconsistent with the obligations of this Agreement or cause nullification or impairment in the sense of Annex 2004.

Annex 2004: Nullification and Impairment

1. If any Party considers that any benefit it could reasonably have expected to accrue to it under any provision of:

(a) Part Two (Trade in Goods), except for those provisions of Annex 300-A (Automotive Sector) or Chapter Six (Energy) relating to investment;

(b) Part Three (Technical Barriers to Trade);

(c) Chapter Twelve (Cross-Border Trade in Services); or

Part Six (Intellectual Property),

is being nullified or impaired as a result of the application of any measure that is not inconsistent with this Agreement, the Party may have recourse to dispute settlement under this Chapter.

We can also find NVNI provision in the following trade treaties: the Mexico-Colombia-Venezuela Free Trade Treaty (entered into force on 1 January 1995); the Mexico-Bolivia Free Trade Treaty and the Mexico-Costa Rica Free Trade Treaty (both 1 January 1995); the Mexico-Nicaragua Free Trade Treaty (1 July 1998); the Centroamerica-Dominican Republic Free Trade Treaty signed by the governments of Costa Rica, El Salvador, Guatemala, Honduras, Nicaragua and the Dominican Republic (16 April 1998).[139]

139 For a more detailed explanation, *see* WTO Document, IP/C/W/124, Council for Trade-Related Aspects of Intellectual Property Rights – Non-Violation Complaints and the TRIPS Agreement (Note by the Secretariat on 28 January 1999) ["WTO Doc. IP/C/W/124"], paras. 101–04.

III. The Development of Non-Violation Complaints

A. Non-Violation Complaints in GATT 47

In the first and seminal NVNI case of *Australian Subsidy* (1950), the Working Party[1] interpreted the difficult language of GATT Article XXIII. It concerned measures by the respondent (Australia) that nullify or impair the trade benefits that accrue to the complainant (Chile).[2] That Article does not expressly discuss the situation where the measures of a Contracting Party that cause harm to the trade benefits of the aggrieved Contracting Party, could not reasonably be anticipated by the aggrieved party. Yet, the decision introduces the concept of *reasonable expectation* whereby benefits are nullified or impaired by the measures that the aggrieved party could not reasonably have been anticipated. The Working Party stated:

> It was agreed that such impairment would exist if the action of the Australian Government which resulted in upsetting the competitive relationship between sodium nitrate and ammonium sulphate *could not reasonably have been anticipated* by the Chilean Government, taking into consideration all pertinent circumstances and the provisions of the General Agreement, at the time it negotiated for the duty-free binding on sodium nitrate.[3] [emphasis added]

1 Initially, trade disputes among GATT Contracting Parties were dealt with at the plenary bi-annual meetings of the Contracting Parties. Later, intercessional committees of the Contracting Parties were assigned the task of resolving disputes, and still later, working parties were used. Their purpose was to clarify the relevant issues rather than to render binding decisions. In 1955, the working party mechanism, which had relied on Contracting Parties designating members of a working party and issuing instructions to them, was replaced by the use of panels comprised of experts acting independently from the Contracting Parties. *See* Raj Bhala, *The Myth about Stare Decisis and International Trade,* 14 American University International Law Review 845, 888–89 (1999).

2 *See Australian Subsidy,* paras. 2–6.

3 *Id.,* para. 12.

This concept was used approvingly in the subsequent cases.[4] From this seed, the jurisprudence on *nullification or impairment* developed. Ultimately, the practice emerged that a Panel would presume *prima facie* nullification or impairment when a Contracting Party had breached a GATT obligation and hence a defending Contracting Party carried the burden of proving that nullification or impairment did not exist.[5]

On the other hand, a NVNI complaint has been treated as an "exceptional" concept and approached "with caution."[6] In one famous NVNI complaint, *EC-Oilseeds I* (1990),[7] the European Eco-

4 Under this significance, Robert Hudec dubs the *Australian Subsidy* case the Marbury *vs.* Madison of GATT jurisprudence, *see* HUDEC (1990), at 159–67; HUDEC (1975), at 483–89.

5 *See* GATT Panel Report, *Uruguayan Recourse to Article XXIII,* at 95. In cases where there is a clear infringement of the provisions of the GATT, or in other words, where measures are applied in conflict with the provisions of GATT and are not permitted under the terms of the relevant protocol under which the GATT is applied by the Contracting Party, the action would, *prima facie,* constitute a case of nullification or impairment and would *ipso facto* require consideration of whether the circumstances are serious enough to justify the authorization of suspension of concessions or obligations'. *Id.,* at 100. *See also* GATT Panel Report, *DISC* (*prima facie* violation of Article XVI); GATT, *Japan – Imports Leather* (*prima facie* violation of Article XI). The *prima facie* concept was also applied in situations involving quotas or domestic subsidies on products subject to agreed upon tariff limitations (i. e. tariffs bound under Article II, and codified in Article 3.8 of DSU). *See generally* JACKSON (1969), at 182; JACKSON (1997), at 124.

6 In *EC – Oilseeds I,* the United States stated that it "concurred in the proposition that non-violation nullification or impairment should remain an exceptional concept. Although this concept had been in the text of Article XXIII of the General Agreement from the outset, a cautious approach should continue to be taken in applying the concept." *EC – Oilseeds I,* para. 114; *See also Japan – Film,* paras. 10.36–37; *Korea – Procurement,* para. 7.97; MCGOVERN (1995), p. 2.27–1 (noting that "if all of these provisions were taken literally their potential scope would be enormous").

7 In this case, the US, a major exporter of oilseeds, complained that the EC subsidies violated the EC's obligations under the GATT on two grounds. First, the US argued that EC subsidies to EC oilseed processors who purchased domestic oilseeds gave the domestic product an advantage over imports,

nomic Community (EC) stated the NVNI concept was exceptional, "since otherwise the trading world would be plunged into a state of precariousness and uncertainty".[8] In the fifty-year history of the GATT 47, few cases considering substantive NVNI complaints were brought to judicial review, and the pattern involved is a rather narrow and consistent fact boundary: product-specific subsidies to a firm that was consistent with the GATT but that undermined specific tariff concessions.[9] A GATT Review Reports (1955) noted that:

> So far as domestic subsidies are concerned, it was agreed that a contracting party which has negotiated a concession under Article II may be assumed, for the purpose of Article XXIII, to have a reasonable expectation, failing

---

violating the national treatment requirement of Article III : 4. Second, the US argued that EC oilseed producer subsidies under the Common Agricultural Policy's price support system also favored domestic products over imported products. Arguing that this favoritism violated the EC's agreement to allow duty-free entry of oilseed products, the US sought redress under Article XXIII because of this impairment of benefits. In considering the *EC – Oilseeds I* report, it is important to keep in mind that production subsidies for agricultural products are not prohibited by the GATT *per se*. Nevertheless, the Panel stated that the principle of negotiated concessions under Article XXIII is such that "the improved competitive opportunities that can legitimately be expected from a tariff concession can be frustrated not only by measures proscribed by the General Agreement but also by measures consistent with that Agreement." For a more detailed explanation, *see* Al J. Daniel, Jr. *Agricultural Reform: The European Community, the Uruguay Round, and International Dispute Resolution,* 46 Arkansas Law Review 873, 905–914 (1994).

8 *EC – Oilseeds I,* para. 113. *Cf. Japan-Film,* para. 10.36; *EC-Asbestos (AB),* para. 36. The preamble to the "Subsidies Code" states that it requires "greater certainty" and "greater uniformity" in interpreting Articles VI, XVI and XXIII, *see* Agreement on Interpretation and Application of Articles VI, XVI, and XXIII of the General Agreement on Tariffs and Trade, *opened for signature* Apr. 12, 1979, BISD 26S/56 (1979) ("Subsidies Code"). The Subsidies Code was adopted by the Contracting Parties as part of the Tokyo Round of Agreements on non-tariff barriers.

9 *See* Durling & Lester (1998), at 214; The pattern is that if country A subsidizes its domestic production, disadvantaging the exports of country B to country A, the country B can bring the case to WTO under the NVNI claim.

> evidence to the contrary, that the value of the concession will not be nullified or impaired by the contracting party which granted the concession by the subsequent introduction or increase of a domestic subsidy on the product concerned.[10]

Subsequently, the ambiguity of NVNI claims has been partly clarified by introducing a higher burden of proof than that of violation claims. A GATT Document (1979) stated, in respect of recourse to Article XXIII: 1(b) or (c), that:

> If a contracting party bringing an Article XXIII case claims that measures that do not conflict with the provisions of the General Agreement have nullified or impaired benefits accruing to it under the General Agreement, it would be called upon to provide a detailed justification.[11]

Furthermore, the more condensed wordings for *causes of action* in some "Tokyo Codes" than that found in GATT have also contributed to the treatment of NVNI claims as exceptional,[12] although the basic concept of NVNI was still present.

The exceptionality of the NVNI concept has led to attempts in the Uruguay Round to clarify its possible scope.[13] However, there

10 GATT Review Reports, Report by the Working Party *on "Other Barriers to Trade,"* adopted on 3 March 1955, BISD 3S/222, para. 13.

11 Understanding on Notification, Consultation, Dispute Settlement and Surveillance; Annex to the 1979 Understanding: Agreed Description of the Customary Practice of the GATT in the Field of Dispute Settlement (Article XXIII: 2), Nov. 28, 1979, BISD 26S/216, para. 5.

12 *See Agreement on Technical Barriers to Trade*, Article 14; *Agreement on Government Procurement*, Article VII; *Agreement on Interpretation and Application of Articles VI of GATT 1994 ("Anti-Dumping Agreement")*, Articles 15; *Agreement on Implementation of Article VII of the GATT 1994*, Articles 19 and 20. *But cf.* Article 6 of the *Agreement on Import Licensing Procedures* referred to Articles XXII and XXIII of the GATT without any reservation.

13 In the *Understanding on the Interpretation and Application of Article XXII and XXIII of the General Agreement on Tariffs and Trade (Draft Understanding)*, which was part of the 'Draft Final Act Embodying the Results of Uruguay Round of Multilateral Trade Negotiations' (Brussels Draft Final Act) there was a provision clarifying the requirements for invoking a NVNI complaint in the Dispute Settlement Understanding with an explanation of reasonable expectation. *See* 2 A NEGOTIATING HISTORY, at 2785–86 (1993).

was no consensus: The EC proposed that in NVNI complaints, no opportunity should be given to appeal unless the parties otherwise agree to binding arbitration or conciliation;[14] on the contrary, the US strongly opposed a different procedure for NVNI complaints.[15] Therefore, the NVNI concept has been retained by the WTO Agreement as it is.

B. Non-Violation Complaints in WTO Agreements

1. *In General*

After WTO inception, the DSU applies to all "covered agreements"[16] which includes the Multilateral Trade Agreement listed in Annexes 1, 2 and 3 of the WTO Agreement.[17] Hence the NVNI complaints are expected to affect the GATT,[18] the GATS[19] and TRIPS.[20] Nevertheless, the significance of the NVNI concept may differ under these agreements. First, in the Multilateral Agreements on Trade in Goods, there are several provisions modifying conventional NVNI wording. The *Agreement on Subsidies and Countervailing Measures ("SCM Agreement")*,[21] Article 5, contains a specific provision on nullification or impairment of benefits accruing to other Members.[22]

14 1 A NEGOTIATING HISTORY (1993), at 61.
15 *Id.* This US opposition appears to have come from the emphasis on reciprocal tariff concessions. *See* CHO (1998), at 321 n. 46. He also refers to the Section 301 of the Trade Act of 1974 providing a variety of causes of action against "unreasonable" practices by a foreign government, *see id.*, at 321.
16 DSU Article 1(1) and Appendix 1.
17 WTO Agreement, Article II: 2. These include the GATT and other Multilateral Agreements on Trade in Goods in Annex 1A, the GATS in Annex 1B, the TRIPS in Annex 1C and the DSU in Annex 2.
18 DSU Article 26.
19 GATS, Article XXIII: 1(b).
20 TRIPS, Part V, Article 64.2.
21 THE LEGAL TEXT (1995), at 264–314.

The *Agreement on Agriculture,* Article 10, contains certain express non-circumvention obligations, so that any nullification or impairment of the relevant benefits might actually constitute a violation,[23] and Article 13 (Peace Clause)[24] temporarily exempts certain domes-

22 Article 5: Adverse Effects
"No Member should cause, through the use of any subsidy referred to in paragraphs 1 and 2 of Article 1, adverse effects to the interests of other Member, i. e.: [...] (b) nullification or impairment of benefits accruing directly or indirectly to other Members under GATT 1994 in particular the benefits of concessions bound under Article II of GATT 1994." (footnote deleted); *See* WTO Panel Report, *US – Offset Acts*, para. 7.119 ("The presumption arising under Article 3.8 DSU relates to nullification or impairment caused by the violation at issue. Thus, if a measure violates Article 18.1 of the AD Agreement and Article VI: 2 of the GATT 1994, that violation would be presumed to cause nullification or impairment, by virtue of the non-conformity of that measure with the relevant provision(s) of the AD Agreement. *For the purpose of SCM Article 5(b), however, Mexico must show that the use of a subsidy caused nullification or impairment.* It is suggested that the fact that the CDSOA is in violation of AD Article 18.1 and GATT Article VI: 2 does not address this issue, since our finding of violation of these provisions says nothing of the effects resulting from the use of CDSOA as a subsidy") [emphasis added].

23 Article 10: Prevention of Circumvention of Export Subsidy Commitments
"1. Export subsidies not listed in paragraph 1 of Article 9 shall not be applied in a manner which results in, or which threatens to lead to, circumvention of export subsidy commitments; nor shall non-commercial transactions be used to circumvent such commitments."

24 Article 13: Due Restraint
"During the implementation period, notwithstanding the provisions of GATT 1994 and the Agreement on Subsidies and Countervailing Measures (referred to in this Article as the "Subsidies Agreement"): (a) domestic support measures that conform fully to the provisions of Annex 2 to this Agreement shall be: [...] (iii) exempt from actions based on non-violation nullification or impairment of the benefits of tariff concessions accruing to another Member under Article II of GATT 1994, in the sense of paragraph 1(b) of Article XXIII of GATT 1994..."; The "peace clause" provides that domestic support that conforms fully to the reduction commitments and exempt payments consistent with the exemption provisions as well as domestic support within *de minimis* levels, are exempt until 2003 from the imposition of countervailing duties, unless there is a determination of injury or threat thereof domestic support is also exempt from actions based on the GATT 1994, the Subsidies Agreement, or NVNI of tariff concessions, provided that such measures do not grant support to a specific commodity in excess of that provided during the 1992 marketing year.

tic support measures from actions based on NVNI complaints arising from anticipated benefits of tariff concessions.[25] Article 8.10 of the *Agreement on Textiles and Clothing* only refers to invocation of paragraph 2 of Article XXIII of GATT and the relevant provisions of the DSU in cases of non-conformance with recommendations of the Textiles Monitoring Body (TBM).[26] Second, the GATS does not provide for situation complaints *as per* Article XXIII : 1(c) of GATT nor does it provide for any complaints based on an *impediment to the attainment of an objective* of that Agreement.[27] Third, in the TRIPS, even the applicability of NVNI complaints is still controversial, which leaves potential for future disputes.[28]

25 The Peace Clause remains in effect through the end of 2003. This provision renders non-actionable until 2004 the trade-distorting export subsidies and domestic support measures maintained by the US and the EU, thereby deprives developing countries of any recourse to address the unfair competitive advantage conferred by the Agreement on developed countries. *See* CARMEN G. GONZALEZ, *Institutionalising Inequality: the WTO Agreement on Agriculture, Food Security, and Developing Countries,* 27 Columbia Journal of Environmental Law 433, 484 (2002).

26 Article 8.10: "If a Member considers itself unable to conform with the recommendations of the TMB, it shall provide the TMB with the reasons therefore not later than one month after receipt of such recommendations. Following thorough consideration of the reason given, the TMB shall issue any further recommendations it considers appropriate forthwith. If, after such further recommendations, the matter remains unresolved, either Member may bring the matter before the Dispute Settlement Body and invoke paragraph 2 of Article XXIII of GATT 1994 and the relevant provisions of the Dispute Settlement Understanding."

27 The following special provision in relation to NVNI is found in Article XXIII : 3 of GATS: "3. If any Member considers that any benefit it could reasonably have expected to accrue to it under a specific commitment of another Member under Part III of this Agreement is being nullified or impaired as a result of the application of any measure which does not conflict with the provisions of this Agreement, it may have recourse to the DSU. If the measure is determined by the DSB to have nullified or impaired such a benefit, the Member affected shall be entitled to a mutually satisfactory adjustment on the basis of paragraph 2 of Article XXI, which may include the modification or withdrawal of the measure. In the event an agreement cannot be reached between the Members concerned, Article 22 of the DSU shall apply."

28 *See* PART ONE-III-B-3 of this dissertation.

2. *General Agreement on Trade in Services (GATS)*

a. In General

Under the WTO Agreements, the conceptual outline of *cause of action* of the NVNI complaints has changed. Although there are startling differences in the nature of goods and services, GATS has imported the NVNI complaints of the GATT but using different settings.[29] The GATS limits the possibility such complaints to the situations in which the benefit accruing under *specific commitments of another Member under Part III of the GATS* is being nullified or impaired.[30] The NVNI complaint under the GATS is concerned with nullification or impairment of reasonably expected benefits arising from the specific commitments undertaken by each Member. These commitments relate to national treatment, market access or additional commitments with respect to particular sectors and/or modes of supply, and are subject to terms, limitations, conditions or qualifications inserted in each Member's schedule of commitments.[31]

The formal documents of the Uruguay Round Group of Negotiations on Services indicate that during 1990, several delegations had submitted drafts of the Agreement, two of which had specifically addressed NVNI complaints by effectively limiting them in different ways to benefits accruing under specific commitments.[32] At the May/June 1991 meeting of the Group of Negotiations on

29 *See, e.g.* COTTIER & SCHEFER (1997), p. 157; LISA SUE KLAIMAN, *Applying GATT Dispute Settlement Procedures to a Trade in Services Agreement: Proceed with Caution*, 11 University of Pennsylvania Journal of International Journal of Business Law 657, 659 (1990).

30 Part III of the GATS contains the specific commitments that Members have negotiated and specified in their national Schedules attached to the GATS. The other parts of the GATS contain general rules of application as well as certain institutional and procedural provisions.

31 ZDOUC (1999), at 303.

32 *See generally* Uruguay Round Document, MTN.GNS/W/101, Communication from Cameroon, China, Egypt, India, Kenya, Nigeria and Tanzania (4 May 1990) and; MTN.GNS/W/102, Communication from Switzerland (7 June 1990).

Services, many delegations expressed the view that NVNI complaints needed careful circumscription and definition, especially in the light of the possible unintended consequences of requiring Members to deregulate certain markets.[33]

In the GATS, the NVNI complaints are provided for in Article XXIII:3. The Article XXIII reads:

> 1. If any Member should consider that any other Member *fails to carry out its obligations or specific commitments under this Agreement,* it may with a view to reaching a mutually satisfactory resolution of the matter have recourse to the DSU.
>
> 2. If the DSB considers that the circumstances are serious enough to justify such action, it may authorize a Member or Members to suspend the application to any other Member or Members of obligations and specific commitments in accordance with Article 22 of the DSU.
>
> 3. If any Member considers that *any benefit it could reasonably have expected to accrue to it under a specific commitment of another Member under Part III of this Agreement* is being nullified or impaired as a result of the application of any measure which does not conflict with the provisions of this Agreement, it may have recourse to the DSU. If the measure is determined by the DSB to have nullified or impaired such a benefit, the Member affected shall be entitled to *a mutually satisfactory adjustment* on the basis of paragraph 2 of Article XXI, which may include the modification or withdrawal of the measure. In the event an agreement cannot be reached between the Members concerned, Article 22 of the DSU shall apply.[34] [emphasis added]

There are two noteworthy points in the above Article. First and foremost, in terms of *causes of action,* one cause (i.e. the impairment of "the attainment of any objective of the [GATS] Agreement") appears deleted compared with the original text of GATT.[35] How-

33 *See* Uruguay Round Document, MTN.GNS/42, Secretariat note on the meeting of 27 May to 6 June 1991.

34 GATS, Article XXIII.

35 Werner Zdouc mentioned two possible ways to explain this deletion: "On the one hand, one could argue that the latter cause of action has already fallen in desuetude under GATT 1947 for non-violation and violation complaints [...] On the other hand, these differences in the wording of the Articles XXIII of GATS and GATT could be interpreted as a deliberate attempt to contain the scope of the non-violation remedy under GATS..." *See* Zdouc (1999), at 303.

ever, considering the "objectives" of "providing effective market access" of GATS by means of "Specific Commitments,"[36] it must be not so hard to find that the specific commitments of GATS regarding the *causes of action*, are no less than "any objective" of the GATT. More importantly, Article XIV of GATS somewhat confirms the connection of "objective" of WTO Agreements with "market access".[37] Second, the "reasonable expectation" as a constituent of "benefits" is shown clearly in the text. Although "reasonable expectation" is typically activated by reciprocal arrangements like the tariff concessions within GATT,[38] and although the expectation can be discouraged under the progressively liberalising commitments of GATS system, the significance of confirming reasonable expectation can not be underestimated. The GATS has literally recognised the principle of reasonable expectation evolved in case law "in order to contain potentially far reaching and arbitrary use of complaints against legal measures."[39]

36 GATS, Article XIV (Negotiation of Specific Commitments); See also Article XVI (Market Access), XVII (National Treatment), XVIII (Additional Commitments), and XX (Schedules of Specific Commitments).

37 GATS, Article XIV: 1. "In pursuance of *the objectives* of this Agreement, Members shall enter into successive rounds of negotiations [...], with a view to achieving *a progressively higher level of liberalization*. Such negotiations shall be directed to the reduction or elimination of the adverse effects on trade in services of measures as *a means of providing effective market access*" [emphasis added].

38 *See, e.g.* PETERSMANN (1994), at 1231; *See also* CHO (1998), at 325 (claiming "[W]ithout a reasonable expectation requirement, supplementary-mode non-violation cases would be irrelevant because the minimum requirement of a connection between tariff concessions and reasonable expectation therefrom cannot be demonstrated. Therefore, with respect to non-violation cases, the GATS regime would produce only 'independent-mode' cases for which there are no specified precedents or discipline").

39 *See* COTTIER & SCHEFER (1997), pp. 157–58.

b. Requirements for Non-Violation Complaints in GATS

Thus, in a NVNI case under the GATS, it is likely that three important conditions will have to be established: (1) that a *measure* attributable to a government exists; (2) that it *nullified the benefits* of the competitive relationship between foreign and similar domestic services or service suppliers and; (3) that it was *not legitimately anticipated* at the time when the relevant specific commitment was negotiated.[40]

First, regarding *measure,* different issues from those that have arisen under the GATT do not seem to be raised. However, the scope of governmental measures could prove to be broader under the GATS than under the GATT.[41] Related to the *measure,* although the GATS does not regulate dumping, could government inaction on a service dumping give rise to a NVNI complaint? Given the comparison with GATT Article VI on dumping, it appears the GATS does not obligate members to be the source of such dumping.[42] Nevertheless, as the GATT Article VI: 1 does state that "contracting parties recognise that dumping [...] is to be condemned if it causes or threatens material injury to an established industry in the territory of a contracting party", it is arguable that upon presentation of satisfactory evidence by the importing member such an injurious service dumping could lead to a NVNI case.

40 ZDOUC (1999), at 305.

41 For example, according to specific schedules on commitments in basic telecommunications, governments might be held responsible for anti-competitive conduct by major suppliers in telecommunications services even if actions of such suppliers have only a remote link to the government. In this case, government's actions not of preventing anti-competitive practices in telecommunications markets could belong to *measures* in NVNI complaints context. *See* ZDOUC (1999), 305–06.

42 *See* GATT Panel Report, *Canada – FIRA,* para. 5.18 ("The Panel found that there is no provision in the General Agreement which forbids requirements to sell goods in foreign markets in preference to the domestic market. In particular, the General Agreement does not impose on contracting parties the obligation to prevent enterprises from dumping").

Second, along the lines of GATT NVNI practices, the *nullification of benefits* under the GATS means an upsetting of the competitive relationship between foreign and similar domestic services or service suppliers. In this instance, standards for defining *like services or service suppliers* are significant for the interpretation of the competitive relationship.[43] The third requirement, *legitimate expectation* can be realised by the GATT practices: that is, the GATS-consistent measures possibly nullifying other members' benefits could not have been legitimately expected at the time when the relevant specific commitment was negotiated.[44] Anyway, the applicability of the NVNI complaints to GATS is likely to be narrower than that of GATT, mainly because the discretion of member governments is already limited by a number of GATS obligations not to nullify the benefits of specific commitments under GATS Articles XVI–XVIII.[45] On top of this, a *positive* approach of GATS contrasted with the GATT *negative* approach,[46] may be another significant reason for the less applicability of NVNI complaints. What the two reasons imply is that to claim violation complaints, which would be NVNI complaints under GATT, is more likely in GATS. Thus several *positive* GATS Articles are worth reviewing.

43 Zdouc, *id.*, at 307.

44 For more concrete examples, *see* Zdouc, *id.*, at 306–07.

45 *Id.*, at 308.

46 The GATS positive list approach is explained that "WTO Members must observe market access- and national treatment-related disciplines only to the extent they undertake specific obligations (by making the corresponding offer) in a given services sector," *see* Matsushita et al. (2003), at 240; In contrast, other trade agreements like NAFTA have adopted the negative list, that is, "If a services sector is not explicitly excluded or otherwise made subject to reservations under this approach, the sector is automatically subject to the NAFTA's rules." *See* Harry G. Broadman, *International Trade and Investment in Services: A Comparative Analysis of the NAFTA*, 27 International Law 623, 640 (1993).

c. Several GATS Articles Relevant to Non-Violation Complaints

GATS Article VI:5 ("Domestic Regulation") would arguably provide for the opportunity to lodge a NVNI complaint against the nullification or impairment of specific commitments through the application of licensing and qualification requirements (other than those listed in the schedules of commitments) and technical standards that could not reasonably have been expected at the time the specific commitments were made.[47]

GATS Article VIII ("Monopolies and Exclusive Service Suppliers") obliges any member to ensure that its monopoly service suppliers do not violate that member's MFN, national treatment and market access obligations when exercising their monopoly rights,[48] but also when such monopoly suppliers compete in the supply of services outside the scope of their monopoly rights directly or through an affiliated company.[49]

GATS Article IX ("Business Practices") provides in part that "certain business practices of service suppliers, other than the practices mentioned in Article VIII, may restrain competition and thereby restrict trade in services". Members are, therefore, under an obligation to enter into consultations with any other member with a view

47 GATS Article VI:5(a): "In sectors in which a Member has undertaken specific commitments [...] the member shall not apply licensing and qualification requirements and technical standards that nullify or impair such specific commitments in a manner which [...] (ii) could not reasonably have been expected of that Member at the time the specific commitments in those sectors were made."

48 GATS Article VIII:1: "Each member shall ensure that any monopoly supplier of a service in its territory does not, in the supply of the monopoly service in the relevant market, act in a manner inconsistent with that Member's obligations under Article II and specific commitments."

49 GATS Article VIII:2: "Where a member's monopoly supplier competes, either directly or through an affiliated company, in the supply of a service outside the scope of its monopoly rights and which is subject to that Member's specific commitments, the Member shall ensure that such a supplier does not abuse its monopoly position to act in its territory in a manner inconsistent with such commitments."

to eliminating such anti-competitive practices, but the obligation is limited in the sense that "WTO members have a duty to consult and cooperate, but no duty to eliminate offending [anti-competitive practices]."[50]

GATS Article XV ("Subsidies") envisions future negotiations to limit subsidies with respect to service providers and consultations in cases of being adversely affected by a subsidy.[51] Although this Article can be paralleled with the *SCM Agreement*, because the Agreement applies to goods only, subsidies granted to service enterprises will fall entirely outside of its coverage. Thus, GATS-related subsidies can be discussed as a possible NVNI complaints area.

3. Agreement on Trade-Related Aspects of Intellectual Property (TRIPS)

a. In General

Under the TRIPS[52] for dispute settlement, Article 64[53] applies by default the provisions of Articles XXII and XXIII of GATT and the DSU.[54]

50 KENNEDY (2001), at 643.

51 Article XV of GATS.

52 It is useful to remember the connection of TRIPS agreement and DSU, in terms of the AB's reasoning. The AB of *India-Patent I* case noted that: "The *TRIPS Agreement* is one of the new agreements negotiated and concluded in the Uruguay Round of multilateral trade negotiations. The *TRIPS Agreement* brings intellectual property within the world trading system for the first time by imposing certain obligations on Members in the area of trade related intellectual property rights. As one of the covered agreements under the DSU, the *TRIPS Agreement* is subject to the dispute settlement rules and procedures of that Understanding." *See India – Patent I (AB)*, para. 29.

53 For a general overview of Article 64.2 and 64.3, *see* WTO Document, IP/C/W/349, TRIPS Council – Non-Violation and Situation Complaints (Summary Note by the Secretariat on 19 June 2002) and IP/C/W/124 (29 January 1999).

54 During the Uruguay Round negotiations, the concept of NVNI was extended to apply to the other multilateral agreements on trade in goods (in addition to GATT 94) and to trade in services. During the TRIPS negotiations in particular, there was significant disagreement regarding the inclusion of a provision

According to Article 64:2,[55] a five-year transition period for developing countries to enforce intellectual property regimes expired from on January 1, 2000, simultaneously with the five-year moratorium on far-reaching NVNI and situation complaints.[56] With the end of the moratorium, NVNI complaints become available for use in TRIPS disputes, which in contrast to a violation case does not require any literal breach of a TRIPS provision.[57] Article 64.3 of the

---

on NVNI in the context of an intellectual property agreement. As a result, the final text included reference to the concept, but delayed the provision's entry into force until 1 January 2000, and provided that the Council for TRIPS "examine the scope and modalities" for such complaints in the intervening period and submit recommendations to the Ministerial Conference for approval. The Ministerial Conference may decide to approve such recommendations or to extend the moratorium by consensus, *see* Article 64 of TRIPS.

55 Article 64.2: "2. Subparagraphs 1(b) and 1(c) of Article XXIII of GATT 1994 shall not apply to the settlement of disputes under this Agreement for a period of five years from the date of entry into force of the WTO Agreement."

56 *See id.*, Article 65(1) of TRIPS (providing all WTO members a one year transition period from the January 1, 1995 entry into force of the WTO Agreement); Article 65(2) of TRIPS (granting developing countries an additional four-year transition period); Article 64(2) of TRIPS (mandating that non-violation and situation complaints will not apply to TRIPS dispute settlement for a period of five years from the January 1, 1995 entry into force); The contention over whether the WTO should countenance NVNI complaints brought by developed nations against developing nations five years after the TRIPS Agreement is essentially a disagreement over the role of the WTO Dispute Settlement Body. *Compare* GELLER (1995), at 107–14 (advocating the view that it would be useful to have the Dispute Settlement Body clarify and define legal standards which negotiating parties phrased vaguely because of failure to reach consensus), *with* SAMAHON (2000), at 1060–75 (expressing the opposing view that giving the Dispute Settlement Body this power is particularly inappropriate in the case of an agreement as divisive and unsettled as the TRIPs Agreement). These commentators point to the destabilizing effect that largely unsupported legal principles mandated by a three-member panel or the Appellate Body could have.

57 On this textual implication of Article 64.3, there appear two different interpretation among member countries, according to a WTO document of IP/C/M/23 (2 June 1999). While the representative of Philippines understood the Article as, "if ever the Council continued discussing this issue, and it could not achieve a consensus on extension or a consensus on scope and modali-

TRIPS[58] required the TRIPS Council to examine the scope and modalities for NVNI complaints made pursuant to the TRIPS Agreement and make recommendations to the General Council by the end of 1999. The *2001 Doha Decision on Implementation-Related Issues and Concerns* instructs the TRIPS Council to make a recommendation to the Cancún Ministerial Conference in 2003.[59] In May 2003, the TRIPS Council chairperson listed four options for a recommendation: (1) banning NVNI complaints in TRIPS completely; (2) allowing the complaints to be handled under the WTO's dispute settlement

---

ties, there was no way in which Article XXIII : 1(b) and (c) would apply under the TRIPS Agreement," the representative of European Communities said that "it was the understanding of his delegation that, pursuant to Article 64.3 of the TRIPS Agreement, the provisions of Article XXIII : 1(b) and (c) of GATT 1994 would automatically apply to disputes under the TRIPS Agreement as from 1 January 2000, unless a consensus was reached beforehand that established otherwise". *See* WTO Document, IP/C/M/23, TRIPS Council – Minutes of Meeting (Held in the Centre William Rappard on 21 and 22 April 1999) ["WTO Doc. IP/C/M/23"], paras. 120–22; For the Appellate Body's opinion on this point, *see India-Patent I (AB)*. para. 42 ("Whether or not 'non-violation' complaints should be available for disputes under the *TRIPS Agreement* is a matter that remains to be determined by the Council for Trade-Related Aspects of Intellectual Property (the "Council for TRIPS") pursuant to Article 64.3 of the *TRIPS Agreement.* It is *not* a matter to be resolved through interpretation by panels or by the Appellate Body"); Frederick Abbott suggested that in the absence of extending or modifying decisions, NVNI complaints would be permitted. *See* FREDERICK M. ABBOTT, 'WTO Dispute Settlement and the Agreement on Trade-Related Aspects of Intellectual Property Rights', in PETERSMANN (ED.) (1997A).

58 Article 64.3: "3. During the time period referred to in paragraph 2, the Council for TRIPS shall examine the scope and modalities for complaints of the type provided for under subparagraphs 1(b) and 1(c) of Article XXIII of GATT 1994 made pursuant to this Agreement, and submit its recommendations to the Ministerial Conference for approval."

59 *See* WTO Document, WT/MIN(01)/17, para. 11.1 ("The TRIPS Council is directed to continue its examination of the scope and modalities for complaints of the types provided for under subparagraphs 1(b) and 1(c) of Article XXIII of GATT 1994 and make recommendations to the Fifth Session of the Ministerial Conference. It is agreed that, in the meantime, members will not initiate such complaints under the TRIPS Agreement").

rules; (3) allowing NVNI complaints but subject to special modalities; and (4) extending the moratorium.[60] In response, most members favoured banning NVNI complaints completely (option 1), or extending the moratorium (option 4).[61] However, no consensus was possible at Cancún Fifth Ministerial Conference on September 2003.[62] Related to the *causes of action* of NVNI complaints, the scope and conditions remain unclear even though Article 64.1 furnishes same applications of Article XXIII of GATT 94 to TRIPS cases.

First, there have been significant controversies whether the NVNI remedy is relevant to the TRIPS Agreement because it originated from a remedy created to deal with the negating tariff concessions.[63] While one side argues that NVNI remedy is intended to protect reciprocal tariff concessions and is simply inapplicable in the context of the TRIPS Agreement,[64] the other side is counter-arguing that there is no substantial difference between GATT, GATS and the TRIPS Agreement and that, as the TRIPS Agreement is one of the pillars of the WTO system, the claims of NVNI clearly applies also

60 WTO Document, IP/C/M/40, Council for Trade-Related Aspects of Intellectual Property Rights – Minutes of Meeting Held in the Centre William Rappard on 4–5 June 2003 (22 August 2003), para. 144.

61 *Id.,* paras. 145–174.

62 WTO Document, WT/MIN(03)/20, Ministerial Statement (adopted on 14 September 2003).

63 *See* Cottier & Schefer (1997), p. 156; According to Frederick Abbott, developing countries had two concerns: "first, that developed countries would allege that the TRIPS Agreement was intended to grant [intellectual property rights ("IPRs")] holders access to their markets, rather than only obligating them to provide IPRs protection; and second, that developed Members would use the non-violation cause of action to expand the literal language of the TRIPS Agreement in light of whatever their 'expectations' might have been about its effects." *See* Abbott (2000), at 172.

64 WTO Doc. IP/C/M/23, para. 111; In addition, it has been argued that it is difficult to see the analogy between tariff concessions (GATT) or specific services commitments (GATS), on the one hand, and the multilateral recognition of the minimum rights of nationals to be provided for by a WTO Member on the basis of the TRIPS Agreement, on the other hand, *see* WTO Document, IP/C/M/22, TRIPS Council – Minutes of Meeting (Held in the Centre William Rappard on 17 February 1999), para. 142.

to it.[65] The Appellate Body appears to be in favor of the former approach. The contradictory approaches are seen in the Report of *India – Patent I* case:

> "Non-violation" complaints are rooted in the GATT's origins as an agreement intended to protect the reciprocal tariff concessions negotiated among the contracting parties under Article II. [...] The meaning of [Article XXIII : 1(b)] is clear: the *only* cause of action permitted under the *TRIPS Agreement* during the first five years after the entry into force of the *WTO Agreement* is a "violation" complaint under Article XXIII : 1(a) of the GATT 1994. [...] Whether or not "non-violation" complaints should be available for disputes under the *TRIPS Agreement* is a matter that remains to be determined by the Council for Trade-Related Aspects of Intellectual Property (the "Council for TRIPS") pursuant to Article 64.3 of the *TRIPS Agreement.* It is *not* a matter to be resolved through interpretation by panels or by the Appellate Body.[66] [underlining added]

This AB's *positivistic* approach is contrasted with the Panel's *normative* approach:

> However, in order to make an objective assessment regarding the consistency of the current Indian mechanism with the TRIPS Agreement, as required under Article 11 of the DSU, we must ask ourselves the following question: can that mechanism achieve the object and purpose of Article 70.8 and thereby protect the legitimate expectations of other WTO Members, by ensuring the preservation of novelty and priority in respect of products which were the subject of mailbox applications? To answer this, we need to analyze the current Indian system from the viewpoint of whether it ensures the degree of legal security and predictability for patent applicants of other WTO Members that they are entitled to legitimately expect under the provisions of Article 70.8(a).[67] [underlining added]

Thomas Cottier connected the Panel's approach with the problems of interpretation and application of national or regional law by national or regional authorities, observing that "Panels, [...] should

65 WTO Document, IP/C/M/27, TRIPS Council – Minutes of Meeting (Held in the Centre William Rappard on 26–29 June 2000) ["WTO Doc. IP/C/M/27"], para. 177.

66 *See India – Patent I (AB),* paras. 41 and 42.

67 Panel Report, *India – Patent I,* para. 7.34.

assess whether national or regional rules on intellectual property rights, as applied by the Member, live up to the legitimate expectations of [TRIPS] Agreement."[68]

Most WTO Members disagree with incorporating the NVNI complaint into the TRIPS Agreement,[69] whilst the United States and Switzerland are insisting on its incorporation into TRIPS. The main concerns by most Members are: (1) uncertainty of the NVNI scope in TRIPS; and (2) undermining regulatory authority of WTO Members.[70] Contrarily the US argues: (1) TRIPS Agreement is a market access agreement; (2) the Marrakesh Agreement was the result of a single undertaking to cooperate each sectoral agreement.[71]

68 COTTIER (1998b), at 118.

69 Some countries have taken a careful approach. For example, European Union has expressed such an approach as follows: "[...] as the [TRIPS] agreement was not principally concerned with questions of market access [...] However, [EC] wished to make clear that well-developed intellectual property legislation, and strong protection of intellectual property rights, as provided by the TRIPS Agreement, was a means of ensuring market access." *See* WTO Doc. IP/C/M/23, para. 122.

70 (1) "It is very difficult to gauge the degree of liability that would be created through introducing non-violation into the TRIPS regime." (2) "As a result, domestic policy making may be unacceptably constrained." *See* WTO Document, IP/C/W/127, TRIPS Council – Non-Violation Nullification or Impairment under the Agreement on Trade Related Aspects of Intellectual Property Rights (TRIPS) (Communication from Canada on 10/February/1999) ["WTO Doc. IP/C/W/127"], at 2.

71 (1) "When negotiating for reductions in tariffs on certain products for which they had a competitive advantage, or to eliminate a quota on those products, Members anticipated a certain level of market access that would result from such changes. The standards and procedures established by the TRIPS Agreement were for the identification, grant, enjoyment and enforcement of private rights in most cases but, in the same way as the TBT or SPS Agreement, established minimum standards that governments must meet before imposing limitations on goods that might be sold in their markets based on health, environment or other factors. In the absence of such agreements, members' expectations of the level of market access obtained could be frustrated."; (2) "However, the Marrakesh Agreement was the result of a single undertaking, so that it was highly unlikely that a panel would determine that something a WTO Member had agreed to under one part of that single undertaking, in fact, nullified and impaired benefits in another area." *See* WTO Doc. IP/C/M/27, para. 160.

Second, there appear different modalities of trades between GATT/GATS and TRIPS. While goods and services trade requires Members not to interfere or regulate the trades ("passive obligations"), trade in intellectual property inversely demands the members to regulate for protecting trade rights ("affirmative obligations").[72] More specifically, while trade barriers to goods typically prevent market access, trade barriers for intellectual properties involve inadequate intellectual properties enforcement by Member states. This conceivable inadequate enforcement by Members, along with the difficulty of policing non-governmental entities,[73] must offer a big challenge for WTO adjudicator to clarify a measure that does not violate any rule of TRIPS Agreement and yet nullifying trade benefits that members reasonably expected to obtain.[74] In addition, necessity for keeping DSU rules consistent among the various WTO fields must be considered.[75]

Third, the "reasonable expectation" requirement which allegedly developed on the basis of reciprocal tariff concessions, is more required to balance the competing interests in empowering market access and acknowledging legitimate sovereign discretion to fulfill TRIPS obligations. This matter will be more emphasised in reasoning the "objective" element in TRIPS disputes, as contrasted by the benefit element. Related to this point, Thomas Cottier rightly claimed that "intellectual property should not be treated differently from other areas" because of smaller ratio of NVNI cases than in GATT area and well-established legitimate expectation jurisprudence of the NVNI complaints.[76]

72 *See* SAMAHON (2000), at 1068; *See also* COTTIER (1998b), p. 118; COTTIER & MAVROIDIS (2000), p. 4 (using the terms of "negative" and "positive" integration-type of WTO provisions).

73 *See* THOMAS COTTIER, *Intellectual Property in International Trade Law and Policy: The GATT Connection,* 47 AUSSENWIRTSCHAFT 79, 83 (1992).

74 *See* SAMAHON (2000), at 1070–75.

75 COTTIER & SCHEFER (1997), p. 143.

76 COTTIER (1998b), p. 117. He also observed that "To the extent that non-violation complaints are likely to remain as the system evolves, it is difficult to see why the present exclusion of this remedy should stay." *Id.*

Fourth, a NVNI complaint can be brought under the claim that the objective of TRIPS Agreement was impaired by the "application by another contracting party of any measure, whether or not it conflicts with the provisions of [the] Agreement".[77] Yet, because the TRIPS regime is more *results-based* focusing on how much intellectual property protection is practically done,[78] the following observation of Thomas Cottier is noteworthy:

> Rights and obligations of the existing GATT are primarily related to goods. [...] Persons and intellectual property rights are, in other words, merely protected indirectly by way of reflection [...]. Intellectual property is no longer limited to justifying potential trade restrictions in a permissive manner, but itself becomes an essential yardstick to limit such restrictions under the heading of persons' rights. Overall, TRIPs would considerably contribute to a constitutional approach and framework of a future GATT, going much beyond the scope of traditional trade arrangements.[79] [footnotes deleted]

Therefore possible disputes over intellectual property could lean more towards whether or not a measure impairs the objective of TRIPS agreement,[80] which is in line with a *constitutional approach* of WTO judicial bodies.[81]

b. Article 8.1 of TRIPS

Article 8.1 of the TRIPS Agreement, entitled "Principles," authorises members to adopt measures "necessary to protect public health and nutrition, and to promote the public interest on sectors of vital

77 Article XXIII : 1(b) of GATT.

78 *See* SAMAHON (2000), at 1069–70.

79 THOMAS COTTIER, *The Prospects for Intellectual Property in GATT,* 28 Common Market Law Review 383, 394 (1991).

80 *Id.,* at 1060 ("As a standard of this judgment, for example, there is some evidentiary categories suggested by the International Intellectual Property Alliance (IIPA). This evidence includes piracy rates; dollar losses; the number of bootleg seizures and raids; police and prosecutorial action, delay, and success; and the number of arrests, convictions, and sentences imposed or served").

81 *See* PART FOUR-IX-B of this dissertation.

importance to their socio-economic and technological development, *provided that such measures are consistent with the provisions of this Agreement.*"[82] This Article establishes a basis for the adoption of internal measures in language similar to that used in Article XX(b) of the GATT. However, while the Article XX(b) is used to justify internal measures that are necessary yet otherwise inconsistent with the GATT 1994, Article 8.1 of the TRIPS Agreement provides that necessary measures must be consistent with the Agreement.[83] Because WTO Members were certainly expected to adopt necessary internal measures that are consistent with TRIPS Agreement, the Article 8.1 bears directly on the potential scope of NVNI complaints.[84]

4. *Anti-Competition Practices (Competition Policies)*

WTO jurisprudence will be cautious for NVNI claiming for which there are not adequately precise rules contained in the WTO Agreement. One such key area will be competition policies.[85] Although competition law generally applies only to private conduct, government practices can enormously affected international trade.[86] In fact, trade negotiations have considered such laws and policies ever since the GATT was signed in 1947. For example in 1958, a GATT experts group examined applying NVNI complaints against restrictive business practices. The group recommended direct consultations between contracting parties to eliminate the harmful ef-

82 Article 8.1 of TRIPS [emphasis added].

83 *See* ABBOTT (2000), at 174. He assessed the Article 8.1 as "a statement of TRIPS interpretative principle: it advises us that members were 'expected' (in the non-violation sense) to have the discretion to adopt 'necessary' internal measures," *See id.*

84 ABBOTT, *id.*, at 175.

85 *See, e.g.* JOHN H. JACKSON, 'Designing and Implementing Effective Dispute Settlement Procedures: WTO Dispute Settlement, Appraisal and Prospects,' in 2 ANDERSON & HOEKMAN (EDS) (2002).

86 *See, e.g.* TARULLO (2000), at 484–85.

fects of the restrictive practices.[87] The majority of the group noted that, "regardless of the question whether Article XXIII could legally be applied, they should recommend to the CONTRACTING PARTIES that they take no action under this Article".[88] The main reasons for this opposition to the applicability of Article XXIII were *inter alia* that "the complexities of the subject" and "the impossibility of obtaining accurate and complete information on private commercial activities in international trade without [...] adequate powers of investigation". Contemporaneously with these reasons, however, they pointed out that to apply the Article XXIII: 1(b) to restrictive business practices needs to have "necessary consensus among countries" and "sufficient experience of action in this [restrictive business] field".[89]

More recently, in the Working Group of Singapore Declaration[90] the proposal of European Commission is noteworthy: it has proposed a WTO agreement that (1) obliges member states to enact or maintain domestic competition legislation that would include at least "core" rules such as prohibiting cartels and monopolisation (or abuse of dominant position); (2) requires the enforcement of

87 *See* GATT BISD, 9S/170, at 172. However, there were different views on certain points between the majority and minority of the group: "The main difference [...] is that the [majority] does not permit the participation of the expert group in the consultations between individual contracting parties if one of the consulting parties does not agree to such participation". *See id.*, at 173, 179.

88 *See id.*, at 172.

89 *Id.*, at 171 ("The necessary consensus among countries upon which such an agreement could be based did not yet exist, and countries did not yet have sufficient experience of action in this field to devise an effective control procedure").

90 *See* WTO Singapore Ministerial Declaration, WT/MIN(96)/DEC (13 December 1996) ("Singapore Ministerial Declaration"). The Ministers agreed to: "establish a working group to examine the relationship between trade and investment; and establish a working group to study issues raised by members relating to the interaction between trade and competition policy, including anti-competitive practices, in order to identify any areas that may merit further consideration in the WTO framework." *See id.*, at para. 20.

this competition legislation, based on principles of nondiscrimination and transparency; (3) provides for cooperation between competition authorities; and (4) aims for the gradual convergence of national practice.[91]

In *Japan – Film,* the United States asked the Panel to consider some novel claims, related to core issues relating to the structure of the institutions of the economy of Japan.[92] As alleged in the *Film* case and in previously regarding sectors such as auto parts,[93] the history of Japanese industry reflects a complex interaction of governmental and private conduct that has apparently foreclosed important distribution channels to foreign companies, and thus seriously constrained market access of foreign companies in Japan.[94] The US claims were of the kind typically addressed in domestic law and policy regulating restrictive business practices.[95] The US claims

91 *See* WTO Document, WT/WGTCP/W/115 (1999), Working Group on the Interaction between Trade and Competition Policy – Communication from the European Community and its Member States; For a criticism of this proposal in terms of the nature and operation of WTO, *see* TARULLO (2000), at 487–93.

92 *See Japan-Film,* paras. 4.1–4.28; One commentator has even criticized the US position as an attack on local constituency preferences in Japan and as an attack on Japanese culture. *See* DILLON (1999), at 202–03.

93 The dispute between the United States and Japan over automobiles was the first major dispute to arise following the signing of the WTO Agreement in 1995. The United States was asserting that Japan's anticompetitive policies closed its auto industry to foreign competition. The dispute came before the WTO when, after months of negotiations broke down, the United States announced it would impose unilateral sanctions on certain Japanese automobiles, and Japan responded by filing a complaint with the WTO challenging these sanctions. The United States had also announced its intention to bring the issue of anticompetitive practices in Japan's auto industry before the WTO, but argued that unilateral actions were, nonetheless, permissible because the WTO's authority did not explicitly cover the issue. The dispute ended in settlement. *See* ABELS (1996), at 476–83.

94 TARULLO, *id.,* at 484.

95 Section 301 is a controversial section of American trade law that authorizes the President to impose unilateral sanctions on other countries when the USTR determines they have engaged in unjustifiable or unreasonable trade practices. *See* 19 USC 2411 (1994). Originally enacted as part of the Trade Act of 1974, section 301 has been significantly altered by the Trade Agreement

apparently sought to determine whether the existing WTO agreements would sufficiently regulate restrictive business behaviours in the absence of an explicit agreement within the WTO framework that deals with competition policy.[96]

Regarding the three requirements for successful NVNI complaints, just the requirement of *application of a measure* needs to be explained in context of restrictive business behaviours. Although competition related formal norms certainly falls within the concept of a member's measure, it would be more difficult to qualify *inac-*

Act of 1979, the Trade and Tariff Act of 1984, and the Omnibus Trade and Competitiveness Act of 1988. Section 301 defines a trade practice as "unjustifiable" if it violates any trade agreement or otherwise denies expected US benefits under those agreements and burdens US commerce. 19 USC. 2411(d)(4)(A). A trade practice is "unreasonable" if, although it is "not necessarily in violation of, or inconsistent with" US legal rights, it is, nonetheless, otherwise "unfair and inequitable." 19 USC. 2411(d)(3)(A). Under this law, private parties may request that the US government, through the US Trade Representative (USTR), impose unilateral sanctions on a country that maintains measures that block free trade. Eastman Kodak Company, US producer of camera film and paper for photographs, filed a petition under Section 301 with the USTR on May 18, 1995. Kodak's petition alleged that prior to 1976, Japan violated the bilateral US-Japan Friendship Commerce and Navigation Treaty and the Organisation for Economic Co-operation and Development Code of Liberalization of Capital Movements with restrictions on inward foreign investment. *See* DURLING (2000), at 63–86; In fact, the actual text of section 301 has been described as "an intricate maze of mandatory commands in one place and extremely wide loopholes in the other." *See* Robert E. Hudec, 'Thinking About the New Section 301: Beyond Good and Evil,' in AGGRESSIVE UNILATERALISM: AMERICA'S 301 TRADE POLICY AND THE WORLD TRADING SYSTEM 122 (JAGDISH BHAGWATI & HUGH T. PATRICK EDS, 1990). The actions are unilateral because the US government independently determines what foreign trading practices are unfair and because the trading partner must then liberalize its practices with no promise of reciprocal concessions from the United States, *see* Hudec, *id.*; A WTO Panel Report ruled that US statute not inconsistent with US obligations under the WTO, *see* WTO Panel Report, *US–Section 301,* para. 8.1.

96 LINARELLI (2000), at 266–67; DILLON (1999), at 197.

tion of a competition authority as a measure.[97] In addition, it does not cover the more likely case that customs concessions[98] are nullified or impaired by nothing more than private agreements.[99]

Some commentators have furthermore concluded that in some instances, government support for private trade barriers can be attacked as NVNI cases.[100] However, Kevin Kennedy's following observation on practical difficulty of applying NVNI claim to *anti-competitive practices* is worth noting:

> First, an Article XXIII : 1(b) complainant must present "a detailed justification" in support of its claim that the responding member's measure has upset the competitive position of the imported products in issue. [...] Second, in proving nullification or impairment of a benefit in the context of private anti-competitive conduct, the complaining member would have to show that it had a reasonable expectation that at the time it negotiated trade concessions with the responding member, the responding member would enforce its competition laws to prevent private barriers to market access. [...] The burden is on the responding member to show that prejudice to the benefits of the concession could have been anticipated at the time the concession was negotiated. [...] Regarding the third element, a "measure," the failure to investigate or prosecute anti-competitive conduct within a member's territory would not likely qualify as a "measure," unless that failure or refusal was based on a regulation or guideline promulgated by national enforcement authorities stating that certain conduct was exempt under the national competition laws.[101]

97 PETROS C. MAVROIDIS & SALLY J. VAN SICLEN, *The Application of the GATT/WTO Dispute Resolution System to Competition Issues*, 31 JWT 5, 11 (1997).

98 GATT Article II : 1(b) provides certain customs concessions for Contracting Parties:
"The products described in Part I of the Schedule, relating to any contracting party, which are the products of territories of other contracting parties, shall, on their importation into the territory [...] be exempt from ordinary customs duties in excess of those set forth and provided for therein."

99 EHLERMANN & EHRING (2003), at 1558. However, just private conduct combined with the absence of competition laws or their non-application can be reviewed by the so-called "situation complaint." *See id.*, at 1558–59.

100 HOEKMAN & MAVROIDIS (1994), at 140–41.

101 KENNEDY (2001), at 641–42: *See also* EHLERMANN & EHRING (2003), at 1561.

In sum, a sensible problem with considering the coverage of competition policies is distinguishing the fine line between legitimate domestic policies and unacceptable restrictions on trade.[102] As the world becomes increasingly interdependent, and business activities become increasingly transnational, differences in domestic economic institutions, business customs, and corporate behaviour will become new obstacles to international business. The treatment of these differences will be a major challenge in future trade relations.[103]

5. *WTO Jurisprudence*

a. India – Patent I Case (1998)

Although this case was not proceeded in the context of violation complaints, the Panel and the Appellate Body have indirectly revealed important jurisprudential points on the *legitimate expectation* requirement for NVNI complaints. In this dispute, the Panel found, and the Appellate Body confirmed, violations by India of Articles of 70.8 and 70.9 of the TRIPS,[104] because India failed to establish a mechanism that adequately preserves novelty and priority for applications for product patents with respect to pharmaceu-

102 ABELS (1996), at 510.

103 *Id.*, at 512; EHLERMANN & EHRING (2003), at 1560; *Cf.* WTO Document, WT/WGTCP/W/130 (July 12, 1999), *Working Group on the Interaction between Trade and Competition Policy – Communication from the European Community and its Member States*: "It is clear, for instance, that the non-violation remedies of the WTO are not an appropriate means to address the interface between competition law and market access." *Id.*, at 1.

104 Jerome Reichman observed that this interpretation of Articles 70.8 and 70.9 was a "triumph for the rule-oriented approach long favoured by Professor John Jackson and a setback for the kind of diplomatic shilly-shallying in which the government of India had indulged." *See* JEROME H. REICHMAN, *Securing Compliance with the TRIPS Agreement after US v India*, 1 JIEL 585, 594 (1998).

tical and agricultural chemical inventions, and with regard to the absence of a system for granting exclusive marketing rights.[105] The Appellate Body upheld the main findings concerning India's obligations under Article 70.8(a) and 70.9 but reversed the Panel's finding concerning Article 63.[106]

According to the Panel, the standard of *legitimate expectation* was mandated by prior GATT jurisprudence[107] and also supposedly mandated by Article 31 of the Vienna Convention on the Law of Treaties.[108] This required *good faith* which indirectly protected *legitimate expectations.*[109] On the contrary, the Appellate Body, while finding against India on the merits, rejected the *legitimate expectations* standard as derived from GATT jurisprudence concerning NVNI complaints.[110] Moreover, the AB precisely rejected the Panel's interpretation of Article 31 of the Vienna Convention because, under that Article, the "legitimate expectations of the parties to a treaty are reflected in the language of the treaty itself."[111] The Appellate Body also noted that their conclusion is "dictated by two separate and very specific provisions of the DSU. Article 3.2 and Article 19.2

105 WTO Panel Report, *India – Patent I,* para. 8.1 and Appellate Body Report, *India – Patent I (AB),* para. 97.

106 Appellate Body Report, *India – Patents I (AB),* para. 97.

107 *India – Patent I,* para. 7.20 ["The protection of legitimate expectations of Members regarding the conditions of competition is a well-established GATT principle, which derives in part from Article XXIII, the basic dispute settlement provisions of GATT (and the WTO)"].

108 *See infra* p. 88, note 5.

109 *India – Patent I, Id.,* para. 7.18 ["As a number of recent panel reports and Appellate Body reports have pointed out, customary rules of interpretation of public international law are embodied in the text of the 1969 Vienna Convention Law of Treaties (Vienna Convention). Article 31(1) of the Vienna Convention provides: 'A treaty shall be interpreted in good faith in accordance with the ordinary meaning to be given to the terms of the treaty in their context and in the light of its object and purpose'"].

110 *India – Patent I (AB),* para. 36 ("Although the Panel states that it is merely applying a 'well-established GATT principle,' the Panel's reasoning does not accurately reflect GATT/WTO practice").

111 *Id.,* para. 45.

of DSU, stating that the WTO adjudication process "cannot add to or diminish the rights and obligations provided in the covered agreements".[112]

The arguments between the Panel and Appellate Body's interpretation on the *legitimate expectation* relate to systemic questions of *what are the sources of WTO law* and *on what viewpoints interpret the sources*. We shall return to these points.[113]

b. Japan – Film Case (1998)

After the inception of WTO, the NVNI concept has evolved through some important judicial decisions of the WTO. The most insightful was the first Panel decision on NVNI complaint since the Uruguay Round, the *Japan – Film* in which Japan and the United States have disputed measures affecting photographic film and paper. The dispute centered on the question of whether Japanese markets for camera film and paper for photographs were open to the US company of Eastman Kodak. The US contended that the Japanese government engaged in systematic and non-transparent measures designed to protect the two principal Japanese producers of film and paper, Fuji Photo Film and Konica Corporation, from international competition counteracting the tariff concessions that Japan made in several GATT rounds of multilateral negotiations.[114] It had the most extensive discussion of the NVNI complaint by any GATT/WTO Panel.[115]

There are two critical implications of this case:

First, the *Japan – Film* Panel confirmed the exceptional approach continued from the GATT 47 jurisprudence. It reiterated that "[WTO] Members negotiate the rules that they agree to follow and only exceptionally would expect to be challenged for actions

112 *Id.*, para. 47.
113 *See* PART THREE-VII-B of this dissertation.
114 *See* WTO Panel Report, *Japan – Film*, para. 1.2 & part II.
115 *See generally* DURLING & LESTER (1998); *See also* CHO (1998), at 311–13.

not in contravention of those rules."[116] The exceptional nature is likely to have a bearing on the scope of such NVNI complaints entertained under the TRIPS Agreement.[117] Although the Panel followed most judicial opinions that the NVNI complaints should be approached with caution and should remain exceptional, it offered a revealing approach. It opined that the relevant NVNI cases "should be examined on its own merits" taking the NVNI complaints' safeguarding function of reciprocal tariff concessions into account.[118] This Panel's "individualised approach" to the NVNI cases implies a broader scope of NVNI application than traditionally appreciated in most judiciary decisions.

Second, the *Japan – Film* Panel broadened scope of the NVNI complaint by expanding the definition of "measure" of Article XXIII : 1 of GATT[119] and of "reasonable (or legitimate) expectations",[120] and by loosening the standard of causation.[121] Some lawyers have found the *Japan – Film* Panel's interpretation confusing: "In light of the panel's legal interpretations, the only remaining exceptional part of the NVNI remedy appears to be its breadth".[122] In effect, the Panel did not reject the US complaint, which was directed *inter alia* against lax enforcement of Japanese competition laws.[123] Furthermore, it accepted that, if the value of negotiated market access commit-

116 *Japan-Film,* para. 10.36; *See also* WTO Panel Report, *EC-Asbestos,* para. 8.271 ("It appears that members which have negotiated a set of rights and obligations would only exceptionally expect to be challenged for actions not in contravention of those rights or obligations").

117 *See* WTO Document, IP/C/W/212 (27 September 2000), TRIPS Council – Non-violation Complaints under the Agreement on Trade-related Aspects of Intellectual Property Rights (TRIPS) (Discussion Paper: Communication from Australia), at 8.

118 *Japan – Film,* para. 10.37 ("a panel charged with examining claims under Article XXIII : 1(b) is, therefore, to make an objective assessment of whether, in light of all the relevant facts and circumstances in the matter before us").

119 *Id.,* paras. 10.42–10.60.

120 *Id.,* paras. 10.61–10.81.

121 *Id.,* paras. 10.82–10.89.

122 DURLING & LESTER (1998), at 213.

123 BAGWELL, MAVROIDIS & STAIGER (2002), at 66 n. 9.

ments is reduced as a result of lax enforcement of competition laws, such an allegation could constitute a NVNI complaint.[124] The US claim was unsuccessful but this was mainly because the US simply had not proved that the Japanese government measures at issue caused the anti-competitive distribution system.[125]

c. Korea – Procurement Case (2000)

In *Korea – Procurement* case,[126] the Panel analysed the NVNI concept in the context of *pacta sunt servanda*,[127] as codified Article 26 of the Vienna Convention ("Every treaty in force is binding upon the parties to it and must be performed in good faith"). In addition, it linked the NVNI with the concept of error in treaty formation in the context of Government Procurement Agreement (GPA).[128] Spe-

124 *Id.*

125 *Japan – Film,* paras. 10.402–10.404.

126 This dispute concerns the Inchon International Airport project in the Republic of Korea and the entities responsible for its construction. The US (the complainant) argued that all of the entities responsible for the construction are covered under Korea's Appendix I of the Agreement on Government Procurement (GPA), such that Korea is responsible for meeting its obligations under the GPA with respect to procurement involved in the construction of the Airport. Specifically, the United States argued that Korea violated GPA Articles II: 1, VIII(b), XI and XX by imposing improper bid deadlines and improper qualification and domestic partnering requirements for bidding, and by failing to establish effective domestic procedures enabling foreign suppliers to challenge alleged breaches under the GPA. *See* WTO Panel Report, *Korea – Procurement,* part II & IV.

127 *Korea – Procurement,* paras. 7.93–7.94. *Cf.* Yearbook of the International Law Commission (1966), Vol. II at 211 ("Some members felt that there would be advantage in also stating that a party must abstain from acts calculated to frustrate the object and purpose of the treaty. The Commission, however, considered that this was clearly implicit in the obligation to perform the treaty in good faith and preferred to state the *pacta sunt servanda* rule in as simple a form as possible"); For a more theoretical explication on *pacta sunt servanda, see* COTTIER & SCHEFER (1997), pp. 171–72.

128 Vienna Convention Article 48: "1. A State may invoke an error in a treaty as invalidating its consent to be bound by the treaty if the error related to a fact or situation which was assumed by that State to exist at the time when the

cifically errors that took place during negotiations, rather than following the literal text of GATT, led to the nullification or impairment of a benefit by "application".[129] This approach has once again significantly broadened the scope of the NVNI complaint, by linking the NVNI complaint with errors that take place during *negotiations*, rather than occurring when actual *concessions* are made. The reason for including the negotiation stage may be that the Annexes to the GPA are "basically self-styled Schedules whose interpretation may require extensive knowledge of another country's procurement systems and governmental organisation".[130] There may be two occasions of invoking the NVNI complaints under the GPA. One is most likely to be based on measures that hinder access to contracts included the GPA annexes,[131] and the other is to prevent a party undermining the balance of agreed concessions by taking steps that affect the volume of procurement affected by those concessions.[132]

d. EC – Asbestos Case (2001 with the AB Report)

The *EC – Asbestos* case was the third WTO case in which the Panel and Appellate Body have analysed a NVNI complaint. In this dispute, Canada (the appellant) challenged a French decree banning the importation of asbestos and products containing all forms of

---

treaty was concluded and formed an essential basis of its consent to be bound by the treaty. 2. Paragraph 1 shall not apply if the State in question contributed by its own conduct to the error or if the circumstances were such as to put that State on notice of a possible error."

129 GATT, Article XXIII: 1 (b).

130 *See Korea-Procurement,* para. 7.121; Under the GPA a NVNI complaint is most likely to be based on measures that hinder access to contracts included the GPA annexes, *see* SUE ARROWSMITH, GOVERNMENT PROCUREMENT IN THE WTO 362 (2002).

131 *See* ARROWSMITH (2002), *id.*

132 *Id.,* at 364.

that substance. Canada alleged violations of several obligations in GATT.[133] There are two noteworthy points related to this case.

First, with regards to the standard of nullification or impairment, the Panel interpreted it as an upset of the "competitive relationship" between imports and domestic products.[134] This is practically the same standard as applied under GATT Article III:4. Under this approach, any measure that causes nullification or impairment would simultaneously violate Article III:4, which makes the distinction between violation and non-violation complaints meaningless. Against this difficulty, the Appellate Body referred to the concept of "market access" in discussing NVNI complaint. This is a broader notion than anti-discrimination, addressing all barriers to imports even if they are not discriminatory.[135] Second, for the requirement of whether the nullification or impairment of the benefit could be legitimately expected or anticipated, an issue that any measure that is justified under GATT Article XX should be anticipated by other WTO Members was raised. That is, does a measure

133 *See* WTO Appellate Body Report, *EC – Asbestos,* paras. 39–44. The issues raised by this case were questions concerning the national treatment of imported products, non-tariff barriers to imported products, the protection of public health, and technical barriers to trade. In addition to the claims under Articles III:4 and XI (and the related arguments under Article XX(b)) and the claim under the TBT Agreement, Canada (the complainant) made a claim under Article XXIII:1(b) to the effect that, even if the French decree did not constitute a violation of GATT 94, it constituted a NVNI case Canada's legitimate expectations with trade incidences. For a more review, *see* Sydney M. Cone, III, *The Asbestos Case and Dispute Settlement in the World Trade Organization: The Uneasy Relationship between Panels and the Appellate Body,* 21 Michigan Journal of International Law 103 (2001); Irene McConnell, *The Asbestos case at the World Trade Organisation: The Treatment of Public Health Regulations under the General Agreement of Tariffs and Trade 1994 and the Agreement on Technical Barriers to Trade,* 10 Tulsa Journal of Comparative & International Law 153 (2002).

134 In this case, the Panel examined whether the measure "has the effect of upsetting the competitive relationship between Canadian asbestos and products containing it, on the one hand, and substitute fibres and products containing them, on the other." *EC – Asbestos,* para. 8.288.

135 *EC – Asbestos (AB),* para. 190.

restricting market access for products posing a health risk fall within the scope of application of NVNI provision? Upholding the Panel's finding that the measure should reasonably have been anticipated, the AB indirectly recognised the applicability of health-based measures to the NVNI complaint.[136] In so holding, the Appellate Body rejected the EC's [appellant] assertion there may be no nullification or impairment where the GATT Article XX exceptions related to "health objectives" are operable.

6. *Survey of Non-Violation Complaints Cases: 1948 ~ 2005*

There have as of June 2005 been 15 cases in which a claim under Article XXIII : 1(b) has been considered by Working Parties, Panels and the Appellate Body.[137] In six of these cases, the NVNI claims were successful[138] and on three of these occasions, the report was adopted:[139]

136 *Id.*

137 1. The statistics are basically founded on the Appellate Body Report *on European Communities – Measures Affecting Asbestos and Asbestos-Containing Products (Complaint by Canada),* WT/DS135/AB/R, adopted 5 April 2001, para. 186 n. 188. As a NVNI-related case after the *EC – Asbestos (AB), US – Offset Act* (with AB Report) is added according to the *WorldTradeLaw.net Dispute Settlement Commentary (DSC).*
2. There are two other classifications on NVNI cases. (1) CHO (1998), at 352–55. His classification based GATT ANALYTICAL INDEX (1994) and the appendix of HUDEC (1993). The estimated cases are 24 between 1948 – 1990. (2) PETERSMANN (1991), at 200–20. 14 cases were covered from 1948 up to July 1991 under the heading of "Non-Violation Complaints in GATT Practice."

138 The successful claims were made in: *Australia Subsidies* (adopted 3 April 1950), *Germany – Sardines* (adopted 31 October 1952), *EC – Citrus* (unadopted), *EC – Canned Fruit* (unadopted), *EC – Oilseeds* (adopted 25 January 1990) and *EC – Oilseeds II* (unadopted).

139 NVNI complaints have also been raised together with violation claims, in various other requests for consultations or the establishment of a panel. These include: GATT Panel Report, *Spain – Measures Concerning Domestic Sale of Soyabean Oil,* L/5142, circulated 17 June 1981 (unadopted); GATT Panel Report, *United States – Trade Measures Affecting Nicaragua,* L/6053, circulated

Table 2: Jurisprudential Overview of Non-Violation Cases: 1948 ~ 2005

Short Title (Year)	**Jurisprudential Points**
Australian Subsidy (1950)	1. GATT Articles I and III : 4 2. First reference to *reasonable expectation* 3. Common law-styled jurisprudence (dubbed as "Mabury vs. Madison") 4. Competitive relationship as a benefit of NVNI complaints
Germany – Sardines (1952)	Standards for "like products" of GATT Article III : 4: through previous negotiations between parties
Uruguayan Recourse to Article XXIII (1962)	1. NVNI claim failed for lack of a detailed justification ("Failed") 2. *Prima facie* nullification or impairment jurisprudence 3. "Detailed submission" jurisprudence
Spain – Soyabean Oil (1981) (unadopted)	1. GATT Article III : 4 2. Precedential effect of panel reports
EC – Citrus (1985) (unadopted)	1. GATT Article XXIV 2. Benefits of regional tariff preferences rather than tariff concessions in terms of MFN principle
EC – Canned Fruit (1985) (unadopted)	Based on Article XXIII : 1(c)
Japan – Semi-Conductors (1988)	1. "Failed" 2. GATT Article XI and VI 3. Broad scope of "measure"
US – Nicaragua (1986) (unadopted)	Applicability of GATT Article XXI ("Security Exceptions") to GATT Article XXIII
EC – Oilseeds I (1990)	1. GATT Articles II and III : 4 2. GATT Article XXVIII 3. Detailed explanation of "competitive relationship"
US – Sugar Waiver, (1990)	1. "Failed" 2. NVNI claim may be based on other than GATT Article II
EC – Oilseeds II, (1992) (unadopted)	Follow-up report of *EC – Oilseeds I*
Japan – Film (1998)	1. "Failed" 2. Broad definition of "measure" 3. Expanded definition of "reasonable expectations" 4. Loose standard of causation
Korea – Procurement (2000)	1. "Failed" 2. NVNI complaint at the negotiation stage of Government Procurement Agreement 3. *Pacta sunt servanda* principle
EC – Asbestos (2001 with the AB Report)	1. Applicability of GATT Article XX to GATT Article XXIII : 1(b) (not appealed) 2. GATT Article III : 4 and XI 3. Standards for "like products" 4. "Necessity" test of GATT Article XX(b) 5. Article 2 of TBT Agreement 6. Ban on *amicus curiae* briefs
US – Offset Act (2003 with the AB Report)	1. "Failed" 2. "Adverse effects" in *SCM Agreement* context 2. Interpretation on good faith

7. *The Jurisprudential Implications of Non-Violation: Sources Argument*

Therefore three revealing implications from the "significance" and "development" of NVNI concept are to be perceived.

First, WTO Members are able to protect domestic commercial, social and political policy, if the measures used avoid impairing the tariff concessions or agreed trade commitments of the WTO Agreements.[140] This point has a bearing on the meaning of "measures" as a requirement of NVNI complaints. Consequently, there is a basic contradiction in the NVNI concept between discretions of a Member to use domestic measures and other Members' demands for market access to resist such measures. In terms of tariff concessions of GATT, this contradiction can be interpreted that if the balance of the negotiated concessions between the Members becomes

---

13 October 1986 (unadopted); *Japan – Measures Affecting Distribution Services,* request for consultations by the United States, WT/DS45/1; *Brazil – Certain Automotive Investment Measures,* requests for consultations by Japan and the United States, WT/DS51/1 and WT/DS52/1; *United States – The Cuban Liberty and Democratic Solidarity* Act, request for establishment of a Panel by the European Communities, WT/DS38/2; *United States – Import Prohibition of Certain Shrimp and Shrimp Products,* request for consultations by the Philippines, WT/DS61/1; *European Communities – Measures Affecting Butter Products,* request for consultations and establishment of a panel by New Zealand, WT/DS72/1-2; *Brazil – Certain Measures Affecting Trade and Investment in the Automotive Sector,* requests for consultations by the United States and the European Communities, WT/DS65/1 and WT/DS81/1; *India – Quantitative Restrictions on Imports of Agricultural, Textile and Industrial Products,* request for consultations by New Zealand, WT/DS93/1; *European Communities – Measures Affecting Asbestos and Products Containing Asbestos,* request for establishment of a panel by Canada, WT/DS135/3; *European Communities – Anti-dumping Investigations regarding Unbleached Cotton Fabrics from India,* request for consultations by India, WT/DS140/1; and *United States – Certain Measures Affecting the Import of Cattle, Swine and Grain from Canada,* request for consultations by Canada, WT/DS144/1.

140 *See generally* COTTIER & MAVROIDIS (2000), p. 4 ["The WTO contract is not (and should not be interpreted as) an instrument for deregulation. Consequently, governments are free to regulate whenever they deem it appropriate"].

disrupted, the Member whose interests are adversely affected may act to restore it. This point is associated with the meaning of "nullifications of benefits" and "impairment of objectives" in NVNI complaints. That seemingly contradictory combination between "measures" and "nullification of benefits" depicted well in *Japan – Film.*

> To achieve [NVNI complaints'] purpose, in our view, it is important that the kinds of government actions considered to be *measures covered by Article XXIII: 1(b) should not be defined in an unduly restrictive manner.* Otherwise, there is the risk of cases, in which governments have been involved one way or another in the nullification or impairment of benefits, that will not be redressable under Article XXIII : 1(b), thereby preventing the achievement of its purpose. We would stress, *however,* that giving a broad definition to *measure* does not expand the scope of the Article XXIII : 1(b) remedy *because it remains incumbent on the complaining Member to clearly demonstrate how the measure at issue results in or causes nullification or impairment of benefits*, and as explained below, in the final analysis the responding member's government is only responsible for what it has itself caused.[141] [emphasis added]

Second, because the origins of NVNI complaints began with the introduction of "equitable treatment" clause against the "indirect protection" in the 1920s and 1930s, such a *equity* or *good faith* background plays an important role in NVNI jurisprudence.[142] These inquiries contain *legitimate expectation*[143] driven from the good faith and its significance for reviewing the nature of NVNI complaints. Concerning the distinction of *good faith as a source of obligation* with *the specific applicability of good faith obligation*, the following Appellate Bodies' views appear pertinent.

(1) Regarding the chapeau of GATT Article XX ("General Exceptions"), the AB noted that:

> The chapeau of Article XX is, in fact, but one expression of the principle of good faith. This principle, at once a general principle of law and a general principle of international law, controls the exercise of rights by states.[144]

141 WTO Panel Report, *Japan – Film,* para. 10.50.
142 *See* COTTIER & SCHEFER (1997), p. 166.
143 *See generally* 2 GATT ANALYTICAL INDEX (1995), at 657–668.
144 WTO Appellate Body Report, *US – Shrimp (AB),* para. 158.

(2) In the context of *Anti-Dumping Agreement*,[145] the AB found that:

> ... the principle of good faith [...] informs the provisions of the *Anti-Dumping Agreement*, as well as the other covered agreements. This organic principle of good faith, in this particular context, restrains investigating authorities from imposing on exporters burdens which, in the circumstances, are not reasonable.[146]

(3) Related to the *SCM Agreement*,[147] the AB noted that:

> Article 3.10 of the DSU commits Members of the WTO, if a dispute arises, to engage in dispute settlement procedures "in good faith in an effort to resolve the dispute." [...] By good faith compliance, complaining Members accord to the responding Members the full measure of protection and opportunity to defend, contemplated by the letter and spirit of the procedural rules.[148]

(4) Against the Panel's opinion that "Good faith interpretations requires the protection of legitimate expectations derived from the protection of intellectual property rights provided for in the Agreement",[149] the AB opined that:

> ... we do not agree with the Panel that the legitimate expectations of Members *and* private rights holders concerning conditions of competition must always be taken into account in interpreting the *TRIPS Agreement*.[150]

Third, a Member can keep WTO-consistent measures that do not violate a specific provision of the WTO, yet could cause a claim for compensation from an aggrieved Member. This aspect will be connected with the discussion on "remedy". The DSU now codifies separate remedies for violation and NVNI disputes,[151] which makes clear that a finding that a WTO-consistent measure nullifies a ben-

145 THE LEGAL TEXTS (1995), at 168–196.
146 WTO Appellate Body Report, *US – Hot-Rolled Steel*, para. 101.
147 THE LEGAL TEXTS (1995), at 264–314.
148 WTO Appellate Body Report, *US – FSC*, para. 166.
149 WTO Panel Report, *India – Patent I*, para. 7.18.
150 WTO Appellate Body Report, *India – Patent I (AB)*, para. 48.
151 Article 26.1 (b) and (c) of DSU.

efit under any of the WTO Agreements does not entail an obligation to withdraw the measure.[152] Furthermore, a mutually satisfactory adjustment of such a claim may include compensation. A successful NVNI complaint is thus entitled to compensation and may retaliate if suitable compensation is not forthcoming.[153] The Appellate Body on *India – Patent I* noted that:

> Under Article XXIII: 1(b) of the GATT 1994, a Member can bring a "non-violation" complaint when the negotiated balance of concessions between Members is upset by the application of a measure, whether or not this measure is inconsistent with the provisions of the covered agreement. The ultimate goal is not the withdrawal of the measure concerned, but rather achieving a *mutually satisfactory adjustment*, usually by means of compensation.[154] [emphasis added]

To conclude, throughout the GATT years, all but one of NVNI cases involved the *granting of a subsidy* to a domestic producer that led to import substitution. In the WTO era, *Japan – Film* made it clear that *regulatory subsidies* can be the object of a NVNI complaint. And further in *EC – Asbestos*, the Appellate Body held that a NVNI complaint could have a health-based measure with a trade incidence as its subject matter. That is, *any regulatory intervention* that may *indirectly affect market access* could be the object of a NVNI complaint.[155]

The above jurisprudence generally clarifies the origin of controversies for NVNI complaints: it typically involves the *interpretation* of scope and subject-matter of the obligations of WTO law and main foundations of the multilateral obligations. As a next step, we employ the *Vienna Convention* to find out *jurisprudential roots of the obligations* in NVNI complaints.

152 Article 26.1 (b) of DSU.

153 Article 26.1 (c) and (d) of DSU; For 4 possible reactions of a WTO Member that has been found to nullify a tariff concession through a WTO-consistent measure, *See* ROESSLER (1997), p. 131; *See also* ROBERT E. HUDEC, *A WTO Perspective on Private Anti-Competitive Behavior in World Markets*, 34 New England Law Review 79, 83 (1999).

154 *India – Patent I (AB)*, para. 41.

155 BAGWELL, MAVROIDIS & STAIGER (2002), at 65–67.

Part Two

The Established Interpretation of Non-Violation Complaints

The essential condition of [the] arrangements [of nullification or impairment] is a very strong sense of common interest and common views in the relevant community. The debate over nullification provision was the ultimate test of that condition, for it was there that the governments squarely confronted the degree of trust that would be required. Their acceptance of the open-ended final text is the clearest possible demonstration of just how strong that sense of community was.

Robert E. Hudec (1990)

IV. Established Treaty Interpretation

A. Overview of the Vienna Convention Articles 31 and 32

1. *In General*

NVNI complaint is a legal phenomenon in WTO law. Law may be said to be a set of rules that we understand by a system.[1] That means consequently, that legal phenomena would be more clearly understood if interpreted *systematically.* Generally speaking, the paradigm[2] of interpretation can be divided into two parts: one is a "conceptual part" that defines what constitutes law and that analyzes its constituent concepts; and the other is a "normative part" that leads the conceptual part in a certain direction, offering theories of legislation, adjudication, and compliance.[3] The normative part is strongly connected with subjective side. For example, when we adjudicate on conceptual grounds, the adjudicative activity closely relies on the attitude of adjudicators or the majority in a legal community.[4] This

1 *See* KELSEN (1961), at 110.

2 The discourse on paradigm was intensively fuelled by the Thomas Kuhn in the context of estimating the scientific knowledge, but few oppose its application to the social sciences because of its powerful analysing effects. *See* THOMAS KUHN, THE STRUCTURE OF SCIENTIFIC REVOLUTIONS 23–34 (1970); For the modification of paradigm to the social sciences, *see* RONALD H. CHILCOTE, THEORIES OF COMPARATIVE POLITICS 55–61 (1994).

3 *See* DWORKIN (2001), at vii–ix.

4 This is a premise of Dworkin's well-known theory of law as integrity. *See* DWORKIN (1997), at 87. Thus Dworkin asserts that individual subjectivity must play a significant role in the construction of features of the legal system, *id.,* 89–90; *See also* J. M. BALKIN: *Understanding Legal Understanding: The Legal Subject and the Problem of Legal Coherence,* 103 Yale Law Journal 105, 109–10 (1993); At a general international economic law level, this is connected with argument of prevailing order, *see* SEIDL-HOHENVELDERN (1999), at 3–8 (predicting "in the very long run, the free interplay of global market

"subjective" character in adjudicative activity requires some "objective" guidelines of the interpretive activity.

In international jurisprudence such an interpretive paradigm is codified in the Vienna Convention on the Law of Treaties ("Vienna Convention") Articles 31 and 32.[5] Here we observe NVNI complaints in terms of the Articles 31 and 32 of the Vienna Convention.

2. *Uniformity and Flexibility in Interpretation*

Conceptually, interpretation is a dynamic interaction between reader and text as the former attempts to evaluate the different aspects of the latter.[6] Legal interpretation seeks to clarify the normatively correct meaning of words contained in a contract, statute or treaty in a *uniform* manner. Since the different fields of law have a considerably diverse character, the inherent structure and peculiar features recognized in each branch of the law are important for the principles of interpretation.[7] The distinct peculiarities of international law from other branches of law (e.g. the existence of sovereign States as main actors, the procedures of treaty-making, and the system of international dispute settlement) have encouraged developing distinct rules for interpreting international law.[8] These are distinct from the rules applicable in other divisions of law, although analogies to private and public law have influenced interpreting international law.[9] Some of the interpretive rules, as generalized as unified customs in treaty interpretation, are in the Vienna Convention[10].

---

forces between multinational corporations and trad-unions, which likewise will work on a global level will lead to a global equalization").

5 Done at Vienna, 23 May 1969, in BROWNLIE (ED.) (1995), at 388–425; *See also* 8 *International Legal Materials* 679 (1969).

6 FISS (1982), at 739.

7 BERNHARDT (1995), p. 1416.

8 *See* HENKIN ET AL. (1993), at 13–14; *See also* JENNINGS & WATTS (EDS) (1996), at 16–22.

9 BERNHARDT (1995), *id.*

10 Some WTO Members would not be a party to this Convention, *see* KUYPER (1994), at 232; However, non-Vienna Convention parties have been recog-

Difficulties in applying and interpreting international law arise because the rules of international law "are finite, and the subject of it infinite."[11] Moreover, dynamic nature of international reality makes the rules *indeterminate*, in the sense that many future implications of the international rules will not be foreseeable at all.[12] The GATT 47 itself contains virtually no guidelines for the process of interpretation, nor was it clear that international understandings, such as the Vienna Convention on the Law of Treaties applied.[13] With respect to the WTO, no matter how seriously the Uruguay Round WTO negotiators would try, the negotiators often failed to foresee the implications of applying general standards of conduct, even to the specific circumstances known at the time of inception of WTO.[14] Some degree of *flexibility* is therefore inevitable in the provisions and subsequent their interpretations however carefully defined.[15]

This inherent flexibility of treaty-making implies that certain essential *equitable values* of their nature cannot be precisely articu-

---

nised the provisions of the Convention in WTO dispute settlement procedures, *see* LENNARD (2002), at 18.

11 *See* 1 HENRY BALLOW, A TREATISE OF EQUITY 9 (3rd ed., Philadelphia, P. Byrne 1805), quoting from Van Alstine (1998), at 702.

12 VAN ALSTINE (1998), *id.*

13 NICHOLS (1996), at 422; John Jackson argued that the Vienna Convention could be used to interpret GATT because the GATT is an international protocol and the Vienna Convention codifies customary law that existed at the time the General Agreement entered into force. *See* JACKSON (1997), at 121; *See also* Thomas J. Schoenbaum, *Free International Trade and Protection of the Environment: Irreconcilable Conflict?*, 86 AJIL 700, 719 n. 108 (1992).

14 From a general legal system, *see generally* WILLIAM N. ESKRIDGE, JR., *Spinning Legislative Supremacy*, 78 Georgetown Law Journal 319, 333 (1989) ("Every statute is enacted against a congeries of background assumptions about law, society, and the operation of the statute itself"); On the WTO level, a main reason for this uncertainty or indeterminacy of GATT/WTO system is that "trading nations have increasingly relied on separate agreements to establish changes in trading rule. Moreover, because amendments to the GATT are difficult, loopholes in the rules are not easily remedied." *See* 2 A NEGOTIATING HISTORY (1993), at 1911.

15 Robert Hudec pointed out two "serious" problems of "flexible rules" for GATT. One is a possible lack of compliance and the other is difficulty of administering the rules. *See* HUDEC (1993), at 265–66.

lated for all events.[16] The same recognition on the nature of WTO rules is found in the AB Report of *Japan – Alcoholic Beverages*:

> WTO rules are not so rigid or so inflexible as not to leave room for reasoned judgments in confronting the endless and ever-changing ebb and flow of real facts in real cases in the real world. They will serve the multilateral trading system best if they are interpreted with that in mind.[17]

These problems appear particularly when the constituents of international communities span disparate legal and political cultures. There are for instance (1) a heterogeneity of the participants in the successive negotiations, (2) a diversity of conflicted norms in the regulated sphere and finally (3) the possible confusions in interpretation by the diverse adjudicators with differing cultural, legal, and political traditions.[18] These all combine to reduce applicability of the Vienna Convention rules.

Keeping in mind the two contradictory aspects of *uniformity* and *flexibility*, in interpreting international rules, the relevance of the Vienna Convention to WTO dispute resolution mechanism is considered below.

3. *Textualism and Intentionalism*

The relevant provisions that set out the rules an adjudicative body is to use when interpreting a treaty are Articles 31 to 33 of the

16 This unavoidable indeterminacy is a well-known phenomenon in legal theory. For a general introduction on the subject, *see* HART (1997), at 128–36 (discussing the inability of "human legislators" not to bring the "possible combinations of circumstances which the future may bring"); On the WTO level, Peter Sutherland observed that every underlying principles of the GATT/WTO exist to provide balance and equity, in a sense that the principles empower small Members who otherwise have no influence on the powerful Members. *See* PETER D. SUTHERLAND, *Concluding the Uruguay Round: Creating the New Architecture of Trade for the Global Economy,* 24 Fordham International Law Journal 15, 18 (2000).

17 WTO Appellate Body Report, *Japan-Alcoholic Beverages,* at 20.

18 VAN ALSTINE (1998), at 702–03.

Vienna Convention.[19] Those Articles have been referred to as the "customary rules of interpretation of public international law," as specifically authorized by Article 3.2 of the DSU[20] and by the WTO panels and the Appellate Body.[21]

19 *Article 31: General Rule of Interpretation*
"(1) A treaty shall be interpreted in good faith in accordance with the ordinary meaning to be given to the terms of the treaty in their context and in the light of its object and purpose.
(2) The context for the purpose of the interpretation of a treaty shall comprise, in addition to the text, including its preamble and annexes: (a) any agreement relating to the treaty which was made between all the parties in connexion with the conclusion of the treaty; (b) any instrument which was made by one or more parties in connexion with the conclusion of the treaty and accepted by the other parties as an instrument related to the treaty.
(3) There shall be taken into account with the context: (a) any subsequent agreement between the parties regarding the interpretation of the treaty or the application of its provisions; (b) any subsequent practice in the application of the treaty which establishes the agreement of the parties regarding its interpretation; (c) any relevant rules of international law applicable in the relations between the parties.
(4) A special meaning shall be given to a term if it is established that the parties so intended."

Article 32: Supplementary Means of Interpretation
"Recourse may be had to supplementary means of interpretation, including the preparatory work of the treaty and the circumstances of its conclusion, in order to confirm the meaning resulting from the application of Article 31, or to determine the meaning when the interpretation according to Article 31: (a) leaves the meaning ambiguous or obscure; or (b) leads to a result which is manifestly absurd or unreasonable."

20 Article 3.2 of DSU prescribes the following guidelines for the dispute resolution: "The dispute settlement system of the WTO is a central element in providing security and predictability to the multilateral trading system. The members recognize that it serves to preserve the rights and obligations of Members under the covered agreements, and to clarify the existing provisions of those agreements in accordance with customary rules of interpretation of public international law. Recommendations and rulings of the DSB cannot add to or diminish the rights and obligations provided in the covered agreements."

21 *See, e.g.* WTO Appellate Body Report, *US – Gasoline (AB)*, at 17; *Japan – Alcoholic Beverages (AB)*, at 10 ff. The Vienna Convention rules would apply to an Accession Protocol, to any paragraphs of an Accession Working Party Report that are specifically picked up by the Protocol, and to the Member

There have been controversies surrounding the Articles originating from the different approaches of determining the "words and implications" of treaty text itself.[22] These slot into two broad "intentionalist" or "textualist" approaches. The intentionalist believes that the actual *subjective expectations* of the parties should be protected, and therefore, the intentionalist will look for evidence of what each party thought the words meant and which meaning captures the true intent.[23] Such an approach emphasises the *travaux preparatoires* (or "preparatory work")[24] of the treaty. For the intentionalist, the text might be the first step for interpretation, but it is "only" that[25] and the most important goal is to discover and enforce the parties' expectations.[26] Furthermore, this intentionalist approach is analogous to the "teleological" approach,[27] which interprets the text in a way viewed as best adapted to fulfilling that object and purpose.[28] However, because this teleological method is more "dynamic," it will be categorised as another approach for interpretation in this dissertation. The textualist, on the other hand, looks to determine the intention of the parties through analysing

---

Schedules which are annexed to an Accession Protocol, *see* WTO Appellate Body Report, *EC – Poultry (AB)*, para. 79 (citing Article II:7 of the GATT 1994); *EC-Computer Equipment (AB)*, para. 84; *Canada – Dairy (AB)*, para. 131; *Korea – Dairy (AB)*, paras. 81 and 84; The International Court of Justice has also recognized the Vienna Convention rules as reflective of customary international law and they were rarely referred to by GATT 47 Panels, *see* LENNARD (2002), at 18 n. 2.

22 GROTIUS, *De jure belli ac pacis* (Book 2, Chapter 16), quoting from Bernhardt (1995), p. 1418; *See also* LENNARD (2002), at 20–22; MAKI (2000), at 348–52.

23 This approach was taken by the United States delegation at the Vienna Treaties Conference and Sir Hersch Lauterpacht, *see* LENNARD (2002), at 21 nn. 11–12.

24 *See* Article 32 of the Vienna Convention.

25 LENNARD, *id.*, at 20.

26 *See generally* MCDOUGAL ET AL. (1994), at 78–118.

27 BEDERMAN (1994), at 1034.

28 This approach has often been favoured by the European Court of Justice (ECJ). *See* PAUL CRAIG & GRAINNE DE BURCA, EU LAW: TEXT, CASES, AND MATERIAL 96–102 (3rd ED., 2003).

what they said in the text, and it believes that treaties should be *objectively clear* to all the parties to them.[29] This method only studies beyond the text when the text is unclear.[30]

In *EC-Hormones,* the distinct approaches between a panel and the Appellate Body reveal such controversies around *textualist* and *intentionalist* methods. As understanding Article 3.1 of Agreement on the Application of Sanitary and Phytosanitary Measures ("SPS Agreement") to be a binding obligation to harmonise national standards, the panel held that:

> One *purpose* of the SPS Agreement, as explicitly recognized in the preamble, is *to promote the use of international standards, guidelines and recommendations. To that end,* Article 3.1 imposes an obligation on all Members to base their sanitary measures on international standards except as otherwise provided for in the SPS Agreement, and in particular in Article 3.3 thereof.[31]

Thus it concluded that the Article 3.1 contains a general rule and Article 3.3 the exception. However, rejecting the panel's reasoning, the AB argued that the panel had not considered the fact that the Article 3.3 explicitly *prescribes* the autonomous right of a Member to establish a higher level of protection than that set out in an international standard.[32] Consequently, the AB reversed the panel's finding, stating the Article 3.3 as the general rule and Article 3.1 the exception to that rule.[33]

The contradictory directions between a panel and the AB were again highlighted in *EC – Computer Equipment.*[34] First, in overturning a panel's decision that the predictability of the reciprocal ad-

29 Sinclair (1984), at 115.

30 *Cf.* Article 32 of the Vienna Convention

31 WTO Panel Report, *EC – Hormones (Panel) (US),* para. 8.86 and *EC – Hormones (Panel) (Canada),* para. 8.89.

32 WTO Appellate Body Report, *EC – Hormones (AB),* para. 104.

33 *Id.*

34 This dispute arose when the United States claimed that the EC had violated Article II of the GATT by charging a higher tariff for Local Area Network (LAN) computer equipment than it was allowed to under its bound tariff Schedule. *See* WTO Appellate Body Report, *EC – Computer Equipment (AB),* para. 27.

vantageous arrangements cannot be maintained without protecting "legitimate expectations",[35] the AB noted that when interpreting a country's tariff schedule, legitimate expectations over the tariff concessions must be shared by both parties:

> However, nothing in [GATT] Article II:5 suggests that the expectations of *only* the exporting Member can be the basis for interpreting a concession in a Member's Schedule for the purposes of determining whether that Member has acted consistently with its obligations under Article II:1. In discussing Article II:5, the Panel overlooked the second sentence of that provision, which clarifies that the "contemplated treatment" referred to in that provision is the treatment contemplated by *both* Members.[36] [emphasis in original]

Second, as emphasising that the purpose of the Vienna Convention's methods is to find the common meaning of a term and not just one party's meaning, the AB held that:

> The purpose of treaty interpretation under Article 31 of the *Vienna Convention* is to ascertain the *common* intentions of the parties. These *common* intentions cannot be ascertained on the basis of the subjective and unilaterally determined "expectations" of *one* of the parties to a treaty.[37] [emphasis in original]

The AB has clearly tilted towards objective textualist. In *Japan – Alcoholic Beverages,* the AB held for the textual position more clearly:

> The terms of Article III must be given their ordinary meaning – in their context and in the light of the overall object and purpose of the *WTO Agreement.* Thus, the words actually used in the Article provide the basis for an interpretation that must give meaning and effect to all its terms. <u>The proper interpretation of the Article is, first of all, a textual interpretation</u>.[38] [underlining added]

35 *EC – Computer Equipment (AB)*, para. 8.25.
36 *Id.*, para. 81; *But Cf.* Panel Report of *EC – Computer Equipment,* para. 8.26 ("In our view, it may, as a matter of fact, be the case that in nearly all instances, the ordinary meaning of the terms of the actual description in a tariff schedule accurately reflects and exhausts the content of the legitimate expectations").
37 *Id.*, para. 84.
38 *Japan – Alcoholic Beverages (AB)*, at 17.

4. Coherent Interpretation between Two Sides

Because the interpretive methods used by the Vienna Convention include some elements of other methods,[39] there have been two different approaches. First, some scholars claim that the attitude of the Vienna Convention is tilted towards the "textual" approach in that it essentially seeks the "objectively ascertained" intention of the parties as "manifested in the text".[40] Taking this view, the interpretive guidelines of Articles 31 and 32 become clear: (1) an adjudicator should start by looking for the ordinary meaning of the words in light of the context, object, and purpose of the agreement; (2) the adjudicator is also to inquire into subsequent agreements by the parties that may shed light on the meaning; and (3) only if the meaning is still ambiguous or provides absurd results may the adjudicator then inquire into the negotiating history of the agreement. Second, another possible assessment on the Vienna Convention method is that it "has turned out to be flexible, and courts have a fair amount of discretion when applying it".[41] That is, the adjudicative body of WTO that wants to follow intentionalist principles is still able to justify itself by reference to the Vienna Convention.[42]

This dissertation takes these two broad categories to conventionally interpret NVNI complaints. This can be subcategorised into four parts: that is, (1) *objective and textual approaches* of (i) "literal" interpretation (ii) "contextual" interpretation; (2) *subjective and intentional approaches* of (iii) "historical" interpretation (iv) "teleological" interpretation.[43] However, because the Vienna Convention

39 *See, e.g.* MAKI (2000), at 351.

40 LENNARD (2002), at 21–22; *See also* MCDOUGAL ET AL. (1994), at 105–06.

41 *See, e.g.* BEDERMAN (1994), at 95–76; MAKI (2000), at 351.

42 MAKI, *id.*

43 According to Rudolf Bernhardt, five concrete categorisations on the interpretative rules of the Vienna Convention are imaginable: "literal," "contextual" (or "systematic"), "teleological," "historical interpretation," and "subsequent practice and changing social condition, *see* BERNHARDT (1995), pp. 1420–21; Two more classifications of the Vienna Convention interpretive rules are

rules appear designed more likely to lead to a "single coherent" interpretation,[44] these four approaches are mutually supported, as balancing between a relative certainty of contextual approach and an additional necessity of flexibility to have recourse to external materials. The demand for coherent interpretation is likely to encourage the WTO adjudicative body to use a variety of interpretive techniques[45] in a "holistic" manner.[46] This point has been observed by the Panel in *US – Section 301*. The Panel noted:

> Text, context and object and purpose correspond to well established systemic and teleological methodologies of treaty interpretation, all of which typically come into play when interpreting complex provisions in multilateral treaties. [...] *However, the elements referred to in Article 31 [of the Vienna Convention] – text, context and object as well as good faith – are to be viewed as one holistic rule of interpretation rather than a sequence of separate tests to be applied in a hierarchical order.*[47] [emphasis added]

---

noteworthy. (1) One is a classification such as "subjective" (or "intentions"), "textual" and "teleological" approach. For this, *see* GERALD FITZMAURICE, *The Law and Procedure of the International Court of Justice: Treaty Interpretation and Certain Other Treaty Points,* 28 British Yearbook of International Law 1 (1951); *See also* International Law Commission Commentary on the draft Vienna Convention, Yearbook of the International Law Commission, 1966, Vol. II, at 218–20 ["ILC Commentary (1966)"]; SINCLAIR (1984), at 130–31. (2) The other is distinctions among "the ordinary meaning of words in their context," "object and purpose," "other (non-contextual) materials," and "special meanings." *See* LENNARD (2002), at 24–45.

44 LENNARD (2002), at 22.

45 Because each treaty is different and should be treated differently, it appears more appropriate for the WTO adjudicative body to look at the WTO Agreements' formation and other factors and then to decide which method of interpretation is most applicable. *See* ILMAR TAMMELO, TREATY INTERPRETATION AND PRACTICAL REASON: TOWARDS A GENERAL THEORY OF LEGAL INTERPRETATION 4 (1967) (stating that states are discouraged from making agreements and from allowing disputes to be settled by a third party when there is an uncertainty as to which principles of interpretation apply); see also Bederman (1994), at 1034 (concluding that treaties are *sui generis* and that courts should treat them as neither statutes nor contracts).

46 LENNARD (2002), at 22.

47 WTO Panel Report, *US – Section 301*, para. 7.22.

Furthermore, the AB of *Japan – Alcoholic Beverages* recognized the "holistic" interpretive techniques:

> WTO rules are reliable, comprehensible and enforceable. WTO rules are not so rigid or so inflexible as not to leave room for reasoned judgements in confronting the endless and ever-changing ebb and flow of real facts in real cases in the real world. They will serve the multilateral trading system best if they are interpreted with that in mind. In that way, we will achieve the "security and predictability" sought for the multilateral trading system by the Members of the WTO through the establishment of the dispute settlement system.[48] [footnote deleted]

B. Typology of Interpretation of Non-Violation Complaints

1. *Four Types of Interpretation*

There have been various interpretations around the NVNI complaints of GATT Article XXIII : 1(b). With only a few dissenters,[49] most scholars recognize the significance of the complaints and tend to depend on the four types of authority: "textual (or literal)," "contextual," "historical," and "teleological" interpretation, along with the relevant Panel and Appellate Body Reports. Each is defined loosely so as not to exclude arguments that others might classify differently. Although the artificially articulated categories do sometimes blur or are interdependent, there are some important aspects of the complaints within each category. And from a competition among the interpretations arising from such categories, each interpreter purports to determine the proper scope for the NVNI complaints. Despite a different weight of the various interpretations to each interpretive method, they commonly accept that the divergent

48 *Japan – Alcoholic Beverages (AB),* at 20.
49 *See, e.g.* PESCATORE (1993), at 19.

interpretations combine or weigh against each other within the customary norms of treaty interpretation practice, codified in the Articles 31 and 32 of the Vienna Convention.

2. *Textual Interpretation of Article XXIII: 1(b)*

a. In General

Interpretation from treaty text[50] plays, as a starting point of every interpretation, a universally accepted role in treaty interpretation.[51] However, it is generally difficult to rely solely on the text,[52] and most GATT Panels avoided overly literal interpretations relying instead on "natural," "normal" or "generally understood" meanings of words.[53] The language of treaty in and of itself resolves so few "hard cases".[54] This difficulty is aggravated for international treaties

50 It refers to in a WTO context "WTO Agreement," *see* WTO Panel Report, *United States-Transitional Safeguard Measure on Combined Cutton Yarn from Pakistan,* WT/DS192/R, adopted on 5 November 2001, at para. 7.46.

51 In the words of the WTO Appellate Body, which was established by Article 17 of DSU, "The proper interpretation of the Article is, first of all, a textual interpretation." *Japan – Alcoholic Beverages (AB),* at 19. *See also* William N. Eskridge, Jr., The New Textualism, 37 UCLA Law Review 621, 674 (1990).

52 *See generally* Paul Brest, *The Misconceived Quest for the Original Understanding,* 60 Boston University Law Review 204, 234 (1980) (arguing that explicit reliance on the text has played a small role in comparison with elaboration of judicial precedents); Fallon (1987), at 1195.

53 *See* GATT Panel Report, *Value-Added Tax and Threshold,* at 254–55 ("natural meaning"); GATT, *Canada – Alcoholic Drinks,* at 80 ("natural meaning"); GATT, *United States Customs User Free,* at 275 ("generally understood meaning"); *US – Restrictions on Import of Sugar,* at 342 ("ordinary meaning").

54 The concept of "hard cases" refers to cases where the law appears to point strongly towards a particular result, and yet, because the result seems unduly harsh either to an individual or to society at large, it is unpalatable to the reviewing court. *See* Ashutosh Bhagwat, *Hard Cases and the (D)Evolution of Constitutional Doctrine* 30 Connel Law Review 961, 966 (1998); Ronald Dworkin, *Hard Cases,* 88 Harvard Law Review 1057, 1058 (1975). Prof. Hart referred to these as the "unenvisaged" cases, *see* Hart (1997), at 129.

which are typically concluded by notoriously heterogeneous States. At the same time, however, an agreed treaty shows a certain commitment to the relationship of the States concerned. Those two delicate aspects of treaty text (i.e. heterogeneous treaty-makers and homogeneous treaty-texts) not only indicate that the understanding *is* and *must be* an evolving process of constructing the meanings,[55] but also require a set of shared understandings about the meanings of the text.[56]

This exploration on what the drafters of a treaty meant by the specific language used in the treaty is all the more important when considering the transition from GATT to WTO. Before the WTO, a mutually acceptable resolution mattered more than adjudicating the precise legal relations in the phase of "diplomat's concept of legal order" of GATT 47.[57] It was mainly after the emergence of the WTO binding dispute settlement mechanism that the meaning of textual language and the role of legal interpretations became increasingly important, with the emergence of a binding dispute settlement mechanism of WTO.[58] This point is all the more inspiring when the predictability of jurisprudence of panel and the AB will play a key role to command the respect of WTO Members.[59]

If the importance of textual meanings in the WTO dispute settlement is reasonable, then it will be helpful to draw a meaningful distinction between interpretations *from* the text, that is, interpretations

55 The *US – Section 301* Panel said: "Thus [Article 31 of the Vienna Convention] is entitled 'General *rule* of Interpretation' in the singular, not 'General *rules*' in the plural, because the [International Law] Commission desired to emphasize that the process of interpretation is a unity and that the provisions of the Article form a single, closely integrated rule (Yearbook of the ILC, 1966, Vol. II, pp. 219–20)." [emphasis in original] *See US – Section 301,* para. 7.22.

56 "A treaty interpreter must begin with, and focus upon, the text of the particular provision to be interpreted. [...] Where the meaning imparted by text itself is equivocal or inconclusive, or where confirmation of the correctness of the reading of the text itself is desired, light from the object and purpose of the treaty as a whole may usefully be sought." *See US – Shrimp (AB),* para. 114.

57 Hudec (1993), at 7.

58 *See* Waincymer (2002), at 386–96.

59 Chua (1998b), at 173.

that purport to settle a dispute by direct appeal to the treaty's plain language, and interpretations *about* the text of the treaty, namely interpretations that recourse to *context or extra-legal evidence.*[60] Although often used simultaneously, the sharper focus of interpretation *from* text as a distinct method of interpretation assumes that it is possible to read the treaty with a more narrowly textual focus, which will sometimes produce more legitimate conclusions than others.[61] This method of interpretation offers two advantages. First occasionally, an interpretation from text will require a unique conclusion – for example, the Article XXIII : 1(a) of GATT must be raised in case of failing to "carry out [members'] obligation under this Agreement". The literal method achieves the somewhat complicated but significant result of excluding a position that might be argued for on non-textual basis. Thus, even though the text of Article XXIII : 1(b) of GATT may not tell us precisely what "the application by another contracting party of any measure" is, the language does demand that "the measure" applies only to the stage of its "application." Second, among the meanings that are not excluded by arguments from text, a narrowly text-focused reading will sometimes yield the conclusion that is more plausible than others. For example, according to the phrase "as the result of" in Article XXIII : 1, the nullification or impairment has to be "the" result of the government measure, rejecting a nullification as "a" result of any measure. This exact reading is significant, because "the" requires a closer linkage between the cause and its result.[62] This textual method clearly conforms to the requirement of legal stability in international relations.[63]

60 *See generally* FALLON (1987), at 1195–96.

61 FALLON, *id.,* at 1197; *See also* MOORE (1985), at 320–21.

62 DURLING & LESTER (1998), at 251–51; The format of the NVNI clause in the GATS uses the phrase "a result" not "the result." *See* GATS Article XXIII : 3. This textual difference makes the difference between "a" and "the" meaningful.

63 BERNHARDT (1995), p. 1420.

b. Relevance of Textual Interpretation to Contextual Interpretation

In a sense, all treaty interpretation must be *about* the text, in the sense that we are interpreting what a treaty should be held to mean. Since treaty language often will bear more than one reading, or "open-textured",[64] it is very difficult to segregate the two aspects in actual interpretive practices. It seems moreover that in interpreting the WTO Agreements there is far little distinction between the *from* and *about* parameters. This is largely because of the broad coverage of the Agreements and the ambiguities and *lacunae* in such Agreements,[65] which calls for the guidance of *non-textual* factors for a selection among the plausible alternatives. Even in case of interpretation *from* text (or the *literal* meaning of the specific language of the text), the language of the text is situated in the international community concerned and must be read in line with an awareness of the range of extra-textual concerns that treaty interpretation traditionally considers. This is the reason why *contextual* interpretation is to be reviewed.

3. Contextual Interpretation of Article XXIII: 1(b)

In line with its essentially *textual* approach, the Vienna Convention Article 31 employs a possible *contextual* interpretation. Few would ever have doubted the need to consider words in their context,[66] but an important question is that of how widely "context" is to be

64 This idea is originally developed in HART (1997), at 124–36.
65 *See* HILF (2001), at 112.
66 According to Philip Nichols, one of the most frequently invoked common law rules by GATT Panels was that words and provisions under examination must be analyzed in context. *See* NICHOLS (1996a), at 425; As GATT cases in this contextual method, *see* GATT Panel Report, *Korea – Polyacetal Resins,* para. 296; GATT, *US – Malt Beverages,* paras. 5.9 and 5.71; *EC – Dessert Apples,* para. 12.12; *Canada – Herring and Salmon,* at 113.

understood for Article 31 purposes.[67] *Context* here can be *narrowly* defined to mean the text (including the preamble and annexes)[68] as well as agreements made by all the parties to a treaty in connection with the conclusion of that treaty,[69] and any instrument made by one or more parties in connection with the treaty that was accepted by the other parties as an instrument related to the treaty.[70] If the *context* is *broadly* defined, then it can consider texts and events outside the framework of the treaty,[71] which allows three rational interpretations through the use of reasoning and abstract legal principles ("logical interpretation").[72]

a. Interpretation based on Legal Theories

One end of the contextual spectrum on the NVNI complaints is based on "common-law jurisdiction" such as that propounded by Robert Hudec.[73] According to Hudec's theory, the nullification provision of Article XXIII : 1 of GATT including the NVNI complaints is "a grant of common-law jurisdiction" to deal with relevant disputed cases.[74] Hence, the complaints create a broad balancing mechanism to sustain the original exchange of tariff concessions,[75] and subsequently grant rights which enable each Member to bring the

67 LENNARD (2002), at 24; The Article 31 embodies a relatively narrow contextual interpretation to comprise only the rest of the treaty and documents directly connected with the conclusion of that treaty, *see id.*, n. 29.
68 *See, e.g. US – Cotton Yarn (AB)*, para. 94.
69 *See, e.g.* WTO Panel Report, *US – Copyright Act*, para. 6.45.
70 *See generally* LENNARD (2002), at 24–27.
71 Bernhardt (1995), p. 1420.
72 VILLIGIER (1985), at 327; A necessity for considering a broader stance is that GATT Panels regularly turned to secondary material as a matter of course, which does not comport with the Vienna Convention's interpretive scheme. *See* NICHOLS (1996a), at 430.
73 *See* HUDEC (1975), at 464–81.
74 The broad grant of jurisdiction was severely criticized and compared by Dr Holloway of the South African Delegate as "a sort of vague and general 'sword of Damocles'." *See* HUDEC (1990), at 42.
75 HUDEC (1975), at 487.

GATT/WTO-consistent measures to the DSB, regardless of whether they conflict with the provisions concerned.

The other side of the theoretical ambit argues about the influence of State responsibility theory on the GATT legal system as explored by Ernst-Ulrich Petersmann.[76] Presenting an example of the International Law Commission (ILC)'s works on State responsibility, namely Part 1 of its draft Articles on "origin of international responsibility" and "international liability for injurious consequences arising out of acts not prohibited by international law", he asserts that "GATT law proceeds from the principle of 'strict liability' and 'objective responsibility for result' independent of a subjective element of fault".[77] Furthermore, he explains the "strict liability" employing terms such as "'reasonable' or 'appropriate' which necessitates a value judgment like the 'due diligence standard' of general international law".[78]

b. Interpretation based on Good Faith Principle

Although the normative or evaluative claims used in reasoning NVNI complaints (e.g. reasonable expectation principle) have drummed up support from most trade lawyers,[79] there is no consensus over the standard for determining when such a label as "reasonable" is proper. Putting this differently, to decide when or how an essentially arguable concept aptly applies requires the conscious undertaking of moral and political commitments.

The jurisprudence of "reasonable expectation" in NVNI complaints reveals the difficulty of managing the contestability of *values.* Consider the connection of "nullification or impairment of a benefit" with the unspecified concept of "reasonableness" in the Article. An early Panel held that the nullification was done *inter alia* through the respondent government's measure "which could not have been reasonably anticipated by the [complaining] Gov-

76 *See* Petersmann (1991), at 175–79.
77 *Id.*, at 178.
78 *Id.*
79 *See, e.g.* Cottier & Schefer (2000), p. 58.

ernment."[80] While the connection between "nullification and impairment of benefit" of Article XXIII : 1 and "reasonably anticipated" does not stem from either the text of the Article or any of its official comments, the Panel held that the existence of nullification or impairment must be construed in light of whether the measure in question causing "upsetting the competitive relationship" could reasonably have been anticipated by the complainant.[81]

c. Interpretation based on Policy

International lawyers make overt or covert interpretations that refer directly to policies, and this approach is generally accepted under some conditions by customary international law. If we use the term *interpretation from policies* to refer to claims about the *descriptive* significance of the current realities in international trade, although various other definitions would be predictable, this interpretation in the context of NVNI complaints is largely related to the conflicts between the WTO and national governments.

The NVNI complaints are depicted as "the counterpart of the policy autonomy the member enjoys under the GATT".[82] In other words, by employing the concept of "nullification" or "impairment" instead of the question of "breach" of treaties, the original GATT dispute settlement system was designed to take into account the contracting parties' *policy autonomy*, alongside the responsibility of a contracting party impairing benefits accruing under the GATT. However, this method can be related to policy benchmarks that are independent of what the treaty text or provision concerned, e.g. "how much deference should [an] international organisation give to national government decisions?"[83] Thus, those policies from pre-

80 GATT Working Party Report, *Australian Subsidy*, para. 12.

81 GATT Panel Report, *Germany – Sardines*, para. 16.

82 Roessler (1997), p. 131.

83 John H. Jackson, *Fragmentation or Unification among International Institution: The World Trade Organisation*, New York University Journal of International Law and Politics 823, 830 (1999).

vailing international practices are basically contestable, especially in interpreting an international treaty as the consents of various States. In addition, having considered the enormously broadened context and competence of WTO against those of GATT 47, and the plausible resistance of national governments to protect their own domestic regulations, the policy elements could cause more contestable or important arguments in the legal reasoning of NVNI complaints.

This *policy* approach is more relevant in the arguments of whether NVNI complaints should be extended into TRIPS. For opponents of the extension, the NVNI would reduce the level of policy discretion open to national decision-makers in the implementation of TRIPS standards.[84]

4. *Historical Interpretation of Article XXIII: 1(b) of GATT*

Searches for the meaning of a treaty provision frequently involve inquiries into the *intent of the drafter* because of the difficulty of determining the original meaning of text. As a matter of fact, some GATT Panels posited that analysis of the GATT's language was the method by which panels could ascertain the intent of the drafters of the GATT.[85] For Article XXIII: 1(b), this intent is mainly based on

84 JEROME H. REICHMAN, *Securing Compliance with the TRIPS Agreement After US v India,* JIEL 1(4), 585, 597 (1998) (stating that the developing countries are free to adopt their own policies that were not expressly harmonized in the TRIPS); FREDERICK M. ABBOTT, 'WTO Dispute Settlement and the Agreement on Trade-Related Aspects of Intellectual Property Rights', in PETERSMANN (ED.) (1997A), at 433–34; *But Cf.* COTTIER & SCHEFER (2000), p. 182 ("As good faith forms parts of international law and therefore will apply to all fields of international law, the issue of non-violation in TRIPS rests on an outdated premise").

85 *See, e.g.* GATT Panel Report, *Italian Agriculture Machinery,* para. 11 ("It was considered, moreover, that the intention of the drafters of the Agreement was clearly to treat the imported products in the same way as the like domestic products once they had been cleared through customs"); GATT, *Canada – Ice Cream,* para. 80.

the "preparatory work" as well as the circumstances of the conclusion of the GATT.[86] As is clear from the Article 32 of the Vienna Convention, an historical interpretation considering the *travaux préparatoires* (preparatory work) and the circumstances of conclusion of a treaty are "supplementary means". That is, the interpretive method may ultimately be considered under Article 32 only where an Article 31 examination leaves the meaning of a term ambiguous or obscure, leads to a manifestly absurd or unreasonable result, or where it is only considered in order to confirm the Article 31 result.[87] Although the term "supplementary means" is not clear from the words of Article 32, there is some relevant WTO jurisprudence on the term, indicating the negotiating history of the GATT 47,[88] records relating to the Havana Charter and the GATT,[89] and documents of Uruguay Round negotiations.[90]

The significance of historical interpretation in the NVNI complaints context is that without relying on this method, the words of NVNI provision leave the meaning of the words ambiguous.[91] And from the historical interpretation, it is possible to give a "special meaning" to a term, "if it is established that the parties so intended".[92]

86 Generally speaking, the significance of the preparatory works of the GATT/WTO has been recognized, *see* CHARNOVITZ (1991), at 37–55; *But cf.* JACKSON (2000), at 429 ("Thus, unlike certain schools of thought concerning the United States Supreme Court's interpretation of the United States Constitution, it is this author's view that one cannot rely too heavily on the original drafting history").

87 ILC Commentary (1966), at 223; LENNARD (2002), at 45.

88 *See, e.g.* WTO Appellate Body Report, *Canada – Periodicals (AB)*, at 34.

89 *See, e.g.* WTO Panel Report *US – Anti-Dumping Act of 1916*, paras. 6.201–6.202. The Panel Report was upheld on appeal, but this issue was not addressed.

90 *See, e.g.* WTO Panel Report, *US – Lamb*, para. 7.110 ff.; *See also* WTO Panel Report, *Korea – Beef*, para. 539.

91 *See* DURLING & LESTER (1998), at 241–55; *See also* Article 32(a) of the Vienna Convention.

92 Article 31(4) of the Vienna Convention. However, the provision does not indicate exactly how the special meaning is to be established. In fact, this provision was nearly deleted by the International Law Commission in a late

Because the drafters designed to attribute "the special meaning" to the term of "benefits" and "objective" of Article XXIII:1, with a view to keeping the balance of tariff concessions, historical interpretation plays a critical role in crafting the most logical interpretation on these terms.

In addition, a study concerning the types of GATT/WTO drafters' intent should be worthwhile. Generally, searches for intent divide into several types.[93] One helpful division distinguishes between *specific* and *general* intent.[94] *Specific intent* involves the relatively precise intent of the drafters to control the outcomes of particular types of NVNI complaints. For example, scholars generally agree that the drafters of the GATT 47 had the clear objective of employing the NVNI complaints for preventing the "indirect protection" measures as a replacement for tariff protection. This was a specific intent of the drafters contained in the terms of "any benefit [...] nullified or impaired" of Article XXIII:1. *General intent* refers to aims that are defined at a higher level of generality, sometimes entailing consequences that the drafters did not specifically consider. An example comes from "any objective of the Agreement" of Article XXIII:1. The drafters of the GATT 47 apparently did not specifically intend to eliminate all domestic measures having adverse effects on the arranged tariff concession. Yet they did intend generally to establish a regime in which the benefit of tariff concession could be recovered if negated – an aspiration that can be conceived abstractly as reaching far more broadly than the drafters themselves specifically had intended.[95]

---

draft of what became the Vienna Convention, on the basis that the so-called "special" meaning would in any case be the "ordinary" meaning in the particular context, in terms of the Article 31(1) rules. *See* LENNARD (2002), at 44.

93 *See, e.g.* DWORKIN (2001), at 134–37 (distinguishing the "concept of fairness" that the framers incorporated into the Constitution from their specific "conception" of fairness what, in particular, the concept require); DWORKIN (1985), at 44 (distinguishing the framers' interpretive hopes from their interpretive expectations).

94 *See* FALLON (1987), at 1198–99.

95 *See* DURLING & LEISTER (1998), at 217–19.

It would be an important question what was the general intent of the drafters when expanding the GATT 47 to all the WTO Agreements? This dissertation will return to this issue in section XI.

5. Teleological Interpretation of Article XXIII: 1(b)

A fourth and normative kind of interpretation of NVNI complaints involves the purpose, generally or theoretically, of the international community taken as a whole or within the GATT/WTO context. Interpretations of this sort usually undertake to push beyond what could feasibly be observed the textual meaning of the NVNI complaints. The aim is to discover the purpose of the WTO members.[96] Furthermore, they strive to understand the Article XXIII: 1(b) as a materialisation of the purpose in light of what kind of structures of the international community and the GATT/WTO are most desirable.

Generally speaking, it seems to be undisputed that the purpose of a given treaty in its entirety is relevant. But a teleological interpretation whereby an interpreter makes the most extensive plausible meaning of a treaty text is neither recognised nor acceptable in international law.[97] Article 31(1) of the Vienna Convention clari-

96 WAINCYMER (2002), at 431; *See also* Appellate Body Report, *EC – Computer Equipment,* para. 84.

97 BERNHARDT (1995), p. 1420; "The principle of interpretation expressed in the maxim: *Ut res magis valeat quam pereat,* often referred to as the rule of effectiveness, cannot justify the Court in attributing to the provisions for the settlement of disputes in the Peace Treaties a meaning which... would be contrary to their letter and spirit." *See* ICJ Reports (1950) at 229. Interpretation of Peace Treaties with Bulgaria, Hungary and Romania (Advisory Opinion); MCDOUGAL, LASSWELL & MILLER supported teleological approach to treaty interpretation, emphasizing "objectives and basic values" of agreement, while Sir Gerald Fitzmaurice was fearful that such a teleological approach would lead to anarchy in interpretation, *See* MCDOUGAL ET AL. (1994), at 154–88 & 193–94 and Sir Gerald Fitzmaurice, *Vae Victis or Woe to the Negotiators! Your Treaty or Our "Interpretation" of It?,* 65 AJIL 358 (1971). The Vienna Convention is, however, somewhat more forgiving of the use of materials shedding light on later interpretations by the parties.

fies that an interpretation of the text and context of a treaty is to be made "in the light of its object and purpose". Mostly, this method *is not accepted* by the AB as an independent basis for interpretation.[98] However, in case of NVNI complaints, a clear reference to "any objective" of Article XXIII:1 is made in the text and therefore an adjudicator can offer the extensive interpretation. Therefore most scholarly articles and resolution decisions on NVNI complaints start with the purpose of GATT/WTO in disentangling the complexities of the complaints.

It is generally suggested that the basic purpose of GATT/WTO system is to facilitate *free trade*:

> In short, international [free] trade is of incalculable importance to the world economy and is a significant contributor to human well-being. International trade increases the possibilities of production and promotes an efficient allocation of resources. International trade increases the variety of goods available to the consumer and lowers the prices of those goods. International trade facilitates better world citizenship by facilitating peaceful cooperation and exchange.[99]

98 *See, e.g.* Appellate Body Report, *Japan – Alcoholic Beverages (AB)*, at 20; *But cf.* Appellate Body Report, *US – Gasoline (AB)* at 17 ff.; *Argentina – Footwear Safeguards (AB)*, para. 91. On these AB's Reports, Michael Lennard commented that "the Appellate Body has sometimes expressed its task as examining the object and purpose of a particular provision, which does not appear strictly accurate under the Vienna Convention rules, but so long as it is shown that the provision's apparent 'object and purpose' reflects one of the objects and purposes of the relevant WTO Agreement as a whole." *See* Lennard (2002), at 28.

99 Nichols (1996b), at 667. In addition, he mentioned several secondary benefits of free trade for economies and societies: (1) Free trade increases contact and promotes cooperation; (2) Free trade helps emerging economies to develop; and (3) Greater consumer satisfaction; (4) Increased technical efficiency; (5) Decreased monopoly power, *see id.*, at 666–67. At the same time he made such a caveat as "It should be recognised, however, that societies will at any point in time have a number of values and goals, and that some of these may come into conflict with the pursuit of unfettered international trade." *See* Nichols, *id.*, at 667; For a collection of the classical and contemporary arguments in support of free trade and the arguments for protectionism, *see* Raj Bhala, International Trade Law: Cases and Materials 5–78 (1996).

In order to achieve the basic purpose, the four pillars of GATT are said to be employed. They are: (1) the unconditional most-favoured nation (MFN) obligation of GATT Article I;[100] (2) tariff concessions from the GATT Preamble and Article XXVIII *bis*; (3) the national treatment obligation of Article III; and (4) the elimination of quotas on imports of Article XI.[101]

Interpretations emphasising the purpose of the GATT/WTO, *free trade,* regard the GATT as a system of "providing a legal framework for the exchange of tariff concessions".[102] According to this viewpoint, the GATT has been created for securing market access opportunities by way of tariff concessions, and this predominantly tariff-centered structure of GATT demands the connection of a nullification or impairment with *a tariff concession*. Subsequently, NVNI complaints are most concerned with the *indirect* nullification or impairment of "benefits accruing under GATT".[103] Hence, the Panels and Appellate Bodies generally read the NVNI complaints to invalidate government measures where an equitable treatment is necessary to correct the distorted market access opportunities.[104]

100 Article I: 1 provides that with respect to (1) customs duties and charges of any kind imposed on importation or exportation, (2) the method of levying those duties and charges, (3) all rules and formalities in connection with importation and exportation and (4) all matters referred to in paragraphs 2 and 4 of Article III concerning national treatment in internal taxation and regulation: any advantage, favour, privilege or immunity granted by any contracting party to any product originating in or destined for any other contracting party shall be accorded immediately and unconditionally to the like product originating in or destined for the territories of all other contracting parties. The text of Article I: 1 is plain that the rule of non-discrimination among WTO Members applies unconditionally. *See* Article I: 1 of WTO Agreement.

101 *See generally* KENNEDY (1998), at 426–35.

102 *See, e.g.* ROESSLER (1997), p. 133.

103 *See* Appellate Body Report, *US-Wool Shirts,* at 13 ("The foundation of dispute settlement under Article XXIII of the GATT 1994 is the assurance to Members of the benefits accruing directly or indirectly to them under the GATT 1994").

104 *See, e.g.* GATT Panel Report, *EC – Oilseeds I,* paras. 150 and 151; Appellate Body Report, *EC – Asbestos (AB),* para. 190.

On the other hand, possible conflicts of other legitimate social policies with unilateral market access are also relevant to future NVNI complaints in teleological interpretation context. This is seen in the balancing mechanism of *principles* and *exceptions* of WTO rules, which has been succeeding with jurisprudential significances in many WTO Panels and the Appellate Body Reports, especially in connection with interpretation over GATT Article XX ("General Exceptions").[105] For example, in *US – Shrimp (AB)*, the Appellate Body reviewed whether the protective measures for certain species of sea turtles are related to "the conservation of exhaustible natural resources" of Article XX(g).[106] In making this determination, the Appellate Body noted that: "the treaty interpreter essentially looks into the relationship between the measure at stake and the legitimate policy of conserving exhaustible natural resources."[107] In the Panel report of the same case, the Panel is expressing in a more general manner:

> Therefore, we are of the opinion that the chapeau Article XX, interpreted within its context and in the light of the object and purpose of GATT and of the WTO Agreement, only allows members to derogate from GATT provisions *so long as, in doing so, they do not undermine the WTO multilateral trading system, thus also abusing the exceptions contained in Article XX.*[108] [emphasis added]

To the extent of "not abusing" the exceptions of GATT Article XX, the *EC – Asbestos* AB implied the intervention of NVNI complaints like this:

105 A basic doctrine of GATT is that "exceptions" are to be interpreted narrowly, *see* 1 GATT Analytical Index (1995), at 563–95; Mcgovern (1995), p. 13.11–10; *See also* Nichols (1996b), at 705–06.

106 WTO Appellate Body Report, *US – Shrimp*, paras. 135–36.

107 From this reasoning, a "substantial relationship" between domestic measures and its legitimacy from the exceptions of the Article XX(g) is needed, *id.; See also* WTO Appellate Body Report, *US – Gasoline (AB)*, at 19.

108 WTO Panel Report, *US – Shrimp*, para. 7.44.

> Rather, the European Communities' argument relates to the substance of a claim that has been determined to fall within the scope of application of Article XXIII : 1(b) and, in particular, *concerns the issue whether a "benefit" has been "nullified or impaired" by a measure restricting market access for products posing a health risk.*[109] [emphasis added]

6. *Summary: Coordination of Various Interpretations*

As reviewed above, the various interpretations over NVNI complaints raises a *coordination* demand among the different interpretations. The problem arises because a wide variety of interpretations are accepted as reasonable. The challenge will be how the WTO judicial bodies use these various interpretations together in a single framework.[110]

An old but famous occasion in GATT 47 practice illustrates the challenge. The first and seminal GATT decision involving NVNI complaints, *Australian Subsidy,* contained *inter alia* the theoretical argument of whether the requirements of tariff concessions and reasonable expectation would be essential for claiming the NVNI complaints. Based on its factual context of whether Australia's removal of parallel subsidies on two competing fertiliser products has nullified or impaired the benefits of tariff concessions received by one of the Chilean producers, the following *hypothetical interpretations* could be feasible.

First and foremost, according to a *textual interpretation* based directly on the plain text of the Article XXIII : 1(b), the *hypothetical Panel* could decide what the nullification or impairment would be if only the Australian measure nullified or impaired "any benefit" accruing to the Chilean producers "directly or indirectly".[111] Hence, if the plain language alone were determinative, the argument of

109 WTO Appellate Body Report, *EC – Asbestos,* para. 190.

110 WAINCYMER (2002), at 431; LENNARD (2002), at 22–24.

111 The plain language of the Article XXIII : 1(b) provides: "the application by another contracting party of any measure, whether or not it conflicts with the provisions of this Agreement".

Chile that the new subsidy policy of Australia seriously threatens the tariff concessions of Chile, regardless of the existence of reasonable expectation for the NVNI complaints, would have *easily* been accepted.

Second, possible interpretations from various contextual meanings would have produced much more generous outcomes. (1) Suppose that the *hypothetical Panel* was most affected by the *legal theory* of State responsibility based upon three different types of international legal obligations (i.e. "obligations of conduct," "obligations of result" and "obligations to prevent a given event")[112] and the notion of "international liability for injurious consequences arising out of acts not prohibited by international law".[113] The interpretative focus easily tilts towards a broad interpretation of not requiring the existence of the reasonable expectation for the NVNI complaints. If the Panel on the other hand, advocates "common law jurisdiction" over the NVNI complaints, then the Panel may conclude it must review the Australian government intention from the reasonable expectation. (2) Interpretation from *values or legal principles* by the Panel would have strengthened the claim of the Chilean government. If the Panel were determined to introduce the component of "reasonable expectation" as a realisation of general principle of good faith, its overall evaluation would have supported the Chilean claim. (3) If the Panel kept *policy-oriented interpretations* of a cautious deference to the Sovereignty of Contracting Parties by regarding the Article XXIII:1(b) as a "subtle compromise between trade integration and domestic policy autonomy",[114] it would have hesitated to accept the Chilean argument. On the contrary, if the Panel had a less cautious deference to the Sovereignty and comprised *free trade* proponents, the NVNI clause would be considered as a "source of hope"[115] for the Chilean government.

112 PETERSMANN (1991), at 177.
113 *Id.*, at 175.
114 *See, e.g.* ROESSLER (1997), p. 141.
115 VON BOGDANDY (1992), at 98–99.

Third, turning to the interpretation of seeking *historical meaning* of the Article XXIII : 1 in terms of drafters' intention, they might have found that it is reasonable that Chile was to be protected from the unexpected Australian subsidy policy *which could circumvent the tariff concessions.* In addition, although the idea that the nullification connects what Chilean government may expect from the standpoint of reasonableness, does not come from the very text of Article XXIII : 1, the Panel might have reasoned that supplementation of "reasonable expectation" was required from the drafters, intention extracted from the text of GATT and other official documents. If this historical interpretation *independently* controls the outcome, the Panel must have reasoned for accepting the NVNI complaint in the context of whether there was an *indirect protective* measure or not. Fourth, if a *hypothetical Panel* reasoned from a *teleological* viewpoint, then it would have decided the same as the Panel for the historical interpretation.

What in these circumstances ought the WTO judicial bodies or academic interpreters to have done? Should interpretations in one or more of the categories necessarily have taken precedence? Or was some sort of balancing required and if so how? These two questions seem to vitiate a dispute settlement on NVNI complaints and ultimately call for cooperation among various legitimate interpretations. Furthermore, the cooperation will reflect an equilibrium in the dispute settlement process, balancing each possible interpretation with others. Indeed, without a comprehensive theory of how different interpretative aspects properly contribute to a single decision in dispute settlement calculus, it is almost impossible to rationalise the correct decision in "hard cases" like NVNI complaints (i.e. cases made hard by the actual or apparent treaties or judicial precedents).

In sum, through a review of the Vienna Convention, it was confirmed that the interpretations on NVNI complaints are typically involved in the *scopes and subject-matters of the obligations of WTO law* and *main foundations of the multilateral obligations* centering around the interpretations of "benefits" and "objective" of Article XXIII : 1. Now, three specific requirements of NVNI complaints zoom in on the foundations of the multilateral obligations.

V. Three Requirements of Non-Violation Complaints

A. In General

The text of Article XXIII : 1(b) which has been repeatedly confirmed by major judiciary decisions,[1] establishes three criteria that a complaining party must demonstrate in order to successfully claim under Article XXIII : 1(b):[2] (1) *application of a measure* by a WTO member; (2) *a benefit accruing* under the relevant agreement; and (3) *nullification or impairment of the benefit as the result of* the application of the measure.[3] In addressing these three criteria there have been two different approaches in the judiciary decisions of the GATT/WTO. One approach encourages minimal use of NVNI concept, mainly limiting the scope of "measure" to domestic subsidies in connection with tariff concessions.[4] The other advocates a wider use of the NVNI concept claiming unlimited scope of the

1 *See, e.g. Australian Subsidy*, para. 12; *EC – Oilseeds I*, paras. 142–152; *Japan-Film*, para. 10.36; *Korea – Procurement*, para. 7.85.

2 Article XXIII : 1(b) of GATT provides in relevant part:
"If any Member should consider that any *benefit* accruing to it directly or indirectly under this Agreement is being *nullified or impaired* [...] as the result of [...] (b) the *application* by another Member of any *measure*, whether or not it conflicts with the provisions of this Agreement ..." [emphasis added].

3 *See, e.g. EC – Oilseeds I*, paras. 142–152; *Australian Subsidy*, paras. 12; *Japan – Film*, para. 10.41.

4 Most NVNI cases of GATT 47, except the cases of the previous footnote, belong to this category.

measure with specific negotiated concessions[5] or with a possible disconnection with the tariff concessions.[6]

The original text of the Article XXIII: 1(b) drafted in a potentially broad manner, however, never really took shape. The cases brought under the NVNI claims tended to be very narrow disputes with little attention to careful textual analysis: new subsidies that focused on a specific product.[7] Moreover, the lack of NVNI cases may be due to the nature of the dispute settlement system under the GATT 47, in which a losing party could block the establishment of a Panel.[8] As a result, GATT Panels did not have the opportunity to test and define the requirements of the NVNI complaints seriously and neither did the Uruguay Round in negotiation.[9] In these terms, it is noteworthy of the statement of *Japan – Film* Panel that the relevant NVNI cases "should be examined on its own merits," taking the NVNI complaints' safeguarding function of negotiating reciprocal tariff concessions into account.[10] The implication of this Panel's opinion of *individualised approach* to the NVNI cases may broaden the scope of NVNI complaints more than they have been used in GATT *acquis.*[11]

5 Tariff concessions are also relevant in this case group. *See, e.g., Japan – Film,* para. 10.38; *EC – Asbestos (AB),* para. 190; In GATS, specific commitments are relevant with slightly different casts to different service sectors, *see Korea-Procurement,* para. 7.103.

6 *See* GATT Panel Report, *EC – Citrus,* paras. 4.36–4.37; GATT, *EC – Canned Fruit,* para. 50; GATT, *Japan – Semi-conductors,* para. 131; GATT, *US – Sugar Waiver,* para. 5.20.

7 Durling & Lester (1998), at 255.

8 *Id.,* note 262.

9 *Id.,* at 255.

10 *Id. See also Japan – Film,* para. 10.37 ("a panel charged with examining claims under Article XXIII: 1(b) is, therefore, to make an objective assessment of whether, in light of all the relevant facts and circumstances in the matter before us").

11 The term *acquis,* commonly used in EC law, has found its way into the jurisprudence of the WTO Appellate Body, *see, e.g. Japan – Alcoholic Beverages (AB),* at 14; *India – Patent I (AB),* para. 43. In EC jurisprudence, *acquis communautaire* refers to "the whole body of rules, principles, agreements, declarations, resolutions, positions, opinions, objectives and practices con-

B. Application of a Measure

1. *Notion of Measure*

Article XXIII : 1(b) of the GATT provides that a complaint under that provision must concern the application by another Member of "any measure," whether or not it conflicts with the provisions of GATT. As implied by its plain meaning,[12] the term of "measure" suggests a pattern of concrete actions, not isolated items or general suggestions. For example, the Panel of *Japan – Film* stated that:

> The ordinary meaning of measure as it is used in Article XXIII : 1(b) certainly encompasses a law or regulation enacted by a government. But in our view, it is broader than that and includes other governmental actions short of legally enforceable enactments. At the same time, it is also true that not every utterance by a government official or study prepared by a non-governmental body at the request of the government or with some degree of government support can be viewed as a measure of a Member government.[13]

Furthermore, an action must be taken by the *government* of a WTO member to be a measure, because "the WTO Agreement is an international agreement, in respect of which only national governments and separate customs territories are directly subject to obligations".[14] Hence, a sufficient degree of government involvement must exist for government action to rise to the level of a measure.[15] However,

---

cerning the European Communities [...] whether or not binding in law, which has developed since their establishment and which has been accepted by the Community [...] as governing their activities." Mary Footer, *The Role of Consensus in GATT/WTO Decision-Making*, 17 New York Journal of International Law and Business 653 (1996–1997).

12 One dictionary offers the definition of measure: "[a] plan or course of action intended to attain some object, a suitable action." *See* OXFORD ENGLISH DICTIONARY (1993), at 1726. This dictionary has been cited in several Appellate Body decisions.

13 *Japan – Film,* para. 10.43.

14 *Id.,* para. 10.52.

15 *See* DURLING & LESTER (1998), at 241.

in comparing to Article III of the GATT that prohibits only "laws, regulations and requirements" discriminating against imports,[16] Article XXIII consciously covers all measures – a much broader term.[17] Thus, the NVNI provision encompasses more than just official legislative acts.[18]

In GATT/WTO jurisprudence, there are two important aspects in defining "measures": one is what kinds of governmental "policies" are involved; the other is what types of governmental "actions"[19] belong. First, while traditional GATT NVNI cases had dealt with the introduction or modification of a subsidy,[20] the *Japan – Film* Panel applied the NVNI complaints to governmental actions other than subsidies policy. Specifically, they assessed a member's *industrial policy*:

> we wish to make clear that we do not *a priori* consider it inappropriate to apply the Article XXIII : 1(b) remedy to other governmental actions, such as those designed to strengthen the competitiveness of certain distribution or industrial sectors through non-financial assistance.[21]

16 Article III is designed to avoid protectionism in the use of internal taxes and regulations by obliging WTO members to provide equality of competitive conditions as between imported and domestic products, *see EC – Asbestos (AB),* para. 98.

17 *EC – Asbestos (AB), Id.* In *Japan – Film,* this difference was largely ignored, *see Japan – Film,* paras. 10.36–10.37.

18 Actually, the *Japan – Semi-conductors* Panel also took a broad view of the scope of "measures" – not just laws or regulations – as support for looking at the substance of the Japanese governmental action, not just its legal status. The Panel looked to the discussion of administrative guidance in *Japan – Agriculture Products* Panel decision (1987), which had found that "administrative guidance in the special circumstances prevailing in Japan could [...] be regarded as a governmental measure enforcing supply restrictions." *See Japan – Agriculture Products,* para. 107.

19 For a different usage between "measures" and "actions," DURLING & LESTER (1998), at 261 (claiming the term of "action" was used to cast a broader sweep in other trade agreements).

20 *See, e.g. Australian Subsidyate,* paras. 5–6; *EC – Canned Fruit,* para. 14; *EC – Oilseeds,* para. 36.

21 *See Japan – Film,* para. 10.38.

The broadening of measure was confirmed by the AB of *EC – Asbestos*:

> Once again, we look to the text of Article XXIII : 1(b), which provides that "the application by another Member of *any measure*" may give rise to a cause of action under that provision. The use of the word "any" suggests that measures of all types may give rise to such a cause of action. The text does not distinguish between, or exclude, certain types of measure.[22]

These decisions have expanded the scope of "measure" correctly, when we consider the *liberal* assumptions of Bretton Woods system and the literal wording of Article XXIII : 1(b). That is, there is no logical reason to limit "measure" to only subsidies,[23] even though this opinion is not mainstream of GATT jurisprudence. In theory, there is no need to limit the NVNI complaint just within the subject matter of domestic subsidies. In addition, a report of the International Economic Conference held at Geneva in 1927 listed four types of "indirect protection," which originally comprised the contents of the "measure" in Article XXIII : 1: (1) subsidies (direct and indirect); (2) dumping and antidumping legislation; (3) discrimination arising from the conditions of transport; and (4) fiscal measures discriminating against foreign goods.[24]

22 *EC – Asbestos (AB),* para. 188.

23 DURLING & LESTER (1998), at 261.

24 Report and Proceedings of the World Economic Conference, at 443–45, League of Nations Doc. C.356 M.129 1927 I, (1927), quoting from Durling & Lester (1998), at 221. The report further noted that "tariff questions, important as they are, only cover a part of the field of the commercial relations between nations." *See* DURLING & LESTER, *id.*; In the London Monetary and Economic Conference held in 1933, Henry Chalmers, a delegate of United States, divided the indirect protectionism into three general categories: (1) those government acts "operating in connection with duties"; (2) "Indirect Protectionism in Connection with Restrictions or Other Controls of Trade" and; (3) government acts taken in connection with consular regulations and customs administration. *See* HENRY CHALMERS, Types of Administrative or Indirect Protectionism, May 25, 1933, pp. 2–5, in Special Memoranda Prepared for the American Delegation to the International Monetary and Economic Conference (June, 1933); *See also* DURLING & LESTER (1998), at 220–21.

Second, on the question of what types of government actions are elevated to "measure" under Article XXIII: 1(b), there have been two approaches in GATT/WTO jurisprudence primarily related to Article XI. In two Article XI cases involving administrative guidance inJapan, measures were found to exist under the "incentives or disincentives" test:

> In order to determine [the measures taken would be such as to constitute a contravention of Article XI], the Panel considered that it needed to be satisfied on two essential criteria. First, there were reasonable grounds to believe that *sufficient incentives or disincentives* existed for non-mandatory measures to take effect. Second, the operation of the measures to *restrict* export of semi-conductors at prices below company-specific costs was essentially dependent on Government action or intervention.[25] [emphasis added]

The other approach that broadened the scope of measure can be found in the *Japan – Film* case:

> Moreover, we also consider it conceivable, in cases where there is a high degree of cooperation and collaboration between government and business, e. g. where there is substantial reliance on administrative guidance and other more informal forms of government-business cooperation, that even non-binding, hortatory wording in a government statement of policy could have a similar effect on private actors to a legally binding measure or what Japan refers to as regulatory administrative guidance. Consequently, we believe we should be open to a broad definition of the term *measure* for purposes of Article XXIII: 1(b), which considers *whether or not a non-binding government action has an effect similar to a binding one.*[26] [emphasis added]

25 *Japan – Semi-conductors,* para. 109.

26 *Japan – Film,* para. 10.49. *Cf. id.*: "In our view, a government policy or action need not necessarily have a substantially binding or compulsory nature for it to entail a likelihood of compliance by private actors in a way so as to nullify or impair legitimately expected benefits within the purview of Article XXIII: 1(b). Indeed, it is clear that non-binding actions, which include sufficient incentives or disincentives for private parties to act in a particular manner, can potentially have adverse effects on competitive conditions of market access"; In this context, the following statement of the Panel also is worth noting: "a Member's industrial policy, pursuing the goal of increasing efficiency in a sector, could in some circumstances upset the competitive relationship in the market between domestic and imported products in a way that could give rise to a cause of action under Article XXIII: 1(b)". *See id.,* para. 10.38; *See also* WTO Panel Report, *Argentina – Bovine Hides,* para. 11.19.

This "binding or non-binding" test for defining the measure has been criticized as ignoring "proper interpretation of the text itself."[27]

Besides, measures need not be only "commercial" measures. In the *EC-Asbestos,* the EC tried to claim that measures with health objectives must be excluded from the scope of application of Article XXIII : 1(b).[28] The AB countered that the distinction of health and commercial measures would be difficult in practice and that health objectives of many measures may be attainable only by means of commercial regulation.[29] Hence, the AB did not see merit in the argument that *only* commercial measures have been the subject of Article XXIII : 1(b) claims.[30]

2. *Application*

An action must be *currently applied* to be a measure. Only an action that continues in operation, and not the market structure that resulted from past actions, constitutes a measure under Article XXIII : 1(b). This is justified on the plain meaning of Article XXIII : 1(b) because it uses the present tense, "[i]f any Member should consider that any benefit accruing to it [...] *is being* nullified or impaired [...] as a result of [...] (b) the application by another Member of any measure, whether or not it conflicts with the provisions of the Agree-

27 DURLING & LESTER (1998), at 262; *But Cf.* "The panel's formulation of a legal test focusing on the binding or non-binding nature of the particular item was not wrong; it was just incomplete." Thus, the *Film* panel leaves open the possibility that even measures no longer being applied may be covered if the underlying policies continue to be applied through administrative guidance. *See Japan-Film,* para. 10.59; Robert Hudec criticised the Panel's broader interpretation on "measure" ("doing nothing would not normally be considered a 'measure'and on this point WTO tribunals are certain to require strict conformity with the words of the [non-violation nullification or impairment] remedy, given its exceptional character"). *See* HUDEC (1999), at 99.

28 *EC – Asbestos (AB),* para. 182.

29 *Id.*, para. 189.

30 *Id.*

ment."[31] In other words, NVNI complaints concern a measure that has a "continuing effect" and not a measure that has "ceased to exist".[32]

C. An Accruing Benefit

1. Nature of "Benefit"

The Article XXIII : 1(b) states that "any benefit accruing" under the GATT shall not be nullified or impaired. As we shall explore the drafting history, the notion of "benefit" is to be materialised between the literal wording of the specific commitments of WTO Agreements and larger standard guided by the "objective" of WTO Agreements of Article XXIII.

First, the experience with NVNI complaints under GATT usually concerned the benefits of negotiated tariff concessions.[33] This has been interpreted in the academic literature that a tariff concession is necessary to keep a certain expectation of market access in terms of a competitive opportunity.[34] On the other hand, four GATT

31 *Japan – Film,* para. 10.57.

32 MATSUSHITA ET AL. (2003), at 85. They assessed that the Panel on *Japan – Film* added one more condition of "continuing effect" to the three traditional requirements for NVNI complaints. *Id.*

33 WTO Doc. IP/C/W/124, paras. 27–28.

34 *See, e.g.* ROESSLER (1997), p. 125–42 (arguing that "In the absence of a tariff concession, a WTO Member may impose tariffs of any level and the legitimate expectation of market access therefore arises under the GATT only from a tariff concession"); *See also* ROBERT E. HUDEC: 'Regulation of Domestic Subsidies Under the MTN Subsidies Code' in INTERFACE THREE: THE LEGAL TREATMENT OF DOMESTIC SUBSIDIES 7 (DON WALLACE, JR., FRANK J. LOFTUS & VAN Z. KRIKORIAN, EDS, 1984) ("If there is no concession on the product, then the other GATT rules do not really promise any particular level of commercial opportunity; they merely promise the avoidance of trade barrier forms specified in the rule").

Panel reports considered NVNI claims based on general obligations rather than specific tariff concessions and found that GATT Article XXIII: 1(b) is not limited to tariff benefits.[35] For example, in the GATT jurisprudence of *EC-Citrus*, the Panel stated that point persuasively:

> [...] the panel considered that although complaints brought previously under Article XXIII: l(b) had related to benefits arising from Article II, it believed that this did not signify that Article XXIII: 1(b) was limited only to those benefits. The drafting history of Article XXIII confirmed that this Article, including paragraph l(b) thereof, protected any benefit under the General Agreement (p. 7 of document E/PC/T/A/PV/12 of 12 June 1947).[36]

Also, the 1985 Panel Report of *EC – Canned Fruit* stated:

> The Panel found no legal justification in either Article XXIII or past GATT practice for limiting the right of contracting parties to challenge under Article XXIII an alleged nullification or impairment of tariff concessions which have to be applied on a most-favoured-nation basis. The Panel noted that neither past Panel proceedings concerning "non-violation complaints" in respect of tariff concessions (BISD II/188; 1S/53; 11S/95) nor the parties to this dispute had suggested any such limitation of the rights of contracting parties under Article XXIII.[37]

The 1990 Panel Report on *United States – Sugar Waiver* considered a NVNI complaint in relation to a non-tariff measure and a general obligation, namely import restrictions in breach of Article XI of GATT 1947. The Panel noted:

> The EEC has not claimed that benefits accruing to it under a tariff concession made by the United States in accordance with Article II have been nullified or impaired as a result of measures taken under the Waiver. The main justification for its claim of nullification or impairment that the EEC presented to the Panel was that the restrictions, in spite of the Waiver, have remained inconsistent with the General Agreement. The Panel recognised that Article

35 GATT Panel Report, *EC – Citrus*, paras. 4.36–4.37; GATT, *EC – Canned Fruit*, para. 50; GATT, *Japan – Semi-conductors*, para. 131; GATT, *US – Sugar Waiver*, para. 5.20.

36 *EC – Citrus*, para. 4.36.

37 *EC – Canned Fruit*, para. 50.

XXIII : 1(b) does not exclude claims of nullification or impairment based on provisions of the General Agreement other than Article II.[38]

In practice under the GATT, a commitment must have established conditions of competition – sometimes referred to as a competitive relationship or the creation of competitive opportunities. These have usually concerned the competitive relationship in a country between imported and domestically-produced goods, although the competitive relationship in a country between imports from other countries has also been at issue.[39] The standard of competitive relationship was first made clear in *Australian Subsidy* (1950). The Working Party's consideration of the NVNI part of the claim begins:

> The working party next considered whether the injury which the Government of Chile said it had suffered represented a nullification or impairment of a benefit accruing to Chile directly or indirectly under the General Agreement and was therefore subject to the provisions of Article XXIII. It was agreed that such impairment would exist if the action of the Australian Government which resulted in *upsetting the competitive relationship between sodium nitrate and ammonium sulphate could not reasonably have been anticipated by the Chilean Government*, taking into consideration all pertinent circumstances and the provisions of the General Agreement, at the time it negotiated for the duty-free binding on sodium nitrate.[40] [emphasis added]

More recently, the *Japan – Film* (1998) also stated that

> [...] to show nullification or impairment as a result of the application of a measure, it must be demonstrated that the competitive position of the imported products subject to and benefitting from a relevant market access [tariff] concession is being upset by the application of a measure not reasonably anticipated [...].[41]

38 *US – Sugar Waiver*, paras. 261–262.

39 The cases of *EC – Citrus* and *Japan – Semi-conductors* concerned the conditions of competition between imports from other countries. *See, e.g., EC – Citrus* para. 4.35; *Japan – Semi-conductors* para. 131.

40 *Australian Subsidy*, para. 12; The complaint was that discontinuance of an Australian subsidy violated Articles XI : 1, III : 2 and XVI of GATT or, in the alternative, nullified or impaired Chilean benefits accruing under the Agreement.

41 *Japan – Film*, para. 10.82.

2. *Legitimately Expected Benefits*

GATT/WTO jurisprudence on Article XXIII : 1(b) provides that to succeed in a NVNI claim, the complainant must show that *a benefit accruing under a relevant WTO Agreement* is being nullified or impaired.[42] This requirement implies that the benefits accruing as a result of a concession or obligation under WTO Agreements are in some way larger than the literal wording of the commitment itself.[43] Over the substances of the larger area, the GATT/WTO jurisprudence has been stated that the accruing benefits of NVNI complaints are *legitimately expected benefits* driven from the commitment goes beyond mere formal compliance with the provision in question.[44] The legitimate expectation element is thus a "temporal" element: a comparison must be made of the competitive relationship between the domestic and imported products at the time when a relevant tariff concession or market access was made and at the current time.[45]

However, the context of *legitimately expected benefits* may be considerably different according to specific WTO Agreements. For example, in the context of TRIPS Agreement, because intellectual property laws and related regulations of Members are constantly being adjusted to reflect changing conditions, the extent of legiti-

42 *See, e.g. Japan – Film,* para. 10.50 ("We reach this conclusion in considering the purpose of Article XXIII : 1(b), which is to protect the balance of concessions under GATT by providing a means to redress government actions not otherwise regulated by GATT rules that nonetheless nullify or impair a Member's legitimate expectations of benefits from tariff negotiations"); *See also EEC – Oilseeds,* BISD 37S/86, para. 144.

43 *See, e.g. Korea – Procurement,* para. 7.93 ("the basic premise is that Members should not take actions, even those consistent with the letter of the treaty, which might serve to undermine the reasonable expectations of negotiating partners. This has traditionally arisen in the context of actions which might undermine the value of negotiated tariff concessions").

44 Without the *legitimate expectation* limitation, the potential breadth of a NVNI complaint would be amazing. The drafters of the GATT recognized how broad this scope would be and had lengthy discussions about whether to grant such power to the organisation. *See* Hudec (1990), at 37–47.

45 Kennedy (2001), at 640.

mate expectation involved in GATT may be different than that likely to arise in respect to TRIPS Agreement.[46]

D. "Nullified or Impaired ... as the Result of" (Causation)

Two key questions arise in relation to legal reasoning of NVNI complaints: one is to articulate what is the nullified or impaired benefit, which is closely related to the matter of legitimately expected benefit *(nullification* or *impairment)*; the other is to prove whether or not nullification or impairment is caused by the measure concerned, which is formulated as "the principle of causal relationship" *(causation* or *causality)*.[47]

1. *Nullification or Impairment*

a. Significance of Nullification or Impairment

The Article XXIII of GATT provides two broad options for the complainant which wants to bring measures of another party before the DSB: it must either prove that any benefit accruing to it directly

46 Frederick Abbott observed contextual differences in terms of the reasoning of *Japan – Film* Panel report: "There are several reasons to be reluctant to regard the Japan-Film and Photographic Paper decision as a sound precedent for the TRIPS context. First, as a general proposition, the Appellate Body has often rejected the legal reasoning of panels of the first instance. There is no reason to believe that this case would have been an exception, particularly in light of the relatively uncharted ground that the panel was covering. Second, this case involved trade in goods, a context considerably different than that likely to arise in respect to TRIPS. Third, some of the general statements made by the panel in this case seem suspect as proper interpretations of WTO law-particularly as they might be extended to the TRIPS Agreement." *See* ABBOTT (2000), at 176.

47 BLACK'S LAW DICTIONARY (1999), at 212.

or indirectly is being "nullified or impaired" or that "the attainment of any objective of that agreement is being impeded" as the result of the measures.[48] To date, all GATT and WTO complaints have focused on the *nullification or impairment* test as contrasted with the *attainment of any objective* test.[49] Thus, WTO jurisprudence centers around the concept of *nullification or impairment.*[50]

First, the nullification or impairment of benefits under GATT Article XXIII : 1 puts more weight on *practical harms against benefits* of GATT rather than violation of legal arrangements. This was certainly created by a delicate effort to form a legal system that would accommodate the political liberalism of the Bretton Woods design for trade policy. Furthermore, in terms of the drafting history, "nullification or impairment" originated in the historical experiences of bilateral trade agreements in the 1930s and the 1940s. These were tools to prevent potential divergences from negotiated balance of tariff concessions or interests. This is because the GATT did not include any substantive commitments on such possible deviating measures by Contracting Parties.[51]

Second, the terms of "nullified" or "impaired" of Article XXIII : 1 was thus to provide a balancing tool for keeping the negotiated tariff concessions if adverse governmental measures were introduced. Hence, all the nullification or impairment languages formed in the drafting history have similar meanings; that is, when benefits are sufficiently undermined, the aggrieved party is entitled to an adjustment of the agreement.[52] Against this background, the CON-

48 *See* the chapeau of Article XXIII of GATT.

49 WAINCYMER (2002), at 88.

50 Article XXIII of GATT; *See also* WAINCYMER (2002), at 88; According to the Oxford English Dictionary, "impair" is defined as "make less effective or weaker; devalue; damage, injure," (at 1318) and "nullify" is defined as "make of no value or use; cancel out" (at 1953). Thus, in their plain meaning, these terms appear reasonably clear implying a varying degree of undermining something. *See* the Oxford English Dictionary (1993), at 1318 and 1953.

51 *See* PART ONE-II-B of this dissertation.

52 DURLING & LESTER (1998), at 250. The literal text was shifted from the phrase "capable of materially altering the de facto situation created by the present

TRACTING PARTIES recognised that GATT-*consistent* measures with domestic subsidies incidences could cause nullification or impairment of benefits.[53]

Third, in a practical sense, the nullification or impairment notion has constrained the United States, the most powerful Member of WTO, into a multilateral resolution mechanism for most of its grievances, which prevents the US from justifying unilateral action.[54] This applicability of nullification notion to multilateral trading system possibly extends Article XXIII under WTO to serve as a "catch-all" and govern some marginal situations.[55]

b. Meaning of Nullification or Impairment

First, in the context of *violation complaints,* the GATT jurisprudence presumed that a *WTO-inconsistent measure* (or the breach of the WTO Agreement concerned) caused *nullification or impairment.* For example, in *Uruguayan Recourse to Article XXIII* (1962), the Panel stated that:

> In cases where there is a clear infringement of the provisions of the General Agreement, or in other words, where measures are applied in conflict with the provisions of GATT and are not permitted under the terms of the relevant protocol under which the GATT is applied by the contracting party, the action would, *prima facie*, constitute a case of nullification or impairment and

---

treaty, to the prejudice of the other Party" (Equitable Treatment Clause) through the phrase "has the effect of nullifying or impairing" (Suggested Charter), then finally to the current GATT text, "is being nullified or impaired... as the result of." *See id.*

53 *See, e.g. Australian Subsidy,* para. 13.

54 *See* ABELS (1996), at 504–05 (1996); HUDEC (1993), at 238; Especially, the US in many of the bilateral disputes with Japan succeeds her allegations through GATT-based arguments concerning deprivation of national treatment and NVNI complaints, *see* FREDERICK M. ABBOTT, *Changing the Dynamics of Dispute Settlement and Avoidance in Trade Relations Between Japan and the United States,* 16 Arizona Journal of International and Comparative Law 185, 205–09 (1999).

55 ABELS (1996), at 514.

> would *ipso facto* require consideration of whether the circumstances are serious enough to justify the authorisation of suspension of concessions or obligations.[56] [footnote deleted]

This practice was codified in one of "Tokyo Round Codes"[57] and is now reflected in Article 3.8 of DSU:

> In case where there is an infringement of the obligations assumed under a covered agreement, *the action is considered prima facie to constitute a case of nullification or impairment.* This means that there is normally a presumption that a breach of the rules has an adverse impact on other Members parties to that covered agreement, and in such cases, *it shall be up to the Member against whom the complaint has been brought to rebut the charge.*[58] [emphasis added]

This provision suggests that the presumption of nullification or impairment is rebuttable and that the demonstration of an absence of an "adverse impact" is sufficient for the rebuttability.[59] However, as the jurisprudence has developed, this presumption has become essentially *irrebuttable.*[60] The established jurisprudence has con-

56 GATT Panel Report, *Uruguayan Recourse to Article XXIII,* para. 15; *See also Japan – Semi-conductors,* para. 131; *US – Sugar Waiver,* paras. 5.20–5.23.

57 *Paragraph 5 of the Annex to the Understanding Regarding Notification, Consultation, Dispute Settlement and Surveillance,* adopted on 28 November 1979 ("In cases where there is an infringement of the obligations assumed under the General Agreement, the action is considered prima facie to constitute a case of nullification or impairment").

58 *Cf. US – Wool Shirts (AB),* at 13–14 ("However, the issue in [the Article 3.8 of DSU] is not what happens after a violation is established; the issue in this case is which party must first show that there is, or is not, a violation. More specifically, the issue in this case is which party has the burden of demonstrating that there has, or has not been, an infringement of the obligations ...").

59 *Id.*; ROESSLER (1997), p. 127.

60 ROESSLER, *id.*: GATT Panel Report, *US – Superfund,* para. 3.1.6 ("... that there was an irrefutable presumption that a breach of the rules of the General Agreement caused nullification or impairment within the meaning of Article XXIII ...").

firmed that it is *trade potential or competitive conditions* rather than *impact on trade flows* that are being protected.[61]

The reason for considering the *trade potential* was well explained in *Japan – Imports Leather* case (1984). Against the respondent Japan's argument that since the quotas had not been fully utilised, they had not restrained trade, and consequently not caused a nullification or impairment of benefit, the Panel noted that:

> In any event, the Panel wished to stress that the existence of quantitative restrictions should be presumed to cause nullification or *impairment not only because of any effect it had on the volume of trade but also for other reason, e.g. it would lead to increased transaction costs and would create uncertainties which could affect investment plans.*[62] [emphasis added]

Accordingly a member's potential trade benefit is sufficient to establish a dispute settlement Panel.[63]

Second, in light of NVNI complaints, such a *prima facie* nullification presumption like in violation complaints does not exist. Although a NVNI complaint can be raised by claiming that the specific rules of WTO Agreements are violated,[64] a general type of NVNI complaint will be a claim that the measures of another Member are nullifying or impairing *any benefit of the relevant WTO Agreement.* Although the proof of the adverse change in the competitive conditions like the violation case is required, the burden of proof is different between two causes of action.

61 *See* Roessler (1997), pp. 127–30. Waincymer (2002), at 90; *See also* GATT Panel Report, *EC – Oilseeds II*, para. 77 (describing that "the subsidies concerned had impaired the tariff concession because they upset the competitive relationship between domestic and imported oilseeds, not because of any effect on trade flows"); *Australian Subsidy*, para. 12: *Germany – Sardines*, para. 16.

62 GATT Panel Report *Japan – Imports Leather*, para. 50.

63 WTO Panel Report, *EC – Bananas III (Ecuador)*, para. 7.50.

64 Cho (1998), at 319. He labelled this type of NVNI complaints as "independent-mode" in that "this type of case does not call for the existence of specific tariff concession or its connection with a reasonable expectation as the basis for invoking a complaint." *See also id.*, note 34.

2. *Causation ("As the Result") of Non-Violation Complaints*

The wording of "as the result of" in Article XXIII : 1 of GATT implies that the NVNI complaint is only available where the causation between the relevant measures and nullified or impaired benefits is confirmed. The *Japan – Film* summarised the point as follows:

> ... In other words, the United States [the complainant] must show a clear correlation between the measures and the adverse effect on the relevant competitive relationship.[65]

The Panel of *Japan – Film* articulated for the first time the standard of causation,[66] referring to four parameters: (1) the degree of causation that must be shown (standard of proof); (2) the relevance of "origin-neutral" measures; (3) the relevance of intent and; (4) the extent to which the collective effect of measures may be considered.[67]

First, the standard of proof will be dealt with under the heading "burden of production." Second, the Panel noted that, even if measures do not discriminate *de jure* on the basis of origin, they may do so *de facto*. In these situations the complainant would need to detail any claimed disproportionate impact on imports.[68]

65 *Japan – Film,* para. 10.82.

66 Durling & Lester (1998), at 265. Actually, neither the specific language of Article XXIII : 1(b) nor prior GATT panel decisions explicitly articulated the degree of causation required to prove nullification or impairment.

67 *Japan – Film,* para. 10.83

68 *Id.,* para. 10.85: "In our view, even in the absence of *de jure* discrimination (measures which on their face discriminate as to origin), it may be possible for the United States to show *de facto* discrimination (measures which have a disparate impact on imports). However, in such circumstances, the complaining party is called upon to make a detailed showing of any claimed disproportionate impact on imports resulting from the origin-neutral measure. And, the burden of demonstrating such impact may be significantly more difficult where the relationship between the measure and the product is questionable"; In GATT/WTO jurisprudence, the issue of *de facto* discrimination has been well-developed, both in regard to the principle of most-favoured-nation treatment under GATT Article I, *see, e.g.* GATT Panel Report,

Third, with respect to intent, the Panel stated that what matters for purposes of establishing causality is the impact of the measure (i.e. whether it upsets competitive relationships). However, a showing of intent to restrict imports might make a panel more inclined to find a causal relationship in specific cases involving measures which on their face appear to be origin-neutral.[69] Fourth, with regard to the collective impact of measures, the Panel did not reject the possibility of undertaking such a collective examination, but indicated its apprehension that the technique to determine causation was subject to potential abuse and therefore must be approached with caution and circumscribed as necessary.[70]

To claim causation *procedurally*[71] is associated with the question of *burden of proof*, which means a party's duty to prove a disputed assertion.[72] This can be divided into: (1) *burden of persuasion* (or *standard of proof*), in the sense that a party's duty is to convince the fact-finder to view the facts in a way that favours that party;[73] and (2) *burden of production* (or *evidentiary standard of proof*), whereby a party's duty to introduce enough evidence on an issue to have the issued decided by the fact-finder.[74] Generally

---

EC – Beef from Canada, paras. 4.2, 4.3; In regard to that of national treatment under GATT Article III, *see* GATT, *US – Section 337*, para. 5.11; GATT, *Canada – Alcoholic Drinks*, paras. 5.12–5.14 and 5.30–5.31; GATT, *US – Malt Beverages*, para. 5.30; GATT, *US – Gasoline*, para. 6.10; WTO Panel Report, *Japan – Alcoholic Beverages*, para. 6.33 and WTO, *EC – Bananas III (Ecuador)*, paras. 7.179–7.180.

69 *Japan – Film*, para. 10.87.

70 *Id.*, para. 10.88: "It is not without logic that a measure, when analyzed in isolation, may have only very limited impact on competitive conditions in a market, but may have a more significant impact on such conditions when seen in the context of – in combination with – a larger set of measures."

71 For elucidations on causation from *substantial* viewpoints, *see* H. L. A. HART AND TONY HONORÉ, CAUSATION IN THE LAW, PART I (1996).

72 BLACK'S LAW DICTIONARY (1999), at 190.

73 *Id.* In civil cases, the plaintiff's burden is usu. "by a preponderance of the evidence," compared to the prosecution's burden of "beyond a reasonable doubt" in criminal cases. *Id.*

74 *Id.*

speaking, the two aspects of burden of proof on causation (i.e. who bears the burden of producing evidence to support the degree of confidence and how high the degree of confidence must be), is a distinct issue of policy or principle.[75] Although a common usage of *burden of proof* means *burden of persuasion* and the two aspects of burden of proof (i.e. burden of persuasion and production) are interwoven, the two aspects are dealt with separately for analytic clarification.

a. Burden of Persuasion (Standard of Proof)

At the outset, the initial burden of proof is always on the complainant in GATT/WTO proceeding, which is a generally-accepted canon of evidence in civil and common law.[76] This is because any system of judicial settlement would be impractical if it proposed that the mere assertion of a claim might amount to proof.[77] Hence, if a party adduces evidence sufficient to raise a presumption that what is claimed is true, the burden then shifts to the other party, who will fail unless it adduces sufficient evidence to rebut the presumption.[78] Jurisprudentially, this requirement is mundane and its purpose is probably to check frivolous or unjustified complaints. The jurisprudence of GATT/WTO supports this proposition that the burden of establishing a violation under Article XXIII:1(a) of the GATT was on the complainant. As early as 1950, the *Australian Subsidy* Working Party clearly put the burden of establishing a violation of the GATT obligations at issue on the complainant:

75 *See* RICHARD W. WRIGHT, *Causation in Tort Law*, 73 California Law Review 1735, 1812 (1985).

76 JACKSON, DAVEY & SYKES (1995), at 355; M. N. HOWARD, P. CRANE AND D. A. HOCHBERG, PHIPSON ON EVIDENCE 52 (14TH ED., 1990) ("The burden of proof rests upon the party, whether plaintiff or defendant, who substantially asserts the affirmative of the issue").

77 *See* WTO Panel Report, *US – Wool Shirts*, at 14; MOJTABA KAZAZI, BURDEN OF PROOF AND RELATED ISSUES: A STUDY ON EVIDENCE BEFORE INTERNATIONAL TRIBUNALS 117 (1996).

78 *US – Wool Shirts*, *Id.*

> Within the terms of reference of the working party, the examination of the relevant provisions of the General Agreement thus led it to the conclusion that no evidence had been presented to show that the Australian Government (the respondent) had failed to carry out its obligations under the Agreement.[79]

The important issue of burden of persuasion is whether the complainant *always* has the burden of persuasion in WTO dispute settlement, or whether the burden *may shift* to the challenged Member in certain conditions.[80] Several WTO decisions have addressed this issue. For example, in *US – Wool Shirts*, India (the complainant) argued that it should not have to prove that the US (the respondent) had violated the *Agreement of Textiles and Clothing* ("ATC"), but that instead the United States should have to prove that the United States was justified in relying on the "exception" to WTO disciplines created by the safeguard procedure of Article 6 of the ATC.[81] The Panel stated that because India had initiated the proceedings, India had to establish that the US restriction was inconsistent with the United States' obligations. In addition, the AB affirmed the panel's conclusion, holding that:

> We agree with the Panel that it was up to India [the complainant] to present evidence and argument sufficient to establish a presumption that the transitional safeguard determination made by the United States was inconsistent with its obligations under Article 6 of the *ATC*.[82]

However, the AB also issued a caveat that "precisely how much and precisely what kind of evidence will be required to establish such a presumption will necessarily vary from measure to measure,

79 *Australian Subsidy,* para. 11; *See also German – Sardines,* para. 15; GATT Panel Report, *Canada – Alcoholic Drinks,* paras. 5.2–5.3; GATT, *US – Tabacco* paras. 82 and 124.

80 In principle, the concept of burden of proof "only applies to facts, not to issues of law," *see* PAUWELYN (1998), at 242. However, most contested issues are mixed questions of fact and law, making this distinction problematic to apply in practice.

81 *See* WTO Panel Report, *US – Wool Shirts,* para. 6.6.

82 *US – Wool Shirts (AB),* at 13.

provision to provision, and case to case."[83] This *case-specific approach* of the AB left unclear the manner in which Members and future Panels should determine whether a particular provision or Agreement is an "exception" that shifts the burden of proof, or whether there are other situations where the complaining country does not have the burden of proof.[84] Along with the "exception" case, generally speaking, the burden of proof will also be imposed on the defending member when the member relies on an "affirmative defense."[85] However, it is unclear what the standard will be for identifying an affirmative defense.[86]

b. Burden of Production (Evidentiary Standard of Proof)

The issue of burden of production is related to the degree of causal confidence that needs to be shown,[87] and this evidentiary degree varies according to the *causes of action* of Article XXIII : 1. First, for a violation complaint, the complainant needs only show that a violation is exists.[88] In this case, evidentiary standard of proof would be the common "but for" (necessary condition) test of causation which is the most widely used test of actual causation in tort adjudication.[89] This test states that a measure of respondent was a cause

83 *Id.*

84 Lichtenbaum (1998), at 1250.

85 *See, e.g. US – Shrimp*, para. 30. In this case, the panel cited the "well-established practice" of allocating the burden of establishing an affirmative defense to the defending member, imposing the burden of establishing the applicability of Article XX on the United States, as the party asserting the affirmative defense. *Id.*

86 Lichtenbaum (1998), at 1252; Pauwelyn (1998), at 252 (stating that the AB "did not really explain" why certain provisions are deemed exceptions and others are not).

87 Waincymer (2002), at 108.

88 Debra P. Steger and Susan M. Hainsworth, 'New Directions in International Trade Law: WTO Dispute Settlement,' *in* Dispute Resolution in the World Trade Organization 28, 41–3 (James Cameron and Karen Campbell, eds, 1998); *See also* GATT Panel Report, *EC – Sugar*, para. 2.29.

89 *See* Wright (1985), at 1775–77.

of a violation *if and only if, but for* the act, the violation would not have occurred:[90] that is, the act must have been a necessary condition for the occurrence of the violation.

Second, in contrast, the *exceptional nature* of the NVNI claim has led to the development of specific elements that must be proven to satisfy such a claim. The complainant must show that benefits accruing under the Agreement have been nullified or impaired as the result of the application of a measure.[91] For an evidentiary standard of proof of NVNI complaint, the Panel of *Japan – Film* articulated for the first time the standard of causation.[92] In regard to the evidentiary degree of causation, the Panel found that the issue at that stage of the proceeding was whether a measure had made *more than de minimis*[93] contribution to nullification or impairment.[94] However this *more than de minimis* standard is "extremely low" given the NVNI complaint' exceptional character and its drafting history.[95] Generally speaking, although the requirement of standard of proof is common with the three sorts of complaints, Article XXIII : 1(a) (b) and (c), because of different extent of rebuttability presumption, the violation complaints is more favorable to the complainant. While infringing the rules of GATT Agreements is considered as *prima facie* nullification or impairment, by contrast, the exceptional nature of the NVNI claim has led to requiring that the complainant must justify *in detail* that benefits accruing under the Agreement have been nullified or impaired as the result of the application of a measure.[96] For example, in *Uruguayan Recourse to Article XXIII* case, the Panel noted that:

90 *Id.*, at 1775.

91 GATS Article XXIII; GATT Article XXIII.

92 DURLING & LESTER (1998), at 265. Actually, neither the specific language of Article XXIII : 1(b) nor prior GATT panel decisions explicitly articulated the degree of causation required to prove nullification or impairment.

93 This Latin word means "of the least." *See* BLACK'S LAW DICTIONARY (1999), at 443.

94 *Japan – Film,* para. 10.84.

95 DURLING & LESTER (1998), at 265–66.

96 See Article 26.1(a) of DSU.

> While it is not precluded that a prima facie case of nullification or impairment could arise even if there is no infringement of GATT provisions, it would be in such cases incumbent on the country invoking Article XXIII to demonstrate the grounds and reasons of its invocation. Detailed submissions on the part of that contracting party on these points were therefore essential for a judgment to be made under this Article.[97]

The GATT codified this practice relatively early by requiring the complainant which brought a NVNI case to submit a "detailed justification."[98] This must be tangible and concrete, going beyond a mere description of the measure at issue.[99] Under the WTO, Article 26.1(a) of the DSU which applies to NVNI complaints, requires "the complaining party to present a detailed justification in support of any complaint relating to a measure which does not conflict with the relevant covered agreement." The failure to meet the burden of demonstrating actual nullification and impairment was decisive in several cases of NVNI claims, including *Japan – Semi-conductors* (1988), *US – Sugar Waiver* (1990) and *Japan – Film* (1998).

However, the *Japan – Film* Panel is assessed to essentially eliminate the "detailed justification" concept from NVNI complaints.[100]

97 *Uruguayan Recourse to Article XXIII*, para. 15.

98 Paragraph 5 of the Annex to the Understanding Regarding Notification, Consultation, Dispute Settlement and Surveillance, adopted on 28 November 1979: "If a contracting party bringing an Article XXIII case claims that measures which do not conflict with the provisions of the General Agreement have nullified or impaired benefits accruing to it under the General Agreement, it would be called upon to provide a detailed justification." In other words, the complainant must show that benefits accruing under the Agreement have been nullified or impaired as the result of the application of a measure.

99 *See, e.g. Japan – Semi-Conductors*, para. 131.

100 Durling & Lester (1998), at 267; *But cf.* "It appears that the [*Japan – Film*] panel did impose a higher standard when it stated that: 'the United States responds that the 'measures' at issue have had a disparate impact on imported products in their application, thereby upsetting competitive conditions of market access for imported film and paper. In our view, even in the absence of *de jure* discrimination (measures which on their face discriminate as to origin), it may be possible for the United States to show *de facto* discrimination (measures which have a disparate impact on imports). However, in such circumstances, the complaining party is called upon to make a detailed showing of any claimed disproportionate impact on imports resulting

As implicitly recognising the US argument that the "detailed justification" was required in the pleading and not just a standard of proof that must be met as a substantive matter, the Panel stated:

> ... the United States argues that the interim report construes the "detailed justification" requirement as imposing a heightened evidentiary standard in non-violation cases, while for the United States it is rather a pleading requirement, i.e. a screen to dismiss inadequately articulated non-violation claims from a panel's consideration. [...] In our view, we did not apply the "detailed justification" requirement as a heightened evidentiary standard.[101]

This finding was criticised by some lawyers as follows:

> The panel's decision implicitly to accept the US characterization of the detailed justification standard as a pleading requirement was misguided. The "detailed justification" requirement is not a procedural or pleading standard. The DSU provides the procedural requirements of a claim in Articles 4.4 and 6.2. Article 4.4 provides that requests for consultations must be submitted in writing and include an "identification of the measures at issue and an indication of the legal basis of the complaint." Similarly, Article 6.2 directs complaining parties, when submitting requests for the establishment of a panel, to "identify the specific measures at issue and provide a brief summary of the legal basis of the complaint sufficient to present the problem clearly." These requirements are the initial "pleading" requirements. They ensure that claims are made properly and sufficiently and that parties are given adequate notice. *By contrast, the "detailed justification" standard has nothing to do with notice; it sets the evidentiary standard that a claim must meet.*[102] [emphasis added] [footnote deleted]

The higher evidentiary standard for NVNI claims than for violation claims is also related to the *remedy* for NVNI complaints.[103] Before the ITO negotiations, no remedy existed for successful NVNI com-

---

from the origin-neutral measure. And the burden of demonstrating such impact may be significantly more difficult where the relationship between the measure and the product is questionable (para. 10.85).'" *See* CHARLES M. GASTLE, *The Convergence of International Trade and Competition Law Through a WTO Market Access Code,* 8 Currents: International Trade Law Journal 3, n. 146, 16 (1999).

101 *See Japan – Film,* para. 9.5.

102 DURLING & LESTER (1998), at 267–68.

103 *Id.* at 254 & 266.

plaints.[104] During the ITO negotiations, NVNI was considered in conjunction with a true dispute settlement procedure for the first time and distinguished the different types of complaints with some legally meaningful remedy.[105] The historical development of a more effective remedy for NVNI complaints provides an important contextual background of demanding a higher evidentiary standard.

Since the remedial modalities of NVNI complaints are relevant to explore the legal nature of NVNI concept, remedy is reviewed in more detail.

3. Remedy

a. Relevant Drafting History

The original remedy for NVNI provided in the League of Nations' equitable treatment clause was just a *recommendation of bilateral consultations.*[106] Consequently, the typical formulation in the US bilateral agreements was that "the government which has adopted any such measure shall consider such representations and proposals as the other government may make with a view to effecting a mutually satisfactory adjustment of the matter".[107] By contrast, the

104 *Id.* Main tool of the equitable treatment clause and the bilateral agreements in the 1930s for successful NVNI complaints was bilateral consultations when one party considered itself to be aggrieved. *See id.*, n. 258.

105 *See* U.N. Conf.–12th Mtg., at 26. Here, the Belgian delegate noted: "[...] the onus of the proof is in direct relation with the oddity and strangeness of the case envisaged; and one should ask the Organisation in a case of that kind for more proof and for the discovery of more facts. [...] We should ask for more facts and guarantees for the application by another Member of any measure [not conflicting with the Agreement]." *See id.*

106 SAUL H. MENDLOVITZ & BURNS H. WESTON, *The United Nations at Fifty: Toward Humane Global Governance*, 4 Transnational Law & Contemporary Problems 309, 313 (1994), quoting from DURLING & LESTER (1998), at 252 n. 241.

107 *See, e.g.* Reciprocal Trade Agreement, Dec. 18, 1935, US-Hond., Article XIV, Stat. 3851, 3862.

NVNI provision, which was included in the various versions of the ITO Charter, provides a much more effective remedy, because the ITO was to be an organisation to administer the trade rules. The Suggested Charter first tries to promote a *mutually satisfactory solution* to the dispute, but when the parties cannot reach such a solution, the Suggested Charter allows the ITO to investigate the dispute on its own and make recommendations.[108] The London Draft maintained a virtually identical provision,[109] and, during the Geneva discussions, the NVNI provision was moved to the general dispute settlement section for the ITO Charter as a whole,[110] which was retained in the present GATT Article XXIII. This aspect was also confirmed by reference to the drafting history of Article XXIII: 1 in *US – Nicaragua* case.[111]

b. "Mutually Satisfactory Adjustment"

Remedies under WTO are different where the complaints are concerned. If WTO judicial bodies find a measure inconsistent with a covered agreement (*violation* complaints), they *shall* recommend that the WTO Member concerned bring the measure into conformity.[112] In addition the judicial bodies *may* suggest ways the Mem-

108 Suggested Charter, Article 30, at 23.
109 London Draft, at A17.
110 Durling & Leister (1998), at 253.
111 *US – Nicaragua,* para. 5.8: "It is clear from the drafting history that in case of recommendations on measures not found to be inconsistent with the General Agreement, the contracting parties are under no specific and contractual obligations to accept those recommendations' (EPCT/A/PV/5, p. 16). The report of the Sixth Committee during the Havana Conference notes with respect to the power of the Executive Board to make recommendations to member States in any matter arising under Article 93:1(b) or (c) of the Havana Charter (which corresponds to Article XXIII: 1(b) and (c) of the General Agreement): "It was agreed that subparagraph 2(e) of Article 94 does not empower the Executive Board or the Conference to require a Member to suspend or withdraw a measure not in conflict with the Charter [...]."
112 Article 19.1 of DSU.

ber could implement the recommendation.[113] In contrast, there is no obligation to withdraw the measure where NVNI complaints under Article XXIII: 1(b) are concerned,[114] because of the compatibility of the measure of the losing party with WTO law.[115] This was made clear in the first NVNI case considered under GATT 47 in *Australian Subsidy*. The Working Party stated that:

> [T]here is in [the working party's] view nothing in Article XXIII which would empower the CONTRACTING PARTIES to require a contracting party to withdraw or reduce [the measure found not to be inconsistent with the General Agreement], and the recommendation made by the working party should not be taken to imply the contrary. The ultimate power of the CONTRACTING PARTIES under Article XXIII is that of authorising an affected contracting party to suspend the application of appropriate obligations or concessions under the General Agreement.[116]

In such NVNI cases, the Panels or the Appellate Body shall recommend that the relevant Members make a "mutually satisfactory adjustment," as indicated in the Article XXIII: 2 of GATT and 26.1(b)

113 *Id.* These suggestions are not binding on their addressee, *see* MATSUSHITA ET AL. (2003), at 80; *See also* WTO Panel Report, *Guatemala – Cement,* para. 8.2 ("Article 19.1 of the DSU is explicit concerning the recommendation a panel is to make in the event it determines that a measure, or in this case, action, is inconsistent with a covered agreement: 'it shall recommend that the Member concerned bring the measure into conformity with that agreement.' Article 19.1 goes on to provides that: 'In addition to its recommendations, the panel or Appellate Body may suggest ways in which the member concerned could implement the recommendations.' *Such suggestions on implementation, however, are not part of the recommendation, and are not binding on the affected Member*") [emphasis added].

114 Article 26.1(b) of DSU provides: "... where a measure has been found to nullify or impair benefits under, or impede the attainment of objectives, of the relevant covered agreement without violation thereof, there is no obligation to withdraw the measure. However, in such cases, the panel or Appellate Body report shall recommend that the member concerned make a mutually satisfactory adjustment."

115 MATSUSHITA ET AL. (2003), at 86.

116 *Australian Subsidy,* para.16. It was quoted with approval in the para. 5.2 of *EC – Citrus* and the para. 82 of *EC – Canned Fruit*; *See also US – Nicaragua,* para. 5.8.

of the DSU.[117] This provision of the DSU draws on experience under GATT 47. The *EC – Canned Fruit* Panel (1985) noted that in previous NVNI cases of tariff concessions (referring specifically to *Australian Subsidy* and *Germany – Sardines*):

> the CONTRACTING PARTIES had recommended that the party against which the finding had been made consider ways and means to remove the competitive inequality brought about by the measure at issue.[118]

It then submitted a draft recommendation of that kind.[119] The recommendation in the *EC – Oilseeds I* (1990) was to the same effect, although drafted differently.[120] Related to such recommendations, Article 19.2 of DSU provides that "In accordance with paragraph 2 of Article 3, in their findings and recommendations, the panel and Appellate Body cannot add to or diminish the rights and obligations provided in the covered agreements".

However, it is not clear how such a *mutually satisfactory adjustment* could be made, because the losing party does not have to do anything it does not want to do if it must be *mutually* satisfactory,[121] and because so far no case law makes the term *mutually satisfactory adjustment* more clear.[122] The parties themselves should determine a satisfactory adjustment, which the arbitration provisions in DSU Article 21 could be utilised.[123] That is, Article 26.1(c) of the DSU puts the responsibility for making suggestions on ways and means of reaching a mutually satisfactory adjustment on an arbitrator who

117 Article XXIII: 2 of GATT; *See also* 2 GATT Analytical Index, at 680–84.

118 *EC – Canned Fruit*, para. 82.

119 *Id.*, para. 83.

120 *EC – Oilseeds*, para. 157. The Panel concluded that the EC processor subsidies violated Article III: 4 and that the processor subsidies were a violation even though the complex EC pricing and subsidy scheme did not always result in discrimination against imports for every individual purchase. The Panel also concluded that the EC oilseeds producer subsidies nullified or impaired the duty-free tariff concession the EC had accorded the United States in its Schedule of Concessions under Article II.

121 Waincymer (2002), at 636.

122 Matsushita et al. (2003), at 86.

123 Waincymer (2002), at 637.

may be requested by either party under Article 21.3 of the DSU. He may be asked to determine the level of benefits which have been nullified or impaired as well as to suggest ways and means of reaching a mutually satisfactory adjustment.[124] In addition, Article 26.1(d) of the DSU states that, notwithstanding the normal rule that compensation should be a *temporary* remedy,[125] in the case of NVNI complaints, "compensation may be part of a mutually satisfactory adjustment as *final* settlement (emphasis added)".

In relation to this point, some Panels have recommended or suggested particular guidelines for a mutually satisfactory adjustment. The Working Party on *Australian Subsidy* explained its reasoning in the following passage:

> The sole reason why the adjustment of subsidies to remove any competitive inequality between the two products arising from subsidisation is recommended is that, in this particular case, it happens that such action appears to afford the best prospect of an adjustment of the matter satisfactory to both parties.[126]

As a concrete suggestion, for example, the Panel on *EC – Oilseeds I* suggested that the tariff concessions impaired could be remedied either by modifying the new European Community's support system for oilseeds or by the EC renegotiating its tariff concessions for oilseeds under Article XXVIII of the GATT 47.[127] On the other hand, Article XXIII:3 of the GATS specifies that a *mutually satisfactory adjustment* in NVNI claims under that Agreement, which can only apply to alleged nullification or impairment of benefits accruing from a specific commitment, shall be "on the basis of paragraph 2 of Article XXI ('Modification of Schedules')." This requires renegotiating specific commitments contained in the national Schedules.[128]

124 Article 26.1(c) of DSU.
125 Article 22.1 of DSU.
126 *Australian Subsidy*, para. 16.
127 *EC – Oilseeds I*, para. 132; *See also EC – Citrus*, para. 5.3.
128 Article XXI:2 of the GATS reads: "(a) At the request of any Member the benefits of which under this Agreement may be affected (referred to in this Article as an "affected Member") by a proposed modification or withdrawal

In summary, the following observation by Matsushita, Schoenbaum & Mavroidis is noteworthy to investigate the conceptual identity of NVNI complaints in the *remedy* context.

> [That the withdrawal of the measure in NVNI complaints is not required] is presumably why the DSU does not provide for such a remedy and merely specifies a solution where the *effects* of [the measure] will be mitigated without the [*measure*] *itself* being put into question at all.[129] [emphasis in original]

E. Different Scope of Interpretation

1. *Narrow Interpretation (Restrictive Approach)*

Most GATT 47 judiciary decisions[130] seem to try to narrow the applicability of NVNI complaints with some requirement,[131] while WTO decisions have taken a broader approach.[132] In the forty-seven year history of the GATT 47, the substantive claims related to the NVNI complaints usually involved product-specific subsidies that undermined specific tariff concessions.[133] Some scholars also considered the complaints to be a narrow remedy whose potential application became significantly diminished because specific GATT disciplines

---

notified under subparagraph 1(b) [of Article XXI], the modifying Member shall enter into negotiations with a view to reaching agreement on any necessary compensatory adjustment. In such negotiations and agreement, the Members concerned shall endeavour to maintain a general level of mutually advantageous commitments not less favourable to trade than that provided for in Schedules of specific commitments prior to such negotiations. (b) Compensatory adjustments shall be made on a most-favoured-nation basis."

129 MATSUSHITA ET AL. (2003), at 86.

130 The following review of the GATT panel jurisprudence is quite brief. For a more complete review, *see* Petersmann (1991), at 201–20.

131 *See, e.g.* PETERSMAN (1991), *id.*

132 *See, e.g.* BAGWELL, MAVROIDIS & STAIGER (2002), at 66.

133 MCGOVERN (1995), p. 2.27–6.

extended to and limited the use of subsidies.[134] Several reasons for the narrow interpretation were given. First, some scholars contended that a broad interpretation would result in "wrong cases" and would contravene the bargains that WTO members make in multilateral trade negotiations.[135]

Second, another common argument is that Article XXIII: 1(b) has diminished in importance because the WTO Agreements increasingly restrict non-tariff barriers, regulate government measures that occur inside the borders of countries, and constrain the domestic policy autonomy of governments when domestic policy affects international trade.[136] In restricting the NVNI complaints, most judiciary opinions of GATT 47 have attempted to impose a certain level of requirements for the success of NVNI complaints.

a. Requirement of Connection with Tariff Concession

The NVNI complaints have only been successful if the impairment of tariff concessions could be proved, that is, the challenged measure has to *impair the balance of tariff concessions.*[137] Thus, the NVNI complaints prevent a measure from impairing the competitive relationships, established by the binding of the relevant tariff position, between foreign and domestic products. In *Germany – Sardines* (1952), the Panel concluded that granting favorable treatment to similar imported products upset the competitive relationship of the imported product concerned.[138] The *EC – Oilseeds I*

134 Hudec (1993), at 7; Cho (1998), at 321–33; Cottier & Schefer (1997), pp. 181–82; Hudec (1980), at 167; Petersmann (1994), at 1188; Roessler (1997), p. 134.

135 Cho (1998), at 313; Hudec (1980), at 167.

136 Roessler (1997), p. 134.

137 *See* 2 GATT Analytical Index (1995), at 660–61; Only in *EC – Citrus* did the complaining party claim that the benefit denied was not improved market access from tariff concessions granted under GATT Article II, but rather GATT Article I: 1 with respect to unbound tariff preferences granted by the EC to certain Mediterranean countries; *See id.*, at 661; *See also* Petersmann (1994), at 1230.

138 *Germany – Sardines,* para. 16.

case (1982) demonstrates that a relevant point for proving deterioration of a competitive relationship is an abstract adverse change in competition, rather than an actual decline in imports.[139]

b. Requirement of Frustration of Legitimate Expectation

To qualify the measure in question cannot reasonably have been anticipated by the complainant at the time of tariff negotiation. In the first pertinent case, *Australian Subsidy* (1950), concerned the abolition of a domestic (Australia) subsidy for a foreign (Chile) product, the Panel noted that:

> It was agreed that such impairment would exist if *the action of the Australian Government* which resulted in upsetting the competitive relationship between sodium nitrate and ammonium sulphate *could not reasonably have been anticipated by the Chilean Government,* taking into consideration all pertinent circumstances and the provisions of the General Agreement, at the time it negotiated for the duty-free binding on sodium nitrate.[140] [emphasis added]

In this context, Cottier and Scheffer observed that the most important element of legitimate expectation jurisprudence is the requirement of "non-foreseeability" of the measure in question, which can function as "an objectivisation of a fundamentally subjective view of the [benefits] impairment."[141] In addition, if the measure in question is one which GATT Article XX is available to justify the measure, a stricter burden of proof will fall on the member that invokes NVNI complaints, particularly regarding the existence of legitimate expectations.[142]

139 *EC – Oilseeds I,* para. 151 ("The provisions of Article XXIII : 1(b) could therefore in practice hardly be applied if a contracting party claiming nullification or impairment had to demonstrate not only that an adverse change in competition has taken place but also that the change has resulted in a decline in imports").

140 *Australian Subsidy,* para. 12.

141 COTTIER & SCHEFER (1997), pp. 162–63.

142 *See* WTO Panel Report, *EC – Asbestos,* para. 8.282; For the relevancy of burden of proof to "foreseeability", *see* MCGOVERN (1995), p. 2.27–3 & 4.

In general, on the necessity of the reasonable expectation, the Panels' viewpoints have shifted in favour of the complainant: in the *Australian Subsidy* case, a working group stated that a contracting party can generally not rely on the same treatment between a domestic and foreign product if a new subsidy is introduced, on the grounds of the respective autonomy under the GATT.[143] However, in later cases, the interpretation changed. In the *EC– Oilseeds* case, the Panel accepted the US argument that the US was assumed to have based their tariff negotiations with the EC on the expectation that the price effect of the tariff concessions would not be systematically offset.[144] The Panel further ruled that EC production subsidies nullified or impaired the value of duty-free tariff bindings for oilseeds, which was reasonably to be expected by the US from the reciprocal exchange of tariff concessions.[145] In *Japan– Film* case the Panel stated that since the Japanese measures in dispute technically existed *before* the US negotiated tariff reduction on film and photographic papers, the US should not have anticipated more market access as a result of the tariff concessions.[146] Now, reasonable expectations can assume no subsequent introduction of a measure against the tariff concessions unless the complainant has positive knowledge to the contrary.[147]

In all cases the measure in question had to be that of the respondent and most cases dealt with positive actions.[148] It is, however, recognised that the frustration of expectation can happen from even an omission, as the *Germany– Sardine* case of Norway against

143 *Id.*, para. 9 ("Even if it is assumed that the maintenance of the Australian subsidy on ammonium sulphate is covered by the terms of Article XVI, it does not seem that the Australian Government's action can be considered as justifying any claim of injury under this article"); Cottier and Schefer interpreted this as an illustration of abuse of rights methodology in the NVNI context, *see* COTTIER & SCHEFER (1997), p. 178.

144 *EC– Oilseeds,* para. 148.

145 *Id.*

146 *Japan – Film,* para. 10.80.

147 *See, e.g.* CHUA (1998), at 30.

148 Von BOGDANDY (1992), at 105.

Germany shows: Germany had promised to enhance the competitive position of a Norwegian product without entering into an international obligation. Later, it did not carry out its promise, which led to a successful NVNI complaint by Norway.[149]

2. *Broader Interpretation (Expansive Approach)*

a. Comparison with Narrow Interpretation

Supporters of a broad interpretation[150] tried firstly to make the case that fears of "wrong cases" may be unfounded, given the constraints imposed on the DSB by the rules and institutions of the world trading system.[151] Second, the supporters specified the fact that a "catch-all type provision" of Article XXIII : 1(b) exists and that the Uruguay Round drafters took care to extend the provision to the WTO and to limit Article XXIII : 1(c)'s application seems to indicate that the provisions were intended to have some force.[152] In addition, they maintained that the cases in which NVNI complaints was found to exist all date prior to 1960 and were decided when the GATT was in its infancy.[153] Third, one commentator suggested that "the purpose of Article XXIII : 1's generous extension was to lock the United States into a multilateral settlement proceeding for nearly all its grievances".[154] Finally, as regards domestic policy choices, Bagwell, Mavroidis and Staiger observed that active use of NVNI complaints leads to enhanced transparency with regard to the domestic policy choices, if members expect a positive prospect

149 *German – Sardine,* para. 13.
150 Benedek (1990), at 290–91; Abels (1996), at 526; Bagwell, Mavroidis and Staiger (2002), at 67; Daul (1995), at 148–50; Hindley (1996), p. 333; Linarelli (2000), at 334–35; Von Bogdandy (1992), at 98–99.
151 Linarelli (2000), at 334–35.
152 Abels (1996), at 505 n. 204.
153 Linarelli (2000), at 266.
154 Abels (1996), at 504.

of the NVNI remedy of DSU 26.1(b) ("mutually satisfactory adjustment") works to secure market access commitments against another member's unilateral infringement.[155]

Most GATT 47 Panels adopt a restrictive attitude, centering on tariff concessions, with some requirements to the NVNI cases. However, four Panel Reports have considered NVNI claims based on general obligations rather than specific tariff concessions and found that GATT Article XXIII: 1(b) is not limited to tariff benefits.[156] For example, The *EC – Citrus* Panel held that Article XXIII: 1(b) protected any benefit under the GATT, not merely those arising from tariff concessions under Article II.[157] The Panel then stated that benefits accruing under the GATT included benefits attaching to Article I: 1 which applied to bound and unbound tariff items alike.[158] The causation between measures in question and its nullification or impairment of benefits under the GATT system is equally required like the narrow interpretation.

b. Adverse Effect

In the above exceptional cases, the connection with tariff concession is not required for proceeding with NVNI complaints. Alternatively, an *adverse effect* of an alleged measure on the attainment

155 BAGWELL, MAVROIDIS AND STAIGER (2002), at 67.

156 GATT Panel Report, *EC – Canned Fruit* (not adopted); GATT, *Japan – Semiconductors*; and GATT, *US – Sugar Waiver*; *Cf.* In *Japan – Nullification and Impairment of Benefits and Impediment to the Attainment of GATT Objectives* (L/5479) case, the EC, without establishing any connection to tariff concessions, simply argued that persistent trade imbalances between the EC and Japan constituted both nullification and impairment of benefits.

157 GATT Panel Report, *EC – Citrus,* para. 4.37; This case was also related to the issue of institutional balance between the political organ and the judicial organ of GATT, regarding the overall consistency of a regional agreement with Article XXIV of GATT, *see* FRIEDER ROESSLER, 'The Institutional Balance between the Judicial and the Political Organs of the WTO,' in BRONCKERS & QUICK (EDS) (2000), p. 327.

158 *EC – Citrus,* paras. 4.36–4.37

of the GATT objective is sufficient.[159] The *EC – Citrus* Panel stated the "adverse effect" in this way:

> The Panel, considering that [...] reached the conclusion that in this particular situation the balance of rights and obligations underlying Articles I and XXIV of the General Agreement had been upset to the disadvantage of the contracting parties not parties to these agreements and that the United States [the complainant] was therefore entitled to offsetting or compensatory adjustment to the extent that the grant of the preferences had caused *substantial adverse effects* to its actual trade or its trade opportunities.[160] [emphasis added]

In some cases this concept has accompanied the concept of reasonable expectation[161] and, in the case where a tariff binding is not in question, this concept has its own importance.[162] Because a legitimate expectation would be overextended if the expectation were applied to the improvement of trade opportunities regardless of a tariff binding,[163] the requirement of adverse effect in the cases absent from the tariff binding would be effective to limit the NVNI claim.

3. Two Variables Differentiating the Approaches

The difference between the restrictive and expansive attitude starts with whether tariff concessions are required for NVNI complaints. Suppose the requirement of a tariff concession is abolished, the applicable scope of NVNI complaints could be extended over whole provisions of the GATT[164] as long as the provisions have beneficial

159 *See, e.g. Japan – Semi-conductors,* para. 131; *Cf. EC – Oilseeds I,* para. 148 ("The main value of a tariff concession is that it provides an assurance of better market access through improved price competition").

160 *Id.,* para. 4.37.

161 *EC – Canned Fruit,* para. 76; *US – Sugar Waiver,* para. 4.2; *See also* VON BOGDANDY (1992), at 103.

162 *See, e.g. Japan – Semi-conductors,* paras. 92 & 93.

163 VON BOGDANDY (1992), at 103.

164 *See, e.g.* CHUA (1998), at 40.

character for any contracting party within the GATT system. Consequently, this type of case does not call for the binding to tariff concession[165] or might not demand a specific connection with reasonable expectation as the basis of the NVNI complaint shown in *EC – Citrus* case. On the contrary, if the tariff concessions become to be an essential constituent for NVNI complaints, a legitimate expectation of market access arises only from the tariff concessions.[166] In conclusion, general differences from the restrictive and expansive approach lie in the different *interpretive considerations* between *tariff concessions* as a benefit of Article XXIII: 1 of GATT and *legitimate expectation* as another benefit of the Article XXIII: 1.

The results of the above investigation on three requirement for NVNI complaints clarify that the *jurisprudential root* of NVNI complaints generally concern the *sources* of obligations in WTO law centering around the interpretations of "any benefit" and "any objective" of Article XXIII: 1. We thus examine the *sources* of legal obligations generally and introduce *liability* as a *conceptual constituent* of a source which procedurally triggers the NVNI complaints. Moreover, the examination invokes a more refined interpretation to *clarify the liability* and *applicable scopes of the liability* in the NVNI complaints.

165 *Id.*

166 *See, e.g.* ROESSLER (1997), p. 133. Based on this assumption, he criticized the *EC – Citrus* report as a "moral hazard" in the dispute settlement procedures, *see id.*

Table 3: Different Scope of Interpretation of Non-Violation Cases: 1948 ~ 2005

	Narrow Interpretation	Broad Interpretation
Definition of NVNI Concept	"Any measure that does not appear to directly violate the provisions of the GATT, but is nevertheless disadvantageous to the exports of one country, can fall within the category of non-violation complaints." [Cho (1998), at 313]	"Article XXIII: 1(b) prohibits nullification or impairment of WTO obligations by methods that do not expressly violate the WTO Agreement, but that evade basic WTO obligations." [Linarelli (2000), at 265]
Supporting Arguments	1. Resulting in "Wrong Cases" 2. Regulatory chilling-effect 3. Hindrance from making in multilateral trade negotiations	1. Codified treaty provision 2. Potential importance for WTO architecture: Migration to common law jurisprudence 3. Containment of unilateral retaliation
References	HUDEC (1993), AT 7; JACKSON, DAVEY & SYKES (1995), AT 363–64*; Cho (1998), at 321–33; Cottier & Schefer (1997), at 181–82; Petersmann (1994), at 1188; Roessler (1999), at 418	BENEDEK (1990), AT 290–91; Abels (1996), at 526; Bagwell, Mavroidis and Staiger (2002), at 67; Daul (1995), at 148–50; Hindley (1996), at 333; Linarelli (2000), at 334–35; Von Bogdandy (1992), at 98–99
GATT/WTO Panel Reports	1. *Australian Subsidy* (BISD II/188) 2. *German – Sardines* (BISD 1S/53) 3. *EC – Oilseeds* (BISD 37S/86) 4. *EC – Canned Fruit* (L/5778) 5. *EC – Oilseed* II (BISD 39S/91)	1. *EC – Citrus* (L/5776) 2. *Japan – Film* (WT/DS44/R) 3. *Korea–Procurement* (WT/DS163/R) 4. *EC – Asbestos* (WT/DS135/R)
Appellate Body Reports (Broad Approach)	1. *US-Wool Shirts* (WT/DS33/AB/R) The foundation of GATT Article XXIII is the "assurance to Members of the benefits accruing directly or indirectly to them under the GATT 1994" (at 13) 2. *India – Patent I* (WT/DS50/AB/R) The purpose of NVNI complaint is to prevent WTO Members from "using non-tariff barriers or other policy measures to negate the benefits of negotiated tariff concessions." (para. 41) 3. *EC – Asbestos* (WT/DS135/AB/R) A benefit can be nullified by "a measure restricting market access for products posing a health risk" (para. 190)	

* It is not clear whether they are in favour of a narrow interpretation or not. *See also* JACKSON (1997), at 114–15 (John Jackson just pointed out the conceptual ambiguity of "nullification or impairment").

Part Three

Refining the Interpretation of Non-Violation Complaints

Despite the obvious fact that [the] correlations [between multilateral agreements and agreements generalised to all values] are frequently far from complete, the simultaneous increase in the importance of multilateral and value-general agreements have at least caused observers to give passing notice to the relevance of value range in their examinations of the great modern constitutive instruments.

Myres S. McDougal, Harold D. Lasswell &
James C. Miller (1967)

VI. Non-Violation Complaints in International Jurisprudence

A. General Jurisprudential Relevance of Non-Violation to Sources Argument

1. In Public International Law

It is clear from the provision of the DSU and from existing WTO jurisprudence that WTO legal system cannot be construed in "clinical isolation" of the widespread *sources* of public international law.[1] Hence the *sources* argument of public international law is important when interpreting the WTO rules and specifically NVNI complaints. In *Korea – Procurement,* the Panel progressively employed rules and principles of customary international law to fill unintended gaps in the WTO agreements. It stated:

> We take note that Article 3.2 of the DSU requires that we seek within the context of a particular dispute to clarify the existing provisions of the WTO agreements in accordance with customary rules of interpretation of public

1 *See* MARCEAU (1999), at 107–09; *See also* Appellate Body Report, *US – Gasoline (AB)*, at 17. It provides: "The 'general rule of interpretation' set out above has been relied upon by all of the participants and third participants, although not always in relation to the same issue. That general rule of interpretation has attained the status of a rule of customary or general international law. As such, it forms part of the 'customary rules of interpretation of public international law' which the Appellate Body has been directed, by Article 3(2) of the *DSU*, to apply in seeking to clarify the provisions of the *General Agreement* and the other 'covered agreements' of the WTO Agreement. That direction reflects a measure of recognition that the *General Agreement* is not to be read in clinical isolation from public international law." [footnote deleted]; *US – Shrimp (AB)*, para. 158 n. 157.

> international law. However, the relationship of the WTO Agreements to customary international law is broader than this. Customary international law applies generally to the economic relations between the WTO Members. Such international law applies to the extent that the WTO treaty agreements do not "contract out" from it. To put it another way, to the extent there is no conflict or inconsistency, or an expression in a covered WTO agreement that implies differently, we are of the view that the customary rules of international law apply to the WTO treaties and to the process of treaty formation under the WTO. [footnote deleted][2]

WTO legal system comprises various bundles of rules of behavior and principles that derive from different *sources* that basically originate from either "positivism",[3] or "counter-positivism."[4] The doctrine of sources concerns verifiable conditions for validating legal rules in international law.[5] Theoretically, discussion of the substan-

2 WTO Panel Report, *Korea – Procurement*, para. 7.96.

3 For a general overview, Alfred P. Rubin, *Enforcing the Rules of International Law*, 34 Harvard International Law Journal 149 (1993); For an overview in context of WTO context, *see* COTTIER & SCHEFER (1997), pp. 151–52 and 163–66; H. L. A. Hart's descriptions of positivism is one of classic view. He identified five meanings of positivism:
(1) the contention that laws are commands of human beings, (2) the contention that there is no necessary connection between law and morals, or law as it is and ought to be, (3) the contention that the analysis (or study of the meaning) of legal concepts is (a) worth pursuing and (b) to be distinguished from historical inquiries into the causes or origins of laws, from sociological inquiries into the relation of law and other social phenomena, and from the criticism or appraisal of law whether in terms of morals, social aims, "functions," or otherwise, (4) the contention that a legal system is a "closed logical system" in which correct legal decisions can be deduced by logical means from predetermined legal rules without reference to social aims, policies, moral standards, and (5) the contention that moral judgments cannot be established or defended, as statements of facts can, by rational argument, evidence, or proof. *See* HART (1958), at 601–02 n. 25 (citations omitted); *But see* KOSKENNIEMI (1989), at 106–30 (surveying other definitions of "positivism" and suggesting that its "deep structure" is not altogether different from what is sometimes assumed to be its polar opposite, natural law).

4 KOSKENNIEMI, *id.* (suggesting that positivism's "deep structure" is not altogether different from what is sometimes assumed to be its polar opposite, natural law).

5 *See generally* HENKIN ET AL. (1993), at 35–6; For a various opinions on defining *sources*, *see* JOHN KING GAMBLE, JR. 'The Treaty/Custom Dichotomy,' in

tive bases of the sources in international system tends to identify two broad types of source: either *consents* of states or *justice* of natural law.[6] As a jurisprudential matter, the two broad sources of obligation (i.e. consents or justice) to abide by international law is a matter of debate. Perhaps the most popular theory is that states become bound to the international legal system because of a social contract, actual or tacit *consent*.[7] Yet the justice-based theories principally maintain either (1) that natural law imposes a duty on states to abide by it, especially when it is legitimate and just;[8] or (2) that principles of good faith bind those who benefit from the legal system to respect its rules;[9] or (3) that utilitarian considerations based on the value of the rule or of the system to individuals obligate them to abide by the law.[10]

Although the traditional international system has mainly organized on the positive and inductive *consent* of individual state, the significance of the *justice* factors have been considerably increased, in the sense that the international system is supported not only by individual state's interests, but also by his collective interests in preserving and promoting the system as a whole.[11] Furthermore,

---

INTERNATIONAL LAW: CLASSIC AND CONTEMPORARY READINGS 77–8 (CHARLOTTE KU & PAUL F. DIEHL EDS, 1998) (understanding the sources as "recognised manifestation" of international law).

6 Actually, because the customs as a source of international law consists of (1) state practice ("material element") and (2) its acceptance as law ("subjective element"), they are belonging to the "consents" base.

7 *See, e.g.* JAMES LESLIE BRIERLY, THE BASIS OF OBLIGATION IN INTERNATIONAL LAW 1–67 (HERSCH LAUTERPACHT & C.H.M. WALDOCK EDS, 1958) (claiming that the basis of individuals' obligation to abide by domestic law is the same as states' obligation to abide by international law, at 56–65.

8 *See, e.g.* THOMAS M. FRANCK & STEVEN W. HAWKINS, *Justice in the International System*, 10 Michigan Journal of International Law 127, 129 (1989).

9 *See, e.g.* STEVEN J. BURTON, *Review Essay: Law, Obligation, and a Good Faith Claim of Justice*, 73 California Law Review 1956, 1964 (1985).

10 *See, e.g.* KENT GREENAWALT, CONFLICTS OF LAW AND MORALITY 94–111 (1989). *See also* Schachter (1971), at 9–10 (identifying 13 theories put forward as potential bases of obligation in international law).

11 *See* JONATHAN I. CHARNEY, *Universal International Law*, 87 AJIL 529, 532 (1993); It is quite likely for an effective decentralised international system to impose

the two bases of sources can be narrowed into one framework. We can ascertain the unified tendency, for example, by a reference to Article 38(1) of the Statute of the International Court of Justice ("ICJ").[12] This Article addresses the "general principles of law". These "general principles" merit more in-depth review for determining the importance of "legitimate expectation" in reasoning NVNI complaints. Although some categories of general principles have been suggested,[13] the most relevant for NVNI complaints are: general principles of municipal law; general principles of international law; and principles of legal systems generally.

In regard to legal reasoning on the NVNI complaints, a more analytically relevant tool of the above three classes of general principles must be whether or not they are codified. While the codified bases are usually seen as relatively precise formulation, the unwrit-

---

sanctions on violators of the law through individual state and collective acts of disapproval and penalties. For a more explanation, *see* HENKIN (1979), at 49–68; *See also* ELISABETH ZOLLER, PEACETIME UNILATERAL REMEDIES: AN ANALYSIS OF COUNTERMEASURES 4–44 (1984).

12 "The Court, whose function is to decide in accordance with international law such disputes as are submitted to it, shall apply:
a. international conventions, whether general or particular, establishing rules expressly recognised by the contesting states; b. international custom as evidence of a general practice accepted as law; c. the general principles of law recognised by civilised nations; d. subject to the provisions of Article 59, judicial decisions and the teachings of the most highly qualified publicists of the various nations, as subsidiary means for the determination of rules of law."; Article 59 of the Statute, referred to in Article 38(1)(d), states: "The decision of the Court has no binding force except between the parties and in respect of that particular case."

13 HENKIN ET AL. (1993), at 104–19: He distinguishes five categories of general principles: (1) general principles of municipal law "recognised by civilised society"; (2) principles "derived from the specific nature of the international community"; (3) principles "intrinsic to the idea of law and basic to all legal systems"; (4) principles "valid through all kinds of societies in relationships of hierarchy and co-ordination"; (5) principles of justice founded on "the very nature of man as a rational and social being." And "... these are analytically distinct, it is not unusual for a particular general principle to fall into more than one of the categories".

ten ones are seen as less precise requiring some references from outside in their applications. These unwritten grounds are seen as allowing or prompting a more purposive approach, so affording flexibility in their applications, but also entailing uncertainty. They are thus associated with substantive rationality: decisions made on an individualized basis in accordance with an instrument for achieving the overall goal of the legal system.

With respect to the NVNI complaints, the instrumental function in the general principles of international law (e.g. "equity" or "reasonable expectation") plays a critical role in interpreting the complaints. Both the preamble of GATT and Article 3 of DSU justify applying "general principles" of international law. The background or function for applying the general principles to international trade law, which can critically affect the argument of NVNI complaints, can be shown more clearly by comparison with different legal orders.

2. *In WTO Law*

The fundamental sources of WTO law consist firstly of the texts of the relevant "covered agreements," as a "particular" international convention within the meaning of Article 38(1)(a) of ICJ Statute,[14] and secondly of the rules of the DSU for dispute settlement procedures, as "establishing rules expressly recognised by the contesting states" of the Article of ICJ Statute.[15] The discussion on the further

14 It provides: "The Court, whose function is to decide in accordance with international law such disputes as are submitted to it, shall apply: a. international conventions, whether general or particular, establishing rules expressly recognised by the contesting states; b. international custom as evidence of a general practice accepted as law; c. the general principles of law recognized by civilized nations; d. subject to the provisions of Article 59, judicial decisions and the teachings of the most highly qualified publicists of the various nations, as subsidiary means for the determination of rules of law."

15 *See* McGovern (1995), §1.121; Palmeter & Mavroidis (1998), at 399; Trachtman (1999), at 342.

sources is controversial. While one group of scholars[16] favours including the rest substances of Article 38(1) of ICJ Statute, others disagree with such an expanded approach on sources of WTO law.[17]

The first approach is preferable for the following reasons. First, because dispute resolution process is necessarily involved in law-making process,[18] Article 3.2 of DSU stating that recommendations and rulings of the DSB cannot add to or diminish the rights and obligations, should be understood in this context. Second, although the Articles 3.2 and Article 7[19] of DSU refer only to interpretation of relevant provisions of WTO agreements "in accordance with customary rules of interpretation of public international law",[20] the interpretation process for clarifying existing provisions is open for considering other sources. In relation to this point, the ICJ in 1962 recognized the "purpose" of the United Nations as a foundation of financial obligations of Member countries.[21] This 1962 Advisory Opinion of ICJ can be also construed in support of the *estoppel*

16 PALMETER & MAVROIDIS (1998), *id.* They view Article 7 of the DSU as "the WTO substitute, *mutatis mutandis*, for Article 38 of ICJ." From this perspective, they consider, as sources of law, the texts of the WTO Agreements; panel and Appellate Body reports; custom; the teachings of publicists; general principles of law; and other international instruments, *id.*, at 399.

17 *See, e.g.* TRACHTMAN (1999), at 342.

18 *See, e.g.* VAN ALSTINE (1998), at 702.

19 Article 7 specifies that the terms of reference for panels shall be "to examine, in the light of *the relevant provisions in* (... *the covered agreement(s)* cited by the parties to the dispute), the matter referred to the DSB" and to "*address the relevant provisions in any covered agreement or agreements* cited by the parties to the dispute".

20 TRACHTMAN (1999), at 342 n. 41.

21 *See* Advisory Opinion on Certain Expenses of the United Nations, 1962 ICJ.(Report of Judgments, Advisory Opinions and Orders) 151, at 179; In this case, the question on which the Court is requested is whether certain expenditures which were authorized by the General Assembly to cover the costs of the United Nations operations in the Congo and of the operations of United Nations Emergency Force in the Middle East constitute expenses of the United Nations within the meaning of Article 17, paragraph 2, of the Charter of the United Nations.

principle.[22] Third, Article 11 of the DSU authorizes panels and the Appellate Body to make "such other findings as will assist the DSB in making the recommendation or in giving the rulings provided for in the covered agreements." This can be interpreted as allowing the panels and Appellate Body to decide all international legal issues involved in a dispute properly before them.[23] This ostensible conflict must be harmonised through legal theory and concrete interpretive discourse.

Furthermore, as the dispute resolution mechanism of WTO moves from negotiation to adjudication, the decisions of the WTO judicial bodies are increasingly prominent on the international trade landscape and in relations between countries. These decisions are ranked as the fourth source in international law[24] and have not been traditionally considered as binding as treaties or customary law. We are faced with a pattern of extensive judicial law-making, yet an international consensus on the force of this law is lacking. This will be an additional reason for exacerbating the confusions over NVNI complaints.

More exactly, we examine the *sources* of legal obligations in terms of their *procedural relevance (causes of action)*.

22 *See* COTTIER & MUELLER (1995), p. 118.

23 SCHOENBAUM (1998), at 653. Schoenbaum saw this Article giving "implied power" to the panel and Appellate Body. *But cf.* TRACHTMAN, note 41 (claiming that Schoenbaum's explanation is "too general to overcome the more specific language of the DSU limiting panels and the Appellate Body to the 'covered agreements'."

24 U.N. Charter, Statute of the International Court of Justice, Chapter II, Article 38.

B. Procedural Relevance of Non-Violation to Causes of Action

1. *Text in terms of Positive and Normative Dimensions*

The original text of NVNI complaints contained Article XXIII of GATT 47 is now part of GATT 94. This Article headed "Nullification or Impairment" is divided into two sub-sections: Article XXIII : 1 provides for two causes of consultation in three occasions; and Article XXIII : 2 presents three kinds of remedies if the consultation fails to reach a satisfactory settlement. Under the Article XXIII, a member may request consultations with other Members and recommendations, rulings, and an authorisation by Dispute Settlement Body to suspend the application of concessions or other obligations in appropriate circumstances.

Article XXIII : 1 of the GATT states:

> 1. If any contracting party should consider that *any benefit accruing to it directly or indirectly under this Agreement* is being nullified or impaired [first cause of action] or that *the attainment of any objective of the Agreement* is being impeded [second cause of action] as the result of
>
> > the failure of another contracting party to carry out its *obligations* under this Agreement [in GATT practice, this complaints is referred to as "violation complaints"], or
> >
> > the application by another contracting party of *any measure, whether or not it conflicts with the provisions* of this Agreement [referred to as "non-violation complaints"], or
> >
> > the existence of *any other situation* ["situation complaints"],
>
> the contracting party may, with a view to the satisfactory adjustment of the matter, make written representations or proposals to the other contracting party or parties which it considers to be concerned. Any contracting party thus approached shall give sympathetic consideration to the representations or proposals made to it. [emphasis added]

The provision consists of two *causes of action* and three allegations of legal consequence necessary to support each actionable cause.

Thus six points matrix of complaints seem *superficially* possible.[25] Two of these complaints are "violation" complaints requiring that a WTO member violate a provision of an applicable WTO agreement to trigger a violation of Article XXIII: two complaints are "non-violation" complaints, which do not require a separate violation of other WTO agreements. Finally, two complaints are "situation" complaints, which are very broad complaints that WTO members can raise when "any other situation" leads to a circumvention of WTO obligations.[26]

Given a distinction between "legal policy studies" and "explanatory studies of law," which roughly equivalent parallels to the distinction between *normative* and *positive* studies,[27] the two causes of action in the NVNI complaints are actually two sides of the same object: that is, they regulate same object but in different approaches. They only differ by the extent each cause covers the object. Consider the distinction between *positive* and *normative* analysis in regulating

25 *See* PETERSMANN (1991), at 192.

26 The first two sorts of violation complaint are as follows: "If any contracting party should consider that any benefit accruing to it directly or indirectly under this Agreement is being nullified or impaired (*or* that the attainment of any objective of the Agreement is being impeded) [...] as the result of [...] the failure of another contracting party to carry out its obligations under this Agreement." There are two kinds of "non-violation" complaints, both found in Article XXIII : 1(b): "If any contracting party should consider that any benefit accruing to it directly or indirectly under this Agreement is being nullified or impaired (*or* that the attainment of any objective of the Agreement is being impeded) [...] as the result of [...] the application by another contracting party of any measure, whether or not it conflicts with the provisions of this Agreement." Finally, there are two kinds of "situation" complaints, which have their basis in Article XXIII : 1(c). The first one provides: "If any contracting party should consider that any benefit accruing to it directly or indirectly under this Agreement is being nullified or impaired [...] as the result of [...] the existence of any other situation." The second one provides: "If any contracting party should consider [...] that the attainment of any objective of the Agreement is being impeded as the result of [...] the existence of any other situation." *See* GATT, Article XXIII : 1.

27 FRANK I. MICHELMAN, *Norms and Normativity in the Economic Theory of Law*, 62 Minnesota Law Review 1015, 1031–32 (1978).

economic activities.[28] Within the dichotomy, positive or descriptive dimension of the WTO Agreement is involved in giving exact accounts of what happened in the world trade activities and draws a line of which activity is to be protected through the terminology of "benefit." The *descriptive* character of benefits is apparent when enforcing Panel and Appellate Body's recommendations: the level of suspension of concessions authorised by DSB must be proportional to the benefit nullification or impairment suffered by a prevailing party. On the other side of the dichotomy, *normative* prospects of the Agreement lead the way of the trade activities in a prescriptive manner and are interpreted by lens of moral backgrounds or world politics which hide themselves in the word of "objective." Thus, the accumulation of the descriptive "benefit" is nothing less than a *part* of the normative terminology of "objective of Agreement." Not a single GATT panel decision connected with the allegation of objective impediment as a basis for a consultation under Article XXIII appears to reflect such epistemological concerns.[29]

These dual expressions from *positive* and *normative* dimensions are worth attention in analysing the WTO system. Since international rules often unaccompanied by effective enforcement procedures which domestic legal rules retain convincingly, the normative dimension urging greater considerations in legitimate trade policy is much more crucial for interpreting the WTO system. This is even more important when exploring the NVNI complaints. Studies of State practices and the decisions of the DSB, although often strictly positive in content and purpose, have an important role in forming world trade policy and therefore contribute to the normative analysis of the objectives of the WTO. The essence is that the causes of action of NVNI complaints can be reduced into either: nullification or impairment of benefit *(benefits approach)*; *or* impediment of the attainment of any objective of the Agreement *(objectives approach)*. Important is that the objectives approach includes such an approach

28 *See, e.g.* RICHARD. POSNER, *Some Uses and Abuses of Economics in Law,* 46 University of Chicago Law Review 281, 285 (1979).

29 *See* 2 GATT ANALYTICAL INDEX (1995), at 654–55.

concentrating on the benefit. Additionally, why the dispute resolution system of WTO employs such a crossed or confused approaches, and of where is the legitimate place of each approach should be addressed.

2. *Text in terms of Consistent Rule-Making*

The wording of Article XXIII : 1 of the GATT read:

> If any contracting party should consider that any benefit accruing to it directly or indirectly under this Agreement is being nullified or impaired or that the attainment of any objective of the Agreement is being impeded as the result of;
>
> (a) the failure of another contracting party to carry out its obligations under this agreement; or
>
> (b) the application by another contracting party of any measure, whether or not it conflicts with the provisions of this Agreement; or
>
> (c) the existence of any other situation…

While the Article XXIII : 1 (a) describes revolving around *protected objects* (i.e. *obligations under GATT/WTO Agreements*) regardless of contracting parties' measures, Article XXIII : 1 (b)(c) focus on *the effect of the measure* against the GATT/WTO system. Even though they are codified in an unusual way, we can infer the direction of the two provisions; if the drafters had been more careful, the confusion of the structure of Article XXIII : 1 would have been avoided. If the Article XXIII : 1 of GATT had drawn up either following the *objects* of obligations (or rights) of the CONTRACTING PARTIES or following the *effect* against the obligations, the provision may have kept a systematic coherence.

In the context of coherent wording of the provision, it is worth noting the provision concerned in the Havana Charter.[30] In Ar-

30 In 1948, the Havana Sub-committee finalised the formation of a dispute settlement provision for the proposed International Trade Organisation (ITO). *See* Final Act and Related Documents, U.N. Conf. On Trade and Employment, 24

ticle 93(1) and (2) of the Charter, members of the ITO were given the right to call for arbitration of disputes if one believed:

> that any benefit accruing to it directly or indirectly, implicitly or explicitly, under any of the provisions of this Charter other than Article 1, is being nullified or impaired as a result of (a) *breach by a Member of an obligation under this Charter* [...], *or* (b) *the application by a Member of a measure not conflicting with the provisions of this Charter.*[31] [emphasis added]

The subsection (a) is made on the ground of *protected objects (obligations)* of the Charter like Article XXIII:1(a) of GATT. However, the subsection (b) clearly *excludes the measure of conflicting with any provision of the Charter*, leaving such measure to jurisdiction of subsection (a). Unlike the subsection (b) of the Charter, Article XXIII:1(b) of GATT *contains any measure whether or not it conflicts with the provisions of Agreements* leading to an inevitable collision with the subsection (a). This is another factor which caused a confusion with Article XXIII:1.

The next step is to find out an appropriate model of interpretation based on the above jurisprudential aspects.

March 1948, U.N. Doc. ICITO/1/4 (1948). Chapter VIII of the Havana Charter, consisting of Articles 92 through 97, established an ITO dispute settlement mechanism. Significantly, Article 96 created a right to appeal interpretive legal issues to the ICJ. *See* U.N. Doc. E/CONF.2/C.8/1–28 (1948).

31 Article 93 of the Havana Charter.

VII. Theoretical Presumptions of the Refined Interpretation

A. Non-Violation Complaints in Legal Theory

a. In General

The process of interpretation can be divided into two interconnected but intellectually separable meanings, namely "interpretation" and "construction" in Anglo-American parlance. The interpretation refers to determining the meaning of terms of a treaty while the construction seeks establishing the parties' intent in case of a matter not specifically addressed in the text of the treaty.[1] NVNI complaints are a *construction* in the sense that they can be justified without specific treaty languages to remedy measures that nullify or impair benefits of WTO Agreements. Thus, a construction of a NVNI complaint must frame a coherent, logical explanations, because the possible legal consequences that are implicit in the text of Article XXIII : 1(b) are not expressly articulated,[2] and because adjudicators with different backgrounds could interpret the vague text of NVNI provision arbitrary.[3]

1 TRACHTMAN (1999), at 339.

2 *Id.*, at 340 ("Construction occurs where concepts that are intended are implicit in the text though they are not expressly articulated"); *See also* WTO Panel Report, *Japan – Film,* paras. 10.35–10.40.

3 This kind of construction, except the cases of NVNI complaint, has been normally rejected by WTO jurisprudence. In *India-Patent I,* the Appellate Body noted that: "The duty of a treaty interpreter is to examine the words of the treaty to determine the intentions of the parties. This should be done in accordance with the principles of treaty interpretation set out in Article 31 of the *Vienna Convention.* But these principles of interpretation neither require nor condone the imputation into a treaty of words that are not there or the importation into a treaty of concepts that were not intended." [emphasis in original] *See* WTO Appellate Body Report, *India – Patent I (AB),* para. 45.

Two main *implicit* elements of NVNI complaints concern articulating *legitimate expectation* and *market access related to tariff concessions or specific trade commitments*. Since we shall delve into these two elements later, it is enough here just to overview on the interpretive approach of GATT/WTO jurisprudence. For example, on the *legitimate expectation,* while panels consistently use the principle outside of traditional GATT contexts,[4] the Appellate Body has repeatedly rejected such uses.[5] The different approaches around the *implicit* elements may reflect different interpretive practices on an internal normative structure of WTO Agreements. This may be a reason why so various interpretations over the NVNI complaints have been appeared, and why an analytical interpretation must be supplemented by "macroscopic standards"[6] which provide "social legitimacy" with a decision of WTO dispute resolution.[7]

This interpretive paradigm applies equally to NVNI complaints. In our legal reasoning on the causes of action of Article XXIII : 1(b), on the one hand, the *conceptual* part falls into the substantial contents of "benefit" in Article XXIII : 1, which provides a general picture of "causes of action" of disputes and shows their internal structure. On the other, the *normative* part addresses the cause of "objective" with its invoked principle of "legitimate expectation" as a general principle of international law.[8] Those two parts guide

4 *See, e.g.* WTO Panel Report, *India – Patent I,* para. 7.21; According to the AB on *India – Patent I,* there are two kinds of well-settled "legitimate expectations" in GATT/WTO jurisprudence: one is as to competitive relationships between products which used in the context of violations of GATT Articles III and XI; the other usage is related to a WTO Member's market access concessions under the non-violation provision in GATT Article XXIII : 1(b). *See* Appellate Body Report, *India – Patent I (AB),* para. 36.

5 *See, e.g. EC – Computer Equipment (AB),* para. 80

6 *See* DWORKIN (1997), at 45–86.

7 *See* Howse (2000), p. 36.

8 *See* Article 38.1 of ICJ Statute. For instance, "the principle of reciprocity," "the equal treatment between foreigners and nationals," "the most-favoured-nation," and so on. In these principles both a procedural and substantive area in international economic law is included. *See* PIETER VERLOREN VAN THEMAAT, THE CHANGING STRUCTURE OF INTERNATIONAL ECONOMIC LAW 16–24 (1981).

interpreting NVNI complaints and provide a good source of the Members' obligations of WTO.

b. Non-Violation Complaints as Standard in Adjudication

Norms in adjudication theory arise broadly in two ways. First, there is the well-known dichotomy of rules and standards.[9] Although most legal norms share both rule- and standard-oriented elements,[10] the rules are more mechanical legal norms triggered by a few easily identified factual backgrounds. This contrasts with the standards that are more flexible, "context-sensitive" legal norms that apply evaluative judgments.[11] In the WTO, this dichotomy is cited as explanatory tools of treaty-making and dispute settlement respectively, as well as institutional and strategic dimension.[12] Relevance of this

9 Several scholars have observed this fundamental distinction between rules and standards. *See, e.g.* ALEXANDER (1997), at 541; ALEXANDER & KRESS (1997), at 740; SULLIVAN (1992), at 22; For a general discussion on the rules versus standards in law and economics, *see* LOUIS KAPLOW, *Rules Versus Standards: An Economic Analysis*, 42 Duke Law Journal 557 (1992); This rule-standard dichotomy has been a favorite topic of the Critical Legal Studies School of American scholars. *See generally* DUNCAN KENNEDY, *Legal Formality*, 2 The Journal of Legal Studies 351 (1973).

10 *See* ALEXANDER (1997), at 541 ("Rules are often described as 'bright-line' (clear and easy to follow), 'formal' (to be applied without regard to substance of the results but only with regard to the rule's terms) and 'opaque' (to the rules' background justifications"); SULLIVAN (1992), at 58 ("Rules aim to confine the decisionmaker to facts, leaving irreducibly arbitrary and subjective value choices to be worked out elsewhere").

11 *See* ALEXANDER, *id.* ("Standards are norms that have the opposite characteristics. A standard can be applied only by engaging in evaluation. Therefore, to the extent that evaluation is contentious and uncertain, standards will be as well. Standards are thus vague, substantive (as opposed to formal), and transparent (to background values)").

12 TRACHTMAN (1999), at 350–51 ("A law is a 'rule' to the extent that it is specified in advance of the conduct to which it is applied. Thus, a law against littering is a rule to the extent that 'littering' is well-defined [...] On the other hand, a standard is a law that is, in relative terms, farther toward the other end of the spectrum. It establishes general guidance to both the person governed and the person charged with applying the law but does not, in advance, specify in detail the conduct required or proscribed").

dichotomy to causes of action of WTO is that violation complaints have more the character of "the rule," and the NVNI complaints have of "the standard."[13]

c. Non-Violation Complaints and Legal Principles

The second way that legal norms can be classified is into rules and principles.[14] In light of the rule/principle dichotomy, rules and principles are distinguishable by "whether they are posited in a canonical form by a specific institution at a particular time, and by whether they are determinative of the outcomes of whatever transactions come within their terms."[15] Because this classification gives seminal clues for reasoning NVNI complaints, it merits a detailed review. In contemporary legal theory, there are two opposite stands over the status of legal principles to legal rules. One group of scholars led by Ronald Dworkin, claim that legal rules are different from legal principles, and that trying to explain legal reasoning in terms of legal rules is descriptively inaccurate and normatively unappealing.[16] The other tendency is represented by Larry Alexander and Ken Kress who claim, with Dworkin, that legal rules are different from legal principles, but disagree with Dworkin about their relative desirability. They argue that decision according to legal principles, unlike decision according to moral principles or legal rules,

13 TRACHTMAN (1999), at 370: "[the concept of NVNI] is a super-standard in the sense that it authorises substantial construction of norms by dispute resolution." He also picks up other examples of the standard, such as "like products" under Article I or III, the necessity test of Article XX(b) and XX(d), the "primarily related" test of Article XX(g) or the *chapeau* of Article XX of GATT. *See id.*, at 356.

14 Here one caveat must be issued. "The rule-principle dichotomy should be clearly distinguished from the rule-standard dichotomy. This distinction should be observed because the term 'rule' appears in both but means something different in each, and because frequently the term 'principle' is used in place of the term 'standard' in discussions of the rule-standard dichotomy," *see* ALEXANDER & KRESS (1997), at 740.

15 ALEXANDER & KRESS, *id.*

16 DWORKIN (2001), at 22–23.

combines the worst features of both.[17] Both sets of standards (i.e. rules and principles) point to particular decisions about legal obligation in particular circumstances. The crucial distinction, which is mainly drawn by Dworkin and assessed to be in line with an entire jurisprudential tradition[18] between legal principles and legal rules, is that they differ in the character of the direction they give. When we make a particular decision, rules are applicable in "all-or-nothing fashion,"[19] but principles are merely "a reason that argues in one direction."[20] To put it still differently, in contrast to *rules* that lay down specific rights and obligations, *principles* formulate flexible imperatives and they are regularly not eligible for direct application in a specific dispute.[21]

Thus, the rules in this second dichotomy can be characterized by their canonical specificity of forms and substances, thereby they can include both rules and standards of the first dichotomy.[22] Conversely, the main proprieties of principles in the second dichotomy are that they are not normally posited and have no canonical form, thereby they leave legal outcomes in all cases in which they apply *infinitive*, although they can influence legal outcomes "through adding normative weight to one outcome as opposed to another."[23] Those elements of *infinity* and "adding normative weight"[24] will become considerably more important in reasoning the NVNI remedies in context of *legitimate expectation* and the *equity* principle.

17 *See* LARRY ALEXANDER & KEN KRESS (1997), *id.*

18 *Id.,* at 745.

19 DWORKIN (2001), at 24.

20 *Id.,* at 26 ("Principles have a dimension that rules do not – the dimension of weight or importance").

21 HILF (2001), at 112.

22 The first sense of rules is characterized by how mechanical they are in form, or by how factual they are in substance. *See* ALEXANDER & KRESS (1997), at 740.

23 *Id,* at 741; At the GATT level, *see* BENEDEK (1990), at 50 ("Waehrend Rechtssaetze Anweisung geben, liegt die Rolle der Prinzipien in ihrer Funktion als *ratio legis,* [...] als Hintergrund der Anweisung").

24 ALEXANDER & KRESS (1997), at 741 ("Moreover, *principles do not determine legal outcomes in all cases in which they apply, though they can influence legal outcomes through adding normative weight to one outcome as opposed to another*") [emphasis added]. Contrasted with the principles, rules are some-

The Preamble of the WTO Agreement confirms the existence of "basic principles" in the WTO context.[25] They could include not only WTO-intended principles of trade liberalisation (or market access),[26] non-discrimination,[27] transparency,[28] but fundamental legal principles such as due process,[29] good faith,[30] proportionality,[31] or natural justice.[32] Such principles are not often positively referenced in the given rules, and to a large extent may originate from legal

---

times said to have no weight; but the more accurate way of characterizing rules is to say that "their weight is infinite" under some conditions, *see* ALEXANDER & KRESS (1997), *id.*

25 The Preamble provides: "The *Parties* [...] *determined* to preserve the basic principles and to further the objectives underlying this multilateral trading system." *See* THE LEGAL TEXTS, at 6. In addition to these principles, some basic "objectives" of a more substantive nature are also mentioned in the Preamble, including sustainable development and raising the standard of living, *see id.*

26 A textual reference to this principle is given in the Preamble of the WTO Agreement ("liberalisation efforts") as well as in the Preamble of GATT 1994, viewing, *inter alia*, the substantial reduction of tariffs and other barriers to trade, and in Articles II and XXVIII*bis* of GATT 1994*; See also* Preamble and Art 2.2 of the TBT Agreement.

27 *See, e.g.* Article I (MFN) and Article III (National Treatment) of the GATT; *See also Japan – Alcoholic Beverages (AB)*, at 19; *EC – Bananas (AB)*, paras. 160, 161, 232, 241; Appellate Body Report, *Australia – Salmon (AB)*, paras. 159, 161; *Korea-Alcoholic Beverages*, para. 119.

28 *See, e.g.* Article X of GATT, Article 10 of TBT agreement, Article 7 and Annex B of SPS agreement.

29 *US – Shrimp (AB)*, para. 182.

30 *Id.*, para. 158; *See also* PART FOUR – XI – A of this dissertation.

31 The basic idea of proportionality (i. e. the due balancing of competing rights) is reflected in several WTO agreements. Article 2.2 of the TBT Agreement and Article 5.4 of the SPS Agreement are the examples; For judicial decisions, for example, *US – Shrimp (AB)* employed the principle of proportionality in its interpretation and application of the chapeau of GATT 1994 Article XX. *See US – Shrimp (AB),* para. 159; *See also* AXEL DESMEDT, *Proportionality in WTO Law,* 3 JIEL 441, 441–80 (2001).

32 HILF (2001), at 112: Recognitions of this fundamental legal principles are found for example in the following decisions of the Appellate Body: *US – Cotton and Underwear (AB)*, para. 18; *EC – Hormones (AB)*, paras. 133, 154; *EC – Computer Equipment (AB),* paras. 70, 79, 83; *Australia – Salmon (AB)*, paras. 223, 264, 266, 272, 278.

sources "outside" the WTO system, mainly from the *corpus* of public international law or WTO members' domestic legal system.[33]

The significance of "basic principles" regarding NVNI complaints is well presented in *Korea – Procurement*:

> we [the Panel] will review the claim of nullification or impairment raised by the United States [the complainant] within the framework of principles of international law which are generally applicable not only to performance of treaties but also to treaty negotiation. To do otherwise potentially would leave a gap in the applicability of the law generally to WTO disputes and we see no evidence in the language of the WTO Agreements that such a gap was intended. If the non-violation remedy were deemed not to provide a relief for such problems as have arisen in the present case regarding good faith and error in the negotiation of [Government Procurement Agreement] commitments (and one might add, in tariff and services commitments under other WTO agreements), then nothing could be done about them within the framework of the WTO dispute settlement mechanism if general rules of customary international law on good faith and error in treaty negotiations were ruled not to be applicable.[34] [footnote deleted]

B. Theories Underlying the Refined Interpretation

1. *Different Theories of International Law*

Because any account of legal reasoning makes assumptions about the approaches of international law, broadly *positivistic* or *counter-positivistic* approach, a legal reasoning must indicate the approach it uses to credible bases. For most of its history, international law has been virtually synonymous with the natural law.[35] Only by the middle of the twentieth century did it with customs and treaties become hegemonic in the jurisprudence of international law.[36]

33 Hilf (2001), at 113.
34 *Korea – Procurement*, para. 7.101.
35 Hall (2001), at 269.
36 *Id.*, at 270.

a. Positivism

"Positivism" is the theory that legal rules are valid only because they are enacted by an existing political authority.[37] It has a broad array of differing approaches to international legal theory.[38] Legal positivism's most important founders were Jeremy Bentham (1748–1832) and, especially, John Austin (1790–1859). According to the Austinian positivists, international law is not law in the sense that rules governing conduct which are not supported by the central organs cannot usefully be studied as a system of community-based obligations.[39] Furthermore, in Austin's view, international law fails the test of law because it does not emanate from a sovereign to an independent political society.[40] However, the concept that all law flowing from the will of a sovereign state to its human subjects is obviously incompatible with the observable facts of real international life. This discordance called for some revision of Austin's theory.[41] For example, Georg Jellinek (1851–1911) argued that, although states are sovereign persons with their own wills which are subject to no external limitation, states can consent to subject themselves to legal obligations on the international plane by limiting their own sovereignty, to the extent necessary to achieve that re-

37 BLACK'S LAW DICTIONARY (1999), at 906; For the positivism in international law, HENKIN ET AL. (1993), at 53–54.

38 *See generally* HALL (2001); SIMMA & PAULUS (1999), at 302–305.

39 Austin believed that law was the enforced command of a sovereign to a subject, thus he rejected international law as a system not enforced by the sovereign command. *See* JOHN AUSTIN, THE PROVINCE OF JURISPRUDENCE DETERMINED 119–20 (Wilfred E. Rumble ed., 1995) (1832). This Austinian view has been basically shared by later positivistic critics, *see, e.g.*, KELSEN (1966), at 185–86; *See also* HART (1997), at 213–237; BRIERLY (1945), at 18 ("But there has been no fundamental change in the attitude of states towards the law that it explained: normally they find it a useful lubricant for their relations and they use it accordingly, but in the last resort they regard its observance as optional rather than, as the nature of law requires, as compulsory and unconditional").

40 AUSTIN, *id.*, at 171.

41 HALL (2001), at 280–82.

sult.[42] This revision enabled us to deduce that all international norms emanated from state will ("Voluntarism"). Combining positivism and voluntarism found its classic expression in the famous *Lotus* judgment of the Permanent Court of International Justice.[43] From this viewpoint, the role of the lawyer is limited to interpreting the authentic will of the states concerned.[44]

Furthermore, a more sophisticated form of positivism claims that because an international system lacks a "legislature, courts with compulsory jurisdiction, and centrally organised sanctions," international law is foremost among the examples of "simple form of social structure, consisting only of primary rules of obligation," in contrast with a developed legal system.[45] This form strictly separates the law in force, as derived from formal sources that are part of a unified system of law, from extralegal factors such as natural reason, moral principles and political ideologies.[46] This separation, however, does not allow legal positivism to explain why international law is binding. Furthermore, the extension of the separation

42 HALL, *id.,* at 282.

43 "International law governs relations between independent States. The rules of law binding upon States therefore emanate from their own free will as expressed in conventions or by usages generally accepted as expressing principles of law and established in order to regulate the relations between these co-existing independent communities or with a view to the achievement of common aims. Restrictions upon the independence of States cannot therefore be presumed," S. S. "Lotus" (Fr. v. Turk.), 1927 PCIJ (ser. A) No. 10, at 18 (Sept. 7).

44 SIMMA & PAULUS (1999), at 304.

45 HART (1997), at 214. Hart argues that modern municipal legal systems consist of two different kinds of rules: primary rules and secondary rules, and he distinguishes a mature legal system from both its primitive counterpart and from international law by way of the existence of a developed secondary rules; For a dissent against Hart's jurisprudence, *see, e.g.*, LON LUVOIS. FULLER, THE MORALITY OF LAW 133–51 (REVISED ED., 1969); DWORKIN (2001), at 16–45. For a compromising analysis that concedes some of Dworkin's points but generally supports Hart, *see* MACCORMICK (1995), at 229–64.

46 *See* HART (1958), at 71; KELSEN (1966), at 3–5; For a naturalist response, *see* LON LUVOIS. FULLER, *Positivism and Fidelity to Law*, 71 Harvard Law Review 630 (1958).

using voluntarism does not explicate observable realities of international life.[47] This discordance reveals itself in considering the *sources* of international law, especially Article 38(1) of the Statute of the International Court of Justice ("ICJ"): Only two of the three primary sources – treaty and custom – are clearly positive in character. That is, they specify obligations and entitlements pursuant to acts of human will.[48] Although the Article 38 strictly applies only to the work of the ICJ, it is nevertheless generally accepted as setting out the sources of international law at large.[49]

b. Counterarguments to Positivism

There are two types of counterarguments against the positivists from international lawyers. One approach is to prove that international law is very similar to the positive law applicable within states.[50] In line with Hart's categories of "primary rules" and "secondary rules,"[51] this approach analyses the whole system of WTO in the two distinct group of rules.[52] The WTO Agreements are the primary rules and then fitting three subcategories of secondary rules (i.e. "rule of recognition,"

47 HALL (2001), at 284.

48 Article 38(1) provides that, in deciding in accordance with international law such cases as are submitted to it, the Court shall apply treaties, international custom and the general principles of law recognised by civilised nations. The Court may also have regard to "judicial decisions and the teachings of the most highly qualified publicists of the various nations as subsidiary means for the determination of rules of law."

49 *See, e.g.* 1 JENNINGS & WATTS (1996), at 24.

50 *See generally* D'AMATO (1995), at 1–26 (CH 1: "Is International Law Really Law?"); *See also* PALMETER (2000).

51 "[W]hile primary rules are concerned with the actions that individuals must or must not do, secondary rules are all concerned with the primary rules themselves. They specify the ways in which the primary rules may be conclusively ascertained, introduced, eliminated, varied, and the fact of their violation conclusively determined." *See* HART (1997), at 94. A society with only primary rules is assessed by him to face problems because these disparate primary rules do not amount to a legal system in the modern sense of the term.

52 *See, e.g.* PALMETER (2000), at 444.

"rule of adjudication," and "rule of change")[53] into the corresponding rules in the WTO law.[54] This approach concludes that the WTO legal system shares many characteristics of international law generally, but "is by any reasonable measure very far from primitive."[55]

The other approach would start with an empirical insight that "most states observe systemic rules much of the time in their relations with other states".[56] Many empirical works seem largely to have confirmed this arguable but optimistic description.[57] With such

53 Hart describes three kinds of secondary rules: (1) rules of recognition: rules that used for the identification of primary rules of obligation; (2) rules of adjudication: rules that empower certain individuals to make authoritative determinations as to whether a primary rule has been broken; (3) rules of change: rules that effect change of a legal system. *See* HART (1997), at 96–100.

54 According to PALMETER: (1) In the WTO, like other all treaties, the basic 'rule of recognition' is the treaty text itself; "Article I of the WTO Agreement establishes the organization while subsequent Articles define, inter alia, its scope, functions, and structure, as well as accession, acceptance, and entry into force. The WTO's ultimate rules of recognition lie in these provisions. Article II(2) provides the agreements and associated legal instruments included in Annexes 1, 2, and 3 ('Multilateral Trade Agreements') are integral parts of the WTO Agreement and binding on all members." *See* Palmeter (2000), at 467; (2) The WTO's Dispute Settlement Understanding is main source of 'rules of adjudication' to the trading system's primary rules (*id.*, at 468); (3) While the WTO's 'rules of change' are more complex, the two most important are Articles IX and X of the WTO Agreement, which deal with Decision-Making and Amendments, respectively, *see id.*, at 474.

55 *Id.*, at 480.

56 FRANCK (1988), at 705; *See also* HENKIN (1979), at 47 (claiming almost all nations observe almost all principles of international law and almost all of their obligations almost all of the time).

57 For a general review, FRANCK (1988), at 705 (assessing most states observe systemic rules much of the time in their relations with other states); Koh (1997); For particularly in the fields of international trade, HUDEC (1993), at 352–55; CURTIS REITZ, *Enforcement of the General Agreement on Tariffs and Trade*, 17 University of Pennsylvania Journal of International Economic Law 555 (1996); According to Hongju Koh's evaluation, these studies tend to confirm not only that most nations obey international law most of the time, but also that, to a surprising extent, even non-complying nations gradually come back into compliance over time with previously violated international legal norms, KOH (1997), at 2599.

unenforced compliance in international communities, the observation throws a revealing question of why should rules with little effective coercion, nevertheless elicit so much compliance.[58] An answer to the question is possibly that "the normative structure of the international system is perfectly capable of being studied with a view to generating a teleological jurisprudence".[59] In a context of WTO dispute resolution history, Robert Hudec shows that from 1947 to 1992, the losing party in dispute resolution eventually accepted the results of an adverse panel report in approximately 90 per cent of the cases.[60]

2. *New International Law Process as a Counterpositivistic Approach*

This dissertation is influenced by the International Legal Process (ILP) discourse and its divisions of "Classic ILP" (CP) and "New ILP" (NP). The ILP emphasises the understanding of how international law works.[61] They can be developed into a far more com-

58 FRANCK (1988), at 707.

59 *Id.*, at 706.

60 HUDEC (1993), at 278.

61 ILP began its existence with the book, CHAYES ET AL. (1968); For a general survey on ILP, *see* KOH (1991); O'CONNELL (1999). Actually, there are two versions of the ILP. One is "Classic ILP" focusing on understanding how international law works, and the other is "New ILP," retaining the contents of the "Classic ILP," which also suggests that the method should have certain normative values, values different from or in addition to those of positivism and inspired by the insights of other contemporary methodologies, like the critical legal studies movement, feminism, critical race theory. For the New ILP, *see* WILLIAM N. ESKRIDGE, Jr., & GARY PELLER, *The New Public Law Movement: Moderation as a Postmodern Cultural Form*, 89 Michigan Law Review 707 (1991); DANIEL B. RODRIGUEZ, *The Substance of the New Legal Process*, 77 California Law Review 919 (1989); The "New Legal Process" movement builds on the scholarship of the Legal Process school of Henry Hart and Albert Sacks. At the center of the new legal process movement, William Eskridge has contributed an agenda for further legislation. *See* ESKRIDGE & FRICKEY (1994); *See also*, KOH (1991), at 2398–2402; KOH (1997), at 2599.

plete legal methodology for international law.[62] These processes assist in understanding the presumptions underlying NVNI complaints. In the following part, *descriptive/normative, positivism counter-positivism* categories are compared to the CP and the NP.

a. Descriptive and Normative Aspect

First and foremost, ILP departed from formal positivism by not focusing *only* on the content of rules and their analysis although CP is something of an adjunct to positivism. The CP is positivism in that the process participates in the role of positive international law in international politics being analysed.[63] Furthermore NP departs from positivism far more than CP because it incorporates *values* beyond the positive international system and it challenges positivism's doctrine of sources in achieving those values.[64] More important, NP advocates that, in achieving international community's normative values, international institutions should have the authority to make decisions in support of those values.[65] Specifically, the

62 KOH (1997), *id.*

63 *See* O'CONNELL (1999), at 335 (1999) ("[I]t was not a theory of law such as positivism, Marxism, or natural law but, rather, *a method for understanding*, using and improving upon positivism") [emphasis added].

64 *Id.*, at 334; According to Jurgen Habermas, "values" are differentiated from "norms" along four dimensions. First, norms obligate, whereas values attract; the fulfillment of a norm consists in its non-violation, whereas the fulfillment of a value consists in the successful pursuit of it by purposive action. Second, that which is proposed as a norm either obligates (is valid as a norm) or it does not (is not valid as a norm), whereas values fix relations or orderings of preference among various, perhaps alternative or competing, states or outcomes. Third, norms are unconditionally binding on everyone, whereas values are relative to culture and belief. Fourth, norms within a system of norms cannot point in conflicting directions, whereas values can be competitive. *See* JURGEN HABERMAS, 'Reconciliation Through the Public Use of Reason,' in JURGEN HABERMAS, THE INCLUSION OF THE OTHER STUDIES IN POLITICAL THEORY 55 (CIARIN CRONIN & PABLO DEGRIEFF, EDS, CIARIN CRONIN, TRANS., 1998)

65 O'CONNELL (1999), at 336.

NP pays more attention in interpretation of the elements of a *purposive whole system of law*, exploring "both functionally and formally institutional competence and the role of process".[66]

The NP can be criticised *as per* any method, to the effect that the primary source of authority in international law is *positive consensus* in recognising legitimacy of an international norm. Basically positivism has the great advantage of "legitimacy," because international rules are to be legitimised by the states, main players in the international community. However, the legitimacy of NP would presumably rise when states or organisations of states have established institutions for decision-making in legislation or adjudication. More specifically, the act of applying WTO law will necessarily involve interpretation, entailing possible judicial actions of law-making. Moreover, ILP can justify the outcome of ever more decisions in WTO law today – decisions wanted by international society, especially when they are called for under consideration of human rights, the environment or labour standards. ILP has the great advantage of being open to resolve global issues of complexity in an efficient and principled way. ILP also avoids allegedly central weakness of positivism, i.e. indeterminacy,[67] and considering the dynamic developments of international legal system, the legitimacy of ILP's approach is all the more strong.

66 ESKRIDGE & FRICKEY (1994), at cxxvi: Mary O'Connell compared ILP with the other methods like this ("Comparing ILP with positivism reveals that ILP builds on positivism and so has much in common with it. It also shares much with the New Haven approach, though ILP can be distinguished in ways similar to the distinctions American legal process scholars drew between themselves and the legal realists. As for the other methodologies, new ILP can surely draw on critical legal studies to understand international law's pathologies, as well as insights from law and economics and feminism to determine what the values of the system should be. Moreover, much of the study of international relations is today consistent with classic ILP's interest in the role of law and institutions in international relations and how institutions, in particular, can be improved"). *See* O'CONNELL (1999), at 349.

67 It is raised by supporters of critical legal studies, especially in finding rules of customary international law. *See generally* HENKIN ET AL. (1993), at 48–50.

In conclusion, strict positivistic approaches have not been intellectually convincing, nor can they be empirically sustained. Both approaches of positivism and counter-positivism appear to be converging on where this dissertation stands. Legal reasoning here will seek to understand the role of *positive international law* in international affairs, but also to explain international law with some *fundamental teleological aspects.*[68] This general approach can address criticism towards the *realist charge* that international law is not really law, because it cannot be enforced,[69] and towards the *rationalistic claim* that nations obey international law only to the extent that it serves national self-interest.[70]

b. India – Patent I Case with ILP Relevance

The theoretical arguments between the Panel and the Appellate Body on *India – Patent I* case appears to reveal the different *CP/positivistic* and *NP/counterpositivistic* approaches to WTO law. The approaches connect and can be compared using two focusing points of original ILP derived from the Hart and Sacks perspective.[71] First, the "allocation of decision-making competence in international affairs" in the ILP context is associated with how much WTO judicial

68 FRANCK (1988), at 706.

69 *See, e.g.* HART (1997), at 216.

70 *See, e.g.* HENKIN (1979), at 49 (claiming "since there is no body to enforce the law, nations will comply with international law only if it is in their interest to do so; they will disregard law or obligation if the advantages of violation outweigh the advantages of observance").

71 The questions were these: "First, the allocation of decision-making competence in international affairs [...] Second, the reasons why a particular regulatory arrangement is adopted for a particular subject-matter area, rather than another mode of control or none at all. Third, the ways in which particular institutions and the system as a whole develop to restrain and organise national and individual behaviour. And finally, the elements of the political, economic and cultural setting that predispose to success or failure in that development." *See* CHAYES ET AL. (1968), at xii.

bodies can intervene in a NVNI case within the WTO. On this, the AB on *India – Patent I* followed the *CP/positivistic* approach, while the Panel favoured the *NP/counterpositivistic* approach recognising an active role for the Panel:

> However, in order to make an objective assessment regarding the consistency of the current Indian mechanism with the TRIPS Agreement, as required under Article 11 of the DSU, we must ask ourselves the following question: can that mechanism achieve the object and purpose of Article 70.8 and thereby protect the legitimate expectations of other WTO Members, by ensuring the preservation of novelty and priority in respect of products which were the subject of mailbox applications?[72] [underlining added]
>
> Whether or not "non-violation" complaints should be available for disputes under the *TRIPS Agreement* is a matter that remains to be determined by the Council for Trade-Related Aspects of Intellectual Property (the "Council for TRIPS") pursuant to Article 64.3 of the *TRIPS Agreement.* It is *not* a matter to be resolved through interpretation by panels or by the Appellate Body.[73] [underlining added]

Second, the approaches "in which particular institutions and the system as a whole develop to restrain and organise national and individual behaviour" in ILP context can be compared with what *sources* of a legal obligation are used to interpret a NVNI complaint. As in the first incidence, here the AB took the *positivistic* argument on the customary rule of interpretation of public international law, contrasted with the Panel's *counterpositivistic* reasoning:

> ... we first deal with a general interpretative issue, namely standards applicable to interpretation of the TRIPS Agreement. In the first instance, Article 3.2 of the DSU directs panels to clarify the provisions of the covered agreements, including the TRIPS Agreement, "in accordance with customary rules of interpretation of public international law." As a number of recent panel reports and Appellate Body reports have pointed out, customary rules of interpretation of public international law are embodied in the text of the 1969 Vienna Convention on the Law of Treaties ("Vienna Convention")... In our view, good faith interpretation requires the protection of legitimate expectations

72 Panel Report, *India – Patent I,* para. 7.34.

73 Appellate Body Report, *India – Patent I (AB),* para. 42.

> derived from the protection of intellectual property rights provided for in the [TRIPS] Agreement.[74] [underlining added]

> The Panel misapplies Article 31 of the *Vienna Convention*. The Panel misunderstands the concept of legitimate expectations in the context of the customary rules of interpretation of public international law. The legitimate expectations of the parties to a treaty are reflected in the language of the treaty itself. The duty of a treaty interpreter is to examine the words of the treaty to determine the intentions of the parties. This should be done in accordance wit h the principles of treaty interpretation set out in Article 31 of the *Vienna Convention*. But these principles of interpretation neither require nor condone the imputation into a treaty of words that are not there or the importation into a treaty of concepts that were not intended.[75] [underlining added]

Although both Reports referred to same provision of Article 31 of the Vienna Convention, and they both recognized the significance of "legitimate expectation" in the TRIPS Agreement, different emphasis on *positivistic* or *counterpositivistic* render *conflicting* conclusions. It is time to consolidate the two approaches.

c. Consolidation of Two Approaches in Context of Non-Violation Complaints

Conventional approaches to NVNI complaints have revealed considerable weakness to address some key *normative* issues pertaining to the complaints. This dissertation will emphasise the *normative* arguments, mainly connecting the conceptual categorisations of "benefits" of GATT Article XXIII: 1 with equity or good faith, to end up with a constructive structure of obligations (i.e. general/uncodified obligations and specific/codified obligations).[76] From these categorisations, a *liability* concept can be shaped for the so-called NVNI complaints. This dissertation will describe the aspects of the *liability* (a conceptual constituent of legal obligation) beyond the familiar *positive* approach by focusing on a *normative* approach using *three interpretive dimensions*.

74 Panel Report, *India – Patent I,* para. 7.18.

75 *India – Patent I (AB),* para. 45.

76 *See* PART FOUR-X-C of this dissertation.

C. Dimensional Interpretation

This dissertation considers an interpretation (or legal reasoning) process, ranging from certain general peculiarities of the WTO legal system, through an overview of its dispute settlement mechanism, finally leding to the area of NVNI complaints. Legal reasoning is a branch of our Reason or Practical Reasoning that is involved in a process of applying rules and of studying the rational structure of the process.[77] Legal reasoning is specifically used here to analyse a host of critically interrelated questions on the role of the DSB and interpretation of the WTO treaties. Because the NVNI complaint has provoked major controversies about its legal nature, this dissertation is intended to set up a model of legal reasoning that will give some necessary and broad perspective to the complaint. In addition, this model may help the legal reasoning of WTO law in general. Therefore, before discussing the specific aspects of the NVNI complaints, it is useful to outline the general dimensions of NVNI reasoning.

1. Dimension of Gathering Legal Data of Non-Violation Complaints

Although there are many significant ways of applying legal reasoning,[78] this dissertation employs "dimensional thinking" coined by Timothy Terrell[79] with some modifications of his original compari-

77 MACCORMICK (1995), at vx.

78 *See, e.g.* POSNER (1990); LARRY ALEXANDER, *The Banality of Legal Reasoning,* 73 Notre Dame Law Review 517 (1998); SCOTT BREWER, *Exemplary Reasoning: Semantics, Pragmatics, and the Rational Force of Legal Argument by Analogy,* 109 Harvard Law Review 923 (1996); RONALD DWORKIN, *"Natural" Law Revisited,* 34 University of Florida Law Review 165 (1982); HUHN (2003); NEIL K. KOMESAR, *In Search of a General Approach to Legal Analysis: A Comparative Institutional Alternative,* 79 Michigan Law Review 1350 (1981); NEIL MACCORMICK, *On Legal Decisions and Their Consequences: From Dewey to Dworkin,* 58 New York University Law Review 239 (1983).

79 TIMOTHY P. TERRELL, *Flatlaw: An Essay on the Dimension of Legal Reasoning and the Development of Fundamental Normative Principles,* 72 California Law

sons and explanations.[80] According to his taxonomy, there are four possibly dimensions of legal reasoning. First dimension is about the identification of bits of legal data and their links to various cases or provisions, or both, which ultimately provides a general picture of the NVNI complaints, metaphorically labelled "linelaw".[81] The basis for the links is some common feature shared by the "straight" legal data of the NVNI – e.g. the historical background, the relevant provisions, the judicial decisions and three requirements for the NVNI complaints. The links to the NVNI complaint reflect further characteristics and their significance within WTO law. At this stage, it makes possible configurations far more complicated than simple continuous "lines" of various parts of NVNI concept, suggesting that each part of the NVNI concept may be fitting tightly to one another under a broader umbrella. Thinking of the NVNI in terms of connections and patterns from the mass of data,

---

Review 288 (1984) [Terrell (1984)]. The origin of the title of his Article and the foundation for the discussion to follow came from the book by Edwin Abbott entitled "Flatland," *see* TERRELL (1984), at 290. Flatland was an imaginary place of only two dimensions where one of the inhabitants – the narrator of the story – struggled to understand the concepts of one and three dimensions. This allegory serves as a vehicle for describing and assessing legal reasoning.

80 Terrell breaks down the dimension of legal reasoning into four parts, here I just proceed with three dimensions like the allegory of Abbott. That means that Terrell's forth dimension of reasoning will not be considered, since a concept of transcendence, his key concept of the fourth dimension, may be basically explained in the third dimension. But, for the fourth dimension, *see id.,* at 328–341.

81 *Id.,* at 293–95. In Abbott's allegory, in Flatland two-dimensional creatures inhabit. The inhabitants' relative social status is established by the number of sides in the individual's figure. The narrator of the tale is a square. Two incidents give the narrating square a unique perspective on his homeland. The first is a dream in which the Square imagines an encounter with the inhabitants of "Lineland," a region of only one dimension. *See* E. ABBOTT, FLATLAND 57–62 (5th ed., 1963); TERRELL (1984), at 291–92. He makes big efforts to explain the concept of "width" to the King of Lineland, but fails because the kingdom is constituted entirely just of "length"; In Richard Posner's terms, this stage can be called "syllogistic reasoning," *see* POSNER (1990), at 38–39.

comes to indicate a "foundation of obligation" of the WTO law to avoid "nullification of benefits" to other members. This invokes discussions of the *sources* of the obligations and their procedural claiming tool of *causes of action* in dispute settlement.

2. *Dimension of Analytic Studies of Non-Violation Complaints*

Second interpretive dimension of NVNI complaints concerns a "linear" pattern established by points of legal data, metaphorically "flatlaw" by Timothy Terrell.[82] For our NVNI complaints it means a reasoning stage to concentrate on where the higher converged "flat" (i.e. "nullification of benefits" as cause of action) is in the sequential lineal pattern.[83] However, this is only a transitory stage in our legal reasoning, because at this stage of reasoning only a limited group of factors related to the positive sources can be identified. Thus this reasoning is about a particular subset of connections among *positive* rules or state practices within the institution of the WTO itself, and in this context main reasoning will be done in the realm of legal positivism.[84] This can be called "institutional support" for a given rule or legal principle.[85]

82 TERRELL, *id.*, at 297.

83 This pattern has a certain coherence to be a pattern, because without such a property we cannot categorise the just isolated lineal data. *See id.*, n. 34 ("[T]he pattern into which the points fall contains the rudiments of a deeper theory of the law. That is, any pattern must show a certain coherence or consistency in order to be a pattern and not a formless jumble, but this coherence or consistency cannot itself *justify* the pattern. We are forced to ask another 'Why?' Why must we have coherence or consistency here? The answer to that question will necessarily be found outside the realm of Linelaw, and indeed outside the realm of Flatlaw").

84 Although positivism contains broad theoretical possibilities, it connotes at a minimum the idea that the term "law" is reserved for "positive" or observable forms of social control. *See generally* HART, *Legal Positivism, in* 4 ENCYCLOPEDIA OF PHILOSOPHY (P. EDWARDS ED., 1967). Another more controversial description of the "skeleton of positivism," from the viewpoints of natural law, appears in DWORKIN (2001), at 17.

85 DWORKIN (2001), at 40–45.

The key to "flatlaw" reasoning is the *recognition of relevance* by an accepted legal source.[86] From this standpoint, the first ("linelaw") and second ("flatlaw") dimension are therefore closely related, since both depend on "institutional support" to connect specific data on NVNI complaints and to extract a more broad "figure," but differing in "analytic sophistication."[87] At this stage, analogy is a main tool to link the "linelaw" and "flatlaw".[88] This moment, we can outline the "figure" of NVNI concept, albeit vaguely, from our legal calculus: a kind of *obligation* being liable to damages from other members. Problem is how could the "feeling" be sophisticated and justified in a more persuasive legal manner? This requires another analytical way of legal reasoning, labeled as "spacelaw" by Timothy Terrell.[89] This is needed to "transcend" two-dimensional reasoning to account for the "phenomenon of change".[90] Because WTO law is not a static system but a dynamic social form, it cannot survive unless its system copes with developing agenda of the international economic area. Hence no two-dimensional sketch of the NVNI concept made solely within the WTO law can ever be "final," no matter how accurate the source. This is also a strong counterargument to the positivistic viewpoint over the complaints. We have covered the two stages in PART ONE and PART TWO.

86 TERRELL (1984), at 297; Richard Posner indicated this stage as "reasoning by analogy," *see* POSNER (1990), at 86–87.

87 TERRELL, *id.*

88 Over the past decade analogical reasoning has received much attention from legal scholars. *See, e.g.* CASS SUNSTEIN, *On Analogical Reasoning*, 106 Harvard Law Review 741, 743–49 (1993) (explaining operation of analogical reasoning within law).

89 TERRELL, *id.*, at 302–3 ("[T]he traveler who has departed Flatlaw will argue to the remaining residents that they see only the shadows of the true legal reality. To this traveler, law has another dimension giving it the depth of solid objects, rather than the flatness of geometric configurations. Thus, the resident of Flatlaw, he argues, is perceiving the law in a distorted, reduced form, either as the two-dimensional shadow of a three-dimensional object").

90 *Id.*, at 300.

3. Dimension of Normative Studies of Non-Violation Complaints

What is then the third perspective that permits us to enter another dimension of legal reasoning? Stated most generally, it is the recognition that international legal rules are only *evidence* of larger social phenomena associated with the other disciplines in the international community. Relevant to discussing NVNI complaints, international community's standards of morality and justice, or equity must be one of the phenomena.[91] From this equity or justice perspective, the "institutional" view of NVNI complaints may well appear as only imperfectly representing NVNI complaints. Under this perspective of equity in yearning for "justice," the NVNI concept could also be viewed as part of a deeper philosophy assessing normative implications of other members' expectations: *legitimate expectation.*

Incorporating *extra-positive values* like justice into legal reasoning can cause disorder in the reasoning process. It involves "not only widely diverse in analytic method but entirely different in focus and purpose".[92] However, the dichotomy between objective/positive analyses of observable state practices and subjective/normative assessments of those events converges at some points. This helps us get to a more exact view of the events.[93] Consolidating these two dimensions is useful in two aspects: (1) the consolidation helps us see NVNI complaints as bits of evidence portraying a more exact reality. More specifically, by reviewing the legal data of NVNI complaints from extra-positive perspective, subsequent to exhausting purely legal analysis, our understanding of WTO dis-

91 Stated most generally, others include: economic efficiency, group behavior, social and political forces, primal or socio-biological urges or necessities. *See id.*, at 304 and the notes of 53–57.

92 TERRELL, *id.*, at 305; Richard Posner used the terms of "practical reasoning" pointing at this stage, *see* POSNER (1990), at 71.

93 *Cf.* "One possible but unfortunate implication of this discussion is that these nonlegal disciplines, affording perspectives which reduce law to evidence of a larger theory, are somehow of a 'higher' order of analysis. Therefore 'institutional' legal analysis is inherently inferior and must worship at the shrines of these non-legal disciplines." TERRELL (1989), at 306.

pute settlement mechanism has more depth;[94] (2) amalgamating the two aspects provides insights for examining the legal data relevant to the NVNI complaints.

The third stage of legal reasoning is needed to make the legal data cohesive. The perspective that reduces the two aspects of NVNI complaints into a larger theory is therefore somehow a "'higher' order of analysis".[95] This reveals that "institutional" legal analysis is inherently inferior and the perspective must consider the extra-positive disciplines of equity. International law is a complex social phenomenon involving far more than the narrow institutional concerns explicitly recognised by the states. More specifically in investigating NVNI complaints, there are legitimate demands outside analytic elements of the "flatlaw." This must satisfy *normative* demands through evaluating the "objectives" of the WTO Agreements. This is the allegorical stage of "spacelaw" by Timothy Terrell,[96] where the question of what will be the *consolidating interpretive principle* for the new prospect and how can we find it. This is required to understand the full and exact reality surrounding NVNI complaints, which necessitates a more refined interpretation.

94 *Id.*, at 306 ("[B]y the same token, we could approach any other discipline through the same progressively expansive forms of reasoning. For example, the first dimension of economic analysis would be the rudimentary connection of bits of economic data in various simple lines of cause and effect; the second dimension would reveal more sophisticated geometric figures reflecting an understanding of more complex economic factors. To arrive at a third dimension the economist would have to view the economic data as part of some larger social whole. Inevitably the economist would have to move beyond economics; at the very least, he or she would have to turn to philosophy to justify his or her myopic dedication to economic data and economic analysis"); *See also* POSNER (1981), at 1–115.

95 TERRELL, *id.*, at 306.

96 *Id.*, at 300–09 ("Transcending Flatlaw"); HUHN (2003), at 316. He matched this stage with "realism," claiming that "Legal realism is a method of legal reasoning that determines what the law is, not by invoking categorical legal principles, but rather by considering the law's probable consequences." *See id.*; According to Richard Posner's terms, the three stages of legal reasoning can be rephrased such as "syllogistic reasoning," "reasoning by analogy" and "practical reasoning." *See* POSNER (1990), at 38–39, 86–87, 71.

VIII. Institutional Presumptions of the Refined Interpretation

A. Non-Violation under Rule-Oriented Dispute Settlement Mechanism

1. *Dispute, Negotiation and Adjudication*

As an institutional question, we must evaluate whether the NVNI complaints under WTO DSM should be adjudicated or mediated. Mediation can allow *political considerations* between members to be considered and interpretation is less important. Adjudication, however, is likely to increase in the number of cases considered by WTO judicial bodies, strengthening the importance of *interpretation* in the NVNI complaints.

Disputes of interests between two or more states, and their settlements are unavoidable in the international community. Dispute settlement is a communally inherent governance mechanism in international trade relations and an effective dispute settlement system can provide predictability and stability in the trade relations.[1] Although most international disputes may either be resolved by "negotiations" given political considerations based on the relative power of the states involved, or by "adjudications" of stricter rules and formalised procedures. There has been a recent gradual evolution from a "power-oriented" approach towards a "rule-oriented"[2] approach in international economic law.[3]

1 *See* WEINCYMER (2002), at 65–70; William J. Davey, *The WTO Dispute Settlement System,* 2000 JIEL 15, 15 (2000).

2 This terminology was coined by John Jackson. *See* John. H. Jackson, *Perspective on the Jurisprudence of International Trade: Cost and Benefits of Legal Procedures in the United States,* 82 Michigan Law Review 1570, 1571–72 (1984); *See also* JACKSON (1997), at 109–112.

3 JACKSON (1997), at 110.

In GATT/WTO history, the preference between "negotiations" or "adjudications" in constructing dispute settlement mechanisms can be found. Historically some countries, particularly the members of the European Union (EU), have preferred a more diplomatic or flexible approach to dispute resolution in the context of the GATT.[4] These countries, highlighting the ambiguity of GATT rules, the sovereign nature of trade disputes, and the complex trade-offs of competing interests that go into formulating any trade rule, have suggested that GATT dispute resolution should be characterised by consultations, negotiations and diplomatic compromises.

On the other hand, other countries, mainly led by the United States, have preferred a more adjudicatory and legalistic approach to GATT dispute resolution. According to this side, the GATT rules will become much clearer and more predictable if GATT dispute resolution is characterised by rule-based decisions rendered through an adjudicatory dispute-resolution process.[5] Moreover, proponents of the more adjudicatory approach also argue that a rule-oriented approach will reduce the potential disputes applying GATT rules and will help stave off protectionist pressures in various countries.[6]

4 *See, e.g.* R. PHAN RAN PHI, *A European View of the GATT,* 14 International Business Lawyer 150 (1986); *See also* MEINHARD HILF, *EC and GATT: A European Proposal for Strengthening the GATT Dispute Settlement Procedures, in* GATT AND CONFLICT MANAGEMENT: A TRANSATLANTIC STRATEGY FOR A STRONGER REGIME 63 (REINHARD RODE ED., 1990).

5 *See* JOHN H. JACKSON, *Governmental Disputes in International Trade Relations: A Proposal in the Context of GATT,* 13 JWT 1 (1979); Hudec (1980); ERNST-ULRICH PETERSMANN, *Strengthening the GATT Dispute Settlement System: On the Use of Arbitration in GATT,* in PETERSMANN & HILF (EDS) (1991), pp. 323–29.

6 Against this, the following observation is worth noting: "In its present form the new 'judicialised' WTO dispute settlement system is substantively and politically unsustainable. Substantively, there is no real consensus among WTO members on many of the complex regulatory issues that the panels and the AB will be asked to rule upon, and in many instances the underlying treaty text contains gaps, ambiguities, and contradictory language. Politically, the imbalance between the ineffective rulemaking procedures and the highly efficient judicial mechanisms will increasingly pressure the panels and the

The Uruguay Round negotiations on dispute resolution has ultimately moved the GATT significantly towards a more adjudicatory, legalistic approach,[7] although the WTO Agreements are not free from ambiguity and the movement to legalism is not complete.[8]

In conclusion, there are principally two models to resolve disputes: one relies on mediation or conciliation to encourage a voluntary agreement between the parties *(mediatory or conciliatory model)*; the other model uses impartial rules with binding decisions by an authority *(adjudicative or legalised model)*. What are the distinctive qualities of each system?

2. Characteristics of the Two Models

The *conciliatory model* of dispute settlement: (1) operates in a more *pragmatic* or *power-based* manner; (2) is flexible in its procedures giving the control over the dispute by the parties; (3) allows a discretionary acceptance of a proposed settlement considering each

---

AB to 'create' law, raising intractable questions of democratic legitimacy." *See* BARFIELD (2001), at 408.

7 JACKSON (1997), at 133–37. John Jackson assessed that if WTO DSU works, it "should considerably enhance the *predictability* and *rule-based nature* of the trading system." [emphasis added] *Id.*, at 133; *See also* William J. Davey, 'The WTO/GATT World Trading System: An Overview,' in 1 HANDBOOK OF WTO/GATT DISPUTE SETTLEMENT (1998), PART ONE, at 75–77. He suggested that as a result of the creation of the WTO and its Dispute Settlement Body, the approach to bilateral trade disputes has changed from a pragmatic model to a legalistic model, installing a more judicial-like system.

8 HUDEC (1993), at 357–66. Robert Hudec more focused on "effectiveness" of international legal institution: "The effectiveness of international legal system is normally measured *by the extent to which they succeed in influencing the behavior of governments.*" [emphasis added] *Id.*, at 358; *See also* Susan M. Hainsworth and Debra P. Steger, *World Trade Organization Dispute Settlement: The First Three Years*, 1 JIEL 199 (1998). They evaluated that the balance between pragmatism and legalism continues under the WTO.

party's political situation.[9] From this perspective, it has been said that the main value of the GATT is that "it provides a process through which trade problems are negotiated and compromised within a general framework of rules."[10] These scholars, although recognising some role of the rules in international trade relations, stress the limitations that the law finds in this context.

The *legalised* (or *adjudicative*) *model* through adjudication is when the contended parties want to proceed with their dispute through a set of legal rules to get a binding decision in conformity with their agreed long-term rights and obligations within the legal rules. It is also a precondition for the effectiveness of many general principles of international law.[11] According to this view, GATT is a model of a legalistic type system of international regulation.[12] In a more compromising stand with some scepticism about the role of law in international trade relations, some commentators note that the international trade system has followed in a more legalised track than do other areas of public international law.[13]

3. Desirable Model

Critics of the adjudicative model of WTO argue that increasing reference to the DSB would poison the atmosphere within the WTO system and it could lead to the collapse of WTO.[14] Negotiated so-

9 *See* Colin Teese, *A View from the Dress Circle in the Theatre of Trade Disputes,* 5 The World Economy 43, 505 (1982); Phillip R. Trimble, *International Trade and the "Rule of Law,"* 83 Michigan Law Review 1016, 1017 (1985).

10 Trimble, *id.*; *See also* Barfield (2001), at 410–11.

11 *See* Ernst-Ulrich Petersmann, 'How to Promote the International Rule of Law? Contributions by the WTO Appellate Review System,' in Cameron & Campbell (eds) (1998), p. 83.

12 Jackson, Davey & Sykes (1995), at 252.

13 *See, e.g.* Daniel K. Tarullo, *Logic, Myth and International Economic Order,* 26 Harvard International Law Journal 533, 533 (1985).

14 *See* Waincymer, at 66 ("Critics of [adjudicative approach] [...] argue that there can be no normative effect of rules without sanctions to support them"); Von

lutions are required not only for dispute resolution but also for reducing the trade distorting barriers. The adjudicative approach is viewed as counterproductive because it poisons the atmosphere in which those negotiations can take place. The criticism seems particularly persuasive when "wrong cases" are brought.[15] Two kinds of wrong cases have been suggested. One is the case where a country has violated the rules of the WTO, but has done so inescapably.[16] The other is one that is initiated in respect of an issue on which the WTO community has either not yet reached a consensus or on which past consensus has broken down.[17] This latter type is closely related to the discussion on NVNI complaints. In most cases of the NVNI complaints, respondents claim that it is not possible for a member, without a clear substantive consensus – normally described by a provision of "covered agreements" of WTO – to bring a case to the Panel.[18]

Proponents in favour of a relatively more legalistic model argue that it would better promote compliance with WTO rules than a mediation model. They place compliance or consistent application with WTO rules as the first priority in order to promote the efficiency of the dispute settlement mechanism in two ways. First, since the legalistic approach would produce more judicial decisions and the decisions tend to be implemented, the compliance

Bogdandy (1992), at 110 ("[...] an overly legalistic approach neglects the fact that the GATT order remains mainly an order of co-ordination").

15 Hudec (1980), at 159–66. Robert Hudec explained that negotiators in the Tokyo Round sought to prevent "wrong cases" from entering an open and strong panel process, or at least from going through the process to judgment, whenever possible. In pursuit of the former goal, they attempted to discourage the filing of potentially troublesome complaints, and limited access to the dispute resolution process by continuing to require a consensus decision by the GATT Council to establish a panel. *Id.*

16 Jackson, Davey & Sykes (1995), at 330.

17 *Id.*, at 331.

18 *See, e.g.*, GATT Document, C/M/101, at 8; GATT Panel Report, *United States Tax Legislation (DISC),* at 98; Therefore they argue the cases have to be considered as political and not appropriate to the GATT procedure, *see* Von Bogdandy (1992), at 105 n. 61.

with WTO rules will improve.[19] Moreover, even if a member initially refuses to comply with a dispute settlement decision, that decision will affect the relative negotiating positions of the two contending members.[20] Second, to the extent that countries know that they will incur a cost if they violate the rules, they will be less likely to do so.[21] The second suggestion for the legalistic model is that it could enhance the predictability of trade conflicts by means of the constant application of international legal principles.[22] Before making a conclusion on this problem, let us examine the present characteristics of WTO's dispute settlement mechanism.

4. *Characteristics of Present WTO System: Mixed Character*

Generally a dispute settlement system significantly promotes making rules effective in any treaty by adding an essential measure of predictability and effectiveness to operating the treaty system in the otherwise relatively weak realm of international norms. The early days of GATT were dominated by a pragmatism-driven diplomatic style of negotiated solutions.[23] In this process, differences and disputes could often be resolved in a mutually advantageous

19 The DSU of WTO provides for surveillance of implementation, and compensation and the suspension of concessions in detail in its Article 21 and 22. Further, to avoid confusion and conflicts, the DSU provides clarification for dealing with 'NVNI' complaints and 'other situation' complaints in Article 26.

20 JACKSON, DAVEY & SYKES (1995), at 333.

21 *Id.,* at 332. William Davey assessed that an adjudicative system would promote compliance with GATT rule in two ways; First, "it would discourage infractions of GATT rules." Second, "to the extent that an adjudicative approach produces more panel decisions, compliance with GATT rules will improve simply because panel decisions tend to be implemented, if not immediately, then over time." *See id.*

22 *See* CHUA (1998a), at 29; COTTIER & SCHEFER (1997), p. 48.

23 *See* HUDEC (1990), at 211–12. As comparing GATT with the EC, he observed that the GATT became in favor of a "pragmatic" approach in order to solve "all the basic legal problems." *See id.,* at 212.

or relative power-oriented manner.[24] However, as the dispute settlement procedure was utilised more frequently[25] and as it gained momentum along with the growing importance of the GATT/WTO system, a more "rule-oriented"[26] approach emerged. One major factor for the shift was the feeling that the rapidly expanding and deepening world economic system needed a stable and reliable legal framework.[27]

Yet, the WTO system still has elements of a power-oriented system in which conflicts are mainly resolved by negotiations and consent: (1) The members still retain the competence to decide to bring a dispute under the DSU or to seek a mutually satisfactory negotiated solution; (2) Even during the formal dispute settlement process, a negotiated settlement between the parties remains possible; (3) Panels are encouraged to consult regularly with the parties and give them adequate opportunity to develop a mutually satisfactory solution;[28] (4) With regard to compliance with recommendations of the DSB, Article 22.2 of the DSU provides for negotiations with a view to developing mutually acceptable compensation if the member concerned fails to comply; (5) Articles 3.3 and 3.4 of the DSU also point in this direction by promoting outcomes that maintain the proper balance between the rights and obligations of members and by aiming for achievement of satisfactory settlements of the matters under dispute.

According to Article 3 of the DSU, the primary purpose of the DSU is to provide "security and predictability to the multilateral trading system" and the mechanism contributes to "preserve the rights and obligations of the member under the covered agreements".[29] More clearly, the DSU considers that a prompt settlement

24 PETERSMANN (1997B), at 66–68.

25 HUDEC (2000), at 17–76.

26 *See* JOHN H. JACKSON, *The Crumbling Institutions of the Liberal Trade System*, 12(2) JWT 93 (1978), 98–101; John H. Jackson, *Governmental Disputes in International Trade Relations: A Proposal in the Context of GATT*, 13 JWT 1, 3–4 (1979).

27 HILF (2001), at 114.

28 Article 11 of the DSU.

29 Article 3.2 of the DSU.

is "essential to the effective functioning of the WTO and the maintenance of a proper balance between the rights and obligations."[30] The objectives of WTO dispute settlement system are to achieve "a satisfactory settlement of the matter"[31] rather than to make final decision on the matter. The emphasis is on securing a positive solution to a dispute preferring "solutions mutually acceptable."[32] These statements suggest that the DSU is principally a mediatory system.

Notwithstanding these mediatory elements, the main function of the DSU seems to be to serve the rule of law. Otherwise the dispute settlement system could not provide "security and predictability to the multilateral trading system" and the mechanism contributes to "preserve the rights and obligations of the member under the covered agreements".[33] The Singapore Ministerial Declaration points in a similar direction and clearly refers to the WTO system as being a "rule-based" system.[34]

The adjudicative character is evident in the DSU in several aspects:[35] (1) In integrating both the GATT and those of the Tokyo Round side agreements into the legal structure of WTO,[36] the DSU improves the legal coherence of the structure; (2) By establishing the DSB and Appellate Body, the DSU intensifies the legal framework of multilateral dispute mechanism with the well organised

30 Article 3.3 of the DSU.

31 *Id.*, para. 4.

32 *Id.*, para. 7.

33 Article 3.2 of the DSU.

34 Singapore Ministerial Declaration, WT/MIN(96)/DEC, adopted on 13 December 1996.
"6. In pursuit of the goal of sustainable growth and development for the common good, we envisage a world where trade flows freely. To this end we renew our commitment to: a fair, equitable and more open rule-based system [...]."

35 *See* PALITHA T. B. KOHONA, *Dispute Resolution under the World Trade Organisation: An Overview*, 28 JWT 23, 25–46 (1994).

36 The WTO Agreements are composed of the Establishing Agreement and four groups of Annexes. It integrates about 30 Uruguay Round Agreements and 200 previous GATT Agreements, mainly based on the legal structure made in 1947.

procedures of the panels and strengthened implementation systems;[37] (3) Through the "negative consensus system" whereby panel report are effectively automatically adopted, the credibility of panel as a third party adjudicator, is much enhanced; (4) By introducing the appellate review system on limited issues of law by the Appellate Body, the uniformity of the legal interpretations by the panels is likely to improve which should consolidate judicialism; (5) The DSU stipulates strict time-scales for a dispute settlement procedure; and (6) the dispute settlement system "serves to preserve the rights and obligations of members, and to clarify the existing provisions of those agreements in accordance with customary rules of interpretation of public international law."[38]

The two models for resolving WTO disputes (mediation or adjudication) do not in most stages, operate in tandem throughout the course of the dispute. The diplomatic means is generally applied, and is more successful prior to, the initiation of formal dispute settlement proceedings. Such means resurfaces during the period between the panel decision and Appellate Body review and after Appellate Body review. During these latter stages however, the effects of the Panel and Appellate Body decisions and the binding nature of such decisions tend to affect the relative bargaining power of the parties. During each of the stages discussed above, the players in WTO dispute settlement can contribute to, or undermine, the efficient and meaningful resolution of disputes.[39]

As a whole, the DSU has a mixed character: At the first phase of conciliation, a rather diplomatic compromise between the members is taken, but if irreconcilable a legal decision of disputing parties' rights and obligations is made by the Panel. Since the decision-making has an objective character, the second stage tends towards an adjudicative character on the basis of a conciliatory

37 Articles 21,22 and 23 of DSU.

38 Article 3.2 of the DSU.

39 James Cameron & Stephen J. Orava, 'GATT/WTO Panels between Recording and Finding Facts: Issues of Due Process, Evidence, Burden of Proof, and Standard of Review,' in Weiss (ed.) (2000), p. 198.

process. The legalistic approach may, in the long run, assist in enhancing the confidence of members in the WTO system, but may not necessarily contribute towards effective dispute resolution in the short term, given the political, economic, and social pressures that invariably have a bearing on international trade. Thus the model of the present DSU appears a "more legalised based on conciliation" [rule-oriented].[40]

B. Rule-Oriented WTO Dispute Settlement Mechanism

1. *Dispute Settlement Mechanism of GATT 47*

Dispute Settlement Mechanism (DSM)[41] under GATT 47[42] developed based upon Article XXII and XXIII and the subsequent prac-

40 PETERSMANN (1997B), at 84–86.

41 DSM is to be used to contain the underlying principles of GATT/WTO's organizational structure and the character of its legal system, as well as on the dispute settlement system itself, *see* THOMAS OPPERMANN & JOSE CHRISTIAN CASCANTE, 'Dispute Settlement in the EC: Lessons for the GATT/WTO Dispute Settlement System?,' in PETERSMANN (ED.) (1997A), p. 469. They assert that when assessing the character of dispute settlement systems, three factors must be taken into account: (1) the organisational structure in which the dispute settlement system has been integrated; (2) the character of the legal system which forms the material basis for dispute settlement; and (3) the structure and enforceability of the dispute settlement system itself. *See id.*

42 According to Robert Hudec, the history of the GATT dispute settlement process can be divided into four parts. In the first period, from 1948 to 1959, the GATT was comprised of fewer than forty countries. Fifty-three complaints were filed in this period, of which twenty proceeded to panels. The 1960s were a period of significant growth in the GATT's membership but of stagnation in the dispute settlement process. Virtually no complaints were filed during this period, which reflects more the inattention paid to the dispute settlement system than it does harmonious trading relationships. The dispute settlement system was largely rebuilt in the 1970s. Thirty-two cases were filed in these years. The 1980s were a decade of contrast. One hundred and

tices. Under GATT Article XXII:1, CONTRACTING PARTIES are to provide adequate opportunities for consultation with respect to any matter arising out of the operation of GATT. Reflecting its nature as a multilateral treaty and its diplomatic roots, GATT required that every action affecting the treaty be consented to by all of the parties. Under the GATT dispute settlement procedures, Contracting Parties who did not receive a satisfactory adjustment of an alleged impairment or nullification could submit complaints to the GATT Council (the executive committee of the membership)[43] which then referred the matter to a panel for decision. However, after receiving a positive decision from the Panel, it became an enforceable decision only after approval by the GATT Council which required unanimity. Therefore, it was possible for the losing party in a dispute to block adoption of a Panel report and in some cases block the very formation of a Panel. From those weak points, despite its crucial role in having handled international trade disputes in goods, GATT revealed a couple of serious systemic shortcomings in dispute settlement procedures.[44]

---

fifteen complaints were filed, yielding forty-seven decisions by panels – more than in the three previous decades combined. The 1990s marked a period of waiting for the conclusion of the Uruguay Round of Multilateral Trade Negotiations. Several possible complainants delayed filing reports while waiting on the results of those negotiations. Dispute settlement panels delayed making decisions, and the Contracting Parties delayed voting on whether to adopt the reports that panels had made. *See* HUDEC (1993), at 11–13; *See also* Nichols (1996a), at 392–99.

43 Under the pre-Uruguay Round procedure, three-member panels would hear the parties, prepare findings of fact and usually reach reasoned conclusions as to whether or not the challenged measure was in violation of the GATT. But panel reports had to be approved by the GATT Council, acting by consensus. Thus, a dissatisfied party could block adoption of a panel report, and sometimes could even block establishment of a panel in the first place, simply by refusing to join the consensus. *See* JACKSON (1969), at 153–162.

44 Numerous complaints and dissatisfactions with the GATT 47 dispute resolution mechanism were raised. The main stumbling block was the consensus approach. Consensus of all Contracting Parties was necessary for the establishment of panels and the adoption of their reports. This impediment was eventually removed for panel establishment, but remained for adoption of

In dispute settlement procedures, two complementary motives prevailed: a preference for flexibility over certainty in interpreting legal commitments; and the settlement of disputes within the organization. Thus in the early years of GATT dispute settlement, adaptability, not legal consistency or certainty, was the goal to be achieved. The dominant aspect of GATT disputes was that of "settlement" of a balanced accommodation of interests[45] rather than of a vindication of rights in a "victory versus defeat" pattern.[46] Additionally, because of the GATT dual nature (i. e. semi-administrative and semi-judicial), both the substantive and dispute settlement provisions of the GATT 47 were found difficult to understand, respect and comply with.[47] This preference for flexibility in settlement to certainty in rule application was reflected in the wide choice offered to GATT contracting parties for settling their disputes.[48]

---

reports. There were also complaints about the time it took to arrive at a panel report and the implementation of reports. More frustrations about the GATT 47 dispute resolution mechanism included: a long and unproductive consultative phase; barriers to the establishment of panels; a long panel process; unsound panel decisions; the blocking of panel reports; and the lack of enforcement of adopted panel reports.

45 *See, e.g.* PESCATORE (1993), at 32 (observing that Panel hearings took "place in a mode of diplomatic exchange, not in the tense atmosphere of court proceedings").

46 *See generally* WAINCYMER (2002), at 67–70.

47 HUDEC (1970), at 665.

48 WEISS (ED.) (2000), at 21. Moreover, the dispute settlement system of GATT was divided into three different regimes of "general" regime of GATT Article XXIII, "special" regime of BISD 14S/18 ("Procedures under Article XXIII"), and "special" regimes provided for in some of the 1979 Tokyo Round Agreements. *See* WEISS (ED.) (2000), at 22 n. 20; PETERSMANN (1997B), at 177–82.

2. *Dispute Settlement Mechanism of WTO*

a. Major Changes under WTO DSU

When the GATT 47 was transformed into the WTO in 1994,[49] one of the most important features was a considerably more effective procedure for adjudicating disputes regulated by Dispute Settlement Understanding.[50] Under the DSU, the WTO DSM received its own governing body, the Dispute Settlement Body. The DSB is authorised to administer the rules and procedures under the Understanding, including establishing panels, adopting panel reports, maintaining surveillance of implementation of the rulings and recommendations, and authorising suspension of concessions. This shift has been receiving enthusiastic support from trade diplomats,

49 Although a sea change was made by this transformation, the continuity of the WTO with the GATT 47 is confirmed in particular by two provisions: one is Article XVI : 1 of WTO Agreement ("[t]he WTO shall be guided by the decisions, procedures and customary practices followed by the Contracting Parties of the GATT 1947"); the other exemplary provision is Article 3.1 of DSU ("[M]embers affirm their adherence to the principles for the management of disputes heretofore applied under Article XXII and XXIII of the GATT 1947"); *See also* the Appellate Body Report on *Japan – Alcoholic Beverages,* at 14 ("Adopted panel reports are an important part of the GATT *acquis.* [...] They create legitimate expectations among WTO Members, and, therefore, should be taken into account where they are relevant to any dispute. However, they are not binding, except with respect to resolving the particular dispute between the parties to that dispute. In short, their character and their legal status have not been changed by the coming into force of the *WTO Agreement*").

50 THE LEGAL TEXTS (1995), at 404–33; Dispute settlement is first mentioned in Article III.3 of the WTO Agreement. Pursuant to Article III : 2 of the WTO Agreement, the DSU is made an integral part of the constitutive instrument of the WTO. The DSU is composed of twenty-seven Articles bearing broadly on the structure of the system, procedure, and implementation of the dispute settlement, and is complemented by four appendices: Appendix 1 defines the scope of the understanding; Appendix 2 lists a number of special rules and procedures for dispute settlement; Appendix 3 mandates some complementary working procedures; and Appendix 4 adds some rules on the functioning of the expert review groups.

scholars and international businesses of more "rule-oriented" dispute resolution and of more effective legal protection of market access.[51] At the political level however, it has encountered quite vigorous opposition from various interest groups concerned about the threat of legal powers and the broad jurisdictional scope of the resolution system.

More specifically, unlike the GATT, the new WTO DSU gave Members automatic access to tribunals and made legal rulings by tribunals automatically binding with stricter time limits.[52] Most importantly, the DSU fundamentally changes the procedures for establishing[53] and adopting panel[54] and Appellate Body decisions.[55]

51 *But cf.* ALAN WM. WOLFF, *Problems with WTO Dispute Settlement,* 2 Chicago Journal of International Law 417 (2001) (assessing that the new dispute resolution system of WTO has increased animosity among major trading Members).

52 The time limits set out under the DSU improve upon and give legal force to those set up under the previous Improvements to the GATT Dispute Settlement Rules and Procedures Decision of 12 April 1989, which was only applied on a trial basis, *see* GATT BISD 36S/91 (1990); In general, the period from the establishment of a panel to the time the DSB considers the panel or appellate report for adoption must not exceed nine months if the panel report is not appealed, or twelve months if the report is appealed, unless the panel or Appellate Body decides to extend the deadline for issuance, *see* Article 20 of DSU.

53 Previously, to establish a panel, the Contracting Parties had to agree by consensus, which meant that establishment could have been blocked by any Contracting Party, *see* Understanding Regarding Notification, Consultation, Dispute Settlement, and Surveillance, GATT BISD 26S/210 (1980), at 212; Now, at the request of the complaining party, a panel is established no later than the next DSB meeting unless the DSB decides by consensus not to establish a panel, *see* Article 6.1 of DSU.

54 Previously, a panel report had to be adopted by consensus, therefore allowing any contracting party to block the adoption of the report, *see* Ministerial Declaration, 38th Session at Ministerial Level, GATT BISD 29S/9 (1983); Now, the DSU provides that the panel report is considered adopted unless either (1) a party to the dispute appeals the finding of the report or (2) the DSB decides by consensus not to adopt the report. *See* DSU Article 16.4.

55 Once the Appellate Body issues its report, the report is adopted by the DSB and unconditionally accepted by the parties to the dispute unless the DSB decides by consensus not to adopt the report, *see* DSU Article 17.14.

The procedures are rendered automatically unless a consensus of members opposes the establishment of the panel and adoption of the decisions.[56] It also introduced the Appellate Body review on legal issues decided at the panel level of settlement.[57] This legal review by the Appellate Body will have some sensitive issues that will require judgments affecting sovereignty and regulatory discretion in a minefield of important topics including NVNI complaints.[58] Finally it made trade sanctions automatically available in cases of noncompliance[59] and separate treatment of NVNI complaints.

b. NVNI Complaints under DSU

With the dramatic shift of WTO DSU to the "rule-oriented" system, an "objective adjudication"[60] for guarding the trade activities is proportionally more important. Hence "adjudicatory fairness," which is characterised by applying a reasoned and neutral elaboration of principles in a given context so as to resolve a dispute,[61] is becoming more imperative over causes of action (i.e. violation and NVNI complaints) of GATT Article XXIII:1.

56 *See, e.g.* PETERSMANN (ED.) (1997A), at 54–69: Bessko (1996), at 291; *Cf. unadopted* panel reports have no legal status in the GATT or WTO system since they have not been endorsed through decisions by the CONTRACTING PARTIES to GATT or WTO Members. *See, e.g.* JACKSON (2000), at 165.

57 Article 17.6 of DSU.

58 *See, e.g.* C. MICHAEL HATHAWAY, *Operation of the Appellate Process and Functions, Including the Appellate Body: Commentary on "the Appellate Body,"* 31 Law and Policy in International Business 697, 697–98 (2000).

59 Article 22.6 of DSU.

60 The "objective adjudication" is well-known notion of Owen Fiss. According to him, "the question is whether *any* judicial interpretation can achieve the measure of objectivity required by the idea of law." *See* FISS (1982), at 744. He believes that legal interpretation is objective to a much greater extent than literary interpretation, primarily because of the institutional hierarchy of the decision-making process and the binding force of interpretive rules.

61 The "adjudicatory fairness" is a notion of Christopher Edley. *See* Christopher EDLEY, JR., *The Governance Crisis, Legal Theory, and Political Ideology*, Duke Law Journal 561, 568 (1991); *See also* HUDEC (2000), PART II ('Concept of Fairness in International Law'); WAINCYMER (2002), at 70–73.

First, to improve the adjudicatory fairness of the DSU, the separation and distinction between a violation and NVNI complaint was made in the WTO DSU. This distinction makes sense under the view that no articulated provisions are actually transgressed in the NVNI complaint. This observation leads to encouraging negotiations, in the cases of NVNI complaint, to come to a mutual settlement rather than forcing the aggrieving party to abide by the rules of the WTO Agreements.[62]

Second, because a NVNI complaint is not involved in breaching express WTO provisions but just in impairing benefits accruing to WTO Agreements, a higher burden of proof is applied to the NVNI complaint.[63] In contrast, for a violation complaint, the complainant only has to provide a brief summary of the legal basis of the complaint that sufficiently presents the issue.[64]

Third, in case of finding a violation of the relevant covered agreement, the panel or Appellate Body recommends that the aggrieving party bring the violating measure into conformity with such agreement.[65] In contrast, where a measure is found to be a NVNI under the relevant covered agreement, the aggrieving party has no obligation to withdraw the measure. In such cases, the panel or Appellate Body only recommends that the aggrieving party make a "mutually satisfactory adjustment".[66] Then, if the losing party does not implement the recommendation to conform within the stipulated period of time determined under Article 21.3, the aggrieved party may seek compensation[67] or be authorised to sus-

62 Article 26.1 of DSU.

63 Article 26.1(a) of DSU.

64 Article 6.2 of DSU.

65 Article 19.1 of DSU. In the violation case, the approach of sanction is clear: the complainant first seeks withdrawal of the offending measure; next seeks compensation "only if the immediate withdrawal of the measure is impracticable…"; finally, and only as a last resort, the complaining Member seeks suspension of concessions, or retaliation. *See* Article 3.7 of DSU.

66 Article 26.1 (b) of DSU.

67 Under Article 21 and 22 of the WTO DSU, if the party does not, within thirty days, state intentions for implementing recommendations of the adopted panel report and set a time period for compliance, the parties must commence

pend concessions.[68] However, this sanctions stage in NVNI case is less clear.[69]

C. Dual Approach in Resolving Non-Violation Complaints

1. *Two Aspects of WTO Rules*

a. Operating and Normative Aspects

Public international law is the aggregate of the legal norms governing international relations.[70] Therefore the legal norms of international law are safely approached by both a normative order ("aggregate of the legal norms") and an operating descriptive order of international communities ("governing international relations").[71] These dual approaches to any international legal norm (i.e. an "operating" dimension of designating international relation and a

---

negotiations for mutually accepted compensation. Compensation is regarded as a temporary substitute measure until compliance in most cases. Only in cases of NVNI complaint is compensation a final solution, *see* Article 26.1(d) of DSU.

68 Article 22.2 of DSU; The WTO DSU is said to have both general and specific weaknesses. On a general level, the DSU still allows delay; those applying the DSU retain a strong aversion toward retaliatory sanctions; and, the make-up of the panels excludes the most qualified individuals. On a more specific level, the DSU fails to remedy weaknesses in the area of NVNI. While the DSU does make it easier to sanction of a violation case, it is still difficult to sanction a Member for a NVNI case. *See* TKACIK (1997), at 170.

69 TKACIK, *id.*, at 186.

70 *See* PROSPER WEIL, *Towards Relative Normativity in International Law?*, 77 AJIL 413, 413 (1983).

71 While the first kind of dimension is about 'empirical facts', the second is about 'values'; the former attempts to depict what 'is', while the latter seeks to justify a vision of what 'ought' to be. *See* PART THREE – VIII – C of this dissertation.

normative dimension of formatting the relation) reflect an interrelation between international politics governing the international relations, and international law organising the politics by way of legal norms.[72] WTO legal system as a part of public international law,[73] must have the same interdependent characteristics in its system.

This observation suggests that the WTO would fulfill better its designated function of controlling international economic interactions by considering the interdependent characteristics. Furthermore, the DSB which is to resolve disputes on WTO rules, should consider the interdependent aspects of the rules to win more support from the members and to legitimize its own decisions. Hence, the dual dimension of dispute resolution is implicitly embedded into NVNI complaints as a specific tool for resolving WTO disputes.

Because the WTO rules law mainly contributes to limiting the behaviours of the members, the dual aspects of international law appear as "obligations" at specific instances. The conceptual aspects of *operating* and *normative* are somewhat converging in the

72 *See, e.g.* HENKIN (1998), p. 18 (depicting that "[L]aw keeps international society running, contributes to order and stability, provides a basis and framework for common enterprise and mutual intercourse").

73 *See, e.g.* JACKSON (1997), at 25; Donald McRae, *The WTO in International Law: Tradition Continued or New Frontier?* 3 JIEL 27 (2000); Donald McRae, *The Contribution of International Trade Law to the Development of International Law,* 260 RECUEIL DES COURS 111 (1996); PAUWELYN (2001), at 538–540; Ernst-Ulrich Petersmann, *Dispute Settlement in International Economic Law: Lessons for Strengthening International Dispute Settlement in Non-Economic Areas,* 2 JIEL 189 (1999). For earlier sources confirming that the GATT was no more than a specialised branch of public international law, *see* SEIDL-HOHENVELDERN (1999), at 3–8; Georg Schwarzenberger, *The Principles and Standards of International Economic Law,* 87 RECUEIL DES COURS 1 (1996). The possible exception is Judith Bello, *The WTO Dispute Settlement Understanding: Less Is More,* 90 AJIL 416, 416–17 (1996) (stating that "WTO rules are simply not 'binding' in the traditional sense").

74 *See generally* SCHACHTER (1971), pp. 9–31. In contemporary theory this problem is treated under *sources* discussion, centered around Article 38 of the Statute of the International Court.

intellectual confusions called "foundation of obligation"[74] of WTO rule. Although for some practical international lawyers this topic matters little and no single theory on the foundation has received general agreement,[75] this basis of obligation is critical. It is vital not only in the theoretical discussion on the binding force of the WTO law but also in concrete controversies such as whether an event is a violation of the law under NVNI complaints.[76] Thus the contents of the WTO obligations could be arranged in two contrasting characteristics: *descriptive* (operating) and *normative* (prescriptive) one.[77] The former explains the WTO in the context of economic transactions happened in the daily international trade and the latter in the context of establishing a set of standards of behaviors or particular values to the transactions.[78] The dichotomy should be useful to analyse the NVNI complaints and relate theoretically to how law-making of international trade can be optimised in combining rules and principles.

b. NVNI as an Operating Concept

The concept of NVNI constitutes an *operating* concept in broadly three ways. *First*, it guards against a governmental measure impeding the basic operating system of WTO by negating tariff concession or other negotiated commitments. It does so by bringing some members' measures to the judicial bodies of WTO, checking acceptability of the measures in terms of whether the measures nullified any benefit accruing to WTO Agreement. In this way, the NVNI concept makes the overall WTO system flexible and dynamic for

75 For the various foundations of obligation, SCHACHTER, *id.*, pp. 9–10.
76 *Id.*, at 11.
77 *See generally* KU & DIEHL (EDS) (1998), at 3–15.
78 The "normative" characteristic is mainly related to regulations of governmental institutions to the transactions. Thus it could be called "regulatory." *See* KU & DIEHL (EDS) (1998), *id.*

judging the nullifications or impairments of accruing benefits under the WTO Agreements. This aspect was described by the Panel in *EC – Oilseeds I*:

> In order to encourage contracting parties to make tariff concessions they must therefore be given a right of redress when a reciprocal concession is impaired by another contracting party as a result of the application of any measure, whether or not it conflicts with the General Agreement.[79]

Second, it indicates where to find applicable WTO law. This is a process to search its organising principles and how they work (i.e. sources of WTO law). Those dynamic aspects of the concept can indicate what is the current trade behaviour and corresponding applicable norms. Hence the NVNI concept guides us on how to fill possible loopholes of WTO law and what might be the substance of future rule-making. The *Film* Panel stated:

> The underlying purpose of Article XXIII ... [is] the safeguarding of the process and the results of negotiating reciprocal tariff concessions under Article II is fundamental to the balance of rights and obligations to which all WTO Members subscribe.[80]

c. NVNI as a Normative Concept

Normative approach seeks ideal values in the world.[81] The NVNI's normative functions in contrast with its operating functions, are seen in a few facets. First, the NVNI concept promotes communica-

79 *EC – Oilseeds,* para. 144.

80 *Japan – Film,* para. 10.35.

81 *See generally* NEIL MACCORMICK, *Institutional Normative Order: A Conception of Law,* 82 Cornell Law Review 1051, 1053 (1997) (stating "[N]ormative order, of course, is ideal in the sense of the favoured or preferred idea, not merely the neutral idea, yet it falls short of any 'best of all possible worlds' perfectionism. Normative order is practical, both in the sense that it guides praxis, guides what we do, and therefore, is also practical in the sense of practicable. It is an order that is envisaged as a practically realisable state of the world, given things as they are and persons as they are here and now"); For an international level, KU & DIEHL (EDS) (1998), at 12–15.

tion among the members by providing some broad evaluative languages in the Article XXIII : 1(b) through which members can make known expectation of their fellows in the trade interactions. Moreover, it indicates whether trade interactions among members are compatible with what is required for a reasonable attitude for promoting the interactions. This point relates to what is the role of general principles in WTO law and more specifically good faith or legitimate expectation in the case of NVNI complaints. The *Korea – Procurement* Panel assessed:

> In our view, the non-violation remedy as it has developed in GATT/WTO jurisprudence should not be viewed in isolation from general principles of customary international law.[82] [...]
>
> If the non-violation remedy were deemed not to provide a relief [...] regarding good faith and error in the negotiation of [Government Procurement Agreement] commitments (and one might add, in tariff and services commitments under other WTO Agreements), then nothing could be done about them within the framework of the WTO dispute settlement mechanism if general rules of customary international law on good faith and error in treaty negotiations were ruled not to be applicable.[83]

Second, the NVNI bridges the WTO legal system to international trade politics. International law interacts with international politics in two ways, sometimes as an object over and through which political power is exercised, and sometimes as a control upon the use and abuse of power.[84] Hence, WTO law has been clearly identified with global policies specifically free trade, which is based on the broader demands of international communities. In this respect, the NVNI concept represents a policy-oriented tendency strongly from the standpoint of "objectives" of WTO Agreements. It shows that law always identifies with legal policy with the broader demands

82 *Korea – Procurement,* para. 7.93.

83 *Id.,* para. 7.101.

84 *See generally* KENNETH W. ABBOTT, *International Relations Theory, International Law, and the Regime Governing Atrocities in Internal Conflicts,* 93 AJIL 361.

of a society in which law is one of the instruments for achieving social goals. The AB of *EC – Asbestos* implied the significance of NVNI complaints in context of different nature of WTO-consistent measures.

> Nor do we see merit in the [appellant] argument that, previously, only "commercial" measures have been the subject of Article XXIII: 1(b) claims, as that does not establish that a claim *cannot* be made under Article XXIII: 1(b) regarding a "non-commercial" measure.[85]
> [...]
> Rather, the European Communities' argument relates to the substance of a claim that has been determined to fall within the scope of application of Article XXIII: 1(b) and, in particular, concerns the issue whether a "benefit" has been "nullified or impaired" by a measure restricting market access for products posing a health risk.[86]

2. *Two Modes for Resolving Non-Violation Complaints*

a. In General

Given the potential broad applicability of NVNI complaints and their impacts on global trade interactions, to effectively resolve the complaints must be an important task facing WTO DSM. Hence an effective dispute settlement mechanism[87] is important for the smooth functioning of the NVNI complaints and generally for the *reinforcement of controlling power* of the WTO law over the present multilateral trading system.[88]

85 *EC – Asbestos (AB),* para. 189.
86 *Id.,* para. 190.
87 According to the words of the ex-Director General of the WTO, Mike Moore, dispute settlement "is the backbone of the multilateral trading system." Mike Moore, *WTO's Unique System of Settling Disputes Nears 200 Cases in 2000,* Press Release (June 5, 2000).
88 *See* WERNER MENG, 'WTO-Recht als Steuerungsmechanismus der Neuen Welthandelsordnung' in DIE NEUE WELTHANDELSORDNUNG DER WTO 19–74 (KLEIN/MENG/RODE, EDS, 1998).

One of the most significant goals of the WTO is to free markets on a global level. To support this cause, many legal tools have been invented to prevent unnecessary intervention by Members and therefore strengthen stability and predictability of WTO system. If WTO Agreements are an important factor in international trade activities, it must facilitate the daily international trade and the relevant politics. Along with these "operating aspects," there are some factors which have played an important role of manipulation of actual legal phenomena in the WTO system. That comes from *normative* aspects of WTO rules underlying in the WTO rules irrespective of the written form.

Those two aspects of WTO law can be recategorised in terms of dispute settlement as settlement for the primacy of Members' interests (*Consent-oriented Settlement*) or as settlement on behalf of common interests of Members (*Justice-oriented Settlement*).[89] The usefulness of such a dichotomy is to seek a satisfactory settling way by opening WTO law to social values surrounding the WTO law.[90] Thus, the method for realising this usefulness is "regressive analysis,"[91] a working backwards from particular legal phenomena or arguments to their underlying oppositional structure, and finally to the point that their conceptual differentiation collapses and competing arguments appropriate each other's content under "legitimacy" umbrella. Robert Howse's assessment on the operation of WTO dispute settlement reveals this point well. As analysing the early results of the disputes settlement, he employs three "perspectives":

89 This dichotomy identifies concreteness and normativity as conflicting requirements of WTO law. For an international law, *see, e.g.,* MARTI KOSKENNIEMI, FROM APOLOGY TO UTOPIA: THE STRUCTURE OF INTERNATIONAL LEGAL ARGUMENT 6 (1989) (noting law must reflect "the concrete wills and interests of individuals," yet the "normative order" binds these individuals against their wishes).

90 *See generally* NICHOLS (1996b) (discussing the World Trade Organization in the context of the conflict between free trade and other societal values).

91 KOSKENNIEMI, *id.,* at xvii.

> One obvious perspectives would be that of practical success, the ability to effectively settle disputes in a timely and cost-efficient fashion. Another perspective would be that of trade liberalisation as a value: to what extent has the jurisprudence generated by the new system produced rulings that unleash the liberalising and integrating potential of WTO legal structures? [...] yet another perspective – that of *legitimacy*. What are the characteristics of international adjudication that tend to allow for the rulings of [these] tribunals to be considered as *legitimate by those whose values or interests are implicated or affected*.[92] [emphasis added]

Although simple in concept, this endeavor proved far more complex in practice. Clearly, many disputes of GATT/WTO have reflected the fact that trade exists in a social context and that completely unrestrained commerce could be inimical to a moral society,[93] and the dispute settlement process sometimes came under special criticism for its failure to accommodate other values.[94] Thus, a reason for distinguishing the two aspects of dispute settlement is to find a theoretical alternative of overcoming "cleavage between the enthusiasts of globalization through law and its critics."[95]

b. Consent-Oriented vs. Justice-Oriented Settlement

When settling a trade dispute in the WTO, we must consider on the one hand, the perspectives of *positivistic* arrangements among Members underlying the present issue and therefore of the legal certainty of WTO law. From this viewpoint, the critical standard of

92 HOWSE (2000), p. 36.

93 The *US – Tuna* case is one manifestation of the difficulty that the GATT had in reconciling free trade and environmental values. *See* GATT Panel Report, *US – Tuna I,* paras. 3.1–3.59; For a discussion of the relationship between trade and social values, *see, e.g.* NICHOLS (1996b), at 672–90; GATT, for example, allowed countries to prohibit the importation of goods made by prison labor. *See* GATT, Article XX (e).

94 *See, e.g.* JACK I. GARVEY, *Trade Law and Quality of Life – Dispute Resolution Under the NAFTA Side Accords on Labor and the Environment*, 89 AJIL 439, 439 (1995).

95 HOWSE (2000), p. 36.

judging the efficiency of WTO dispute settlement may be its "practical success."[96] Such a focus on the positivistic arrangements in dispute settlement will provide the framework for the WTO system to *operate presently*. An approach that emphasises such an operating framework[97] can be categorised as "consent-oriented" settlements.

On the other hand, the WTO dispute settlement seeks the *right* decisions *correctly* allocating the social values among states and hence among their citizens. From this prospective, the settlement also tries to identify and correct improper members' measures. The *rightness* largely depends on how the measures relate to the whole WTO system through *purpose* of WTO and consequently includes *prescriptive values* of members'. The quest of rightness in the dispute settlement can be referred to as "justice-oriented" settlement.

In practice, the above two distinct but related approaches have been employed by GATT/WTO dispute settlement. For example, the main approach during GATT era relied heavily on the *consent-oriented* settlement with the consideration of free trade purpose, setting aside more delicate and value-related matters in negotiating process.[98] This in turn would depend on institutional and technical expertise sharing the *unilateral* purpose of free trade:[99] that is, the GATT provisions have been manipulated to give priority to improve the traditionally assumed purpose of free trade.[100] However, after the inception of WTO, based on expanded trade agenda and

96 HOWSE (2000), p. 36.

97 *See* KU & DIEHL (EDS) (1998), at 6.

98 *See, e.g.* HUDEC (1993), at 12: "Legal ruling were drafted with an elusive diplomatic vagueness."

99 HOWSE (2000), p. 37.

100 One of the most challengeable tasks in International Economic Law is some tension between national order (sovereignty) and international order (economic interdependence). But if we changed the concept or feeling of sovereignty, that is, from absolute sovereignty to more flexible one, most problems can be solved. *See* JACKSON (1997), at 367–95 ('The Great 1994 Sovereignty Debate: United States acceptance and implementation of the Uruguay Round result').

coverage, the WTO dispute settlement has been embroiled into various players and multi-faceted values which are basically deemed to be conflicted.[101]

The ideal solution for each disputed issue and generally for WTO law would be consensus at a point between positive and prescriptive demands.[102] Absent that, legal reasoning techniques must be applied where consensus is not achieved,[103] but always with the understanding that an overall search for justice is necessary.

In summary, the *consent-oriented* approach attempts to consider the generally agreed procedures for the conduct of international trade, and it could provide the *operating outlines* of for real disputes. In contrast, the *justice-oriented* approach suggests directions for international trade relations by identifying the *normative values and goals* to be advanced. Thus, assuming that such dual aspects in resolving disputes are deeply embedded into the WTO DSM is reasonable, and it would apply to interpreting the NVNI complaints.[104]

101 *See* Howse (2000), pp. 38–42.

102 Authoritative interpretation mechanism of Article IV of WTO Agreement is an example. This provision indicates the realization by the drafters that an authoritative interpretation could result in a significant modification of the agreement. The authoritative interpretation provision also signifies a shift of responsibility of interpretation away from the dispute settlement panels and toward the policymaking body. *See generally* Eric J. Pan, *Authoritative Interpretation of Agreements: Developing More Responsive International Administrative Regimes,* 38 Harvard International Law Journal 503 (1997).

103 *Id.*, at 514–17.

104 Other various approaches suggested for explaining on the international relations and dispute settlements have been advanced in different ways such as: "power-oriented" versus "rule-oriented" in Jackson (1997), at 109–11; "rules" versus "standards" in Louis Kaplow, *Rules Versus Standards: An Economic Analysis,* 42 Duke Law Journal 557 (1992). The "rules" spoken of in the rules and standards literature are said to be narrower than the category referenced in John Jackson's dichotomy of "rule- oriented" versus "power-oriented" dispute resolution, *see* Trachtman (1999), at 350–51.

IX. Coherence as Interpretative Guideline of Article XXIII: 1

A. Institutional Necessity for Coherent Interpretation: "Constitutionalisation"

1. Necessity from Institutional Presumption

Harmonising the interpretative guidelines from *consent-oriented* and *justice-oriented* approaches is the additional theoretical subject of this dissertation. The effort of harmonisation is also related to enhance "legitimacy" of WTO dispute settlement.[1] The guidelines to harmonise the two distinct but related approaches, in interpreting specific provisions, can be roughly divided into two types: one is to prevail a general purpose of WTO Agreement (i.e. free trade over other social values); and the other is to consider the social values of members *to some extent.*[2] The former guideline draws more attention to the economic welfare of mankind while the latter

1 Robert Howse distinguishes "formal or positivistic legitimacy" and "social legitimacy," *see* HOWSE (2000), p. 37. For the concept of "social legitimacy," *see* J. H. H. WEILER, *The Transformation of Europe,* 100 Yale Law Journal 2403, 2466–77 (1991).

2 HOWSE (2000), p. 36; For an economical explanation on origins of the Free Trade, *see* DOUGLAS IRWIN, AGAINST THE TIDE: AN INTELLECTUAL HISTORY OF FREE TRADE, PART ONE (1996); For alternative perspectives on free trade and the GATT/WTO system, *see* JOEL P. TRACHTMAN, *The International Economic Law Revolution,* 17 University of Pennsylvania Journal of International Economic Law 33 (1996); Leonard Bierman, Donald R. Fraser & James W. Kolari, *The General Agreement on Tariffs and Trade: World Trade From A Market Perspective,* 17 University of Pennsylvania Journal of International Economic Law 821 (1996).

seeks to balance protecting other values, e.g. the environmental value with preserving the economic welfare. More directly, the presumption of *tariff binding* which many regard the crowning success of GATT/WTO system and the reasonable expectation of market access thereof, has steadily influenced the subordinate interpretative guideline of the DSU. For example, a DSU interpretive guideline of serving "to preserve the rights and obligations of Members under the covered agreements"[3] can be influenced by the general purpose of *market access.*

In reviewing WTO dispute settlement, such interfaces between the two interpretive guidelines impress their own types of settlements on the current disputes. Since those embracing guidelines are only partly expressed and the details of such expression issue into the derivative specialised questions of WTO DSM, coordination between the two types of guidelines having contradictory potentials should be called for. In this context, the following observation of Phillip Nichols deserves attention:

> Unfortunately, the rigidity of [the WTO DSM] may have a darker aspect: it may become so inflexible as to actually hinder the prospects for free trade. Disputes arise when a country's laws or administration of laws interferes with the ability of another member to enjoy the benefits of a trade agreement. Often these laws are protectionist in nature, designed and intended principally to shelter a domestic industry or market from international competition. Some laws, however, are enacted not on the basis of opening or closing markets, but instead as reflective of underlying societal values. These laws may also affect trade, and thus may also become the subject of a dispute. The World Trade Organisation system, as currently envisioned, fails to take into account the fundamental nature of societal values, and creates little or no space in which such laws can exist. This intemperance may diminish the already fragile support for the international trade regime, which in turn may hinder the ability of member countries to support the World Trade Organisation.[4]

The demand for coordination is all the more important given the "rule-oriented" WTO DSM facilitating the development of a coher-

3 Article 3.2 of DSU.
4 Nichols (1996b), at 659–660.

ent system of WTO law.[5] The NVNI complaints stand at the middle of the coordination, which invokes an appropriate standard between *operating* and *normative* aspect of NVNI complaints. This is an institutional presumption under *coherent* interpretation.

2. *Constitutionalisation of WTO DSM (1)*

In international legal system, public international law is said to serve the function that a constitution serves in domestic legal system: it is the fundamental component governing the institutional environment for international organisations and for states. It provides a limited set of rules regarding the formation of law and its interpretation, application and enforcement. Thus, it serves as the background norms for treaties and other less constitutional varieties of customary international law.[6]

With the establishment of the WTO in 1995, members agreed on a shift towards "rule-oriented" structure in their trade disputes with the aim of enhancing stability and predictability in world trade. This trend has accelerated a more "constitutionalised"[7] fabric on the global trade disputes, encouraging the role of independent third party judgments and then integrating various aspects of global economic relations. WTO dispute settlement is then a coordination mechanism for international trade regulation, which facilitates WTO member bargaining and reduces transaction costs for governments to get together to negotiate agreements.[8]

5 *Id.*, at 659.

6 TRACHTMAN (1999), at 349.

7 For an overview of the constitutionalization of the world trading system, *see* JACKSON (1969), at 35 (Part 1 is called "Constitutional Law of GATT"); JACKSON (1998); PETERSMANN (1997B), at 44–65; *See also* Petersmann (1994), at 1158–60; *See* For many approaches to theorize about constitutionalisation in context of dispute settlement, *see* LINARELLI (2000), at 335 n. 278.

8 For a general overview on this point, *see* KENNETH A. SHEPSLE & MARK S. BONCHEK, ANALYZING POLITICS: RATIONALITY, BEHAVIOR, AND INSTITUTIONS 407 (1997).

Although there is some fuzziness around the constutionalization of international trade law,[9] the term "constitutionalisation" has continued to be fashionable with a small but influential subset of international trade lawyers. There might be three subgroups of the term. Some scholars associate it with the establishment of a set of institutions, rules and practices to administer, implement and operate the multilateral trading system.[10] Second usage includes not only institutions, rules and practices, but also rights, including a right to trade, which ultimately could be relied upon by individuals within states.[11] Third group reads constitutionalisation in the WTO law context as "constitution-making by judicial interpretation".[12] According to this approach, the WTO Appellate Body is the driving force behind constitution-building by virtue of its capacity to generate constitutional norms and structures during any dispute resolution.[13]

9 The term "constitutionalisation" varies according to disciplinary perspective, legal orientation, cultural background and analytical objective. For this, *see* CASS (2001), at 40 n. 4.

10 JACKSON (1998), at 36–58.

11 PETERSMANN (1997B), at 53.

12 Cass, *id.*; In European Union Law context, one more category is possible of the consitutionalisation to include a kind of "spirit" without which there can be no durable social contract within the emergent constitutional community, *see id.*

13 CASS (2001), at 42; COTTIER (1998c), at 90–91. Thomas Cottier seems to take a cautious approach on the trend of "constitutionalisation." He argued, based on the third category of constitutionalisation, that factors associated with constitutionalisation, including the adoption by the AB of full *de novo* review of Panel reports, the high rate of appeals, the slowness of any "legislative" response to AB decisions and the lack of facility for the AB to remand cases, will ultimately lead to a "classical" judicial model which in international law and international relations has proved to have limited effect. *Id.*; *See also* COTTIER (2000), at 221. Here he refers to "constitutionalism in a modest sense." That is, "to depict an attitude and a framework capable of reasonably balancing and weighing different, equally legitimate and democratically defined basic values and policy goals of a polity dedicated to promote liberty and welfare in a broad sense". *Id.*

This dissertation focuses on the third aspect of "constitutionalisation," which concentrates on the interpretive roles of WTO judicial bodies, especially that of the Appellate Body. The establishment of the Appellate Body is assessed as a most critical development of the new dispute resolution mechanism.[14] In this context, this caveat to the interpretative role of the Appellate Body is useful:

> First, full *de novo* review [of the Appellate Body] creates concentration of powers. [...] As a result, the concentration of power in the Appellate Body invites political pressure and may jeopardise the independence and authority of the new institution. Second, judicial activism may backfire at the stage of national implementation to the extent that national constituencies politically challenge the authority of a report that is based merely on the absence of negative consensus (DSU Article 17.14). Third, the absence of judicial restraint may create serious resource problems, and the benefits of relatively speedy dispute settlement – the trademark of the WTO – may be eventually lost.[15]

14 *See, e.g.,* Petersmann (1997b), at 186 (assessing that "The strictly legal function and expertise of the appellate body were perceived as a rule-oriented substitute for the political consensus practice"); Waincymer (2002), at 693 (indicating that "The WTO is the first international organization to develop a binding and comprehensive appeal process within its dispute settlement system"); Cottier (1998c), at 87; One of the main features of the constitutionalisation is seen in its rule-based, quasi-obligatory dispute settlement mechanism of WTO, *see* Article 23.1 of DSU. On the other hand, while there is already an abundant and continuously growing amount of specialised literature on GATT/WTO dispute settlement, general treatises on international law and practice have yet to digest that new and vigorous area of dispute from 'dispute settlement within international organisations,' *see* Anthony Aust, Modern Treaty Law and Practice 297–99 (2000).

15 Cottier (1998c), at 90.

B. Theoretical Necessity for Coherent Interpretation

1. Necessity from Theoretical Presumption

Legal reasoning of NVNI complaints involves two types of inquiries: an *analytic* one and a *normative* one.[16] When recognising NVNI complaints as *causes of action* in WTO law, the *analytic* part of reasoning elucidates some *positive* patterns and their connections. It primarily identifies enough conditions for the legal requirements of NVNI provision. This investigation elaborates the criteria of *sources* and *causes of action* discussions in *analytic* manner. Subsidiary concerns analyse various legal concepts such as "provisions," "benefits" and "obligations".[17] This reasoning implicitly distinguishes WTO law from public international law by mainly focusing on "internal point of view".[18] This exploration belongs to "positivism" or "flatlaw" of our metaphor. *Normative portion* of reasoning explores the justice-based elements of the NVNI complaints encompassing broad concerns and perplexing problems of equity. This exploration illuminates the on-going challenge of how international economic

16 Here the word "analytic" indicates that a method of legal reasoning that concentrates on "the logical structure of law, the meanings and uses of its concepts and the terms and the modes of its operation", and "normative" as "legal and moral principles purportedly deriving from a universalised conception of human nature or divine justice rather than from legislative or judicial action". *See* BLACK'S LAW DICTIONARY (1999), at 858 and 1049 ("Natural Law"); These two groups of "analytic" and "normative" reasoning in this dissertation are categorised in terms of "how" we carry out legal reasoning. From "what" is the object of our legal reasoning, the groups can be relabelled as "descriptive" and "normative".

17 *See* Article XXIII : 1(a) of GATT.

18 *See* HART (1997), at 88–89. Hart distinguished the "internal perspective" from an "external perspective," the point of view which sees legal rules not as norms that can be correctly or incorrectly followed but simply as producing regularities of behavior, *Id.* at 89–90. Hart has subsequently acknowledged that this constitutes a third, "hermeneutic" perspective. H. L. A. HART, ESSAYS IN JURISPRUDENCE AND PHILOSOPHY 14 (1983).

community ought to be organised in a multilateral arena. It also raises foundations to base obligations in NVNI complaints. Now the *relationship* between the analytic and the normative is emerging as one of the central and final points in our reasoning.

Legal reasoning is a process of interpretation[19] and the interpretation on the NVNI complaints here includes two different perspectives (i.e. descriptive and normative one) of our international legal *reality*. This statement is concerned with conforming the two perspectives within one interpretive judgment. There needs to be *a mega-interpretative guideline* at conforming two perspectives: *Coherence.*[20] This is a theoretical presumption under *coherent* interpretation. Furthermore, through coherently interpreting the conclusions of *analytic* and *normative* studies, the dissertation pictures NVNI complaints in the light of legal discourse: *Liability.*

2. *Constitutionalisation of WTO DSM (2)*

In terms of general legal theory, "constitutionalisation" may lead to legal entrenchment of some sets of rules over others and the creation of a hierarchy of norms.[21] The norm-hierarchy is also reflecting the artificial dichotomy between *analytic* and *normative* parts of our reasoning on NVNI complaints that are intended to analyse or solve the "indeterminacy of obligations" incorporated in the Article XXIII: 1(b). The analysis, as we will see later, entails some new implications on the nature of NVNI complaints.

19 *See, e.g.* FISS (1982); ROBERT DWORKIN, *Law as Interpretation,* 60 Texa Law Review 527 (1982). For a more limited use of "interpretation," *see* MOORE (1985), at 281 ("... whereas I think there is a part of legal reasoning, but only a part, that can usefully be labelled the activity of 'interpretation'").

20 Thus this is a kind of rational transcendence, *see* TERRELL (1984), 310–16; *See also* JACK M. BALKIN, *Understanding Legal Understanding: The Legal Subject and the Problem of Legal Coherence,* 103 Yale Law Review 105, 112 (1993) ("Judgments of legal coherence result from one particular activity of understanding, an interpretive attitude I call rational reconstruction. This is an attempt to see the substantive reason that emanates from legal materials").

21 KELSEN (1961), at 110.

Now the problem is how can the two parts connect in an *inclusive* manner under the DSU. Interpretation of a particular instance in WTO law will not be possible if the common characteristics of WTO as a legal system are not defined. Put it another way, a key factor for improving *legitimacy* of WTO DSM is for it to deliver clear, rational and predictable results.[22] Therefore, the interpretative process of NVNI complaints should be "coherent," in the sense that the relationship between fundamental values and specific provisions of WTO cannot be viewed in isolation *(external coherence)*, and that each legal terms of Article XXIII: 1(b) should be interpreted in a principled fashion *(internal coherence)*. The coherence demand in interpretation thus can be divided into *internal and external coherence*. This can be further relevant to coherence as an indication of legitimate rules.[23]

C. The Notion of Coherence

The notion of coherence has been addressed by some scholars of legal theory[24] and also discussed in the law of European

22 *See, e.g.* Michael K. Young, *Dispute Resolution in the Uruguay Round: Lawyers Triumph Over Diplomats*, 29 International Lawyer 389, 408 (1995) (noting that people are more likely to accept adverse political decisions if those decisions are made by political institutions they consider legitimate); Steven P. Croley & John H. Jackson, *WTO Dispute Procedures, Standard of Review, and Deference to National Governments*, 90 AJIL 193, 212 (1996) (noting that a reasonable approach by WTO Panels will help the credibility of the dispute settlement system and lessen dangers of unilateral action by governments). Given the practices for dispute settlement panels to routinely follow older decisions, keeping these qualities is all the more important. *But cf.* Bederman (1994), at 1034 (noting that without a clear doctrine, in treaty interpretation, courts have been inconsistent and confusing).

23 *See* Franck (1995), at 30.

24 Robert Alexy, *Juristische Begruendung System und Kohaeranz*, in Rechtsdogmatik und Praktische Vernunft, Symposium zum 80. Geburtstag von Franz Wieacker 95 (Okko Behrends et al., eds, 1990); Dworkin (1997), at 245; MacCormick (1984).

Union[25] and in public international law.[26] Before analysing the concept of coherence, we need to distinguish between coherence and consistency. Consistency in law can be explained by "non-contradiction;"[27] coherence on the other hand refers to "making sense in entirety".[28] Moreover, coherence is a "matter of degree" while consistency is a "static concept".[29]

Exploring the coherence theory in interpreting NVNI complaints is a search for a refined model of interpretation. It facilitates the investigating of *jurisprudential identity* of NVNI concept in stabilising the still evolving WTO DSM. For the stabilisation, we need some holistic evaluative standards on which reviews of various legal rules and principles in WTO DSM are made sense of in entirety. One standard is *coherence, in the sense that a rule should be related in a principled fashion to other rules of the same system.* The coherence conception thus can be divided into *internal and external coherence*, according to how *the principled fashion* relates to the codification of a rule.[30]

25 *See* Tietje (1997), at 212–13.
26 *See* Franck (1995), at 38–41.
27 MacCormick (1984), p. 38 (interpreting it "[A] set of propositions is mutually consistent if each can without contradiction be asserted in conjunction with every other and with their conjunction").
28 *Id.*
29 Tietje (1997), at 212: *See also* MacCormick (1984), p. 38 (exemplifying "A story can be coherent on the whole and as a whole though it contains some internal inconsistencies – and in this case, the sense of the overall coherence of the story may be decisive for us in deciding which among pairs of inconsistent propositions to discard").
30 The following references affect *internal* and *external coherence* theory: (1) the dichotomy of "intrinsic" and "extrinsic" in legal reasoning, *see* MacCormick (1995), at 279–92; On the dichotomy of "analytic jurisprudence" and "sociological jurisprudence" in legal reasoning of international law, *see* Anthony D'Amato (ed.) (1996), at xi ("Analytic Jurisprudence concerns *the internalities of law* – what law is and how we determine what it is, whether it is consistent and by what standards we measure consistency [...]. In contrast, Sociological Jurisprudence [...] deals with [...] *externalities of law* – how law connects to, is informed by, or derives from, social values, policies and norms [...]. Analytic Jurisprudence is general in conception; it applies to any legal system anywhere in the world. In contrast, Social Jurisprudence derives its content from particular legal systems") [emphasis added].

1. Internal Coherence of Text of Article XXIII: 1(b)

As there is a fair appeal for a well-founded constitution of rules, rules must have *internal coherence*, in the sense that the very many rules of a legal system ought to be organised not contradicting each rule with the others. Since rules in a legal system are mainly composed of rights and their corresponding obligations, regardless of their conceptual sub-classification, one of the most effective ways for preventing possible contradictions among international legal rules ought to make the rules, in which the obligations (correspondingly rights) concepts are arranged in a certain predictable or agreed manner. The obligations reflect certain protected objects by the international law concerned, and in WTO law and the concept of *benefit* in Article XXIII: 1 of GATT/WTO imply the objects.

The foregoing idea of *internal coherence* appears to have much persuasive power in the interpretation of the Article XXIII: 1 which consists of three subsections (a)(b)(c). There could be those who unconsciously proceed to analyse Article XXIII under the presumption that the subsections of the Article XXIII: 1 must share a similar character and therefore a would-be interpreter could unravel the crux in the Article XXIII: 1 by legal reasoning. However, we must check whether the terms in the Article XXIII could be used in a consistent way before setting out the interpretation, with a view to avoiding unnecessarily redundant interpretation. For example, in the Article XXIII of GATT, we usually refer to "nullification" or "impairment" in the study of the WTO DSM, but the meaning of "nullification" in this context is very different according to the connotations of the three subsections: when we connect the "nullification" with Article XXIII: 1(a), the meaning of nullification is no more than the infringement of *arranged obligations* which revealed themselves by the forms of written provisions of GATT. However, going into the subsection (b), we might be embarrassed by finding a totally different standard for nullification, judged by a vague and broad concept of "balance of benefits."[31] Thus, main jurispruden-

31 Von Bogdandy (1992), at 97.

tial confusions around NVNI complaints, first and foremost, appear to result from lack of systematic coherence of legal terms in the Article XXIII: 1. This is the reason for a detailed review on "benefit" in respect to the explication of NVNI complaints, under the title of *internal coherence.*

2. *External Coherence of Text of Article XXIII: 1(b)*

Since there are underlying values to set up legal obligations, an exploration of obligations in a legal system are to arrive at *an externally coherent structure,* in the sense that the multitudinous rules of the legal system should be pointless in case of their isolation from the values.[32] From this external coherence, we could confirm an existence of *value-nets* in legal systems which make sets of rules be regarded as their concrete manifestations. The values should present themselves in a form of specific *objective* of the concerned law (e.g. free trade or market access in WTO law), or general principles of international law (e.g. good faith, equity). With a good authority for the values, we could legitimately interpret the rules against unexpected phenomena, as encouraging flexibility of WTO legal system. In this respect, the following observation by Mcdougal, Lasswell & Miller is noteworthy:

> Despite the obvious fact that [the] correlations [between multilateral agreements and agreements generalised to all values] are frequently far from complete, the simultaneous increase in the importance of multilateral and value-general agreements have at least caused observers to give passing notice to the relevance of value range in their examinations of the great modern constitutive instruments.[33]

Based on the above interpretive frameworks of *internal* and *external* coherence, placing NVNI complaints into a proper jurisprudential site is next.

32 *See generally* MacCormick (1995) at 265–74.
33 Mcdougal et al. (1994), at 154–55.

Part Four

Transforming the Non-Violation into Liability

In the WTO, the non-violation clause is used to attain the fairness the system attempted to achieve but could not have under the legal theories prevalent in the first half of this century. As we move into the next century, it is time to re-evaluate the needs of the trading system and act accordingly.

Thomas Cottier & Krista Nadakavukaren Schefer (1997)

X. Internal Coherence as an Analytic Approach

A. Structure of "Benefit" in GATT XXIII : 1

1. *In General: Definitional Exactness and Reciprocity*

In analysing a given system or legal phenomena, a basic problem is to confirm the meaning of legal terms. International law conglomerates concepts[1] which are realised in normative propositions of specific legal terms. The meanings and the underlying context of such terms are central to our legal reasoning processes.[2] In terms of GATT, John Jackson observed the importance of treaty languages in 1969:

> But even if the institution of GATT were to go out of existence or change into a new form, it is clear that the GATT language of treaty obligations will continue to have an important influence on any international attempt to regulate or co-ordinate trade policy.[3]

Thus, reviewing the terms in Article XXIII of GATT can help us find a unifying interpretation of the Article XXIII. We can conceive two aspects of the reviewing process. First, the rearranged conceptualisation of the "benefit" (Article XXIII : 1) can embrace the other pivotal terms such as the "obligations" (Article XXIII : 1(a)), and the

1 *See* LOUIS HENKIN, INTERNATIONAL LAW: POLITICS AND VALUES 7 (1995).

2 For insights on language in legal reasoning, *See, e.g.* AHILAN T. ARULANANTHAM, *Breaking the Rules?: Wittgenstein and Legal Realism,* 107 Yale Law Journal 1853 (1998); Morawetz (1992); Dennis Patterson, *Wittgenstein and Constitutional Theory*, 72 Texas Law Review 1837 (1994); LOUIS E. WOLCHER, *Ronald Dworkin's Right Answers Thesis Through the Lens of Wittgenstein,* 29 Rutgers Law Journal 43 (1997).

3 JACKSON (1969), at 193.

"nullification or impairment" which is an inclusive wording of the two terminologies (i. e. "benefit" and "obligations") in terms of *definitional exactness.* Second, an overall structure underlying important legal terms also plays an important part in understanding the terms. One underlying structure related to the contextual meaning of "benefit" of Article XXIII: 1 is *reciprocity.*

2. *Definitional Exactness and Benefit*

The discourse on *obligation* and its corresponding *rights* in jurisprudence can be analysed from both a theoretical and practical perspective. First, the discourse invokes some basic theoretical questions: "What are the necessary and sufficient conditions for the existence of a right?" "What are the basic values which rights protect?"[4] Simultaneously, it poses a practical ongoing challenge for international lawyers, for if we cannot predict when nation-states will carry out their international legal obligations, how can we count on "multilateralism" as a cornerstone of present international order?[5] Not least, the obligation discourse holds a key to legal reasoning over NVNI complaints, because the following conclusions can indicate what are the main variables in the process of the reasoning.

Definitional exactitude has been "a can of worms" in every academic area, because of the flexible uses of language.[6] Very briefly, consider the *general interrelation among language (terms), meanings and their logical connections.* We tend to think that a word has meaning by its attachment to an object and this primitive idea makes us infer that it is the object that secures the consistency with which it is used. However, it is the consistency with which a word

4 *See* KRAMER ET AL. (2000), at 1.

5 KOH (1997), at 2600.

6 The justification of this general review on linguistic theory is "the formation of the nature of legal language has been drawn from philosophy" and recent philosophical work is mainly related to the linguistic approach. *See* JOHN BRIGHAM, CONSTITUTIONAL LANGUAGE: AN INTERPRETATION OF JUDICIAL DECISION CHP.3 (1978); *See also* KELSEN (1961), at 41.

has a useful meaning that enables us to keep in communication.[7] In terms of the Wittgensteinian view,[8] without a certain stabiliser or explicit agreement, we can never guarantee that other people also share the same meaning of the terms.[9] In other words, under the guarantee of a practical connection[10] between a word and its logical connotation, the word has its own proper meaning. In this statement, particularly in "the guarantee of a practical connection," there is the hint of the theory story.

Although an exact definition of a legal term, for example, "benefits" of Article XXIII: 1(b) of GATT, may accurately summarise the way in which we currently use the term "benefit" in our plain language,[11] there must be some reason why we agree that some variables in the "benefits," and not others, capture the proper meaning of the term in the context of the Article XXIII. That connecting function thus could be supplied by some normative foundations for the very existence of the concept of benefit. And perhaps those foundations could also explain why our definition of "benefit" revolves around the primary variables of advantage or good with trade incidences. One of such foundations is *reciprocity*.

7 LUDWIG WITTGENSTEIN, REMARKS ON THE FOUNDATIONS OF MATHEMATICS 344 (1978) ("Only in the practice of a language can a word have meaning.").

8 *See* Morawetz (1992), at 379 ("[Wittgenstein] stressed that *all* persons – theorists and practitioners alike – inhabit ways of proceeding (thinking, acting, taking things for granted) and cannot step outside. The possibility of doing anything, including the possibility of propounding theories, depends on inhabiting a way of speaking and thinking. If this is true, then the relationship between theory and practice may not be an inside/outside relationship *but a relationship of two different ways of being inside*").

9 *See* IIHAM DILMAN, INDUCTION AND DEDUCTION 12 (1973) ("... It underlies the possibility of our being able to talk and reason in the way we do. Wittgenstein said that a language-game is only possible if one trusts something.").

10 In a legal account by Hans Kelsen, we find a similar statement: "Any attempt to define a concept must take for its starting-point the common usage of the word, denoting the concept in question." *See* KELSEN (1961), at 4.

11 Benefit has been defined as "The advantages of belonging to a privileged order exempted from the jurisdiction or sentence of ordinary courts of law." *See* 1 Oxford English Dictionary (1993), at 214; *See also* BLACK'S LAW DICTIONARY (1999), at 150 ("1. Advantage; privilege. 2. Profit or gain").

3. Reciprocity and Benefit

Reciprocity is often depicted as a "rough equivalence and conditionality – one nation acts only on condition that others do likewise".[12] A basic tenant of *reciprocity* is that trade commitments have to be enforceable in order to ensure performance of the reciprocal obligation promised in exchange for a benefit given.[13] From its very beginning, the GATT 47 provided an international forum for further negotiations to create a mutually advantageous system based on reciprocity, "stimulat[ing] the general code of trade policy rules that traditionally went along with the exchange of tariff reduction".[14] Actually, the idea of reciprocity inspired the tariff reduction at the formative time of GATT 47.[15] Since the tariff reduction could easily be impeded by various "indirect protection" measures of domestic commercial policy, it was urged to invent some legal tools against possible nonreciprocal measures which caused an adverse effect on the balance of the tariff reductions or economic interests: For example, the London Economic and Mon-

12 Alan C. Swan, *"Fairness" and "Reciprocity" in International Trade Section 301 and the Rule of Law*, 16 Arizona Journal of International and Comparative Law 37, 39 (1999).

13 Naboth Van Den Broek, *Legal Persuasion, Political Realism, And Legitimacy: The European Court's Recent Treatment Of The Effect Of WTO Agreements in the EC Legal Order*, JIEL 411, 426 (2001). He classified four types or stages of reciprocity in international law: (1) Formal and substantive reciprocity in the creation of legal obligations; (2) Reciprocity in domestic legal effect of treaty obligations; (3) Reciprocity in the observance or performance of treaty obligations; (4) Reciprocity in sanctioning, *see id.*, at 418; *See also* JACKSON (1969), at 241.

14 HUDEC (1990), at 23; Preamble of the GATT 47 provides: "Being desirous of contributing to ...by entering into reciprocal and mutually advantageous arrangements [...]."; Article XXVIII *bis* of GATT expressly mention that negotiations will be on a "reciprocal and mutually advantageous basis."; John Jackson claimed three major premises underlying GATT 47 negotiations: (1) Reciprocity (2) MFN and (3) Non-tariff barriers, *see* JACKSON (1969), at 240–48.

15 *See generally* L.A. Winters, 'Reciprocity', in 2 ANDERSON & HOEKMAN (EDS) (2002), pp. 290–300.

etary Conference of 1933 brought in a broad provision designed "in terms of the effect (nullification and impairment) rather than the specific cause."[16] More salient evaluation, moreover, lies in that the words of Article XXIII, especially of "nullification or impairment," is related to the concept of "unreasonableness" of Section 301 (a) of the Trade Act of 1974 of the US.[17] Furthermore, the WTO DSM mainly comprises the idea of reciprocity, which can be confirmed in some provisions of DSU.[18]

Therefore the overriding concern for "reciprocity" in WTO context[19] affects the legal structure of the trade agreements. First, related to rule-making aspects, "general codes of trade policy obligations" prohibited such forbidden acts as quantitative restrictions, discrimination and similar trade practices.[20] Furthermore, the WTO DSM mainly comprises the idea of reciprocity, which can be confirmed in some provisions of DSU.[21]

Given the final purpose of reciprocal satisfaction of WTO Members, secondly, little distinction was made between violations of legal obligations and other legal consequences to nullify the reciprocally balanced interests. The balancing of economic interests is fundamental to international trade treaties like the WTO Agreements in legitimizing its legal system. And in establishing and maintaining this balance, reciprocity figures prominently and has played

16 Hudec (2000), at 19.
17 Hudec (1975b), at 464.
18 *See, e.g.* Articles of 3, 4 and 22 of DSU.
19 *See, e.g.* Hudec (1975), at 464; Reciprocity can be approximately depicted in international economy as "each nation extend to imports of goods, services, capital, and technology from its partners essentially the same right of access as its exports receive from its partners." *See* Swan, *id.*; The final guarantee of this reciprocal relation had to be a termination clause which would allow either party to get out altogether, for any reason, on short notice. *See* Hudec, *id.*, 463–464; *See also* Jackson (1997), at 345. He explained reciprocity as "a system of continuous 'trades' or 'swaps' of measures to liberalise (or restrict) trade."
20 Hudec, *id.*, at 464.
21 *See, e.g.* Articles of 3, 4 and 22 of DSU.

a significant role in formatting the WTO legal system.[22] The Appellate Body in *India – Patent I* explained that NVNI complaints are "rooted in the GATT's origins as an agreement intended to protect the *reciprocal tariff concessions* negotiated among the contracting parties under Article II".[23] The reciprocal nature affects on the scope of *legitimate expectation* as noted in the AB Report of *EC – Computer Equipment*:

> [GATT Article II : 5] recognises the possibility that the treatment contemplated in a concession, provided for in a Member's Schedule, on a particular product, may differ from the treatment accorded to that product and provides for a compensatory mechanism to rebalance the concessions between the two members concerned in such a situation. However, *nothing in Article II: 5 suggests that the expectations of only the exporting member can be the basis for interpreting* a concession in a Member's Schedule for the purposes of determining whether that member has acted consistently with its obligations under Article II : 1.[24]

Finally, the reciprocal balance is relevant to the remedy aspects of NVNI complaints. Thus the ultimate goal of NVNI complaints "is not the withdrawal of the measure concerned, but rather achieving a mutually satisfactory adjustment, usually by means of compensation."[25]

In the following part, two points are addressed: internal coherence of legal terminology; and the interrelation of meaning and logical connection in the context of GATT Article XXIII.

22 *See, e.g.* HUDEC (1975), at 464; Reciprocity can be approximately depicted in international economy as "each nation extend to imports of goods, services, capital, and technology from its partners essentially the same right of access as its exports receive from its partners." *See* SWAN (1999), at 39; The final guarantee of this reciprocal relation had to be a termination clause which would allow either party to get out altogether, for any reason, on short notice, *see* HUDEC (1975), at 463–64.

23 *India – Patent I (AB)*, para. 41 [emphasis added].

24 *EC – Computer Equipment (AB)*, para. 81.

25 *India – Patent I (AB)*, para. 41. This is codified in Article 26.1(b) of DSU.

B. Two-Tried Track in "Benefits" of Article XXIII : 1

1. *From "Benefits" to "Rights"*

Law serves to protect a community order and it regulates various relations within a legal community,[26] and the relations consist of various "benefits" in a broad sense. These benefits, through the process of legal recognition in the community, can be converted into a more defined and systematic form of "rights" (correspondingly obligations).[27] Within the GATT/WTO law, this transitional process from "benefits" to "rights" holds true.

In a report on the preparatory committee on trade and employment issued by the United Nations in 1947, the outline of benefit was addressed well by an Australian delegate:

> I should like to emphasise that by the word 'benefits' we conceive not merely benefits accorded for instance, under the provisions of Article 24 [on tariff concessions], but the *benefits which other countries derive from the acceptance of the wider obligations imposed by the Charter*...[28] [emphasis added]

This statement by a drafter of GATT 47 clarifies that the benefits accruing as a result of a concession or obligation under an agreement are in some way larger than the literal wording of the commitment (or obligation) itself. This aspect of the relationship between "benefits" and "obligations" was raised in a note on the subject prepared by the Secretariat in the course of the Uruguay Round negotiations.[29]

26 *See, e.g.*, HART (1997), at 20–21.

27 Roughly stated, the Interest Theory maintains that all rights consist in the protection of individual or corporate interest. For more review, *See, e.g.*, N. E. Simmonds, 'Rights at the Cutting Edge,' in KRAMER ET AL. (2000), pp. 195–211; *See also* NEIL MACCORMICK, H. L. A. HART 88–91 (1981).

28 U.N. Conf.–12th Mtg., at 7.

29 The 1989 Secretariat note raised for consideration the question of whether: "[...] the 'benefits' deriving from the GATT rules on non-tariff trade barriers were larger than the GATT rules themselves (e.g. do they protect also freedom from market-distorting measures other than those explicitly prohibited in these GATT rules)?" *See* Uruguay Round Doc. MTN.GNG/NG13/W/31.

a. Potential Benefits vs. Verified Benefits

When the drafters decided to take a benefits-based approach in principle, not a more tidy approach based on legal obligations like other international treaties, in the rule-applying process of GATT/WTO dispute resolution mechanism, they probably intended to focus their attention on some roles or functions that the mechanism is expected to carry on. Specifically, in the course of outlining the causes of action of Article XXIII : 1, the drafters must have firstly considered an apparatus of imposing each Member's legal obligations – and their corresponding rights –[30] in order to efficiently sustain WTO and to objectively resolve disputes among the members. These claims against breach of the legal obligations are related to Article XXIII : 1(a) of violation complaints.[31]

On the other hand, in organising a universal mechanism like the WTO, the organisation needed to recognise each member's *potential benefits*, being not yet verified as "rights" but existing because of the process of balancing tariff concessions. This consideration of the potential benefits was reflected in the NVNI complaints, reserving the *verified benefits* mainly for the violation complaints. According to literal terms of Article XXIII : 1, *directly* or *indirectly* nullified *benefits*[32] are corresponding to *verified* and *potential* benefit categories.[33]

30 For example, the panel of *Japan – Film* used "legally binding obligations or the substantive equivalent" in the discussion of non-violation. *See Japan – Film*, para. 9.9.

31 Waincymer (2002), at 89. *Cf India – Patent I (AB)*, para. 39: "These are disputes that arise from an alleged failure by a member to carry out its obligations. During nearly fifty years of experience, Article XXIII : 1(a) has formed the basis of almost all disputes under the GATT 1947 and the *WTO Agreement*."

32 Contrary to GATT Article XXIII : 1, which addresses nullification or impairment of "benefits accruing [...] directly or indirectly under this Agreement" to a Member, GATS Article XXIII : 3 refers just to "any benefit [a member] could reasonably have expected to accrue to it."

33 Articl XXIII : 1 of GATT: "If any contracting party should consider that *any benefit accruing to it directly or indirectly* under this Agreement is being nullified or impaired [...]."

In *EC – Oilseeds* case, we can find this categorisation in the conflicting parties' arguments. Rebutting the European Community's claim that "the absence of a prohibition in one GATT Article should take precedence over rights and expectations of contracting parties with respect to other GATT provisions and negotiated commitments," the United States argued that:

> Article XXIII itself recognised in clear terms that nullification or impairment may exist in the absence of any contravention of specific GATT obligations and GATT provisions and rulings established that a finding of nullification or impairment could and should be made in the present dispute.[34]

The statement of the United States clearly implicates the existence of "potential benefits," differentiated from "verified benefits" (i.e. rights) of the applicable WTO Agreements. In this sense, the following EC claim in the *EC – Oilseeds* case is incorrect:

> the protection of the benefits accruing from concessions *could not be extended to the exercise of a right* recognised by the General Agreement being affected *de jure* or *de facto* without a change in the relationships between the various Articles of the GATT and thus in the balance between the rights and obligations of contracting parties.[35] [emphasis added]

The correlation between *potential benefits* and *verified benefits* (i.e. rights) again appears in the Panel Report of *EC-Asbestos*. Rejecting the EC's claim that the rules on NVNI complaint apply only if the measure in question does not fall under other provisions of the GATT,[36] the Panel noted that:

> To begin with, it should be noted that the wording of Article XXIII:1(b) ["measure, whether or not it conflicts with the provisions] shows unequivocally that this provision applies both in situations in which a measure conflicts and in situations in which it does not conflict with the provisions of the GATT 1994.[37] [...]

34 *EC – Oilseeds,* para. 118.
35 *Id.*, para. 116.
36 *EC – Asbestos,* para. 8.246.
37 *Id,* para. 8.261; *See also* GATT Panel Report, *US – Sugar Waiver*, para. 5.21 ("Article XXIII:1(b) applies whether or not the measure at issue conflicts

> it is our opinion that the fact that a measure does not violate Article III:4 does not necessarily mean that [Article XXIII:1 (b)] is not applicable to [the measure].[38]

In agreeing with the US claim that the term "measure" in Article XXIII:1(b) should not be limited only to legally binding obligations or their substantive equivalent, the Panel uses a more encompassing definition of the term "benefit." The broader applicability of benefits more than rights or obligations appears to be a reason for employing the concept of "nullification or impairment." One of WTO Appellate Body Report confirms this reason. In *India-Patent I,* it was stated:

> Article XXIII:1(a) involves so-called "violation" complaints. These are disputes that arise from an alleged failure by a Member to carry out its obligations. During nearly fifty years of experience, Article XXIII:1(a) has formed the basis of almost all disputes under the GATT 1947 and the *WTO Agreement.* In contrast, Article XXIII:1(b) involves so-called "non-violation" complaints. These are disputes that do not require an allegation of a violation of an obligation. The basis of a cause of action under Article XXIII:1(b) is not necessarily a violation of the rules, but rather the nullification or impairment of a benefit accruing to a Member under a covered agreement.[39]

These two tracks of dispute resolution, although they cause considerable vagueness for predictable resolution, must have been created to harmonise the "liberal" political structure of Bretton Wood system with the "conservative" legal structure of GATT. Thus, Ar-

---

with the General Agreement and that therefore, the question of whether a measure inconsistent with Article XI:1 remains inconsistent with the General Agreement even if covered by a waiver cannot, by itself, determine whether it nullifies or impairs benefits accruing under the General Agreement within the meaning of that provision").

38 *EC – Asbestos,* para. 8.263; *See also EC – Oilseeds I,* para. 144 ("The idea underlying [the balance of tariff concessions] is that the improved competitive opportunities that can legitimately be expected from a tariff concession can be frustrated not only by measures proscribed by the General Agreement but also by measures consistent with that Agreement").

39 *India – Patent I,* para. 39.

ticle XXIII effectively allocates "conceptually different rights to challenge violation and non-violation activities."[40]

b. Role of "Objective" Regarding Potential Benefits

The next logical question then is about how much the *potential benefits* can be recognised. Put differently, where can we draw the line between members' legitimate autonomy and regulatory intervention by the GATT? One of the answers provided by Article XXIII:1 of GATT is to use the very "objective" of the GATT,[41] which is closely related to the balance of competitive conditions accorded to imported products in the GATT.[42] Regarding the objective, the five principles of the US representative in the Preparatory Committee in London in 1946 must be worthwhile. These were: (1) Substantial reduction of existing barriers; (2) Importance of multilateralism; (3) Importance of non-discrimination; (4) Consistency of stabilization policies for industry and agriculture; and (5) Equal and fair applicability of international commerce rules.[43]

For the analysis of the "objective" related to the "benefit" of Article XXIII:1, consider some historic reviews of the formation of the NVNI provision, since these terms do not readily submit to a literal analysis. The present NVNI provision states that "any benefit accruing" or "any objective" under the GATT shall not be nullified or impaired[44] which has been derived from the equitable treatment

40 WAINCYMER (2002), at 89.

41 *See* U.N. Conf.–12th Mtg., at 31. ("In fact, the additional phrase "purposes of the Charter" specifically sought to compensate for the narrow meaning of the term 'benefit' [...]").

42 ROESSLER (1997), p. 131; *See also EC – Oilseeds I*, para. 151; GATT Panel Report, *Japan – Customs Duties*, para. 5.11; GATT Panel Report, *US – Superfund*, para. 5.1.9.

43 *See* U.N. Doc. E/PCT/PV.2, at 5 (1946), quoting from JACKSON (1969), at 54. He also mentioned the strongest clashes of objective at the London Conference occurred "(1) how to treat quantitative restrictions; and (2) the degree of control over trade restrictions for economic development purposes." *Id.*, at 55.

44 GATT Article XXIII:1.

clause of the League of Nations.[45] The first version of the clause was superseded by the nullification or impairment of "any objective of the Agreement" of GATT Article XXIII : 1 which was standard in the United States bilateral agreements.[46] Moreover, because the United States drafted the Suggested Charter, this language was the basis for the ITO negotiations.[47] In the course of Geneva discussions in the summer of 1947, the "any objective" standard was narrowed to including only the nullification or impairment of "benefits accruing" under the Agreement.[48] And then, with a view to compensating for the narrow applicability of the term "benefit," the phrase "purposes of the Charter" was added.[49]

In summary, on the significance of "objective" element, a delegate's statement during the International Trade Organisation negotiations is noteworthy:

> the original antecedent of [the NVNI provision]... was a provision developed in the London Economic Conference to deal with matters of protectionism. There the question came up whether we should list all of the things that a country could not do which might destroy the value of concessions made. We got such a long list that they finally hit upon a clause something like the

45 The first version of the League of Nations' equitable treatment clause covered any measure "capable of materially altering the de facto situation created by the present treaty, to the prejudice of the other Party." *See* Equitable Treatment Draft. The "de facto situation" seems to indicate actual trade volumes, in judging the nullification of benefit, a notion explicitly rejected by later GATT panels.

46 *See* Durling & Lester (1998), at 247 n. 211: For example, Reciprocal Trade Agreement, May 6, 1936, US-Fr., Article XI, 53 Stat. 2236, 2250 (effective provisionally Jun. 15, 1936; terminated Dec. 13, 1962) (referring to any "important object"); Reciprocal Trade Agreement, Apr. 1, 1939, US-Turk., Article XIII, 54 Stat. 1870, 1876 (entered into force provisionally May 5, 1939; terminated Aug. 4, 1952) (referring only to "impair[ing] the effectiveness of the Agreement").

47 Durling & Lester, at 247 n. 214.

48 *Id.*, note 216.

49 *See* U.N. Conf.–12th Mtg., at 31.

> one that is here. We took it up, starting with that, but we broadened it. *That clause related only to matters which were not in conflict with the agreement but had the effect of nullifying or impairing its objects.*[50] [emphasis added]

We shall return this aspect later.[51]

2. *Relationship between two Kinds of Benefits*

a. Substantively Inclusive Relationship

The two kinds of benefits *(potential vs. verified)* overlap each other to some extent. This is the question of whether a NVNI complaint can be brought *concurrently* with a violation complaint about the same measure.[52] As a first appeal since the establishment of WTO to examine Article XXIII : 1(b), *EC-Asbestos* clarified this overlap:

> Article XXIII : 1(a) sets forth a cause of action for a claim that a Member has failed to carry out one or more of its obligations under the GATT 1994. A claim under Article XXIII : 1(a), therefore, lies when a Member is alleged to have acted inconsistently with a provision of the GATT 1994. Article XXIII : 1(b) sets forth a separate cause of action for a claim that, through the application of a measure, a Member has "nullified or impaired" "benefits" accruing to another Member, "whether or not that measure conflicts with the provisions" of the GATT 1994. *Thus, it is not necessary, under Article XXIII: 1(b), to establish that the measure involved is inconsistent with, or violates, a provision of the GATT 1994.*[53] [emphasis added]

50 *See* U.N. Conf.–9th Mtg., at 23–24.
51 *See* PART FOUR – XI – B of this dissertation.
52 WAINCYMER (2002), at 115.
53 *EC – Asbestos (AB),* para. 185; *See also* WTO Panel Report, *EC – Asbestos (P),* paras. 8.260–8.265; *But see Korea – Procurement,* para. 7.118: "As discussed above, the United States bases its argument on the claim that it had a reasonable expectation that it had received a commitment with respect to a particular project, but the concessions themselves are based on covered entities. Thus, unlike traditional non-violation claims there is no actual Schedule commitment in this case. If there were a commitment, the case would properly be a violation case because the measures cited by the United States as the basis for the non-violation nullification case (e.g. inadequate bid deadlines

In addition, the border between benefits of violation claims and of NVNI claims is constantly changing as the substantive provisions regulating new trade areas of WTO have been increasing. This supplementation of legislations over time expands violation claims over NVNI claims. The following statement clarifies thus the overlapping relationship:

> The working party [on the Australian Subsidy on Ammonium Sulphate case (BISD II/188–196)] could have concluded that the two fertilizers were like directly competing products within the meaning of the national treatment provisions of Article III and the differentiation between them was therefore *a failure to observe obligations* [...]. The Appellate Body confirmed that fiscal discrimination between directly competing products for the purpose of protecting a domestic industry, as Australia practised in 1949, *violates* the national-treatment of the GATT.[54] [emphasis added]

Given the consistent fact pattern of "domestic subsidies" claimed by NVNI complaints in GATT jurisprudence and new legislation on the subsidies[55] that codified the jurisprudence of Contracting Parties, all three successful NVNI cases in the GATT jurisprudence *would be found* to be *illegal* rather than just impairing measures.[56] Therefore, in terms of the *substantive contents,* the two sorts of benefits have an inclusive correlation.

---

and insufficient challenge procedures) would, if they were substantiated, result in a violation. *A traditional non-violation case could, therefore, not be sustained in this situation.*" [emphasis added]; WAINCYMER (2002), at 115 ("A further reason not to read down the non-violation area is that a finding of non-violation nullification or impairment does not lead to an obligation to withdraw the measure").

54 ROESSLER (1999), pp. 418–19. He also demonstrates the possibility of interpreting another successful NVNI case of *Sardine* as a violation case.

55 Article XVI of the GATT contains general provisions on subsidies and it was expanded in 1955 to include a more specific provision on export subsidies. During the Tokyo Round, the two-track approach was laid out in the *Tokyo Round Code on Subsidies and Countervailing Duties*. Finally, the *Subsidies and Countervailing Measures Agreement* was introduced in the Uruguay Round, which is an integral part of the GATT/WTO and binds all Members, unlike the Tokyo Round Code, *see* TREBILCOCK & HOWSE (2001), at 191–99.

56 *Id.,* at 420.

b. Procedurally Exclusive Relationship

On the other hand, however, while a WTO Member can clearly bring a NVNI complaint against a measure in dispute, although the measure also constitutes a violation of a specific provision of WTO Agreements, it is unlikely that the judicial bodies of WTO would examine the measure under the NVNI provision once the violation has been established. For example, in *EC – Asbestos (AB)* case, the AB noted that:

> It follows that a measure may, *at one and the same time*, be inconsistent with, or in breach of, a provision of the GATT 1994 *and*, nonetheless, give rise to a cause of action under Article XXIII : 1(b). Of course, if a measure "conflicts" with a provision of the GATT 1994, that measure must actually fall within the scope of application of that provision of the GATT 1994.[57] [emphasis in original]

Therefore, *procedurally* there can be an *exclusive* relationship between violation and NVNI complaint to some extent, because of *judicial economy* whereby Panels that find violation allegations to be proven may not address the NVNI complaints.[58]

Regarding the existence of a *benefit* in NVNI complaints, with only one exception,[59] in all the previous cases of GATT/WTO practices in which Article XXIII : 1(b) was invoked, the benefit was related to a legitimate expectation of improved market access opportunities resulting from the relevant tariff concessions.[60]

57 *EC – Asbestos (AB),* para. 187.

58 WAICYMER (2002), at 115; For a general review on judicial economy, *see* WAICYMER (2002), at 367–72.

59 *See EC – Citrus,* para. 4.37.

60 *See generally, Japan – Film,* para. 10.61 n. 1223.

C. Corresponding Structure of Obligations

The above categorisation of benefits or rights[61] can be used for analysing Article XXIII: 1 of GATT. The analysis carefully examines the language used to clarify concepts. This type of work can be sometimes dismissed as an arid exercise in intellectual pedantry in international trade law. However, an insufficient analysis of key terms such as "obligation" or "benefits" will lead to a morass of ambiguity and mere assertion. Analysis of "benefit" (and its corresponding "obligation") is important for a balanced comprehension of GATT XXIII: 1.

1. *Specific Obligations in Article XXIII: 1(a)*

The term "obligation" in GATT XXIII: 1(a) can be first interpreted in terms of *verified benefit*, that is, obligations of members not to nullified *verified benefits* of other members. Thus, compare the Article XXIII: 1(a) with subsections (b), and these obligations are *codified* in concrete provisions within GATT. This is *a specific or codified obligation* in the sense that the obligations have, at the moment of making GATT law, ascertained concrete and consented contents of the GATT law. A complaint against this obligation is customarily called a *violation complaint* – a violation against a member's specific obligation to respect a *verified benefit*.

61 Here the universal correlativity between right and obligation is reviewed, setting aside the arguments on the possible distinction between rights-based and duty-based theories, *see* KRAMER ET AL. (2000), at 38.

2. *General Obligations in Article XXIII: 1(b)*

The contextual meaning of "obligations" in the other subsections (b) corresponds to the second category of "benefit". If we understand the benefit associated with Article XXIII: 1(b) as *a potential benefit,* the status of corresponding obligations appears clear: that is, all WTO members are under the obligation to protect another member's *potential benefits* in the WTO. This concerns *a general or customary obligation* because it serves the basis of the entire WTO or international system.[62] Such complaints against the secondary obligation are customarily called *a non-violation (NVNI) complaint* – it is not a violation of a member's specific obligation but a violation against a general obligation with corresponding *potential benefits.*

In terms of GATT practices, Panels developed a general rule of conduct that countries were not to circumvent the prescriptions of the GATT through GATT-consistent measures, requiring members to comply with GATT obligations in good faith.[63] For example, a government could not escape GATT scrutiny merely by characterising its conduct as a private contract with businesses rather than as a law or measure.[64] Neither could parties require the GATT to scrutinise legislation only in its entirety, because it would be possible for countries to slip violations into the parts.[65] Similarly, in case of dumping determinations, members must accept GATT's authority to review a dumping determination to avoid members' limitless discretion over the antidumping provisions.[66] Philip Nichols's following observation is instructive on the general obligation.

62 *See generally* Arend (1999), at 139.

63 Nichols (1996a), at 436. He mentions additional two kinds of general obligations to govern the behaviour of members. The fundamental principles of the GATT provide the basis for two of these obligations: national treatment and most-favored-nation treatment. *Id.*

64 *See* GATT Panel Report, *Canada – FIRA,* paras. 6.4 & 6.5.

65 GATT Panel Report, *US – Section 337,* at 393.

66 GATT, *New Zealand – Imports of Electrical Transformers,* at 67.

> Clearly, this general proscription against circumvention had an *interpretive effect*, allowing panels to interpret provisions more broadly to prevent circumvention. It also bore some relation to the *expansive definition of nullification and impairment*. Its import, however, is not in these dynamics, but rather is in the relationship the rule indicates between panels and the contracting parties. In contrast to other, more deferential aspects of panel conduct, *this rule bespeaks a willingness to take a stern approach with contracting parties and to keep them in line, not just with the letter of the General Agreement, but also with its spirit*.[67] [emphasis added]

In conclusion, Article XXIII: 1(a) concerns complaints against *specific or codified obligations* in WTO Agreements while Article XXIII: 1(b) concerns a different type of complaint against general or customary obligations of the relevant international economic community. However, designating obligations as either specific or general is not itself important, for it is just helpful to express a distinction between the content of rules in WTO legal system and the results of their breach. But this designation becomes important when the violation and NVNI complaints are applied to real cases because the concept of NVNI is conceived in broader terms than the nullification of codified or verified benefits. These NVNI claims thus include general obligations stemming from good faith and consequently legitimate expectation. This expansion of obligations resulting from NVNI complaints becomes apparent when we consider a clear attempt of GATT drafters to include such general obligations for keeping the GATT system current.

By establishing an interactive obligation structure within the GATT system in this way, this was an effort to keep the bedrock foundation of the GATT effective – balancing the tariff concession. This has raised two questions: what is the relationship between specific and customary obligation; and whether there should be any difference of enforcement for breaching each categorical obligation?

67 NICHOLS (1996a), at 438.

3. Relationship of General Obligation to Legitimate Expectation

a. Legitimately Expected Obligation: Duty of Care

These two types of obligation (*specific* & *general*) can be considered sufficient to establish the overall structure of obligations of WTO Members. However, there are some further requirements for overcoming difficulties surrounding the general obligation. One of these difficulties is the possible inconsistent interpretation of the *general* obligation. While a *specific* obligation, as noted, can be easily perceived by a codified or specified reference, the general obligation may have an unlimited character unless some conditions are imposed. The more WTO rules are predictable, the greater international trade would be stably regulated. This necessity for enhancing clarity of *the general obligation* is closely connected with a *duty of care*[68] as a WTO Member.

The concept of *duty of care* contributes to the improvement of legal clarity of *NVNI complaints* by ensuring that a *liability* extends only to those Members of WTO who stand in such care relationships to the other Members. In addition, the care must be taken within to a *reasonable extent,* since a WTO Member deserves an *expectation* that other Members will take measures within objective reasonableness in a certain trade. The basic function of the *reasonable care* is for the Members to comply with WTO obligations in god faith in the light of any possible measure against WTO's objec-

68 *See generally* A. G. GUEST, ANSON'S LAW OF CONTRACT 78–80 (1984). The following Lord Atkins's famous "neighbour principle" relates the duty of care in commercial law: "You must [he says] take reasonable care to avoid acts or omissions which you can reasonably foresee would be likely to injure your neighbour. Who, then, in law is my neighbour? [This receives a restrictive answer] [...] persons who are so closely and directly affected by my act that I ought reasonably to have them in contemplation as being so affected when I am directing my mind to the acts or omissions which are called into question." *See* M'Alister (or Donoghue) *vs* Stevenson [1932] *Appeal Cases* 562, at 580.

tive.[69] This discourse explains why *legitimate expectation* must be needed in the case of the NVNI complaints.

b. Foreseeability

A dispute arises only if there are some pre-existing relations between the parties by which *expectations* are created as to their future conduct.[70] In multilateral agreements such as the GATT/WTO, the expectations arise from mutual promises, e.g. schedule of tariff concessions or GATS specific commitments. However, although protecting such expectation is a critical element for enhancing the trading system, there is a crucial presumption that the trading system must operate reasonably well within the consents of WTO members. As a result, a member allegedly breaching the expectation should be judged *fairly* and *objectively*. This is the reason why the expectation test needs the concept of *foreseeability* of likely damage of WTO members, which implies the limitation of legitimate expectation.[71]

An interesting NVNI case in context of the *foreseeability* is the *EC – Citrus*. In the case, the US claimed that their reasonably expected benefits of the GATT were being nullified and impaired by the preferential trade arrangements the EEC had established with countries arguably in violation of GATT Article XXIV.[72] In its Article XXIII : 1(b) arguments, the US stressed their view that the EEC preferential tariffs not only were damaging their citrus trade opportunities, but also that the negative impacts of the preferential tariff scheme were objectively serious in the context of an agreement

69 *See generally* WILLIAM PROSSER, HANDBOOK OF THE LAW OF TORTS 224 (1941); at the level of WTO, *see* Von Bogdandy (1992), at 104.

70 P. Behrens, 'Alternative Methods of Dispute Settlement in International Economic Relations,' in PETERSMANN & JAENICKE (EDS) (1992), p. 7.

71 *See* COTTIER & SCHEFER (1997), pp. 162–63.

72 GATT Panel Report, *EC – Citrus,* paras. 3.1 & 3.2.

intended to foster trade.[73] Further, the US went on to claim that the preferential status of the Mediterranean countries was neither *fore-seen* nor *objectively foreseeable* at the time of negotiating their citrus schedules with the EEC. Using non-violation language, the *Citrus* Panel decision found that the rights of the United States, insofar as lemons and oranges were concerned, were indeed frustrated. It therefore recommended that the EC "consider limiting the adverse effects on US exports [...] by reducing the most-favoured-nation tariff rates".[74]

Clarified from the above *analytic* approach on the "benefit", *potential benefit* or *general obligation*, which invokes certain *responsibility of members*, is a conceptual constituent of NVNI complaints. This observation needs to be reviewed in terms of *state responsibility* perspective.

D. Non-Violation as State Liability

Because NVNI complaints establish a state responsibility for a WTO-*consistent* measure[75] and are associated with "objective responsibility for result,"[76] the general study of legal nature of state responsibility in international jurisprudence is worthwhile. More specifically, the resolution of most of the disputes concerning the nullification or impairment of benefits accruing under the covered agreements presupposes both the determination that a member has failed to

73 *Id.*, paras. 3.26 & 3.33.

74 *EC – Citrus,* para. 5.3; *See also* COTTIER & SCHEFER (1997), p. 163. Having analyzed *EC – Canned Fruit* case, they claimed that "while the United States [the complainant] may have *subjectively* expected a certain balance of concessions when it negotiated with the EEC [the respondant], these expectations were not reasonable. Here reasonability and legitimacy merge, and such expectations will not be protected under the General Agreement." *Id.*

75 VON BOGDANDY (1992), at 111.

76 PETERSMANN (1991), at 178; *See also* p. 103 of this dissertation.

carry out its conventional obligations and the establishment of the legal consequences of that measure.[77] This study is inextricably linked to the work of the United Nations International Law Commission (ILC).[78]

There have been three considerations to examine the controversies concerning the application of the general rules of State responsibility to the context of the WTO. First, whether the WTO system is a "self-contained" system has been considered.[79] A second review is concerned with the "attribution of conduct to the states" concerning the states responsibility for internationally wrongful acts.[80] The third consideration has been done in a context of "international liability for the injurious consequences of acts not prohibited by international law".[81] It is the latter that is most relevant to NVNI complaints.[82]

77 VILLALPANDO (2002), at 393–94.

78 The ILC began its examination on state responsibility in 1955 by the request of the UN General Assembly in its resolution 799 (VIII) of 7 December 1953. This study remained part of the ILC's work until 2002. On State Responsibility under general international law, see the Draft Articles on State Responsibility prepared by the International Law Commission, U.N. G.A. A/CN4/L528/Add.2 (16 July 1996). *See also* http://www.law.cam.ac.uk/rcil/ILCSR/Statresp.htm (last visited 4 May 2003).

79 KUYPER (1994), at 251–52. He observed that "It is perhaps too early to say if the GATT, [...] has moved decisively in the direction of such a self-contained system in the form of the WTO. It is obvious, however, that the intention was there." *See id.*, at 252; The term "self-contained regime" was used in 1980 by the International Court of Justice to refer to the rules of diplomatic law, *see* ICJ Reports 1980, at 40, para. 86. For an authoritative study on the concept, *see* BRUNO SIMMA, *Self-Contained Regimes*, VI Netherlands Yearbook of International Law ("NYIL") 111–36 (1985).

80 VILLALPANDO (2002), at 394.

81 This topic has been on the agenda of International Law Commission ("ILC") since 1978. It originated from a belief that states might be responsible in international law not only for their wrongful acts, but also for the harmful consequences of their lawful activities. *See* BOYLE (2002), p. 141; *See generally* BROWNLIE (1998), at 401–03; 1 JENNINGS & WATTS (EDS) (1996), at 501–02.

82 The following assessment of Santiago Villalpando is noteworthy: "In so doing, most authors have concentrated on the specificity of the WTO dispute settlement system, that embraces not only the failure of a member to carry out its

The legal nature of international responsibility or liability has perennially generated considerable theoretical debates, practical difficulties and occupied a central stage in international law.[83] The concept of *state responsibility* is said to include a threefold division within the generic concept of responsibility:[84] distinction of criminal responsibility from general concept of an internationally wrong act;[85] distinction the international liability from other forms of responsibility, and; the consequences ensuing from different forms of responsibility.[86] Here the focus will be on the second point of distinction between *liability* and *responsibility*.

---

obligations under the agreements, but also so-called non-violation complaints. Otherwise, authors have turned directly to the burning issue of remedies, namely the Panel's recommendation that the Member bring its measure into conformity with the covered agreement, compensation and the suspension of concessions, or even counter-measures." *See* VILLALPANDO (2002), at 393.

83 The debates include, for example, the distinction between the secondary obligations of the responsible State and the right of other states to invoke that responsibility and the distinction in principle between "injured states" and other states with a legal interest in the obligation breached, which was widely endorsed. However, a number of substantive issues remained unresolved, including: (1) The definition of "damage" and "injury" in conjunction with the Articles specifying the states entitled to invoke responsibility; (2) The treatment of the consequences of "serious breaches" of certain obligations; (3) The treatment of countermeasures as a circumstance precluding wrongfulness. *See also* JAMES CRAWFORD, JACQUELINE PEEL and SIMON OLLESON, *The ILC's Article on Responsibility of States for Internationally Wrongful acts: Completion of the Second Reading*, 12 European Journal of International Law 963 (2001).

84 BOYLE (2002), p. 143; *See also* KARL ZEMANEK, 'Responsibility of States: General Principles', in 4 ENCYCLOPEDIA (2000), pp. 219–229.

85 The primary consequence of an internationally wrong act, defined as the violation of a state of an international obligation, is classically described "[T]he essential principles contained in the actual notion of illegal act [...] is that reparation must, as far as possible, wipe out all the consequences of the illegal act and re-establish the situation in which would, in all probability, have existed if that act had not been committed." *See* PCIJ, Series A, No. at 17, para. 47.

86 For a general study on this, *see* SANTIAGO M. VILLALPANDO, *Attribution Of Conduct To The State: How The Rules Of State Responsibility May Be Applied Within The Wto Dispute Settlement System*, 5 JIEL 393 (2002).

First of all, the most common usage of *responsibility* in public international law is to refer to the obligations of states, leaving *liability* to refer to the consequences which follow from a breach of those obligations.[87] In other words, "... responsibility is taken to indicate a duty, or as denoting the standards which the legal system imposes on performing a social role, and liability is seen as designating the consequences of a failure to perform the duty, or to fulfill the standards of performance required".[88]

A second possible usage of the term *liability* is in relation to the term "responsibility". Viewed in this way, one may describe *liability* in terms comparable to *responsibility* as follows: "It is not used to mean only the consequences of obligation, but rather to mean the obligation itself, which – like 'responsibility' – includes its consequences".[89] This broad characterisation can conclude that "the word 'liability' is taken in its two meanings, covering all its implications: the host of duties of a person in society in relation to certain conduct and the obligation of reparation which arises as a consequence of injury."[90] This approach corresponds with the ILC's present work,[91] and in this line the NVNI concept can be well understood. In addition, the following observations of Alan Boyle, Michael Akehurst and Joost Pauwelyn are revealing in examining the NVNI concept:

87 *See, e.g.* AKEHURST (1985), at 9–16; GOLDIE (1985), at 180; *Cf.* Article 139.2 of The Law of the Sea Convention: "... (2) Without prejudice to the result of international law [...] damage caused by the failure of a State Party or international organization to carry out its responsibility under this Part shall entail liability." The two words of responsibility and liability here are used with different connotations; *See also* ICJ Reports (1971), at 16, para. 118.

88 GOLDIE, *id.*

89 *See* ILC Yearbook (1980), vol. 2, part 1, at 250, para. 12 (Rapporteur Quentin-Baxer's explanation). Quentin-Baxer also mentioned that "In this report, therefore, the term 'liability' is used, [...] without nuance and in a sense very close to its ordinary meaning: a negative asset, *as an obligation, in contra-distinction to a right.*" [emphasis added] *Id.*

90 *Id.*

91 *Id.*

> Initially, the [International Law] Commission used these [responsibility and liability] terms interchangeably, but it eventually adopted the view that 'responsibility' was appropriate in cases involving a breach of obligation, while 'liability' should be used in connection with activities which are otherwise lawful or involve no wrongful acts.[92] [underlining added]

> The vast majority of lawful acts do not give rise to liability. [...] Some writers go so far to say that liability for non-wrongful acts can exist only when a treaty provides to that effect. There are a few instances of customary international law providing for such liability.[93] [underlining added]

> With one possible exception, no academic author (or any WTO decision or document) disputes that WTO rules are part of the wider corpus of public international law. .... To public international lawyers, [...] WTO rules to "be considered as creating international legal obligations that are part of public international law" is a truism.[94] [underlining added]

These observations imply two important points on *liability* in international law as they relate to the NVNI concept in WTO law. First, liability has the same legal character in that the NVNI is connected with a WTO-consistent measure (i.e. *lawful* measure). In addition, the liability or NVNI concept is mainly associated with the *consequence* of the lawful measure.[95] Second, to demonstrate the exist-

92 Boyle (2000), at 148–49.

93 Akehurst (1985), at 9–10. In this context, Rapporteur Quentin-Baxer has stated that "an obligation in respect of an act not prohibited *arises only when a primary rule of international law so provides*" [emphasis added] *See* ILC Yearbook (1980), vol. 2, part 1, p. 251, para. 13.

94 Pauwelyn (2001), at 538. The possible exception indicated by Joost Pauwelyn is Judith Bello, *The WTO Dispute Settlement Understanding: Less Is More*, 90 AJIL 416, 416–17 (1996); Explaining the relationship between WTO rules and other rules of international law, Joost Pauwelyn set up 5 types. The third type of such relationship which is relevant to the similarity of liability to NVNI concept is "(3) WTO rules that confirm preexisting rules of international law, be they of general international law (such as DSU Article 3.2 confirming that WTO covered agreements are to be interpreted 'in accordance with customary rules of interpretation of public international law') or preexisting treaty law (such as GATT 1994 incorporating GATT 1947 and the TRIPS Agreement incorporating parts of certain WIPO conventions"). *See id.*, at 540; *See also* Jackson (1997), at 26–28.

95 In this context, John Jackson's following remark on "non-violation" complaints is understandable: "In the [nonviolation] case, the draft provisions of [Uruguay

ence of liability, it needs to be justified by treaty provisions and/or customary international law. The second part indicates the significance of *sources* in interpreting NVNI complaints which appears to paraphrase in the Article 3.2 of DSU:

> The [WTO] Members recognize that [WTO dispute settlement system] serves to preserve the rights and obligations of Members under the covered agreements, and to *clarify the existing provisions of those agreements in accordance with customary rules of interpretation of public international law.* [emphasis added]

In sum, the above observations imply that the legal character of *liability* equates with *NVNI concept* and suggests changing the label of NVNI into a *liability* as a more established concept in international jurisprudence. The use of one label or the other is sensitive because the legal consequences of disturbing economically balanced benefits in WTO law has the potential to influence the WTO's direction. In respect of this standpoint, John Jackson's following remark is noteworthy:

> The GATT is the most significant collection of specific legal clauses relating to the regulation of international trade that exists and some of this language has already had an important influence on other treaties and institutions.[96] [footnote deleted]

By exactly labelling the NVNI as *liability*, we can use the conventional international jurisprudence to efficiently interpret future trade disputes under WTO system. Next is to investigate the *possible scope of the NVNI /liability* by reviewing its *external coherence.*

Round] suggest that there is no legal obligation to carry out the conclusions of a GATT dispute settlement process, but there would exist an obligation to negotiate for 'compensation.'" *See* Jackson (2000), at 132.

96 Jackson (1969), at 193.

XI. External Coherence as a Normative Approach

A. General Principles of International Law

a. In General

Rules on international trade are generalisations of a number of transactions. However, in generalising only some features of a particular transaction are focused on and are projected onto future events. The generalisations in rules such as in GATT/WTO law are thus simplifications of complex events or courses of behaviour in the international trade, containing a spectrum of rules that are binding in varying degrees.[1] In the context of subsidies, for example, some types of state subsidies are not illegal *per se* but can nevertheless nullify another Member's benefits invoking the imposition of a retaliatory or counter-measure by the affected Member.[2]

The specifications of WTO rules are likely to leave out some important aspects of treaty-making or drafters' intents for a few reasons. First, in simplifying the substantive contents of international transactions, one cannot include all subject-matters mainly because of the limitations of treaty-making skills.[3] Second, the substantive contents of WTO rules bear simply a "probable relationship" between the possible nullification of benefits to be avoided and the intended purpose of the contents to be achieved.[4] Third, even if a

1 *See, e.g.,* QURESHI (1996), at 10–45.

2 *Id.,* at 10.

3 *See generally* SCHAUER (1991), at 23–4; *See also* VAN ALSTINE (1998), at 702 (claiming that "[M]uch of the friction in the identification and application of law stems from the simple fact that the rules of law 'are finite, and the subject of it infinite'"); On the GATT level, *see* JACKSON (1969), at 9–12.

4 *See generally* SCHAUER (1991), at 27–31; John Jackson mentioned in several occasions the probable relationship, for example, *see* JACKSON (1969), at 214 (related to "tariff concessions"), 413 ("antidumping"), 501 ("export controls").

perfect causal match between the substantive contents of WTO rules and the corresponding events could be achieved, future events may develop in such a way that the causation ceases to be.[5] These three reasons mainly inspire to insert a bit *ambiguous* but *comprehensive standards* in dispute settlement mechanism of WTO.[6]

One of the standards found in GATT XXIII: 1 is the "objective" of GATT. The objective of the GATT is said to protect the balance of rights and obligations stemming from the exchange of scheduled tariff concessions and consequently to keep a predictable market access.[7] Therefore, the purpose of WTO system can be said to aim at eliminating or reducing discrimination and barriers relating to international trade. To achieve the purpose, the GATT/WTO imposes a number of obligations on the Members. As a main obligation, tariff concession becomes the top agenda of the obligations and there are many complementary obligations which are designed to reinforce the tariff concession.[8] In other words, the complementary obligations in the GATT law were designed to inhibit avoidance of a tariff concession by using other non-tariff barriers that would prevent imports.[9] In addition to these obligations, the GATT contains a large number of exceptions[10] which may be necessary

5 *See generally* SCHAUER (1991), at 35; *See also* JACKSON (1969), at 515–32.
6 *See* PART THREE – VII – A – b of this dissertation.
7 In a GATT Panel Reports, we can find the objective as upholding "[...] the improved competitive opportunities that can legitimately be expected from a tariff concession [...]," *see EC – Oilseeds I*, para. 144.
8 *See, e.g.*, JACKSON (1969), at 201–48; VON BOGDANDY (1992), at 98.
9 *See, e.g.*, JACKSON (1969), at 536 ("The escape clause and exceptions provide the necessary flexibility without which the General Agreement might never have been concluded or might never have endured in the face of the pressures that have buffeted it"); JACKSON (1997), at 154–55.
10 For example, there are also many exceptions to GATT's primary obligations, such as Article XIX, the so-called "safeguard" or "escape clause", which allows for the temporary imposition of additional restrictions on imports that cause serious injury to domestic producers, and Article XX, which provides that GATT's primary obligations do not prohibit measures necessary to achieve a wide variety of public purposes, such as the protection of human, animal or plant life (XX(b)); the exclusion of the products of prison labour (XX(e)); or the conservation of exhaustible natural resources (XX(g)). Article XII–XIV

to allow the system to be viable, giving an indispensable flexibility for its survival. Therefore, whenever the substantive contents of a rule mismatch their corresponding events in reality, an *objective-focused* reasoning has emerged despite being in a very vague shape.

The "objective" in the context of causes of action thus performs an *instrumental function* in GATT law in that it tries to narrow the gap between the substantive rules concerned and their expected functions.[11] This is a reason for necessitating various forms of reasoning (e.g. intervention of "general principles" of international law). In effect, from the beginning the rules of the GATT were based on principles of general international law.[12] Because of the GATT's provisional nature, there was still a reluctance to refer to international law, while the legal factors sustaining the whole structure consisted mainly of good faith and the reciprocity of the interests involved.[13] However, the WTO was created by a formal treaty-making process, following the requirements of international practice and national constitutional law. This enables the WTO Agreement to have a strong connection with general international law[14] and the Appellate Body confirmed that the body of general international law includes WTO law.[15]

This jurisprudential calculus of general principles flows in the background of the Article XXIII: 1 (b), which is a reason why NVNI complaints must also be reviewed *normatively*. This reviewing pro-

---

(balance of payments problems), XIX (escape clause), XX–XXI (general exception), XXV (waiver), XXIV (customs unions and free trade areas); *See* JACKSON (1969), at 533–752.

11 In Robert Summer's version, the context of "instrumental" here is that law is "something *for use* and *in use* in daily life," *see* ROBERT S. SUMMERS, INSTITUTIONALISM AND AMERICAN LEGAL THEORY 270 (1982).

12 *See, e.g.* PIERRE PESCATORE, 'Drafting and Analyzing Decisions on Dispute Settlement', in 1 HANDBOOK OF WTO/GATT DISPUTE SETTLEMENT (1998), PART 2, at 11.

13 *See id.*

14 *Id.*

15 *See, e.g.* WTO Appellate Body Report, *US – Gasoline*, at 16; Article 3.2 of DSU explicitly recognises this new legitimacy for the purpose of dispute settlement.

cess becomes inevitably involved in pondering over the *underlying general values or principles of international community* to establish legal obligations in WTO law. The values can be introduced into the WTO system in the form of general principles of international law (e.g. good faith, equity, legitimate expectation)[16] and the introduction has been legitimately encouraged by using a broad cause of action: *impediment of attainment of any objective* of WTO Agreements. Furthermore, with a good authority of the general principles, we could legitimately interpret the rules against the unexpected as encouraging flexibility in WTO's legal system.

In conclusion, the obligations in NVNI complaints are to be *externally coherent* in the sense that the Article XXIII: 1(b) would be pointless if isolated from its operative values. From this external coherence, we can confirm that *values*[17] exist in WTO's legal system whereby sets of rules are regarded as their concrete manifestations. One of the common values in WTO law concerns *legitimate expectation* stemming from Good Faith or Equity principles.[18]

b. Good Faith

Good faith is a well-established principle of international law and several multilateral treaties have incorporated the principle as a general principle of international law.[19] Article 2(2) of the Charter of the United Nations supported by General Assembly Resolution 2625 (XXV), uses the principle for governing friendly relations and

16 *See* Cottier & Schefer (2000), p. 48.

17 *See, e.g.* Thomas Cottier, *Trade and Human Rights: A Relationship to Discover,* 5 JIEL 111 (2002). Here he explores the possible relationship between trade rules and fundamental principles and values in trading system.

18 Cottier & Schefer (2000), p. 54.

19 *Id.,* p. 48; However, a caveat is in order. Because good faith is an elusive idea taking on different meanings and emphases by different context, we have to need examine the particular contexts and the nature of the subject matters, *see generally* Good Faith in Contract: Concept and Context 3–4 (Roger Brownsword et al., eds, 1999).

cooperation among states. Article 26 and 31(1) of the Vienna Convention on the Law of Treaties relies upon the recognition of this principle in state practice. Moreover, the ICJ recognises the principle of good faith as "one of the basic principles governing the creation and performance of legal obligations".[20] In addition, this case also supported the significance of *estoppel* principle founded in the good faith.[21] Although the ICJ did not clearly refer to the estoppel in this *Nuclear Test* case, it was suggested by the ICJ that the French declarations were intended to induce a certain conduct and the other parties would be detrimentally affected by the French declarations, if the declarations were not observed.[22] A relevant GATT NVNI case of estoppel is the *Germany – Starch* (1955).[23] By referring to two facts construing estoppel: (1) a general assurance by Germany that "the duties would be reduced as soon as possible"; and (2) an agreement for Germany to negotiate the tariffs, the Panel implied that Germany would have been estopped from refusing to do so.[24]

The recognition of good faith represents a major advance in modern international law. The impact on reasoning WTO law is considerable for several reasons. First, the sheer volume of case

20 Neclear Tests Cases, ICJ Reports (1974), at 253, para. 268; Although the cases did not proceed to the merits phase, along with the points pertinent to good faith principle, they contains exclusive implication for issues relating to nuclear disarmament; for the doctrine of the freedom of the high seas; and for the general law of state responsibility for environmental damage. *See* BARBARA KWIATKOWSKA, *New Zealand v. France Nuclear Tests: The Dismissed Case of Lasting Significance,* 37 Virginia Journal of International Law 107. 117–118 & 182–190; *See also* GOLDIE (1985), at 219–31.

21 COTTIER & MUELLER (1995), p. 118.

22 *Id.* Cottier & Mueller on the other hand observed that "It is usually very difficult, [...] to prove intention as a subjective element of a party's behaviour." *Id.*

23 *See* COTTIER & SCHEFER (1997), p. 177.

24 GATT Panel Report, *Germany – Starch,* paras. 5–7. Actually, the Germany offered to grant the promised tariff concessions and the Panel suggested that the parties find a mutually acceptable resolution of the problem, reserving the right to adjudicate if it were necessary. *See id,* para. 4.

law is constantly increasing.[25] Second, the broad recognition of good faith symbolises a commitment to one of the most fundamental objectives of international legal system, i.e. Justice.[26] When we speak of justice, it implies a certain acceptable outcome in an evalu-

25 *See, e.g.* Appellate Body Report, *EC – Sardines (AB)*, para. 278 (the US claim); *US – Shrimp (AB)*, para. 158; *US – FSC (AB)*, para. 166; *US – Hot-Rolled Steel (AB)*, para. 101; *But cf. US – Offset Act (AB)*, para. 298 ("Nothing, however, in the covered agreements supports the conclusion that simply because a WTO Member is found to have violated a substantive treaty provision, it has therefore not acted in good faith. In our view, *it would be necessary to prove more than mere violation to support such a conclusion*") [emphasis added].

26 The concept of justice in context of international economic law is often used to consider a legal order with value in legal and social thought. Certain problems in WTO law, including trade linkage problems, are to be examined as problems involving the often conflicting claims of justice in the context of international economic law. *See generally* FRANK J. GARCIA, *Trade and Justice: Linking the Trade Linkage Debates,* 19 University of Pennsylvania Journal of International Economic Law 391, 391–411 (1998). FRIEDER ROESSLER, *Domestic Policy Objectives and the Multilateral Trade Order,* 19 University of Pennsylvania Journal of International Economic Law 201 (1998) (noting links between employment, balance of payments issues, and fair labor standards recognized in 1947–48 conference leading to the Havana Charter and in the Charter itself). On the trade and environment link, *see, e.g.* STEVE CHARNOVITZ, *Free Trade, Fair Trade, Green Trade: Defogging the Debate,* 27 Cornell International Law Journal 459 (1994). Other recognized or asserted linkage fields include: human rights, *see, e.g.* JAMES F. SMITH, *NAFTA and Human Rights: A Necessary Linkage,* 27 University of California at Davis Law Review 793 (1994); Patricia Stirling, *The Use of Trade Sanctions as an Enforcement Mechanism for Basic Human Rights: A Proposal for Addition to the World Trade Organization,* 11 American University Journal of International Law and Policy 1 (1996); competition law, *see, e.g.* ELEANOR M. FOX, *Toward World Antitrust and Market Access,* 91 AJIL 1 (1997); intellectual property, *see, e.g.* FRANK J. GARCIA, *Protection of Intellectual Property Rights in the North American Free Trade Agreement: A Successful Case of Regional Trade Regulation,* 8 American University Journal of International Law & Policy 817 (1993); and culture, *see, e.g.* JOHN DAVID DONALDSON, "*Television Without Frontiers*"*: The Continuing Tension Between Liberal Free Trade and European Cultural Integrity,* 20 Fordham International Law Journal 90 (1996) and W. MING SHAO, *Is There No Business Like Show Business? Free Trade and Cultural Protectionism,* 20 Yale Journal of International Law 105 (1995).

ative or justificatory sense.[27] Thus the particular criteria by which the acceptability of an outcome is evaluated will depend on the theoretical framework used for the analysis. One of the theoretical frameworks for dispute settlement is good faith principle. It is important for constructing coherent interpretation in terms of good faith for improving "fairness"[28] in WTO dispute settlement.

Third, although the general obligation of good faith "has only marginal value as an autonomous source of rights and duties"[29] and although the WTO Agreements do not explicitly refer to the principle of good faith and equity,[30] its relevance in trade law is peculiarly wide-ranging. Moreover, it provides a benchmark for determining the extent and sort of the legal obligations incurred by states within international law. In *US – Shrimp,* the AB stated that:

> The chapeau of Article XX is, in fact, but one expression of the principle of good faith. This principle, at once a general principle of law and a general principle of international law, controls the exercise of rights by states.[31]

27 *See* John Bell & Eric Schokkaert, Interdisciplinary Theory and Research on Justice, in Justice: Interdisciplinary Perspectives 237 (Klaus R. Scherer, ed., 1992).

28 "Fairness is a composite of two independent variables: legitimacy and distributive justice." *See* Franck (1995), at 25 & ch. 1.

29 Virally (1983), at 133; *Cf.* On appeal of *US – Offset Act,* the United States maintains that there is "no basis or justification in the WTO Agreement for a WTO dispute settlement panel to conclude that a Member has not acted in good faith, or to enforce a principle of good faith as a substantive obligation agreed to by WTO Members." *See US – Offset Act (AB),* para. 296; Because of the "marginal value" of good faith, sometimes a legal status of good faith needs to be supported by more proof than mere violation of treaty provision. In *US – Offset Act (AB),* the AB noted that "Clearly, therefore, there is a basis for a dispute settlement panel to determine, in an appropriate case, whether a Member has not acted in good faith. *Nothing, however, in the covered agreements supports the conclusion that simply because a WTO Member is found to have violated a substantive treaty provision, it has therefore not acted in good faith. In our view, it would be necessary to prove more than mere violation to support such a conclusion.*" [emphasis added] *See US – Offset Act (AB),* paras. 297–98.

30 *See, e.g.* Cottier & Schefer (2000), p. 55.

31 Appellate Body Report, *US – Shrimp (AB),* para. 158; *See also* Appellate Body Report, *US – FSC (AB),* para. 166; In relation to GATT Article XXI, the GATT

This benchmark function of good faith or equity could prevent members from executing bad faith in several WTO contexts.[32] Fourth, the good faith principle embodies a fundamental norm that plays an inherently significant role in WTO law. It can operate as a sort of safety valve in the volatile trade disputes which DSB may fill gaps and qualify rights and obligations otherwise arising under the broad or vague languages like in the NVNI complaints.[33] Finally, as a source of an integral part of legal obligations in trade law, the principle can perform as a direct and overt tool to restore the basic demand of "reciprocity" in trade agreements. In some sense, international trade dispute resolution may be historically summarised as a painstaking effort to overcome "indirect protections" by domestic commercial measures which are invented for evading original trade commitments. Leaving such measures of bad faith unredressed will lead to fictionalising the trade agreements or otherwise begetting unpredictability, unclarity, or inequity of international trade. This is the main significance of good faith principle in the context of NVNI complaints.[34]

member states decided that with respect to Article XXI "Security Exceptions"), they "should be cautious not to take any step which might have the effect of undermining the General Agreement," which implies that good faith is a requisite for Article XXI's invocation. *See* 1 GATT ANALYTICAL INDEX (1995), at 600 ("The spirit in which Members of the Organization would interpret these provisions was the only guarantee against abuses").

32 For example, in *US – Hot-Rolled Steel (AB),* the AB found that "... the principle of good faith [...] informs the provisions of the *Anti-Dumping Agreement,* as well as the other covered agreements," *see* Appellate Body Report, *US – Hot-Rolled Steel,* para. 101.

33 In this context, the distinction between "procedural" and "substantive" good faith is useful, *see* COTTIER & SCHEFER (2000), pp. 59–60.

34 *See* COTTIER & SCHEFER (2000), pp. 55–65.

c. Equity

As the conceptual origin of equity goes back to the Aristotelian premise[35] that equity should alleviate the defects of generally worded laws,[36] the concept over time came to penetrate into English jurisprudence through civilian law passed down from the Romans.[37] This historical interaction[38] makes it clear that "the general principle of good faith in international law," which originated from the Roman Law's *fides publica*, "would not be complete without mak-

35 There are three general theories of justice in discussions on equity. The oldest is Aristotle's *equity principle*, which asserts that goods should be divided in proportion to each claimant's contribution. A second theory of justice is *classical utilitarianism*, which states that goods should be distributed so as to maximise the total welfare of the claimants (*the greatest good for the greatest number*). A third approach to social justice is John Rawls's theory, which states the least well-off group in society should be made as well off as possible. *See* H. PEYTON YOUNG, EQUITY: IN THEORY AND PRACTICE 9–10 (1994); *See also* JANIS (1995), p. 109.

36 The concept of equity remains difficult to positively define. It is often defined by listing approximate synonyms that seem equally elusive: fairness, justice, reasonableness, good faith. *See* SCHACHTER (1997), at 55–56. He distinguishes the following five uses of equity and equitable principles: "(1) Equity as a basis for 'individualised' justice tempering the rigours of strict law. (2) Equity as consideration of fairness, reasonableness and good faith. (3) Equity as a basis for certain specific principles of legal reasoning associated with fairness and reasonableness: to wit, estoppel, unjust enrichment, and abuse of rights. (4) Equitable standards for the allocation and sharing of resources and benefits. (5) Equity as a broad synonym for distributive justice used to justify demands for economic and social arrangements and redistribution of wealth". *See id.*

37 The equity administered by the early English Chancellors was borrowed from the *aequitas* and judicial power of the Roman magistrates, *see* SPENCER W. SYMONS, A TREATISE ON EQUITY JURISPRUDENCE 3 (5th ed., 1994).

38 To assess the possible claims raised by equity in context of modern international law, it would be essential to understand the English institutional setting that gave rise to and sustained the equitable practice in England. Traditionally, equity was emerged as a doctrinal artifact of an old English governmental structure, one that had made so little distinction among governmental powers as to made it natural for judicial agency to exercise independent discretion in relation to statutes.

ing reference to the doctrines of equity emanating from the traditions of common law."[39] So viewed, the doctrine does not translate well into WTO Agreements marked by a formally designed system of separated powers.

The use of equity has been discussed by international lawyers and tribunals under three headings of equity *infra legem* (within the law), *praeter legem* (outside the law) and *contra legem* (against the law). The first category is well accepted. It enables the tribunal to apply the law within the margin allowed for interpretation by considering the circumstances of the case.[40] Interpretations from *contra legem* would normally be excluded unless the parties concerned agreed on the desirability of an interpretation *ex aequo et bone.*[41] The category of equity *praeter legem* is most relevant to reasoning NVNI complaints.[42] This usage of equity is still controversial because the questions here raised appear by virtue of the silence of the law on the point at issue.[43] The recent discussion of "treatment equity" for HIV/AIDS patients in developing countries in intellectual property rights will be another concrete example.[44]

In the context of NVNI complaints, the difficult task to judicial bodies has been that no substantive standard for resolving NVNI claims is given to them. The discussion on issues of this kind is reminiscent of the earlier comments on positivists and counter-

39 COTTIER & SCHEFER (2000), p. 54.

40 M. Akehurst, *Equity and General Principles of Law,* 25 International and Comparative Law Quarterly 802 (1976).

41 This Latin phrase means that "According to what is equitable and good," *see* BLACK'S LAW DICTIONARY (1999), at 581; SCHACHTER (1997), at 57; Article 38 (2) of the Statute of the ICJ provides that the court has power to "decide a case *ex aequo et bone,* if the parties agree thereto."

42 *Cf.* JANIS (1995), p. 109 ("In the [*praeter legem*] sense, equity is seen as a gap-filler when the law is silent").

43 SCHACHTER (1997), *id.*

44 "Treatment equity" is the umbrella phrase explaining the need of greater equity in access to treatments between patients in developed and developing countries. *See* J. M. SPECTAR, *Patent Necessity: Intellectual Property Dilemmas in the Biotech Domain & Treatment Equity for Developing Countries,* 24 Houston Journal of International Law 227 (2002).

positivists. The former as proponents of positive WTO law would be more likely to reject *outside sources* on equitable ground as unwarranted judicial legislation, claiming the significance of each Member's regulatory autonomy. The counter-positivists would favor more consideration of intent and "objective" of WTO law and thus allow employment of the outside sources for interpreting NVNI complaints.[45] In other words, this latter group proposes that equity doctrine gives assumed moral values predominance over man-made law and subsequently enables judges to conform the positive law to those natural legal principles.[46]

Both groups would be influenced by their perception of the degree to which the WTO rule in question left discretion for diverse interpretation. However, in recent development of international law, the equity concept and its derivative principles have been recognised as assimilating into general principles of law.[47] Thus, by a doctrinal construction, equity has become part of law.[48] In this context, the following statement by Oscar Schachter is instructive in reasoning NVNI complaints:

> The controversy as to whether they are *contra legem* or *praeter legem* is avoided by recognizing them as general principles of law or as basic factors in legal reasoning applicable to all legal systems. A similar approach has been taken with respect to such substantive concepts of equity as estoppel, unjust enrichment and abuse of rights. These concepts are now often characterised as general principles recognised by civilised nations and therefore applicable as positive law to State conduct and State responsibility. While not free from controversy as to their place in customary law, they are employed widely as general principles in the assertion of rights and obligations.[49] [footnote deleted]

45 *See* PART FOUR – XI – B of this dissertation.

46 COTTIER & SCHEFER (1997), pp. 164–65.

47 *See, e.g.*, WOLFGANG FRIEDMANN, THE CHANGING STRUCTURE OF INTERNATIONAL LAW 188–210 (1964); Janis (1995), p. 110.

48 SCHACHTER (1997), at 58.

49 *Id.*

A highly abstract rule or term like NVNI complaints would open the door more widely to equitable consideration, which needs a theorization in a concrete form.[50]

B. Roles of "Objective" of GATT Article XXIII : 1

1. *In General*

A literal text of WTO Agreements conveys instructions of varying specificity to members that must implement or obey the Agreements. At the same time, it is said that a background purpose underlies those textual commands.[51] Because literal texts are often necessarily drafted in general terms causing indeterminate elements of the texts, none will match its apparent purpose in every application. Thus the purpose of a treaty can play a leading role in resolving the indeterminacy of the GATT/WTO law.[52]

50 *But cf.* As assessing the results of the Uruguay Round, John Jackson observed that "In any event, [the results] seems generally clear that a rule-orientation has now largely prevailed in the GATT context. This brings the GATT into line with most other international dispute settlement procedures, and appropriately focuses attention on the specific treaty obligations, rather than general and arguable notions of 'equity' or 'nullification or impairment.'" *See* JACKSON (2000), at 132.

51 The purpose of international regulation of trade is "essential to prevent the pursuit of self-interested national regulation of international trade in a manner that harms other nations and in a manner that [...] results in a sharp and chaotic restriction in the over-all level of international trade." *See* JACKSON (1969), at 9; *See also* WAINCYMER (2002), at 434; HUHN (2003), at 316 ("Law should be interpreted not by consulting a dictionary, but by inquiring into the underlying purposes of the law").

52 In terms of general contract law, this part can be rephrased as follows: "Traditionally, many of [sic] rules relating to particular contracts are regarded as resting on 'implied terms' in the original contract, and these implied terms are themselves regarded as resting on the presumed intention of the parties." *See* P.S. ATIYAH, AN INTRODUCTION TO THE LAW OF CONTRACT 201–202 (5th ed.,1996);

On the other, the debate on the purpose of WTO is political and multi-faceted.[53]

First, according to the WTO preamble, the parties recognized "the optimal use of world's resources in accordance with the objective of sustainable development, [...]".[54] It further notes that the parties were desirous of "entering into reciprocal and mutually advantageous arrangements directed to the substantial reduction of tariffs and other barriers to trade and to the elimination of discriminatory treatment in international trade relations". Second, Article II of the WTO Agreement states that "the WTO shall provide the *common institutional framework for the conduct of trade relations* among its Members in matters related to the agreements".[55] Third, Article III indicates that "the WTO shall provide the forum for negotiations among its Members concerning their multilateral trade relations in matters dealt with under the agreements [...] [and] may also provide a forum for further negotiations among its Members concerning their multilateral trade relations".[56] If those statements

---

In WTO law, this purpose exploration is closely related to "WTO-linkage" aspects, *see, e.g.*, Steve Charnovitz, *Triangulating the World Trade Organization,* 96 AJIL. 28, 30–34 (2002). *Cf.* BENJAMIN N. CARDOZO, THE NATURE OF THE JUDICIAL PROCESS 66 (1921) ("The final cause of law is the welfare of society. The rule that misses its aim cannot permanently justify its existence [...] Logic and history and custom have their place. We will shape the law to conform to them when we may; but only within bounds. The end which the law serves will dominate them all").

53 In this sense, the purposes of each WTO Agreements indicate various "policies" in the Agreements. The feasible conflicts among the various policies at the WTO level may be big challenges for the WTO. *See* JACKSON (1969), at 26–29; JACKSON (2000), at 414–17.

54 WTO Agreement, preamble; The compliance panel in the *US – Shrimp (21.5)* declared that "we must keep in mind that sustainable development is one of the objectives of the WTO Agreement." *See US – Shrimp (21.5),* para. 5.54. The role of the compliance panel is to see whether the defending government has complied with the recommendations of the WTO Dispute Settlement Body.

55 WTO Agreement, Article II : 1 [emphasis added].

56 *Id.*, Article III : 2.

are right, the purpose of WTO would have far-reaching and conflicting implications regarding the obligations of WTO law.[57]

In effect, the legitimacy of NVNI complaints was stemmed from a dire necessity for achieving balancing acts of preventing any deviations from "substantial reduction of tariffs" (an objective of GATT).[58] Thus an examination of multiple purposes of WTO[59] can yield insight into the normative basis for the NVNI complaints and give an important clue for the applicability of the complaints. The examination can be made two ways. One way is to look at the purpose of particular provisions and the other way is a deduction of purposes of individual provisions from an analysis of the general purpose.[60] Once we have a frame that explicates the functions of current GATT/WTO purpose, that frame can be used to assess which standard is proper for the applicability of the complaints.

2. *GATT/WTO Jurisprudence on Objective*

Article XXIII:1 allows complaints if "the attainment of any objective of an Agreement" is being impeded. In GATT/WTO jurisprudence no Panel report has ever dealt substantively with it even

57 The statement is associated with "WTO-linkage" problem. Regarding "strategic" danger of the linkage, David Leebron observed that "[...] First, linkage might undermine the ability of nations to reach a consensus on the agenda and the resolution of the issues. [...] Second, linkage has the potential to undermine the normative framework for a particular regime or the degree of commitment to that regime. [...] Equally important, linkage or the expansion of the regime's scope might weaken the degree of commitment to the regime, in particular the enforcement mechanisms to which the parties are willing to agree. [...] Third, and relatedly, linkage will sometimes create an additional source of regime instability. [...] In most such situations, linkage is a second-best solution. It would be preferable to develop the unsatisfactory regime independently [...]." *See* DAVID W. LEEBRON, *Symposium: The Boundaries of the WTO: Linkages*, 96 AJIL 5, 25–27 (2002).

58 Preamble of GATT 47.

59 For the multiple purposes of WTO, *see* WAINCYMER (2002), at 437–56.

60 WAINCYMER (2002), at 448.

where the "objective" basis for the complaint is available in respect of all subparagraphs of Article XXIII : 1. Various complaints under GATT 47, however, have alleged impediments to attainment of an objective of that Agreement. For example, in *Japan – Nullification or Impairment of the Benefits* (1983),[61] the European Communities made a complaint under Article XXIII : 2, alleging that "benefits of successive GATT negotiations with Japan have not been realised owing to a series of factors particular to the Japanese economy [...]."[62] Furthermore, the complainant submitted that:

> [...] [t]he present situation constitutes a nullification or impairment by Japan, of the benefits otherwise accruing to the European Community under the GATT, and an impediment to the attainment of GATT's objectives. In particular, the general GATT objective of "reciprocal and mutually advantageous arrangements" has not been achieved.[63]

This complaint however was not pursued.

Another interesting case was Nicaragua's 1986 complaint in *US – Nicaragua*. Nicaragua alleged, among other things, that a trade embargo impeded achieving the objectives of the GATT. On this, the Panel which had limited terms of reference, concluded in its Report:

> The Panel therefore concluded that embargoes such as the one imposed by the United States, independent of whether or not they were justified under Article XXI, ran counter to *basic aims of the GATT, namely to foster non-discriminatory and open trade policies, to further the development of the less-developed contracting parties and to reduce uncertainty in trade relations.* The Panel recognised that the General Agreement protected each contracting party's essential security interests through Article XXI and that the General Agreement's purpose was therefore not to make contracting parties forego their essential security interests for the sake of these aims. However, the

61 GATT Panel Report, *Japan – Nullification or Impairment of the Benefits Accruing to the EEC under the General Agreement and Impediment to the Attainment of GATT Objectives*, L/5479, adopted 8 April 1983.

62 *Id.*, page 1.

63 *Id.*, page 3.

> Panel considered that the GATT could not achieve its basic aims unless each contracting party, whenever it made use of its rights under Article XXI, carefully weighed its security needs against the need to maintain stable trade relations.[64] [emphasis added]

In the 1988 *Japan – Semi-conductors* case,[65] the EC (the complainant) submitted that the third country market monitoring system in question "was contrary to the basic philosophy and objectives of the General Agreement". More specifically, it stated:

> [...] that one of the objectives in the Preamble of the General Agreement was the "substantial reduction of tariff and other barriers to trade," and that the objective of this reduction included the expansion of production and exchange of goods. [...] To achieve these objectives, it was necessary for all contracting parties not to manipulate the system through the imposition of

64 GATT Panel Report, *United States-Trade Measures Affecting Nicaragua,* para. 5.16; In this case, the US used GATT Article XXI(b) to justify the embargo it imposed on Nicaragua in 1985. Nicaragua argued that the security exemptions should only be applied in cases of self-defense, such as when states are subjected to direct aggression. The Panel examining the issue was unable to examine whether the US' use of Article XXI was justified, because its terms of reference precluded it from even considering any invocation of Article XXI. *See* 1 GATT ANALYTICAL INDEX (1995), at 607–08.

65 In this important case, the complainant (EC) challenged the 1986 Japan – U.S. Arrangement on Semiconductor Trade. The Panel found that (1) export regulations that prevent or quantitatively restrict exports below a minimum price level are inconsistent with GATT Article XI; (2) a complex of Japanese government measures including non-legally binding administrative guidance to prevent semiconductor exports below cost were such export restrictions and, hence, inconsistent with GATT Article XI; (3) the GATT's provisions on dumping in Article VI neither justify nor forbid such restraints by exporting countries; and (4) the evidence did not show that Japanese actions to improve market access for foreign semiconductors had discriminated in favor of U.S. products; Here the EC had argued NVNI claims of Article XXIII(1)(b) and (c), but the Panel rejected this argument, as the EC's evidence on the market access issue did not indicate actual discrimination. *See* GATT Panel Report, *Japan – Semi-conductors,* para. 124–27; *See also* Peter D. Trooboff & Amelia Porges, *International Trade – Export Restraint Agreement – Japan-United States – Third Country Dumping,* 83 AJIL 388 (1989).

> arbitrary, unilateral export restrictions especially in areas where they had gained a substantial degree of preeminence in terms of concentration of production of essential products.[66]

In addition, Australia's 1979 complaint in *European Communities – Refunds on Exports of Sugar* claimed impediment to attainment of the objective of General Agreement[67] but because no detailed submissions were made on this point, the Panel Report did not consider it.

In the WTO era, consideration of *objective* or *purpose* of WTO Agreements has become significant and often, mainly because of possible gaps in the broad coverage of the Agreements. Moreover, for filling the gaps, general principles of customary international law have been referred to. This logic is clearly found in the following statement of *Korea – Procurement* Panel:

> In our view, the non-violation remedy as it has developed in GATT/WTO jurisprudence should not be viewed in isolation from general principles of customary international law.[68]
>
> [...]
>
> Thus, [...] we will review the claim of nullification or impairment raised by the United States within the framework of principles of international law which are generally applicable not only to performance of treaties but also to treaty negotiation. To do otherwise potentially would leave a gap in the applicability of the law generally to WTO disputes and we see no evidence in the language of the WTO Agreements that such a gap was intended. If the non-violation remedy were deemed not to provide a relief for such problems as have arisen in the present case regarding good faith and error in the negotiation of GPA commitments (and one might add, in tariff and services commitments under other WTO Agreements), then nothing could be done about them within the framework of the WTO dispute settlement mechanism if general rules of customary international law on good faith and error in treaty negotiations were ruled not to be applicable.[69] [footnote deleted]

66 *Japan – Semi-conductors*, paras. 137–138.
67 GATT Panel Report, *EC – Sugar*, para. 2.1.
68 *Korea – Procurement*, para. 7.93.
69 *Id.*, para. 7.101.

In *Argentina – Textiles and Apparel*, the Appellate Body noted that a basic purpose of the GATT 94:

> In accordance with the general rules of treaty interpretation set out in Article 31 of the *Vienna Convention*, Article II: 1(b), first sentence, must be read in its context and in light of the object and purpose of the GATT 1994. [...] A basic object and purpose of the GATT 1994, as reflected in Article II, is to preserve the value of tariff concessions negotiated by a Member with its trading partners, and bound in that Member's Schedule. Once a tariff concession is agreed and bound in a Member's Schedule, a reduction in its value by the imposition of duties in excess of the bound tariff rate would upset the balance of concessions among Members.[70]

The examination of the functions of *objective* is valuable to rightly assess NVNI complaints in the changed and broad context of WTO law.[71] In this context, the following observation of David Daul is instructive for future discussions on NVNI complaints in WTO era.

> Although never before argued at the former GATT or the WTO, the conditions precedent to a non-violation impediment to objectives claim also appear easy to satisfy. By using the WTO to settle the [*Japan – Film*] dispute, the United States will give the new organisation an opportunity to send a message that free trade is important and every member has an obligation not to impede the attainment by another member of the objectives of the WTO.[72]

3. *Bridging Role between Specific and General Obligations*

The "objective" of GATT Article XXIII: 1 under some conditions materializes *general/customary* obligations which were not clearly regulated at the beginning of the GATT/WTO system.[73] For ex-

70 Appellate Body Report, *Argentina – Footwear and Apparel (AB)*, para. 47.

71 For the various objectives of WTO Agreements, *see* WAINCYMER (2002), at 450–56.

72 DUAL (1995), at 149–50.

73 In general, the objective or principle of a normative system can accommodate situations where the imposition of liability, rights in a broad sense, is felt to be needed. *See, e.g.*, N. MACCORMIC, Defeasibility in Law and Logic in Z. BANKOWSKI (ed.), INFORMATICS AND THE FOUNDATIONS OF LEGAL REASONING, 1995, p. 99.

ample, when any subsidy without infringing *codified* obligation, affects unfavorably the competitive relations between domestic and imported goods, the objective would require a rebalancing between rights and obligations by introducing the *general* obligation in conjunction with the "objective" of GATT Article XXIII: 1.

In order to prevent the unlimited claims for the general obligation, which may hamper the predictable application of WTO law, the general obligation is to be materialized through the codified provisions in a *reasonable* manner. In arguing NVNI complaints, the reasonable expectation *attached* to the codified provisions serves this role. In this context, the AB's opinion on *EC – Computer Equipment* is reasonable:

> However, nothing in [GATT] Article II: 5 suggests that the expectations of only the exporting Member can be the basis for interpreting a concession in a Member's Schedule for the purposes of determining whether that Member has acted consistently with its obligations under Article II: 1. In discussing Article II: 5, the Panel overlooked the second sentence of that provision, which clarifies that the "contemplated treatment" referred to in that provision is the treatment contemplated by *both* Members.[74] [emphasis in original]

The subordinate nature of the general obligation to the codified obligation in terms of their legal effect, on the other hand, is evident in the procedural stage. In many NVNI cases, there has been no clear distinction between violation (corresponding to codified obligations) and NVNI (related to general obligations) complaints.[75] Furthermore, at the initial stage of complaints, the NVNI provision does not provide an independent cause of action: it has played mainly an *auxiliary* role as a foresight against the failure of the codified obligation argument.[76]

The objective of GATT Article XXIII: 1 thus acts as the standard for filling gaps *(lacunae)* in WTO law.[77] In most NVNI complaints

74 Appellate Body Report, *EC – Computer Equipment,* para. 81.

75 HUDEC (1970), at 618.

76 CHO (1998), at 322; *See also Japan – Film,* para. 1.2.

77 *See generally,* KELSEN (1961), at 147 ("The legal order cannot have any gaps. If the judge is authorised to decide a given dispute as legislator in case the

cases, we can find this function of objective. For example,[78] if the *competitive relationships* is undermined by a GATT-consistent measure which is not illegalized by a clear WTO provision, the aggrieved member can bring the measure into DSB under the title of NVNI. In this case the objective of competitive relationships guides interpretation of the NVNI case. This bridging role of "objective" between specific and general obligations is strongly relevant to *what could be a proper standard for the applicable scope of NVNI complaints or liability* in WTO.

legal order does not contain any general norm [...] he does not fill a gap of actually valid law, but he adds to the actually valid law an individual norm to which no general norm corresponds"); At the level of GATT/WTO, *see* Von Bogdandy (1992), at 99 ("The panel could recognise the lawfulness [of the measure in question] because of a certain discretion of the contracting party, or it could leave the question open. In the second case, the possibility of a non-violation complaint based on a 'legal vacuum' persists").

78 *See, e.g.* GATT Panel Report, *EC– Oilseeds I,* para. 144 ("The idea underlying [the provisions of Article XXIII : 1(b)] is that the improved competitive opportunities [of Article II's objective of that can legitimately be expected from a tariff concession can be frustrated not only by measures proscribed by the General Agreement but also by measures consistent with that Agreement"; WTO Panel Report, *Japan – Film,* para. 10.82.

XII. Standards Defining the Scope of Non-Violation Complaints

A. Introduction

Mainly because of the subsequent codifications since GATT 47, the gap between substantive content and the objective has become much narrower. However, due to the limitation on legislating skill and the political considerations of members, it is very difficult to regulate every possible case against the objective. Thus, for accommodating derivations from the objective, the NVNI provision which employs indeterminate elements was born.[1] The indeterminacy[2] arises in part from the nature of terms of the Article XXIII: 1(b) and its anticipatory nature.[3] The indeterminacy matters because GATT/

1 *See, e.g.* ROESSLER (1997), p. 126.

2 The indeterminacy argument was originally developed by the legal realists as a critique of the legal formalism of the late nineteenth and early twentieth centuries. The realists introduced the indeterminacy argument to demonstrate that the application of the principles of deductive reasoning to the set of legal materials did not and could not uniquely determine the outcome of particular cases; that judicial decisions were not reasonably deducible from a closed legal system. The argument was based on two observations. The first was that the law is riddled with contradictory rules such that a judge will always have a choice between competing rules. The second was that it is always possible for a judge to interpret the breadth of the rules and the facts of the case so as to generate conflicting results. *See* JOHN HASNAS, *Back to the Future: From Critical Legal Studies Forward to Legal Realism, or How not to Miss the Point of the Indeterminacy Argument,* 45 Duke Law Journal 84, 86–98 (1995).

3 *See generally* KENN KRESS, *A Preface to Epistemological Indeterminacy,* 85 Northwestern University Law Review 134 (1985); S. Jay Plager, *Challenges for Intellectual Property Law in the Twenty First Century: Indeterminacy and Other Problems,* University of Illinois Law Review 69 (2001).

WTO rules are authoritative statements that are meant to guide behavior and are applicable in an indefinite number of occasions. As Professor Hart properly said, rules in general are described as having a core meaning and fringe of vagueness:[4] The indeterminate elements arise not because the meaning of the word is unclear in itself, but because in applying the rule, the question would always occur as to whether the general term used in the rule applied to a particular situation.[5] The indeterminacy is an inherent property of every legal system which creates both a vagueness of a provision in the law and a possibility of regulating a situation unforeseen when the terms of the provision were defined.[6] The apparent vagueness of Article XXIII: 1(b) thus must be interpreted positively focusing more on openness for future matters and considering its connection with the objective of WTO Agreements.[7] In this context it is difficult to accept the Article XXIII: 1(b) of GATT as "legal fantasy"[8] or "the Achilles' Heel of the dispute settlement process".[9]

More detailed, how does *the objective* and *the WTO code* relate to NVNI complaints? Given the breadth and ambiguity of the "objective," what tests should the DSB apply when it deliberates on Article XXIII claims? This must be a core to reasoning NVNI complaints. Although this dissertation is mainly focused on legal arguments, the following two tests also reflect assumptions made about the economics. The first *compensatory adjustment* test for NVNI complaints may presume that free trade will be good for a member regardless of whether the other Members have agreed to remove them.[10] On

4 Professor Hart contended that the realists had greatly exaggerated the amount of indeterminacy in the law. He argued that although there was indeed a "penumbra of doubt" within which the rules of law did not yield determinate outcomes, there was also a much more extensive "core of certainty." *See* HART (1997), at 122–23.

5 HART, *id.*

6 For this property of GATT law, *see* HUDEC (1990), pp. 3–45

7 *See* Article XXIII: 1 of GATT.

8 PESCATORE (1993), at 5.

9 CHO (1998), at 351.

10 *See, e.g.* PAUL KRUGMAN, *What Should Trade Negotiators Negotiate About?*, 35 Journal of Economic Literature 113, 113 (1997) ("the economist's case for free

the other hand, the *expectation* test reflects free trade will be more generally favorable if the WTO system is based on more *mutual concessions* among Members. In this view, the WTO agreements function as a set of *incomplete contracts.*[11] From this viewpoint, the focus of the WTO regime is on *pacta sunt servanda,*[12] not on welfare maximization and WTO members are permitted to take into account the distributional interests of producers to the potential detriment of consumers.[13]

According to the juristic commentaries on NVNI complaints and GATT/WTO jurisprudence, there might be four tests for deciding possible benefits accrued to NVNI complaints.[14]

---

trade is essentially a unilateral case: a country serves its own interests by pursuing free trade regardless of what other countries may do").

11 LINARELLI (2000), at 347; TRACTMAN (1999), at 346–50. He explained that "Treaties may be optimally incomplete in that they contain appropriate instructions for decision-makers to complete the 'contract' in particular cases. The parameters to consider include (i) the costs of advance specification, (ii) the degree to which the future is unpredictable or stochastic, (iii) the ability to customise to particular facts in specific cases and (iv) the potential value of diversity of compliance techniques," *see id.,* at 346–47.

12 Article 26 of the Vienna Convention translates this principle as follows: "Every treaty in force is binding upon the parties to it and must be performed by them in good faith." At the heart of this rule is the obligation to abstain from acts that would frustrate the object and purpose of a treaty. *See* THOMAS M. FRANCK, THE POWER OF LEGITIMACY AMONG NATIONS 187–88 (1990); JAMES LESLIE BRIERLY, THE BASIS OF OBLIGATION IN INTERNATIONAL LAW AND OTHER PAPERS 21 (1958). *See also* COTTIER & SCHEFER (1997), pp. 171–72.

13 According to John Linarelli, this state of affairs is embedded in the DSU and in the DSB's interpretations on NVNI complaints: "The DSB enforces the WTO bargain of tariff concessions and agreements on non-tariff barriers without regard to economic efficiency. The DSB exists in the nation state system of reciprocity, and it is bound to adhere to an approach resembling the legal doctrine of freedom of contract even when this approach is inconsistent with the maximization of consumer welfare or economic efficiency. In a reciprocity based system, the DSB focuses on the balance of concessions, the competitive relationships between the WTO members, and similar conceptualizations to either preserve or restate the WTO bargain struck by the WTO members." *See* LINARELLI (2000), at 348.

14 An economic background of the following standards has much to do with the extent of free trade. The first standard of "adjustment test" for NVNI complaints

B. Compensatory Adjustment Standard

1. Relevant Cases: Citrus and Uruguayan Recourse

A radical and the broadest standard for NVNI complaints that would depart significantly from the mainstream GATT jurisprudence, would be *compensatory adjustment* test.[15] In 1985 *Citrus*, Panel stated:

> The Panel noted that the basic purpose of Article XXIII : 1(b) was to provide for offsetting or compensatory adjustment in situations in which the balance of rights and obligations of the contracting parties had been disturbed (see page 5 of document E/PC/T/A/PV/6 of 2 June 1947). One of the fundamental benefits accruing to the contracting parties under the General Agreement, therefore, was the right to such adjustment in situations in which the balance of their rights and obligations had been upset to their disadvantage.[16] [emphasis added]

Using the *compensatory adjustment* test, the Panel attempted to rebalance the rights and obligations of the NVNI complainant. The complainant (US) would have to demonstrate that the measures of the defendant unambiguously caused substantial adverse effect to its actual trade or its trade opportunities.[17]

Although following the exact reasoning of the *Citrus Panel* is difficult, main points were that the US had a right to expect certain benefits from the *MFN obligation of GATT Article I,* and that these benefits had been impaired to the extent that preferential agreements between the respondent (EC) and the Mediterranean countries had caused considerable trade damages.[18] Thus this case is fairly different from the conventional type of NVNI cases in that

---

may be presumed of complete free trade, i.e. removal of all trade restrictions regardless of whether WTO Members have agreed to remove them. The neo-classical economic theory of comparative advantage reflects this approach. For a simple case for complete free trade, SYKES (1998), at 60–68.

15 This is similar to John Linarelli's "inefficient test." *See* LINARELLI (2000), at 348–52.

16 *EC – Citrus,* para. 4.37.

17 *Id.*

18 *See* HUDEC (1993), at 160.

Citrus Panel (1) expanded the applicability of NVNI complaints into *any benefit* under the GATT;[19] and (2) did weigh the economic "disadvantage of the contracting parties"[20] rather than on the conventional requirement of reasonable/legitimate expectation.[21] The Panel's approach can be interpreted in its explicit preference of maximizing economic welfare in reviewing the NVNI claim[22] while setting aside the contracting parties' mutual understanding. This broad discretion of the *Citrus* Panel raises the issue of appropriate discretion by panels (and the Appellate Body).[23]

In another relevant case *Uruguayan Recourse to Article XXIII* (1961),[24] the argument of Uruguay guides us about the *compensatory adjustment* test. According to the GATT *Uruguayan Recourse to Article XXIII* Panel, the representative of Uruguay drew the atten-

19 *EC – Citrus*, para. 4.36.

20 *Id.*, para. 4.37.

21 *See EC – Citrus*, para. 4.32 ("[...] the Panel could not find that the United States Government could not have reasonably anticipated in 1973, [...] that the tariff preferences accorded to certain Mediterranean countries by the Community of the Six already in place, would be extended to the Community of the Nine as well as improved in favour of the Mediterranean countries"). But, at the same time, Panel did note that "However, US Government negotiators must have been aware during the negotiation of the new tariff schedule of the Community of the Nine in 1973, that the value of the new tariff concessions that they received, or the old concessions which here confirmed, would be affected by the anticipated extension and deepening of the tariff preferences on citrus to the Mediterranean countries." *See id.*, para. 4.34. Thus, as recognizing the EC preferential measure had been reasonably anticipated by the U.S at the time of the negotiation of the tariff concession, the Panel admitted the U.S's NVNI claims.

22 LINARELLI (2000), at 348.

23 *See, e.g.* VON BOGDANDY (1992), at 99 (noting that a legal vacuum in a NVNI claim depends on the "approach of future panels in relation to judicial self-restraint"); *See generally* WILLIAM J. DAVEY, *Has The WTO Dispute Settlement System Exceeded Its Authority? – A Consideration Of Deference Shown By The System To Member Government Decisions And Its Use Of Issue-Avoidance Techniques*, JIEL 79, 85–86 (2001).

24 GATT Panel Report, *Uruguayan Recourse to Article XXIII*. In 1961, Uruguay complained to the GATT that GATT benefits accruing to it had been nullified or impaired by 562 trade restrictions imposed by fifteen industrialised countries.

tion of the Council of Representatives to the "trade problems concerning temperate primary producers such as Uruguay, both as regards the limited marketing opportunities available to them and the failure of the prices of their products to be maintained at a satisfactory level".[25] This alludes to the extent to which Uruguayan exports were confronted by restrictive measures in force in nineteen industrialized countries.[26] Actually, Uruguay made a kind of *situation claim*, referring to the general difficulties created for Uruguay by the restrictive measures affecting its exports and to the resulting inequality for temperate zone primary producers to participate in world trade.[27] Although the Panel recognised that "nullification or impairment must relate to benefits accruing to the contracting party 'under the General Agreement',"[28] the Panel made recommendations on some measures favouring Uruguay just by the existence of the allegedly restrictive measures.[29] This approach could also have danger of excessive discretion by the Panel.[30]

2. *Some Weaknesses of Compensatory Adjustment Standard*

The *compensatory adjustment* test could face some reasonable concerns.[31] First, the test could provide panels or the Appellate Body with incentives to be intrusively active and to add new substantive

25 *Uruguayan Recourse to Article XXIII,* para. 2.
26 *Id.*
27 LINARELLI (2000), at 349; *Uruguayan Recourse to Article XXIII,* para. 22. Here Uruguay did not provide a detailed demonstration of how each trade restriction impaired or nullified a particular GATT benefit.
28 *Uruguayan Recourse to Article XXIII,* para. 14.
29 The Panel avoided the issue of whether Uruguay' claim was justiciable and instead relied on procedure to decide the case, *see Uruguayan Recourse to Article XXIII,* paras. 16 & 20.
30 For example, in the *Uruguayan Recourse to Article XXIII,* regarding the Belgium's measures of *variable surtax* and *mixing regulation,* the Panel noted that "there are *a priori* grounds for assuming that they could have an adverse effect on Uruguay's exports." *See id.*, at 108.
31 *See* LINARELLI (2000), at 350–52. He picks up six possible objections related to the test.

obligations to the WTO regime on a case-by-case in dispute settlement rather than on a codified or legislative basis in WTO negotiating rounds. Second, by the judicial activism the test may be viewed as impinging on sovereignty in that it may prescribe the domestic policy autonomy of WTO Members. Third, a broad adjustment test thus could easily lead to literal violations of DSU Article 3.2, which provides that "[r]ecommendations and rulings of the DSB cannot add to or diminish the rights and obligations provided in the covered agreements". These concerns may be unfounded to the extent that interpretation on NVNI complaints is effective in constraining DSB preferences in a manner that align with the preferences of Members.

C. Expectation Standard

1. In General

Next standard for NVNI complaints is an *expectations* test. It has been used in all but one case[32] in GATT/WTO jurisprudence. For example, in the *Australian Subsidy* case that has been called the Marbury vs. Madison of the pre-Uruguay Round GATT period,[33] the Working Parties for the first time developed an *expectations* test:

> The working party next considered whether the injury which the Government of Chile said it had suffered represented a nullification of impairment of a benefit accruing to Chile directly or indirectly under the General Agreement and was therefore subject to the provision of Article XXIII. It was agreed that such impairment would exist if the action of the Australian Government which resulted in upsetting the competitive relationship between sodium

32 *See EC – Citrus*, para. 3.47.

33 HUDEC (1975), at 144–53; This *Australian Subsidy* case was also assessed as an example of emerging common law concept of *precedent* or *stare decisis*. *See* Raj Bhala, *The Myth about Stare Decisis and International Trade Law (Part One of a Trilogy)*, 14 American University International Law Review 845, 889 (1999).

> nitrate and ammonium sulphate *could not reasonably have been anticipated by the Chilean Government, taking into consideration all pertinent circumstances and the provisions of the General Agreement, at the time it negotiated for the duty-free binding on sodium nitrate.*[34] [emphasis added]

More recently, the Panel of *Japan – Film* confirmed this test like this:

> In all but one of the past GATT cases dealing with Article XXIII : 1(b) claims, the claimed benefit has been that of legitimate expectations of improved market-access opportunities arising out of relevant tariff concessions. This same set of GATT precedents suggests that for expectations to be legitimate, they must take into account all measures of the party making the concession that could have been reasonably anticipated at the time of the concession.[35]

As for this standard, three questions can be raised. First, it is unclear from where the *expectation* is to be created. Second question is whether there is a distinction between "legitimate expectations" and "reasonable expectations." Third question concerns how many subcategories are conceivable under *expectation standard* in GATT/WTO jurisprudence.

a. Foundation of Legitimate Expectation

There may be three explanations on foundation of legitimate (or reasonable) expectation. First, paying much attention to the increasing incorporation of international trade law into the public international law system, some commentators have argued that Article XXIII : 1(b) has its origin of protection of good faith or equity.[36] In addition, they have claimed that Article XXIII : 1(b) is analogous to the principle of *clausula rebus sic stantibus*,[37] frustration of purpose

34 *Australian Subsidy*, para. 12.
35 *Japan – Film*, para. 10.61.
36 COTTIER & SCHEFER (1997), pp. 171–81.
37 The principle of *clausula rebus sic stantibus* means that a treaty provision is binding only as long as the circumstances in existence when the treaty was signed remain substantially the same, *see* BLACK'S LAW DICTIONARY (1999), at 243. This principle was codified in Article 62 of the Vienna Convention. The deciding elements of the *clausula rebus* are said (1) the non-foreseeability of the change in circumstances (2) the importance of these circumstances to the

doctrine in English contract law,[38] to the principle of promissory estoppel[39] or abuse of rights.[40] Second explanation comes from private law viewpoint. It maintains that legitimate expectation is the foundation for much of contract law and it forms the basis for reliance-based theories of contract law.[41] Third, there is a claim that the legitimate expectation in WTO context can be better understood from both English contract law and English administrative law, because "the WTO agreements are essentially long-term bargains subject to re-negotiation by members in successive negotiating rounds" and "WTO law is regulatory or public in nature".[42]

---

purpose of the agreement as a whole (3) and the extent to which the obligations under the contract as a whole are affected by the change, *see* COTTIER & SCHEFER (1997), p. 173. *But cf.* "A closer look, however, shows that the substantive conditions are necessary to prove *clausula rebus sic stantibus* are more rigorous to fulfill than the normal non-violation complaint and that the legal remedies available in WTO reach less far than those dictated by an honest reading of *clausula rebus*." *Id. See also* VON BOGANDY (1992), at 110–11.

38 The principle implies that, if the entire performance of a contract becomes fundamentally changed, the contract is considered terminate, SEE BLACK'S LAW DICTIONARY (1999), at 679. Although this principle in international treaty is by no means generally accepted, its applicability to long-term contract situations makes it helpful in analysing WTO dispute settlement, *see* COTTIER & SCHEFER, *id.*, p. 175. *But see* Linarelli (2000), at 344. He points out that despite some similarities in the three concepts (NVNI, frustration of purpose and *clausula rebus sic stantibus*), the differences are substantial in that a successful NVNI claim does not excuse or discharge a WTO member from performance of its WTO obligations. *Id.*

39 The doctrine, firmly recognized in international law, recognises that a promise made without consideration may nonetheless be enforced to prevent injustice if the promisor should have reasonably expected the promise, *see* BLACK'S LAW DICTIONARY (1999), at 571 and COTTIER & SCHEFER, *id.*, p. 176.

40 The doctrine prohibits abuse of rights by states in exercising their sovereignty and it is arguably part of contemporary international law, *see* COTTIER & SCHEFER, *id.*, p. 178.

41 *See, e.g.* P. S. ATIYAH, *Contracts, Promises and the Law of Obligations,* 94 L.Q. REV 193 (1978). Reliance-based contract doctrine focuses analysis on a person's reaction to a promise and alternatively stated, the theory focuses on the interaction of contract parties to find contractual obligation.

42 LINARELLI (2000), at 344; In terms of English administrative law, the concept of legitimate expectations comes into play when a party justifiably relies on the

b. Distinction between Legitimate and Reasonable Expectation

According to GATT/WTO jurisprudence, the notion of expectation can be verbally divided into two subgroup of *legitimate* and *reasonable* expectation. In some sense, the *Japan – Film* Panel merged the concept of "legitimate expectations" with that of "reasonable expectations,"[43] which the GATT practice in prior cases was to not make a stark distinction between these two concepts. For example, the *EC – Oilseeds* Panel (1990) stated that the rationale for NVNI claims under Article XXIII:1(b) "is that the improved competitive opportunities that can be legitimately expected from a tariff concession can be frustrated not only by measures proscribed by the General Agreement but also by measures consistent with that Agreement."[44] It also stated in several places that the NVNI provisions protected "reasonable expectations".[45] Other GATT NVNI cases used both phrases interchangeably. The *Australian Subsidy* and *German-Sardines* cases both set forth a *reasonable expectations* test based on the reasonable anticipations of the complainant at the time it negotiated concessions that it alleged the respondent had nullified or impaired. The WTO Appellate Body's opinion on appropriate standards, moreover, is unclear at present, because the US did not appeal the *Japan – Film* case.

However, through the rulings and *obiter dicta* in two other AB decisions on *EC – Computer Equipment* and *India – Patent I*, we can guess the approach of AB on the issue of the appropriate legal standards for NVNI complaints. As upholding most of the findings of the panel except, in the *India – Patent I* case, the AB criticized the panel's interpretation of TRIPS obligations based on the "legitimate expectations" of the parties. The AB found that:

---

promise or action of a public official and it is tied intrinsically to concepts of fairness and justice. *See* P. P. Craig, *Legitimate Expectations: A Conceptual Analysis*, 108 The Law Quarterly Review 79 (1992).

43 *Cf. Japan – Film,* paras. 10.66, 10.67, 10.70, 10.71, 10.74, 10.217, 10.301, 10.315, 10.329.

44 *EC – Oilseeds,* para. 144.

45 *Id.,* paras. 80–88.

> Although the panel states that it is merely applying a "well established GATT principle," the panel's reasoning does not accurately reflect GATT/WTO practice. In developing its interpretative principle, the panel merges, and thereby confuses, two different concepts from previous GATT practice. One is the concept of protecting the expectations of contracting parties as to the competitive relationship between their products and the products of other contracting parties. This is a concept that was developed in the context of violation complaints [...] brought under Article XXIII : 1(a) of the GATT. The other is the concept of the protection of the reasonable expectations of contracting parties relating to market access concessions. This is a concept that was developed in the context of non-violation complaints brought under Article XXIII : 1(b) of the GATT.[46]

In another interesting case, *EC – Computer Equipment,* the AB again reversed the Panel's finding that tariff schedules are to be interpreted in light of the "legitimate expectations" of the parties, as the Panel had confused the concept of "legitimate expectations" with "reasonable expectations" and conflated the two distinct causes of action of violation and non-violation complaints into one cause of action.[47] The AB finalised its finding on legitimate expectations in terms of treaty interpretation:

> The purpose of treaty interpretation under Article 31 of the *Vienna Convention* is to ascertain the *common* intentions of the parties. These *common* intentions cannot be ascertained on the basis of the subjective and unilaterally determined "expectations" of *one* of the parties to a treaty.[48]

46 WTO Appellate Body Report, *India – Patent I (AB)* para. 36. The Appellate Body further noted that "the panel's invocation of the 'legitimate expectations' of Members relating to conditions of competition melds the legally distinct bases for 'violation' and 'non-violation' complaints." *Id.,* para. 42.

47 Appellate Body Report, *EC – Computer Equipment,* paras. 80–111.

48 *Id.,* para. 84; At this stage, three possible forms of legitimate/reasonable expectations suggested by the United Stated are worthy mentioning. Against the European Communities' (the Appellant's) argument that the panel of *EC – Computer Equipment* melds the legally-distinct bases for violation and non-violation complaints under Article XXIII into a uniform cause, the United States (the Appellee) argued that there are three different contextual concepts of legitimate or reasonable expectations, although the phrases may exhibit "accidental linguistic convergence": (1) the context of Articles III or XI of the GATT; (2) the context of NVNI complaint; and (3) the context of GATT Article II. *See EC – Computer Equipment (AB),* para. 42.

John Linarelli assessed this AB's position as an attempt "to restrict the application of the non-violation provisions to a narrow range of cases" and "to avoid a common law approach in WTO dispute settlement cases in which panel members would have substantial discretion to formulate standards for interpreting the WTO agreements".[49] In contrast, Michael Lennard regarded the AB' position as "the correct approach both in interpretation of WTO Agreements generally, and in the consideration of 'legitimate expectations' more specifically;" because "the relevant expectations can only flow from a consensus ad idem objectively expressed in the text of the treaty, when interpreted in accord with applicable international norms."[50]

Under the focus of the *expectation test*, there may be two subcategories of the test conceivable.

2. *Competitive Relationship Test*

One of the subcategory, along with the existence of legitimate expectation, to be considered for assessing NVNI claims is a *competitive relationship* test. This test is the most common approach that has been found in GATT/WTO jurisprudence. For example, the Panel Report on *EC – Oilseeds II* (1990)[51] stated that "it had found [...]

49 LINARELLI (2000), at 343.

50 LENNARD (2002), at 67.

51 The Panel on *EC – Oilseeds II* noted that the changes in the EC's producer subsidy system had failed to bring EC law into compliance with the Panel's earlier Report of *EC – Oilseeds I.* The second Panel decision concluded that the new EC subsidies based on acreage continued to impair the EC's 1962 tariff concessions to the US. The reaction of the EC to the second Panel Report was negative. The EC blocked adoption of the new report. The EC, however, has sought to reform its internal Common Agricultural Policy ("CAP") in an effort to reduce EC commodity surpluses and subsidy costs in agriculture. Reduction of agricultural subsidies has been at the center of the dispute over efforts to bring the agricultural sector under GATT disciplines, which led an accord in the Blair House Agreement in November, 1992. *See* AL J. DANIEL, JR., *The European Community, the Uruguay Round, and International Dispute Resolution,* 46 Arkansas Law Review 873, 908–13 (1994).

that the subsidies concerned had impaired the tariff concession because they *upset the competitive relationship between domestic and imported oilseeds*, not because of any effect on trade flows".[52] The same test was used in the *Australian Subsidy* and *Germany – Sardines* cases.[53] In *Japan – Film,* the Panel reiterated the conventional mainstream of *competitive relationship* approach in NVNI complaint as follows:

> The equation of 'nullification or impairment' with 'upsetting the competitive relationship' established between domestic and imported products as a result of tariff concessions has been consistently used by GATT panels examining non-violation complaints.[54]

In effect, this competitive relationship test distinguishes little from the standard used in the *national treatment provision* of GATT Article III.[55] Considering a subsidiary argument of the United States in the *Japan – Film* was that Japanese distribution countermeasures

52 GATT Panel Report, *EC – Oilseeds II,* para. 77 [emphasis added].

53 The Working Party in *Australian Subsidy* case agreed that that impairment would exist if the Australian action "which resulted in upsetting the competitive relationship [...]," *see Australian Subsidy,* para. 12; The Panel Report *on Germany – Sardines* also based on *competitive relationship* standard, stating that "action of the German Government [the respondent], which resulted in upsetting the competitive relationship between [...]," *see Germany – Sardines,* para. 16.

54 *Japan – Film,* para. 10.82.

55 Article III is one of the central provisions in GATT. It regulates the application of domestic policies to imported products. It requires members of WTO to accord national treatment to imported products. Article III, known as the national treatment obligation, focuses on discrimination against imports for the benefit of domestic production in the importing country. The purpose of this Article is to ensure that that an imported product is treated in the same way in terms of taxation and regulatory treatment as a "like" domestically produced good after that imported product has cleared customs. *See generally* JOHN H. JACKSON, *National Treatment Obligations and Non-Tariff Barriers,* 10 Michigan Journal of International Law 127 (1989); Edward S. Tsai, *"Like" is a Four-Letter Word – GATT Article III's "Like Product" Conundrum,* 17 Berkeley Journal of International Law 26.

violated the national treatment obligation set forth in Article III of GATT,[56] the Panel noted that:

> In this connection, it could be argued that the standard we enunciated and applied under Article XXIII : 1(b) – that of "upsetting the competitive relationship" – may be different from the standard of "upsetting effective equality of competitive opportunities" applicable to Article III : 4. However, we do not see any significant distinction between the two standards apart from the fact that this Article III : 4 standard calls for no less favourable treatment for imported products in general, whereas the Article XXIII : 1(b) standard calls for a comparison of the competitive relationship between foreign and domestic products at two specific points in time, i. e. when the concession was granted and currently.[57]

Thus, the main drawback of using a national treatment test under Article XXIII is that it could render the NVNI language in Article XXIII ineffective or meaningless.[58] However, Article III and its substantial jurisprudence provides useful guidance in understanding how to decide NVNI claims and to properly delimit Article XXIII : 1 (b) coverage.[59]

On the other hand, the *competitive relationship* test is closely related to the criteria included in the Article XX ("General Exception") of the GATT, because the Article XX justifies exceptions to the basic obligation of non-discrimination of the national treatment principle and the constraints thereon, in particular constraints on disguised or unjustified forms of discrimination.[60]

56 The *Japan – Film* Panel found that the Japanese measures did not discriminate, *de jure* ("a measure that discriminates *on its face* as to the origin of products") or *de facto* ("a measure that in its application upsets the relative competitive position between domestic and imported products, as it existed at the time when a relevant tariff concession was granted"), against foreign firms. In addition, the panel found that the activities in question – single brand distribution in particular – were becoming standard industry practices without government intervention, even in the United States. *See id.*, paras. 10.380 & 10.381.

57 *Id.*, para. 10.380; *See also* LINARELLI (2000), at 353–54.

58 LINARELLI, *id.*

59 *Id.*, at 354.

60 *See* MICHAEL TREBILCOCK & ROBERT HOWSE, *Trade Liberalization and Regulatory Diversity: Reconciling Competitive Markets with Competitive Politics*, 6 European Journal of Law and Economics 5, 10 (1998).

3. *Market Access Test*

Given the inevitable difficulty of *competitive relationship* test that draws level with the national treatment standard of Article III:4, that is, if nullification or impairment scope of NVNI complaints gets almost the same area of discrimination already covered by Article III:4, it is difficult to justify the existence of NVNI claims which is supposed to parallel *violation complaints*. Thus an alternative approach to interpreting NVNI complaints would be a broader one. Such a test is based on the concept of market access. In general terms, the GATT/WTO offers a forum within which each Member may negotiate market access. Market access is interpreted in the GATT/WTO as reflecting the *competitive relationship* between imported and domestic products.[61] For example, when an import tariff on a good is reduced, then it alters the competitive relationship between imported and domestic good in favour of imported good and thus provides greater market access to foreign producers. This difficulty again emerged in the *EC-Asbestos* Appellate Body Report. With regard to nullification or impairment of benefits, the panel's standard of "upsetting of the competitive relationship"[62] was broadened by the Appellate Body to "market access":

> Rather, the European Communities' argument relates to the substance of a claim that has been determined to fall within the scope of application of Article XXIII:1(b) and, in particular, concerns the issue *whether a 'benefit' has been 'nullified or impaired' by a measure restricting market access* for products posing a health risk.[63] [emphasis added]

61 Bagwell, Mavroidis & Staiger (2002), at 59.

62 The panel in this case examined whether the French measure "must have had the effect of upsetting the competitive relationship between Canadian asbestos and products containing it, on the one hand, and substitute fibres and products containing them, on the other." *See EC-Asbestos*, para. 8.288.

63 *EC – Asbestos (AB)*, para. 190: *See also India – Patent I (AB)*, para. 36 ("The other is the concept of the protection of the reasonable expectations of contracting parties *relating to market access concessions*. This is a concept that was developed in the context of *non-violation* complaints brought under Article XXIII:1(b) of the GATT") [emphasis added].

Notwithstanding still some confusion over this standard and uncertainty of AB's confirmed position, "market access" is a broader notion than "upsetting of the competitive relationship." It addresses all barriers to imports even if they are not discriminatory.

In effect, the WTO legal system does not contain any provisions that oblige the members to adopt any particular conduct with respect to *market access* standards. To the extent, however, that a change in the WTO-consistent measures adversely affects foreign products, the aggrieved member can bring a NVNI complaint against the measures. From this viewpoint, the NVNI complaints may secure negotiated market access commitments secure against unilateral infringement, recognising that such infringement could occur through measures with legality.[64] Moreover, some scholars argue that after the AB's reasoning in *EC– Asbestos* enabling a NVNI claim based on a health-based measure, a NVNI complaint could well be feasible as regards "relaxation" of labor and environmental standards.[65]

This approach then would provide the NVNI complaints with a more logical and a fairly broad scope, given that the non-discrimination standard already exists in Article III:4 and that WTO law is expected to cover many areas in line with encouraging *free trade.*

64 BAGWELL, MAVROIDIS & STAIGER (2002), at 65.

65 *Id.* From this point, they have proposed the following, with regard to the role of the WTO in addressing non-pecuniary externalities associated with labor and environmental standards: "(1) as a general matter, agreements on labor and environmental standards should not be negotiated in the WTO to address problems that arise as a result of non-pecuniary externalities associated with unilateral standards choices; and (2) as a general matter, explicit links between the WTO and other international labour and environmental organisations should not be established for enforcement purposes, but the existing implicit enforcement links between the WTO and other organisations – as embodied in the nonviolation nullification-or-impairment and renegotiation provisions of the WTO Agreements – should be encouraged." *See id.,* at 74.

Table 4: Standards Defining the Scope of Non-Violation Complaints

<table>
<tr><th colspan="2">Standards</th><th>Relevant Cases</th><th>Notes</th></tr>
<tr><td colspan="2">Compensatory Adjustment Standard</td><td>GATT, EC – Citrus, para. 4.37: "The Panel noted that the basic purpose of Article XXIII : 1(b) was to provide for offsetting or compensatory adjustment in situations in which the balance of rights and obligations of the contracting parties had been disturbed [...]. One of the fundamental benefits accruing to the contracting parties under the General Agreement, therefore, was the right to such adjustment in situations in which the balance of their rights and obligations had been upset to their disadvantage."</td><td>1. Argument of the US on benefits of TRIPS: "overall anticipated economic returns are the proper benefit of an intellectual property right." (WTO Doc. IP/C/W/349)
2. Excessive discretionary power of judicial bodies
3. This standard could include a Pareto or Kaldor-Hicks efficiency theory</td></tr>
<tr><td rowspan="3">Expectation Standard</td><td rowspan="2">Competitive Relationship Test</td><td>GATT, EC – Oilseed, para. 144: "The idea underlying [the provisions of Article XXIII : 1(b)] is that the improved competitive opportunities that can legitimately be expected from a tariff concession can be frustrated not only by measures proscribed by the General Agreement but also by measures consistent with that Agreement.</td><td rowspan="2">1. Most GATT/WTO Panels
• Australian Subsidy
• German – Sardines
• EC – Oilseeds I
• EC – Canned Fruit
• EC – Oilseed II
• Japan – Film
2. Close relationship to GATT Art. III: "Article III : 4 standard calls for no less favourable treatment for imported products in general, whereas the Article XXIII : 1(b) standard calls for a comparison of the competitive relationship between foreign and domestic" (Japan – Film, para. 10.380)</td></tr>
<tr><td>WTO, Japan – Film, para. 10.82: "The equation of 'nullification or impairment' with 'upsetting the competitive relationship' established between domestic and imported products as a result of tariff concessions has been consistently used by GATT panels examining non-violation complaints"</td></tr>
<tr><td>Market Access Test</td><td>WTO, EC – Asbestos (AB), para. 190: "[T]he European Communities' (Appellee) argument relates to the substance of a claim that has been determined to fall within the scope of application of Article XXIII : 1(b) and, in particular, concerns the issue whether a 'benefit' has been 'nullified or impaired' by a measure restricting market access for products posing a health risk</td><td>3. The Appellate Body's opinions on legitimate expectation:
• India – Patent I (AB)
"The legitimate expectations of the parties to a treaty are reflected in the language of the treaty itself." (para. 45)
• EC – Computer Equipment (AB)
"[N]othing in Article II : 5 suggests that the expectations of only the exporting Member can be the basis for interpreting a concession in a Member's Schedule [. . .]." (para. 81)
4. US Argument of three kinds of legitimate expectation in EC – Computer Equipment (AB), para. 45</td></tr>
</table>

Conclusion

It is scarcely surprising that one can find ambiguities, omissions and other troublesome interpretive problems in the WTO Agreements, mainly because they were negotiated among more than 140 participating national governments with different implications of many of the legal obligations in the WTO Agreements. For this reason, the dispute settlement process becomes crucial. It is one of the principal means for resolving the inevitable differences that arise about the various legal obligations in the WTO Agreements.

Thus, a satisfactory dispute settlement in the WTO requires two prerequisites: one is well-thought legal frameworks which connect substantive obligations with efficient procedural mechanisms and; the other is a more standardised interpretation of the WTO Agreements including the predictable application of basic principles of international law. From this viewpoint, the legal structure of WTO has some faults. First, the connection between the substantive obligations and its procedurally enforcing mechanism is said to be unstable: while the substantive obligations have been formed deliberately, by contrast, the procedural mechanism, mainly based on GATT Article XXIII, shows a number of ambiguities which can make the whole framework of WTO weak. Second, related to the aspects of standardised interpretation, how to apply the basic principles of international law incorporated in the Vienna Convention is crucial. A good jurisprudential example is NVNI complaints. To properly interpret the NVNI complaints calls for full investigations from three directions: normative characteristics of WTO law, sources of WTO law especially legitimate expectation, and interpretive rules managing the sources of WTO law.

All legal systems compromise competing elements of certainty/uniformity and flexibility/individualisation. The former elements are associated with the *formal interpretation*, making judgments according to the literal meaning of the provision concerned. The latter elements allow or infer a more *purpose-based interpretation*, so conferring greater discretion in their application but also entailing uncertainty and dangers of such discretion. This general proposition can be applied to the interpretations surrounding Article XXIII : 1 (a) and (b) of GATT/WTO.

In applying Article XXIII : 1(a) of GATT, we see the formal approach, focusing on legal certainty. On the other hand, the interpretation of the GATT Article XXIII : 1(b) is to consider a more purpose-based approach, relying on an individualised basis in accordance with the overall objective of the WTO law. Therefore, the complaints of Article XXIII : 1(b) are not unusual in terms of general legal theory, and the focus must be in their *theorisation* in the context of an acceptable compromise between certainty and flexibility of WTO law. This must be the starting point for interpreting Article XXIII : 1(b).

Having examined the complex viewpoints surrounding the complaints of GATT Article XXIII : 1(b), there are generally two competing arguments on the *sources of obligations* of WTO law. One is the argument that the Article XXIII : 1(b) contains fundamental general principles which members must *normatively* obey for sustaining a multilateral trading system. Thus it is wrong to cause nullification or impairment to another member's benefits notwithstanding the absence of specific provisions in WTO Agreements. The other is the argument that there are several *positivistically* codified provisions in the WTO Agreements prohibiting certain kinds of nullifying activities, therefore leaving all the rest *outside* the sphere of legal responsibility to the political arena among the members.

Challenge to the former approach lies in that WTO law is an international system which is based on the *consent* of WTO members. Equally the latter approach can be criticised by its narrow reference which can lead international trade disputes into deadlocks. If we bear in mind that the present multilateral systems such as the WTO are evolving into a satisfactory forum for settling trade disputes, the dogmatism of sticking to codified sources would cause unfavourable consequences. Hence, neither of these two approaches *at their extremes* achieves the overall intelligibility of the NVNI complaints, which require a more refined interpretation of NVNI complaints. This becomes more important when we consider a more legalised model of WTO DSM and when we consider the future codifications from the current negotiations. In this context, *coherent interpretation* can solve the difficulty of interpreting the NVNI complaints.

First, by an inquiry into *internal coherence* between legal terms and their contexts in Article XXIII : 1(b), especially through the reviewing of "benefit" concept, we came to understand that the NVNI complaint in practice is a form of violation complaint. Based on the classifications of *verified* and *potential benefits* in Article XXIII : 1, we can conceive different obligations, i. e. *specific/codified* and *general/ customary* obligations. These two kinds of obligations correspond to the obligations of the Article XXIII : 1(a) and those of the Article XXIII : 1(b). Thus, we can put the Article XXIII : 1(b) into a different type of violation complaint of Article XXIII : 1(a) as a *liability*.

Second, we can further theorise on the applicable scope of the *liability*. Based on *potential benefits* of Article XXIII : 1(b) and their corresponding *customary* obligations of WTO law, we can incorporate general principles of international law into the NVNI complaints through the consideration of "any objective" of WTO Agreements. Put it differently, by reviewing an *externally coherent interrelation* between the fundamental values of WTO law and further employing legitimate expectation into Article XXIII : 1(b), the *potential benefits* will be clarified by the consideration of "objective" as the applicable scope of *liability* in the Article XXIII : 1(b).

Third, if we consider possible disputes against the WTO-*consistent* measures which are on its face neutral and non-discriminatory, having a disguised discrimination, the NVNI complaints are expected to be raised often in future. Those incidences will increase as the coverage of WTO is ever expanding. Should that occur, the WTO judicial bodies could use *coherent interpretation* to interpret *a nominal non-violation case as a violation of liability case*, which enhances the systematic coherence of WTO. This contributes to improving the normative effect of WTO law. With this legal reasoning, we can avoid unnecessary arguments and interpret Article XXIII : 1(b) consistently and focus more on future trade agendas.

Index

adjudicatory fairness 205, 206
adverse effect 37, 50, 54, 107, 120, 131, 149, 150, 234, 251, 280, 282
benefits 8, 10, 12, 22, 24, 25, 32, 39, 40, 41, 45, 47, 48, 50, 52, 54–56, 63, 64, 69, 70, 81, 104, 107, 109, 110, 112, 114, 120, 122–125, 127, 131, 136, 137, 141, 143, 146, 149, 152, 164, 167, 183, 186, 206, 210, 218, 221, 222, 226, 233, 237–244, 246–248, 250, 256, 257, 265, 271, 279–282, 293, 296, 297
bretton woods system 6, 29, 36, 119
causation 74, 79, 126, 131, 132, 135, 136, 149, 258
cause(s) of action 1, 7, 10, 13, 15, 22, 25, 48, 49, 52, 53, 61, 62, 119, 120, 130, 135, 161–164, 168, 170, 186, 205, 222, 238, 240, 243, 245, 259, 260, 275, 287
coherence 10, 35, 165, 186, 198, 223–227, 236, 256, 260, 297
competitive relationship 45, 55, 56, 77, 79, 104, 120, 124, 125, 130–132, 145, 146, 168, 276, 279, 283, 287–293
consent-oriented approach 216
constitutional approach 65
constitutionalisation 217, 219, 223
counterpositivism 179
dimensional thinking 184
dispute settlement 4, 10, 12, 13, 16, 22, 23, 27, 28, 31, 32, 34, 36, 41–43, 58, 59, 72, 82, 88, 89, 91, 97, 99, 104, 110, 114, 116, 130, 134, 139, 140, 151, 159, 165, 169, 173, 184, 186, 189, 191–193, 195–203, 211–219, 221, 224, 252, 256, 258, 259, 263, 268, 273, 278, 283, 285, 288, 295
embedded liberalism 6, 23, 32
equity 7, 36, 38, 81, 90, 159, 171, 183, 188, 189, 222, 227, 260, 263–268, 284
estoppel 160, 261, 265, 267, 285
foreseeability 250
good faith 36, 72, 75, 79, 81, 82, 91, 96, 105, 113, 157, 172, 173, 182, 183, 211, 227, 247, 248, 259–265, 273, 279, 284
indirect protection 20, 37, 81, 107, 119, 234, 264
International Law Process (ILP) 10, 178–182
interpretation 31, 47, 48, 79, 87, 88, 91, 95–99, 101–105, 108, 110, 112, 113, 144, 148, 152, 167, 173, 184, 191, 216, 217, 222–224, 232, 266
justice-oriented approach 216, 217
legitimate expectation 10, 14, 40, 56, 62–64, 71–73, 77, 81, 82, 94, 122, 125, 126, 146, 150, 151, 158, 168, 171, 182, 183, 188, 203, 211, 236, 245, 248, 250, 260, 281, 284–288, 293, 295, 297
liability 9, 10, 63, 103, 113, 151, 183, 196, 249, 252–256, 274, 276, 297
market access 18, 39, 41, 52, 54, 56, 57, 63, 64, 68, 70, 71, 74, 77, 80, 83, 110–112, 120, 122, 124, 125, 137, 145, 147, 149–152, 168, 172, 204, 212, 218, 227, 245, 258, 272, 287, 291–293

measure 5–8, 11, 13, 16–25, 27–30, 33, 35, 37, 39, 40, 42, 43, 45–48, 50, 51, 53–56, 64–66, 69, 70, 73, 74, 76, 77, 79–83, 93, 100, 103, 107, 110–112, 114, 115, 117–121, 123, 124, 126–128, 130–132, 134–142, 144–147, 149, 152, 155, 158, 162, 163, 165–167, 177, 193, 196, 201, 205–207, 209, 210, 212, 215, 225, 234–237, 239, 240, 242–245, 247, 249, 251, 253, 255, 257, 258, 264, 272, 276, 280–282, 284, 286, 289–293, 297

mutually satisfactory adjustment 22, 24, 27, 51, 53, 83, 139–143, 149, 206, 236

non-discriminatory competition 31

Non-Violation Nullification or Impairment (NVNI) 7–11, 14, 16–26, 31, 35, 37, 38, 40–43, 45–53, 55–61, 63–66, 69–83, 87, 88, 95, 97, 100, 102–116, 118, 119, 122–126, 128, 130, 131, 136–139, 141, 143–152, 155, 158, 159, 161–164, 167, 168, 170, 171, 173, 179, 182–189, 191, 195, 205–212, 216, 219, 222–225, 227, 232, 236, 238, 239, 241–245, 247–252, 254–256, 259–261, 264, 266–268, 270, 272, 274, 275, 277–281, 283, 285–288, 290–292, 295–297

normative 10, 33, 62, 87, 88, 103, 108, 163, 164, 168, 170, 171, 178–180, 183, 188, 189, 194, 207–210, 213, 216, 219, 222, 223, 231, 233, 259, 270, 274, 295–297

nullification or impairment of benefits 12, 49, 50, 81, 127, 128, 143, 149, 251, 291

objective 6–8, 10, 13, 17, 19, 25, 28, 34, 40, 51, 53, 54, 62, 64, 65, 74, 78, 81, 88, 93–95, 103, 107–109, 114, 116, 121, 122, 127, 141, 150, 151, 162–165, 168, 172, 182, 188, 189, 198, 199, 205, 211, 220, 227, 238, 241, 242, 249–251, 258–260, 262, 267, 269–278, 288, 296, 297

positive 10, 56, 64, 147, 148, 157, 163, 164, 172, 176, 179–181, 183, 186, 188, 189, 198, 201, 216, 222, 265, 267, 278

positivism 33, 156, 174, 175, 178, 179, 180, 181, 186, 222

potential benefits 238, 247, 297

principles 6, 14, 33, 34, 36, 59, 68, 88, 90, 95, 96, 102, 111, 113, 116, 155, 156, 158–160, 167, 168, 170–173, 175–177, 183, 189, 194, 196, 200, 203, 205, 209–211, 222, 225, 227, 241, 247, 253, 259–261, 265, 267, 273, 277, 295–297

reasonable expectation 18, 45, 47, 48, 54, 64, 70, 79, 103, 112–114, 125, 130, 147, 150, 151, 159, 218, 243, 275, 284, 286, 287, 291

reciprocity 5, 231, 234–236

rights 3–6, 12, 29, 40, 41, 57, 58, 61, 63–65, 69, 72–74, 81, 82, 91, 102, 123, 142, 147, 150, 160, 165, 171, 172, 180, 183, 194, 197–199, 202, 210, 218, 220, 226, 232, 237–241, 246, 251, 256, 258, 262–267, 272, 274, 275, 280, 283, 285, 293

rules 5, 14, 16–19, 27, 30, 35, 40, 52, 56, 58, 61, 63, 64, 66, 67, 72, 73, 82, 87–91, 95–97, 99, 101, 107, 109–111, 116, 122, 125, 129, 130, 136, 140, 148, 155, 156, 158–160, 164, 169–177, 179, 180, 182–184, 186, 188, 191–196, 199, 203, 205, 206, 208, 211, 213, 216, 219, 220, 222–227, 234, 237, 239–241, 248, 249, 252, 255–257, 259, 260, 268, 273, 274, 277, 278, 295

sources of obligations 15, 151, 296

state responsibility 103, 113, 251, 252, 267

structure of obligations 246
tariff concessions 11, 13, 17, 20, 31, 32, 36, 38–41, 47, 49–51, 54, 61, 62, 64, 73, 74, 79, 80, 94, 102, 107, 110, 112–116, 122, 123, 125, 127, 142–145, 147, 149, 150, 152, 168, 210, 236–238, 240, 245, 250, 257, 258, 261, 274, 279, 281, 284, 288, 289, 293
values 89, 103, 108, 109, 113, 153, 169, 178–180, 188, 207, 209, 210, 213–218, 220, 224, 225, 227, 232, 260, 267, 297
verified benefits 238, 239
Vienna convention 9, 72, 75, 83, 87–96, 98, 99, 101, 102, 106, 108, 109, 114, 167, 182, 183, 261, 274, 279, 284, 287, 295

Studies in Global Economic Law
Studien zum globalen Wirtschaftsrecht
Études en droit économique mondial

edited by THOMAS COTTIER

Vol. 1 MARTIN A. GIRSBERGER – Biodiversity and the Concept of Farmers' Rights in International Law, 1999

Vol. 2 DAVID WYSS – Bankdienstleistungen im Allgemeinen Dienstleistungsabkommen der WTO. Auswirkungen auf das schwiezerische Bankenrecht, 1999

Vol. 3 BENOÎT MERKT – Harmonisation internationale et entraide administrative internationale en droit de la concurrence. Droit du GATT/OMC, droit européen, accords bilatéraux et perspectives pour le droit suisse, 2000

Vol. 4 INGO MEITINGER – Der Schutz von Geschäftsgeheimnissen im globalen und regionalen Wirtschaftsrecht. Stand und mögliche Entwicklungen der internationalen und regionalen Rechtsharmonisierung, 2001

Vol. 5 JOËLLE DE SÉPIBUS – Die Umweltschutzsubvention im Gemeinschaftsrecht. Eine umweltrechtliche Kritik der europäischen Beihilfekontrolle, 2003

Vol. 6 BOBJOSEPH MATHEW – The WTO Agreements on Telecommunications, 2003

Vol. 7 LUKAS ENGELBERGER – Die Unmittelbare Anwendbarkeit des WTO-Rechts in der Schweiz. Grundlagen und Perspektiven im Kontext internationaler Rechtsentwicklung, 2004

Vol. 8 THOMAS M. FISCHER – Die Entbündelung der letzten Meile in der Schweiz im Lichte des GATS, 2004

Vol. 9 DAE-WON KIM – Non-Violation Complaints in WTO Law. Theory and Practice, 2006

Studies in Global Economic Law
Studien zum globalen Wirtschaftsrecht
Études en droit économique mondial

Present and future economic, technological and societal changes and evolutions fundamentally affect traditional legal structures of the territorial state system. They increasingly call for global approaches and solutions, transgressing the tools of classical public international law. This trilingual series publishes monographs, studies and collected papers dedicated to these challenges. The contributions examine existing instruments, in particular within the framework of the international trading system. They explore new approaches and search for innovative solutions within the global process of legal integration. Research efforts are dedicated to different walks of life and areas of regulation, and to the quest for adequate constitutional structures of transnational and democratic processes.

Wirtschaftliche, technologische und gesellschaftliche Entwicklungen der Gegenwart und Zukunft bewirken tiefgreifende Änderungen traditioneller Strukturen des Rechts des Territorialstaats und rufen zunehmend nach globalen Vorgehensweisen und Lösungen, die oftmals über das Instrumentarium des klassischen Völkerrechts hinaus weisen. Die dreisprachige Reihe publiziert Monographien, Studien und Tagungsbände, die sich vertieft mit diesen Herausforderungen auseinandersetzen. Die Beiträge untersuchen das bestehende Instrumentarium namentlich im Rahmen des Welthandelssystems und forschen nach neuen Ansätzen und Lösungen im Rahmen des globalen Integrationsprozesses. Dazu gehören Studien zu den Regelungen einzelner Sach- und Lebensbereiche wie auch zu Fragen adäquater transnationaler demokratischer Verfassungs- und Entscheidungsstrukturen.

Les évolutions actuelles et futures sur le plan technique, économique et social ne cesseront d'influencer profondément les structures traditionnelles du droit de l'état territorial. Par conséquent, des approches et des solutions dépassant les instruments du droit international public classique deviennent de plus en plus nécessaires. Cette collection trilingue publie des monographies, études et actes de colloques qui analysent et font face à ces défis. Les contributions examinent les instruments existants, notamment dans la domaine du système commercial mondiale. Elles cherchent à développer des approches nouvelles et des solutions innovatrices dans le contexte du processus d'intégration globale en incluant des études de droit touchant aux différents secteurs et domaines de vie. De plus, les travaux de recherche seront également destinés à trouver les procédures constitutionnelles et décisionnelles les plus adéquates et démocratiques au niveau transnational.